WOMEN IN EARLY
CHRISTIANITY

WOMEN IN EARLY CHRISTIANITY

Translations from Greek Texts

Patricia Cox Miller

THE CATHOLIC UNIVERSITY OF AMERICA PRESS
Washington, D.C.

LIBRARY OF CONGRESS CATALOGING-IN-PUBLICATION DATA

Women in early Christianity : translations from Greek texts / [edited by]
Patricia Cox Miller.— 1st ed.

p. cm.

Includes bibliographical references and index.

ISBN-13: 978-0-8132-1417-7 (pbk. : alk. paper)

ISBN-10: 0-8132-1417-3 (pbk. : alk. paper)

1. Women in Christianity—History—Early church, ca. 30–600—Sources.

I. Miller, Patricia Cox, 1947–   II. Title.

BR195.W6W66 2005

270.1′082—dc22

2004018079

FOR LIZ

Contents

Acknowledgments

This volume has been many years in the making, and I would like to thank three colleagues for special help. In the early stages of this project, when scanning texts into computer files was more like magic than technological craft, I had the able assistance of Dr. Mary Keller, then a graduate student. I thank her for all the hours she spent in assisting me with the tedious but necessary process of gathering texts. To my husband, Professor David L. Miller, go my love and thanks for supporting me in this, as in all of my work. Finally, I thank the scholar and friend to whom this book is dedicated, Professor Elizabeth A. Clark of Duke University. When I first knew Liz, I was an undergraduate at Mary Washington College of the University of Virginia. My introduction to the field that we now call "Christianity in Late Antiquity" was Liz's seminar entitled simply (I think), "Patristics." Of course there was no "Matristics" in those days, but thanks to Liz's pioneering work in subsequent years on women and gender in late ancient Christianity, students today can feast on such documents as the *Life of Melania the Younger,* who herself was said to have "read the Fathers as though she were eating dessert." I am grateful to Liz not only for her magnificent contributions to the field but also for her generous encouragement and support of my own career as a scholar. My greatest thanks, however, are for the long and sustaining friendship that we share.

The following texts are reprinted with permission. My own interpolations within a given selection are indicated by square brackets and a typeface smaller than that of the surrounding text. Texts are listed here alphabetically by author and, when anonymous, by title.

The Acts of Andrew, selections, from *The Apocryphal New Testament: A Collection of Apocryphal Christian Literature in an English Translation,* trans. J. K. Elliott, copyright © 1993 by Oxford University Press.

The Acts of Paul and Thecla, from *The Apocryphal New Testament: A Collection of Apocryphal Christian Literature in an English Translation*, trans. J. K. Elliott, copyright © 1993 by Oxford University Press.

The Acts of Xanthippe and Polyxena, selections, from The Ante-Nicene Fathers, vol. 10, ed. Allan Menzies, trans. W. A. Craigie, copyright © 1980 (repr. ed.) by Wm. B. Eerdmans Publishing Company.

Apostolic Constitutions 3.9, from *Women in the Early Church*, Message of the Fathers of the Church, vol. 13, trans. Elizabeth A. Clark, copyright © 1983 by Elizabeth A. Clark, used by permission of The Liturgical Press.

Athanasius, *Second Letter to Virgins*, selections, from David Brakke, *Athanasius and Asceticism*, copyright © 1998 by The Johns Hopkins University Press.

Canons of the Council of Gangra, selections, from *Ascetic Behavior in Greco-Roman Antiquity*, ed. Vincent L. Wimbush, trans. O. Larry Yarbrough, copyright © 1990 by The Institute for Antiquity and Christianity, reprinted by permission from Trinity Press International and T and T Clark International.

2 Clement, selections, from *The Apostolic Fathers*, Fathers of the Church, vol. 1, trans. Francis X. Glimm, copyright © 1947 by The Catholic University of America Press.

Clement of Alexandria, *The Instructor*, selections from Book 2, from *Marriage in the Early Church*, ed. and trans. David G. Hunter, copyright © 1992 by Augsburg Fortress Press (located in Section IV of the present volume); *The Pedagogue*, selections from Books 1 and 2, from *Clement of Alexandria: Christ the Educator*, Fathers of the Church, vol. 23, trans. Simon P. Wood, copyright © 1954 by The Catholic University of America Press (located in the present volume in Sections V and II respectively; note that this treatise is translated variously as either *The Instructor* or *The Pedagogue*).

————, *Miscellanies*, selections from Books 2 and 3, from *Marriage in the Early Church*, ed. and trans. David G. Hunter, copyright © 1992 by Augsburg Fortress Press (located in Section IV of the present volume); *Miscellanies* 3.6–8, from Library of Christian Classics, vol. 2: *Alexandrian Christianity*, trans. J. E. L. Oulton and Henry Chadwick, copyright © Westminster John Knox Press, 1954 (located in Section I of the present volume).

Debate of a Montanist and an Orthodox Christian, selections, from *The Montanist Oracles and Testimonia*, trans. Ronald E. Heine, copyright © 2002 by The North American Patristic Society (originally published in 1989 by Mercer University Press).

Didascalia apostolorum, selections, from *Didascalia apostolorum*, trans. R. Hugh Connolly, copyright © 1929 by Oxford University Press.

Epiphanius, *Panarion* 48–49, 79, selections, from *The Panarion of Epiphanius of Salamis*, vol. 2, trans. Frank Williams, copyright © 1994 by E. J. Brill; *Panarion* 48–49, selections, from *The Montanist Oracles and Testimonia*, North American Patristic Society Monograph Series, vol. 14, trans. Ronald E. Heine, copyright © 2002 by The North American Patristic Society, originally published in 1989 by Mercer University Press (the above are all in Section I of the present volume); *Panarion* 78.17–19, from *Mary and the Fathers of the Church: The Blessed Virgin Mary in Patristic Thought*, trans. Luigi Gambero, S.M., English trans. Thomas Buffer, copyright © 1999 by Ignatius Press (located in Section V of the present volume); *Panarion* 78.23, 79, selections, from *Maenads, Martyrs, Matrons, Monastics: A Sourcebook on Women's Religions in the Greco-Roman World*, ed. Ross Shepard Kraemer, trans. Carolyn Osiek, copyright © 1988 by Ross Shepard Kraemer, originally published by Fortress Press (in Section IV of the present volume).

Eusebius of Caesarea, *Ecclesiastical History*, selections, from *The Acts of the Christian Martyrs*, trans. Herbert Musurillo, S.J., copyright © 1972 by Oxford University Press.

Exegesis on the Soul, selection, from *The Nag Hammadi Library in English, 3rd, Completely Revised Ed.*, ed. James M. Robinson, trans. William C. Robinson, copyright © 1978, 1988 by E. J. Brill, reprinted by permission of HarperCollins Publishers, Inc., and Koninklijke Brill NV.

Gerontius, *Life of Melania the Younger*, selections, from *The Life of Melania the Younger: Introduction, Translation, Commentary*, Studies in Women and Religion, vol. 14, trans. Elizabeth A. Clark, copyright © 1984 by The Edwin Mellen Press.

Gospel of Mary, selections, from *The Nag Hammadi Library in English, 3rd, Completely Revised Ed.*, ed. James M. Robinson, trans. George W. MacRae and R. McL. Wilson, copyright © 1978, 1988 by E. J. Brill, reprinted by permission of HarperCollins Publishers, Inc., and Koninklijke Brill NV.

Gospel of Philip, selection, from *The Nag Hammadi Library in English, 3rd, Completely Revised Ed.,* ed. James M. Robinson, trans. Wesley W. Isenberg, copyright © 1978, 1988 by E. J. Brill, reprinted by permission of HarperCollins Publishers, Inc., and Koninklijke Brill NV.

Gospel of Thomas, selection, from *The Nag Hammadi Library in English, 3rd, Completely Revised Ed.,* ed. James M. Robinson, trans. Thomas O. Lambdin, copyright © 1978, 1988 by E. J. Brill, reprinted by permission of HarperCollins Publishers, Inc., and Koninklijke Brill NV.

Gregory of Nazianzus, *On His Own Affairs,* selection, from *Saint Gregory of Nazianzus: Three Poems,* Fathers of the Church, vol. 75, trans. Denis Meehan, copyright © 1987 by The Catholic University of America Press.

_____, *On His Own Life,* selection, from *Saint Gregory of Nazianzus: Three Poems,* Fathers of the Church, vol. 75, trans. Denis Meehan, copyright © 1987 by The Catholic University of America Press.

_____, *Oration 8,* selections, from *Funeral Orations by Saint Gregory Nazianzen and Saint Ambrose,* Fathers of the Church, vol. 22, trans. Leo P. McCauley, S.J., copyright © 1953 by The Catholic University of America Press.

Gregory of Nyssa, *Life of Saint Macrina,* selections, from *Gregory of Nyssa: The Life of Saint Macrina,* trans. Kevin Corrigan, copyright © 1987 by Peregrina Publishing Company.

_____, *On the Soul and the Resurrection,* selections, from *Saint Gregory of Nyssa: Ascetical Works,* Fathers of the Church, vol. 58, trans. Virginia Woods Callahan, copyright © 1967 by The Catholic University of America Press.

_____, *On Virginity,* selections, from *Saint Gregory of Nyssa: Ascetical Works,* Fathers of the Church, vol. 58, trans. Virginia Woods Callahan, copyright © 1967 by The Catholic University of America Press.

Hermas, *The Shepherd,* Mandate 4, from *Marriage in the Early Church,* ed. and trans. David G. Hunter, copyright © 1992 by Augsburg Fortress Press; *The Shepherd,* Parables and Visions, selections, from *The Apostolic Fathers,* Fathers of the Church, vol. 1, trans. Joseph M.-F. Marique, S.J., copyright © 1947 by The Catholic University of America Press.

Hippolytus, *The Apostolic Tradition,* selections, from *The Apostolic Tradition of Hippolytus,* trans. Burton Scott Easton, copyright © 1934 by Cambridge University Press.

_____, *The Refutation of All Heresies,* selection, from *The Montanist Oracles and Testimonia,* North American Patristic Society Monograph Series, vol. 14, trans. Ronald E. Heine, copyright © 1989 by The North American Patristic Society.

_____, *Treatise on Christ and Antichrist,* selections, from The Ante-Nicene Fathers, vol. 5, ed. Alexander Roberts and James Donaldson, trans. S. D. F. Salmond, copyright © 1978 (repr. ed.) by Wm. B. Eerdmans Publishing Company.

Ignatius of Antioch, *To the Smyrneans,* selection, from *Early Christian Fathers,* Library of Christian Classics, vol. 1, trans. Cyril Richardson, copyright © 1953 by Westminster John Knox Press.

Irenaeus, *Against Heresies,* selection, from *Women in the Early Church,* Message of the Fathers of the Church, vol. 13, trans. Elizabeth A. Clark, copyright © 1983 by Elizabeth A. Clark, used by permission of The Liturgical Press.

John Chrysostom, *Discourse 4 on Genesis,* selection, from *Women in the Early Church,* Message of the Fathers of the Church, vol. 13, trans. Elizabeth A. Clark, copyright © 1983 by Elizabeth A. Clark, used by permission of The Liturgical Press.

_____, *Homilies on Matthew,* selection, from *Mary and the Fathers of the Church: The Blessed Virgin Mary in Patristic Thought,* trans. Luigi Gambero, copyright © 1999 by Ignatius Press [note: this volume, originally in Italian, was translated into English by Thomas Buffer].

_____, *Homily 12 on 1 Corinthians,* selections, from *Women in the Early Church,* Message of the Fathers of the Church, vol. 13, trans. Elizabeth A. Clark, copyright © 1983 by Elizabeth A. Clark, used by permission of The Liturgical Press.

_____, *Homily 20 on Ephesians,* selections, from *Marriage in the Early Church,* trans. David G. Hunter, copyright © 1992 by Augsburg Fortress Press.

_____, *Instruction and Refutation,* selections, from *Jerome, Chrysostom, and Friends,* Studies in Women and Religion, vol. 1, trans. Elizabeth A. Clark, copyright © 1979 by The Edwin Mellen Press.

_____, *The Kind of Women Who Ought to be Taken as Wives,* selection, from *Women in the Early Church,* Message of the Fathers of the Church, vol.

13, trans. Elizabeth A. Clark, copyright © 1983 by Elizabeth A. Clark, used by permission of The Liturgical Press.

_____, *On the Necessity of Guarding Virginity,* selections, from *Jerome, Chrysostom, and Friends,* Studies in Women and Religion, vol. 1, trans. Elizabeth A. Clark, copyright © 1979 by The Edwin Mellen Press.

_____, *On the Priesthood,* selection, from *Women in the Early Church,* Message of the Fathers of the Church, vol. 13, trans. Elizabeth A. Clark, copyright © 1983 by Elizabeth A. Clark, used by permission of The Liturgical Press.

_____, *On Virginity,* selections, from *John Chrysostom: On Virginity; Against Remarriage,* Studies in Women and Religion, vol. 9, trans. Sally Rieger Shore, copyright © 1983 by The Edwin Mellen Press.

Justin Martyr, *Dialogue with Trypho,* selection, from The Ante-Nicene Fathers, vol. 1, ed. and trans. Alexander Roberts and James Donaldson, copyright © 1979 (repr. ed.) by Wm. B. Eerdmans Publishing Company.

The Life of Olympias, Deaconess, selections, from *Jerome, Chrysostom, and Friends: Essays and Translations,* Studies in Women and Religion, vol. 1, trans. Elizabeth A. Clark, copyright © 1979 by The Edwin Mellen Press.

Life of Pelagia the Harlot, from *Harlots of the Desert: A Study of Repentance in Early Monastic Sources,* trans. Benedicta Ward, S.L.G., copyright © 1987 by Cistercian Publications.

The Martyrdom of Potamiaena and Basilides, selections, from *The Acts of the Christian Martyrs,* trans. Herbert Musurillo, S.J., copyright © 1972 by Oxford University Press.

The Martyrdom of Saints Carpus, Papylus, and Agathonicê, selections, from *The Acts of the Christian Martyrs,* trans. Herbert Musurillo, S.J., copyright © 1972 by Oxford University Press.

The Martyrs of Lyons, selections, from *The Acts of the Christian Martyrs,* trans. Herbert Musurillo, S.J., copyright © 1972 by Oxford University Press.

Montanist Oracles, selections, from *The Montanist Oracles and Testimonia,* trans. Ronald E. Heine, copyright © 2002 by The North American Patristic Society, originally published in 1989 by Mercer University Press.

Odes of Solomon, selection, from *The Odes of Solomon,* ed. and trans. James Hamilton Charlesworth, copyright © 1973 by Oxford University Press.

Origen of Alexandria, *Commentary on the Song of Songs,* selection, from *Origen of Alexandria: The Song of Songs: Commentary and Homilies,* Ancient Christian Writers, vol. 26, trans. R. P. Lawson, copyright © 1956 by Newman Press, reprinted by permission of Paulist Press.

_____, *Homilies on Genesis,* selections, from *Origen: Homilies on Genesis and Exodus,* Fathers of the Church, vol. 71, trans. Ronald E. Heine, copyright © 1982 by The Catholic University of America Press.

Palladius, *Lausiac History* 46, 54, from *Women in the Early Church,* Message of the Fathers of the Church, vol. 13, trans. Elizabeth A. Clark, copyright © 1983 by Elizabeth A. Clark, used by permission of The Liturgical Press; *Lausiac History* 34, from *Palladius: The Lausiac History,* Ancient Christian Writers, vol. 34, trans. Robert T. Meyer, copyright © 1965 by The Newman Press, used by permission of Paulist Press.

Polycarp, *To the Philippians,* selection, from *Early Christian Fathers,* Library of Christian Classics, vol. 1, trans. Cyril Richardson, copyright © 1953 by Westminster John Knox Press.

Proclus of Constantinople, *Oration to the Theotokos,* selection, from *Religions of Late Antiquity in Practice,* ed. Richard Valantasis, trans. Vasiliki Limberis, copyright © 2000 by Princeton University Press.

Protevangelium of James, selections, from *New Testament Apocrypha,* vol. 1: *Gospels and Related Writings,* ed. and trans. Edgar Hennecke and Wilhelm Schneemelcher, English trans. by R. McL. Wilson, copyright © 1963, used by permission of Westminster John Knox Press and James Clarke and Co., Ltd.

The Sayings of the Desert Fathers, selections, trans. Benedicta Ward, S.L.G., copyright © 1975 by Cistercian Publications.

Theodotus of Ancyra, *On the Mother of God and On Nativity,* selections, from *Mary and the Fathers of the Church: The Blessed Virgin Mary in Patristic Thought,* trans. Luigi Gambero, copyright © 1999 by Ignatius Press [note: this volume, originally written in Italian, was translated into English by Thomas Buffer].

My own translations were based on the following editions. Texts are listed by author and, when anonymous, by title.

Apostolic Constitutions 2.26.6; 2.57.2–4, 10–13; 3.16.1–2; 8.19.1–20.1–2, text in *Les Constitutions Apostoliques,* 3 vols., ed. and trans. Marcel Metzger, Sources Chrétiennes 320, 329, 336 (Paris: Les Éditions du Cerf, 1985–87).

Gregory of Nazianzus, *On the Misfortunes of his Soul* 2.1.45.229–66, text in *Patrologiae cursus completus: series graeca,* vol. 37, ed. J. P. Migne, translation adapted from Carmen-Marie Szymusiak-Affholder, "Psychologie et histoire dans la rêve initiale de Grégoire le théologien," *Philologus* 15 (1971): 302–10.

———, *Oration* 7.4 (*Funeral Oration for his Brother Caesarius*), text in *Patrologiae cursus completus: series graeca,* vol. 35, ed. J. P. Migne.

———, *Oration* 18.8.30 (*Funeral Oration for his Father*), text in *Patrologiae cursus completus: series graeca,* vol. 35, ed. J. P. Migne.

Irenaeus, *Against Heresies* 1.25.6 and 1.13.1–3, text in *Irénée de Lyon: Contre les Hérésies,* ed. and trans. Adelin Rousseau and Louis Doutreleau, Sources Chrétiennes 264 (Paris: Les Éditions du Cerf, 1979); *Against Heresies* 4.38.1, text in *Irénée de Lyon: Contre les Hérésies, Livre IV,* vol. 2, trans. Adelin Rousseau, Sources Chrétiennes 100 (Paris: Les Éditions du Cerf, 1965).

Methodius, *The Symposium,* selections, text in *Méthode d'Olympe: Le Banquet,* ed. and trans. Herbert Musurillo, S.J., Sources Chrétiennes 95 (Paris: Les Éditions du Cerf, 1963).

Origen, *Against Celsus* 5.62, text in *Origène: Contre Celse,* ed. and trans. Marcel Borret, S.J., Sources Chrétiennes 147 (Paris: Les Éditions du Cerf, 1969).

———, *Commentary on 1 Corinthians,* fragment 74, text in Claude Jenkins, ed., "Origen on 1 Corinthians," *Journal of Theological Studies* 10 (1908–9): 29–51.

———, *Commentary on John,* fragment 45, text in *Die griechischen christlichen Schriftsteller der ersten drei Jahrhunderte* 10 (1903), ed. Erwin Preuschen.

WOMEN IN EARLY
CHRISTIANITY

Introduction

From the fictional Thecla in the second century to the very real Olympias in the early fifth century, the history of women in early Christianity was as varied as the religion itself. Even though, as one scholar has remarked, "the presence of women is almost always perceived indirectly,"[1] nonetheless to investigate the history of early Christian women is to immerse oneself in the tangle of competing theologies and religious convictions that characterized Christianity as it developed during its first five centuries. Contemporary historians do not have much direct access to women's own perspectives on their lives and roles as Christians because so few documents written by women have been preserved. However, there are many kinds of texts that can be used both to reconstruct the history of actual women in Christianity as well as to analyze the ideologies of gender that affected how women were perceived in social and religious terms in Graeco-Roman culture.

The ancient materials that concern women in Christianity focus on several, often interlocking, issues: heresy and orthodoxy in both thought and practice, martyrdom, asceticism and virginity, domestic functions concerning family and household, leadership roles in the church, and female theological imagery. In other words, when ancient Christian men write about women, they seem to be most interested (whether negatively or positively) in women's roles as teachers, prophets, martyrs, widows, deaconesses, ascetics, virgins, patrons, wives, mothers and sisters, and metaphors.

This volume is composed of texts written in Greek in Christian communities around the Mediterranean basin and dated from the second

---

1. Monique Alexandre, "Early Christian Women," in *A History of Women in the West,* vol. 1: *From Ancient Goddesses to Christian Saints,* ed. Pauline Schmitt Pantel (Cambridge: The Belknap Press of Harvard University Press, 1992), 412.

century through the sixth. Most of these texts were written by men, although a few are anonymous. Among the unattributed materials are selections from the Apocryphal Acts, which deserve special mention here. Several contemporary scholars have argued that these stories about such fictional heroines as Xanthippe, Polyxena, and Maximilla were tales told by and for women and may also have been written by women.[2] Otherwise, unlike the Latin tradition, little exists in Greek patristic literature by women authors.[3]

Sources and Organization

There are three broad categories of material relevant to the study of women in early Christianity: official documentary sources; popular narrative and poetic sources; and theological sources. Each of these categories is represented here, and each yields its own distinctive perspective on both actual women and the socio-theological construction of "woman."[4] Although distinctive in terms of the kinds of texts they include, these categories are not mutually exclusive insofar as they share a concern to locate women theologically (for example, by defining woman's nature in terms of the biblical Eve) and socially (for example, by defining women's ecclesiastical roles in terms of gendered understandings of public and private space drawn from Graeco-Roman culture).

The first category of material noted above is composed of documen-

2. See Virginia Burrus, *Chastity As Autonomy: Women in the Stories of the Apocryphal Acts,* Studies in Women and Religion 23 (Lewiston: Edwin Mellen Press, 1987); Stevan Davies, *The Revolt of the Widows: The Social World of the Apocryphal Acts* (Carbondale: Southern Illinois University Press, 1980); Dennis Ronald MacDonald, *The Legend and the Apostle: The Battle for Paul in Story and Canon* (Philadelphia: Westminster Press, 1983); Ross S. Kraemer, "The Conversion of Women to Ascetic Forms of Christianity," *Signs: Journal of Women in Culture and Society* 6 (1980): 298–307.

3. The only texts that I know of are by the Empress Eudocia (ca. 400–460 C.E.), who wrote "Homeric Stitchings" (biblical stories told in verses taken verbatim from Homer's *Iliad* and *Odyssey*) and turned a biography of St. Cyprian into Homeric hexameters. These texts are more revealing of the empress's literary ambitions than they are of the relation of late ancient women to Christianity.

4. I have drawn these categories from Elizabeth A. Clark, "Early Christian Women: Sources and Interpretation," in *That Gentle Strength: Historical Perspectives on Women in Christianity,* ed. Lynda L. Coon, Katherine J. Haldane, and Elisabeth W. Sommer (Charlottesville: University Press of Virginia, 1990), 19.

tary sources such as canons of ecclesiastical councils, represented in this volume by the Council of Gangra, and church orders like the *Apostolic Constitutions*. These are prescriptive texts that regulate what women can and cannot do in official positions (for example, as deaconesses and widows) and in matters of religious practice (for example, whether transvestism—dressing in male clothing—is permissible). As the least "literary" of the sources assembled here, and so less marked by rhetorical embellishment and bias, these texts provide valuable resources for knowledge about women's leadership roles in the church.

Unlike the texts in the first category, those in the next two categories are literary representations rather than transparent windows through which to view history "as it really was." As Elizabeth Clark has noted, in dealing with such highly interpretive texts scholars have moved "beyond the stage . . . in which we retrieve another forgotten woman and throw her into the historical mix" and now examine instead "how women and gender are constructed in these texts" as well as "the social forces at work in these constructions" (and, one may add, the theological forces also).[5] As indicated in what follows, one important result of such examinations shows the importance of the female body—whether it be that of a virgin, harlot, martyr, mother, or saint—for symbolizing religious identity and values in early Christianity.

The second category includes more popular narrative and poetic literature such as apocryphal acts, martyrologies, hagiographies, hymns, and homilies. Such texts tend to be celebratory accounts of heroines who, whether fictional or historical, are presented as rebelling against conventional political and social norms of Graeco-Roman society in order to be faithful to their profession of Christianity and their understanding of their roles within it.[6] Martyrs such as Valentina and Ennatha, for

5. Elizabeth A. Clark, "The Lady Vanishes: Dilemmas of a Feminist Historian after the 'Linguistic Turn,'" *Church History* 67 (March, 1998): 30–31. See also Elizabeth A. Castelli, "Heteroglossia, Hermeneutics, and History: A Review Essay of Recent Feminist Studies of Early Christianity," *Journal of Feminist Studies in Religion* 10 (1994): 73–98; Virginia Burrus, "The Heretical Woman as Symbol in Alexander, Athanasius, Epiphanius, and Jerome," *Harvard Theological Review* 84 (1991): 229–48; Kate Cooper, *The Virgin and the Bride: Idealized Womanhood in Late Antiquity* (Cambridge: Harvard University Press, 1996).

6. See Clark, "Early Christian Women," 20, on the themes of regulation and

example, defied the political authority of the Roman Empire by refusing to engage in ritual religious practices regarded as crucial to civic welfare. In similar fashion, fictional heroines like Maximilla are portrayed as defying cultural expectations about women's role in the family, the basic social unit in Graeco-Roman society, by adopting an ascetic lifestyle within marriage. This pattern would later be adopted by historical women like Melania the Younger, whose biography is included in this volume. The impact of this popular literature cannot be underestimated; as Averil Cameron has observed, these were "stories people want."[7]

The third category comprises formal theological works that expound their authors' ideal or normative constructions of womanhood. Sometimes these carry a positive valence, as in treatises on virginity that hold out the promise of an "angelic life" and in funeral orations that praise their subjects' virtues. However, they can also be negatively charged, as in heresiological works that reveal the "orthodox" ideal by exposing its "heretical" opposite. As Virginia Burrus has observed, the figure of the virgin, "closely linked with the construction of orthodoxy, is frequently contrasted with the figure of the heretical harlot, in language that seeks to delineate the boundaries of acceptable theological reflection while also creating a sharp distinction between 'insiders' and 'outsiders.'"[8] Indeed, theological ideas about sinfulness and salvation are often paramount in such texts, and they are closely linked with women's sexual behavior. Especially in the treatises on virginity, women's literally chaste bodies are presented as metaphors of the pure "brides of Christ" that all Christians strive to become. Overall, texts in this category develop mod-

---

rebellion: "Regulation is especially demanded in two areas: within the family and within the leadership of the church. Here, the traditional hierarchical structures of Greco-Roman society prevailed, and Christianity made few early inroads into the existing order. But for heresy, martyrdom and asceticism, rebellion was the issue. Here, women were judged by what they rebelled *against:* if it was the mainline orthodox church (so seen in retrospect, of course), they were condemned. If, however, they rebelled against social and political structures deemed by churchmen to be tainted or even outright evil, they were rather exalted as true heroines of the faith."

7. Averil Cameron, *Christianity and the Rhetoric of Empire: The Development of Christian Discourse* (Berkeley: University of California Press, 1991), 89–119.

8. Virginia Burrus, "Word and Flesh: The Bodies and Sexuality of Ascetic Women in Christian Antiquity," *Journal of Feminist Studies in Religion* 10 (1994): 31.

els of the ideal woman, whether as mentor to husbands and children or as paradigms of the spiritual life.

This collection is organized topically into five major sections: "Women's Roles in the Church," "Women and Virginity," "Portraits of Ascetic Women," "Women and Domestic Life," and "Female Imagery and Theology." All of these sections contain material from at least two of the categories discussed above, and each aims to be as comprehensive as possible in its presentation of women in early Christian thought. Furthermore, the topic of each section demonstrates in a variety of ways how "the question of woman" generated theological controversy, provoked examinations of ecclesiastical hierarchy, prompted the development of new understandings of religious identity and comportment, and provided a novel set of metaphors for expressing Christian values and ideas.

Many of these issues regarding the position of women in Christianity were already present, although not extensively developed, in the earliest Christian writings collected in the New Testament. Unfortunately for interpreters who wanted to use these texts as authoritative guidelines to settle controversial issues, the New Testament itself reflects different perspectives on the roles of women, and its texts can bear a variety of interpretations. As the major topics and themes are introduced in the following pages, some of the most important Scriptural passages will be noted.

Topics and Themes

Leadership

Some of the most controversial material on early Christian women is contained in Section I: "Women's Roles in the Church." From the second century onward, as the church moved toward institutionalization, it adapted to the male-oriented order of Graeco-Roman society, in which public authority and office were the province of men, while women were defined primarily by their roles as wives and mothers.[9] One of the Pas-

9. See Karen Jo Torjesen, "Reconstruction of Women's Early Christian History," in *Searching the Scriptures*, vol. 1: *A Feminist Introduction*, ed. Elisabeth Schüssler Fiorenza (New York: Crossroad, 1993), 290–310; Margaret Y. MacDonald, *Early Christian*

toral Epistles, probably written late in the first century or early in the second, expresses this situation clearly: "Let a woman learn in silence with all submissiveness. I permit no woman to teach or to have authority over men; she is to keep silent. For Adam was formed first, then Eve; and Adam was not deceived, but the woman was deceived and became a transgressor. Yet woman will be saved through bearing children, if she continues in faith and love and holiness, with modesty" (1 Tim 2:11–15).

Prior to the church's gradual elaboration of a male-dominated hierarchy, however, the earliest Christian communities were house-based groups in which women as well as men held leadership roles, especially in the charismatic exercise of the gift of prophecy. This is evident in the community established by the apostle Paul in Corinth; in his first letter to the Corinthians, Paul supports women's public acts of prayer and prophecy, as long as they veil themselves.[10] In other letters, Paul names several women as notable missionaries and fellow "workers in the Lord," and even calls one, Junia, "foremost among the apostles."[11] Some post-Pauline Christians followed Paul's lead in viewing women as capable leaders and prophets: the second-century *Acts of Paul and Thecla* presents its heroine as a teacher who also performs the priestly function of baptism (see Section III for this text),[12] and another text from the same era, the *Gospel of Mary*, presents its heroine as a visionary who, although challenged by the male apostles, delivers an authoritative revelation of the Savior's teaching (see Section V for this text).

Women and Pagan Opinion: The Power of the Hysterical Woman (Cambridge: Cambridge University Press, 1996), 27–40, 154–65.

10. 1 Cor 11; Antoinette Clark Wire, *The Corinthian Women Prophets: A Reconstruction through Paul's Rhetoric* (Minneapolis: Fortress Press, 1990); Dale B. Martin, *The Corinthian Body* (New Haven: Yale University Press, 1995), 229–49.

11. Rom 16:12; see also Phil 4:2–3; see Rom 16:7 for Junia; for a discussion of the roles of women in Pauline communities, see Wayne A. Meeks, "The Image of the Androgyne: Some Uses of a Symbol in Earliest Christianity," *History of Religions* 13 (1974): 197–206; Elisabeth Schüssler Fiorenza, *In Memory of Her: A Feminist Theological Reconstruction of Christian Origins* (New York: Crossroad, 1983), 160–204.

12. In this text, Thecla baptizes herself (*Acts of Paul and Thecla* 34 and 40), but when Paul commissions her to go and teach, he does not mention baptizing as one of her roles. However, shortly after this text was written, some had apparently understood it as authorizing women to perform baptisms; see Tertullian, *On Baptism* 1 and 17, who argues against those who claim the *Acts of Paul and Thecla* as the basis for allowing women to teach and baptize.

This way of thinking about women's activities as Christians did not win the day, however. As the church gradually began to pattern its organization after the conventional gender roles of Roman society, women's leadership roles were diminished.[13] Thus when certain Christian groups in the second century continued to extend leadership roles to women like the teacher Marcellina, and especially to women who were prophets like the female followers of Marcus, they were condemned as heretical in part for this reason.[14] The Montanist prophets Priscilla and Maximilla were sharply denounced by later writers not only as heretical but also as deluded and irrational. They were early instances of what later became a commonplace in theological writing: the "heretical woman" expressed the dangerous condition of a community whose boundaries were permeable and uncontrolled, while the figure of the female virgin symbolized a community that was safely closed to unorthodox ideas and practices.[15]

Despite their exclusion from the highest ranks of the ecclesiastical hierarchy, women played a role in the institutional church. Widows aged sixty and older were organized as an order and charged with the duty of intercessory prayer. Although they were likened to "the altar of God" by the third-century text *Didascalia apostolorum*, the church order included in Section I, they were denied liturgical duties; even so, they were allowed to give some instruction to other women about ethics, faith, and "the refutation of idols."[16] The only office to which women were ordained was that of deaconess, well attested from the third century onward in the

13. Schüssler Fiorenza, *In Memory of Her*, 285–315; see also Bart D. Ehrman, *The New Testament: A Historical Introduction to the Early Christian Writings*, 2d ed. (New York: Oxford University Press, 2000), 363–74.

14. See Ross Shepard Kraemer, "Heresy as Women's Religion, Women's Religion as Heresy," chap. 11 in *Her Share of the Blessings: Women's Religions Among Pagans, Jews, and Christians in the Greco-Roman World* (New York: Oxford University Press, 1992), 157–73; Karen L. King, "Prophetic Power and Women's Authority: The Case of the *Gospel of Mary* (Magdalene)," in *Women Preachers and Prophets in the Christian Tradition*, ed. Beverly Kienzle (Berkeley: University of California Press, 1995).

15. Virginia Burrus, "The Heretical Woman As Symbol"; Peter Brown, *The Body and Society: Men, Women, and Sexual Renunciation in Early Christianity* (New York: Columbia University Press, 1988), 259–84, 341–65; Alexandre, "Early Christian Women," 426–29.

16. See Charlotte Methuen, "Widows, Bishops and the Struggle for Authority in the *Didascalia Apostolorum*," *Journal of Ecclesiastical History* 46 (1995): 197–213.

eastern half of the Roman Empire. Called by one church order "an image of the Holy Spirit," the deaconess assisted in the baptism of women by anointing their bodies with oil and instructing them how to "preserve the seal of baptism in purity." Deaconesses were also charged with care for women who were ill and with helping to maintain decorum during church services (see the *Apostolic Constitutions* in Section I for material on deaconesses).

As Elizabeth Castelli has noted, "Christian women's religious involvement fell into the more dominant pattern of the broader culture, in which women's religiosity was simultaneously revered and distrusted."[17] Although the material discussed above might seem to fall more heavily on the side of distrust, there was also reverence: the bravery of women martyrs and the intellectual abilities of women who founded convents and taught in them, such as Melania the Younger and Macrina, were both extolled as exemplary.

Asceticism and Virginity

Above all, however, it was the figure of the female virgin that captured the imagination of ancient Christian writers, since she was thought to have the power to overcome the disadvantages of the female gender. Since the themes of asceticism and virginity were closely intertwined, the material in Section II on women and virginity and in Section III on portraits of ascetic women will be treated together here. There are complex issues involved in these two themes, but the basic problem is succinctly stated by Kate Cooper in a book-length study that explores "how the civic ideology of marriage, which had served for at least a millennium as a symbolic reinforcement of social stability, lost ground to a model of otherworldly allegiance and a corresponding ideal of Christian virginity."[18]

Early Christians often traced their ideas about physical chastity to certain passages in the New Testament such as Jesus' saying in Matthew

---

17. Elizabeth A. Castelli, "Gender, Theory, and *The Rise of Christianity:* A Response to Rodney Stark," *Journal of Early Christian Studies* 6 (1998): 233.

18. Kate Cooper, *The Virgin and the Bride: Idealized Womanhood in Late Antiquity* (Cambridge: Harvard University Press, 1996), 19.

19:12 ("There are eunuchs who have made themselves eunuchs for the sake of the kingdom of heaven") and Paul's stated preference for the celibate life over marriage in 1 Corinthians 7:1, 7. However, asceticism did not originate with Christianity but was widespread in Graeco-Roman culture, which had developed practices for the "care of the self" that focused on the human body as a significant locus of meaning.[19] Even though it was seen as dangerously associated with the passionate senses and thus with vice, the body had been re-conceptualized in this period as an essential part of the self. Practices designed to control the body's perceived tendency to excess, especially in matters of diet and sex, spanned a continuum from moderation with regard to food and sexual activity to the more extreme forms of Christian asceticism among monastics in the Egyptian and Syrian deserts (see the sayings of the "desert mothers" in Section III).

Although Christian practices of renunciation like fasting and celibacy might seem at first to entail a negative view of the body, in fact asceticism had a very optimistic dimension because it was premised on the belief that human beings could be spiritually transformed in the here and now. Susanna Elm has observed that "asceticism began as a method for men and women to transcend, as virgins of God, the limitations of humanity in relation to the divine. It slowly changed into a way for men as men and women as women to symbolize the power of the Church to surpass human weakness."[20]

The extolling of virginity as a privileged means of closeness to God was an aspect of asceticism that Christians developed in a distinctive manner. Virginity as an ideal state of being for women received fullest expression in the fourth-century theological treatises included in Section II. However, as early as the second century, the legendary heroine Thecla had already provided a model for a woman empowered spiritually and liberated socially by chastity, and she lived on as an ideal in later biographical portraits of historical women like Olympias, Melania the Elder,

---

19. See the ground-breaking work of Michel Foucault, *The History of Sexuality*, vol. 3: *The Care of the Self*, trans. Robert Hurley (New York: Random House, 1986).

20. Susanna Elm, *"Virgins of God": The Making of Asceticism in Late Antiquity* (Oxford: The Clarendon Press, 1994), 384.

and Macrina, who was said to have "Thecla" as her secret name. "The-cla" is also the name of the virgin in Methodius's *Symposium* who gives the crowning speech about the heavenly benefits of female asceticism. The bridal imagery in this third-century work is part of what became a common feature of Christian texts on virginity: the denial of literal sexuality resulted in its metaphorical intensification. When not only the virginal woman but also the church was understood as a "bride of Christ," virginity became a metaphor for Christianity as a whole. Paradoxically, virginity was the true marriage, a union with the divine.[21]

Thecla was notable not only for her embrace of asceticism but also for cutting her hair and dressing like a man. This motif of the "manly woman" also characterizes biographies of historical female ascetics as well as theological discussions of virginity. Since virtues were understood to be "male," virtuous women were declared to have transcended their gender: in his biography of his sister Macrina, for example, Gregory of Nyssa wondered whether "woman" was really a proper name for her, given her supremely virtuous character. Such women were understood to have reversed the sins of the temptress Eve.[22] Yet, as Teresa Shaw has pointed out, even the holiest woman could not, finally, overcome the negative qualities associated with the female body. As she argues, "the male delineation of the contours of female piety seems driven by *fear* of the power and sexual danger ascribed to the female body and to female 'nature,' within the same discourse that praised virginity. Gender, or really the problem of femaleness, intrudes at every level. . . ."[23]

Nonetheless, there is evidence that some women "became male" not only by living the ascetic life with its attendant physical and spiritual practices but also by dressing as men (see the Council of Gangra in Section II). In late antiquity, stories about transvestite saints became very popular. One such saint, Pelagia of Antioch (see her hagiography in Section III), was a "holy harlot," a sinful woman who repented, adopted the

21. See Cameron, *Christianity and the Rhetoric of Empire*, 175.
22. See Elizabeth A. Clark, "Devil's Gateway and Bride of Christ: Women in the Early Christian World," in eadem, *Ascetic Piety and Women's Faith: Essays on Late Ancient Christianity* (Lewiston: The Edwin Mellen Press, 1986), 23–60.
23. Teresa Shaw, *The Burden of the Flesh: Fasting and Sexuality in Early Christianity* (Minneapolis: Fortress Press, 1998), 252 (Shaw's emphasis).

dress of a monk, lived out her life in a monastic cell, and was only discovered to be female after she had died. This phenomenon of the "female man of God"[24] may well have been related to ancient ideas about androgyny, as reflected in Paul's statement in Galatians 3:28: "In Christ there is no male and female." Envisioning a reunified humankind, such thoughts held out the hope of a return to paradise in which the fateful split between male and female was healed.[25]

Marriage

This exaltation of virginity contributed to the creation of a hierarchy in the church in which married Christians were devalued in relation to the ascetic elite.[26] In his treatise *On Virginity*, for example, John Chrysostom wrote that "virginity is as much superior to marriage as heaven is to earth and as the angels are to people" (see Section II). Theologians who placed virginity at the pinnacle of spiritual attainment also regaled their readers with the day-to-day miseries of married life: in his *On Virginity*, Gregory of Nyssa paid special attention to the dangers of pregnancy and childbirth as well as the cares of child-rearing, while John Chrysostom makes the drudgery of married life sarcastically clear in his treatises against the *subintroductae* (see Section II for both authors). Socially, the ascetic lifestyle may well have offered opportunities to women that they would not have had if married. At least for the aristocratic ascetics whose biographies are presented in Section III, such benefits included freedom to travel, to found and lead monasteries, to study and teach, to engage in public theological discussions, and to cultivate friendships with like-minded men.[27]

Christians could not, however, debase marriage completely if they were to honor the authority of Scripture, specifically the divine command in Genesis 1:28, "Be fruitful and multiply." Indeed, as the texts pertaining

24. This phrase is used by Palladius, *Lausiac History* 9.1, to refer to Melania the Elder.

25. See Meeks, "Image of the Androgyne,"165–208.

26. Burrus, "Word and Flesh," 45.

27. See Elizabeth A. Clark, "Ascetic Renunciation and Feminine Advancement: A Paradox of Late Ancient Christianity," in eadem, *Ascetic Piety and Women's Faith*, 175–208.

to marriage in Section IV show, authors like John Chrysostom who highly revered virginity also wrote to commend marriage. Yet even positive Christian presentations of marriage had been affected by ascetic ideas, as in fact they had been in the culture at large. By the fourth century, as one interpreter has noted, "traditionalists both pagan and Christian were elaborating the ideal of marriage in increasingly spiritualized language."[28]

The apostle Paul had recommended reciprocity between husband and wife concerning conjugal relations and advised that "it is better to marry than to be aflame with passion" (see 1 Corinthians 7 in Section IV). Subsequently, under the influence of Graeco-Roman philosophical and medical views that the passions of the body were harmful to the soul, later Christians began to emphasize the importance of continence in marriage. The goal of marital sex was now procreation alone. Indeed, for the late second-century theologian Clement of Alexandria, the sexual act was so dangerous (he compared it to "minor epilepsy") that he counseled his readers that "our aim is not merely to be self-controlled . . . but rather to be self-controlled even over lust itself." Despite this ascetic distrust of marital sex, however, writers like John Chrysostom promoted a view of marriage in which love, harmony, and friendship were the ideals (see Section IV for both authors).

Except for its strong condemnation of divorce, remarriage, contraception, abortion, and infanticide, Christianity largely followed the marital practices and ideologies of Graeco-Roman culture. In terms of practices, Chrysostom gives a lively, if disapproving, picture of wedding celebrations in Antioch, replete with singing, dancing, and drinking (see his homily on 1 Corinthians in Section IV). In addition, as Margaret Schatkin has pointed out, "secular customs of joining right hands, giving a ring, taking a veil, and (in the east) crowning were continued in the [Christian] wedding ceremony. . . . Christian iconography continued the Roman custom of depicting a marriage by showing the couple joining right hands, but Christ replaced Juno as the deity uniting the couple."[29]

28. Cooper, *The Virgin and the Bride*, 97.
29. Margaret A. Schatkin, "Marriage," in *Encyclopedia of Early Christianity*, ed. Everett Ferguson (New York: Garland Publishing, Inc., 1997), 2: 722–23; see also Judith

Ideologically speaking, marriage was regarded by the church not as
a civic duty, as in the culture at large, but rather as a divinely appointed
institution "whose model was the relationship between Christ and his
church" and which fell under the purview of ecclesiastical authority.[30]
On the other hand, Christian marriages followed the Roman convention
that placed men in the public sphere and women in the private domain.
Wives were expected to be modest and submissive, but, as much of the
material in Section IV shows, they were also idealized as mentors to their
husbands and children and trusted managers of the household. Gregory
of Nazianzus, for example, compared his mother Nonna to biblical heroines like Sarah and Anna; excelling both in domestic duties and in piety,
she represents a perfect blend of the Roman matron and the faithful
Christian.

Theological Imagery

The material presented thus far suggests that the history of women
in early Christianity was marked by ambivalence. On the one hand, their
connection with the biblical "first woman," Eve, cast a negative light on
their nature while, on the other hand, the theological function of female
virgins as "brides of Christ" was extremely positive. One of the most important currents in early Christian thought that helps explain the transformation of woman as "Eve" into woman as "bride of Christ" was the
development of the redemptive role of the Virgin Mary. Section V includes texts that explore the Eve-Mary theme as well as the view of Mary
as mother of God. These texts give theological expression to many of the
perspectives that undergird the material in the previous sections of this
volume.

What Eve destroyed, Mary recuperated: this fundamental theme per-
vades early Christian theology. While not all early Christians viewed Eve
as evil, most did: as Epiphanius explained, "Eve became for men the
cause of death, because through her death entered the world" (see "Eve
and Mary" in Section V). As the mother of Christ, however, Mary was the

---

Evans Grubbs, "'Pagan' and 'Christian' Marriage: The State of the Question," *Journal of
Early Christian Studies* 2 (1994): 361–412.

30. Schatkin, 722.

cause of life. In the Marian texts given here, Mary plays a cosmological role in the renewal of creation and humanity's relationship with God. Proclus of Constantinople, for example, called her "the only bridge from God to humanity." So elevated did her status become that some women worshipped her as a goddess (see "Marian Cult" in Section V). The development of Marian theology and the growing popularity of virginity as the highest spiritual calling for women were simultaneous processes, and the materials in Section II on theologies of virginity, and in Section III on portraits of ascetic women, should be read in this light.

Finally, this volume closes with a selection of ways in which early Christian writers appropriated "woman" as a metaphor for spiritual realities. It may come as a surprise, given the power of Eve as a negative image of womanhood, that God, the church, and the human soul were at various times all characterized as having female traits! Of course there was ambivalence here as in so many texts regarding women, since sometimes the soul-as-female was seen as errant and ignorant, and other times as a Bride longing to kiss Christ her Bridegroom. Nonetheless, these texts demonstrate how powerful the image of woman was for the early Christian imagination.

As the themes and images in this introduction suggest, it is not possible to write a neat and tidy history of women in early Christianity. Monique Alexandre has rightly observed that "the contradictions in these seminal texts cannot be ignored. They justified a reinforcement of the traditional subordination of women, yet at the same time they opened up a realm of freedom."[31] Although not tidy, this history is full of fascinating figures: from harlot-saints to aristocratic ascetics, women were intimately involved in the complex history of the church in late antiquity.

31. Alexandre, "Early Christian Women," 410.

SECTION I

WOMEN'S ROLES
IN THE CHURCH

Teachers

Apart from the kinds of teaching roles exercised in monastery and family, like those of Melania the Younger and Macrina included here, public teaching was forbidden to women in the early church. Those who attempted to teach publicly, like Marcellina (below), were eventually stigmatized as heretics. What follows are selections from the biography of Melania the Younger and a dialogue of Macrina with her brother Gregory, as well as passages from heresiologists describing Marcellina. The section concludes with examples of strictures against women as teachers.

1. Marcellina

Marcellina was the leader of a group of Christians in Rome in the mid-2nd century C.E. The group to which she belonged, called "Carpocratians" after the founding teacher Carpocrates (active during the reign of the emperor Hadrian, 117–38 C.E.), was considered by later heresiological writers to be gnostic and so heretical. Marcellina and those with whom she was associated apparently taught a form of Christianity that emphasized equality among men and women and rejected the idea of private property and other conventional arrangements that they thought were restrictive, such as marriage. The presence of strong female leaders and teachers seems apparent from the notices of Irenaeus and Origen, below.

Irenaeus, *Against Heresies* 1.25.6

Among these [the Carpocratians] was Marcellina, who came to Rome during the bishopric of Anicetus [ca. 155–66 C.E.], and since she held these teachings, she caused the downfall of many.

Origen, *Against Celsus* 5.62

Celsus knows also of Marcellians who follow Marcellina and Harpocratians who follow Salome and others who follow Mariamme and others who follow Martha.

Clement of Alexandria, *Miscellanies* 3.6–8

This passage is a summary of the beliefs and practices of the Carpocratians written by an Alexandrian theologian who held the orthodox view of them as heretics.

6. This is what he [Epiphanes, son of Carpocrates] says, then, in the book *Concerning Righteousness:* "The righteousness of God is a kind of universal fairness and equality. There is equality in the heaven which is stretched out in all directions and contains the entire earth in its circle. The night reveals equally all the stars. The light of the sun, which is the cause of the daytime and the father of light, God pours out from above upon the earth in equal measure on all who have power to see. For all see alike. There is no distinction between rich and poor, people and governor, stupid and clever, female and male, free men and slaves. Even the irrational animals are not accorded any different treatment; but in just the same way God pours out from above sunlight equally upon all the animals. He establishes his righteousness to both good and bad by seeing that none is able to get more than his share and to deprive his neighbor, so that he has twice the light his neighbor has. The sun causes food to grow for all living beings alike; the universal righteousness is given to all equally. . . .

7. "And for birth there is no written law (for otherwise it would have been transcribed). All beings beget and give birth alike, having received by God's righteousness an innate equality. The Creator and Father of all with his own righteousness appointed this. . . . As the laws (he says) could not punish men who were ignorant of them, they taught men that they were transgressors. But the laws, by presupposing the existence of private property, cut up and destroyed the universal equality decreed by the divine law." . . . As he does not understand the words of the apostle where he says "Through the law I knew sin" [Rom 7:7], he says that the idea of Mine and Thine came into existence through the laws so that the

earth and money were no longer put to common use. And so also with marriage. . . .

8. "God made all things for man to be common property. He brought female to be with male and in the same way united all animals. He thus showed righteousness to be a universal fairness and equality. But those who have been born in this way have denied the universality which is the corollary of their birth and say, 'Let him who has taken one woman keep her,' whereas all alike can have her, just as the other animals do."

2. Melania the Younger

Melania the Younger (ca. 383–439 C.E.), granddaughter of the Roman aristocrat and ascetic Melania the Elder, was a noted ascetic in her own right. She lived in continence with her husband Pinian and built women's and men's monasteries on the Mount of Olives in Jerusalem. She was also renowned as a teacher. The following excerpt from her biography describes her role as teacher in the first monastery for virgins that she founded. For fuller biographical information, see Section III, "Biographies of Ascetic Leaders," 3: "Melania the Younger," below.

Gerontius, *Life of Melania the Younger* 42–48

The identity of this author is disputed among contemporary scholars. At the very least, he was a priest in Jerusalem during the period when Melania lived there and knew her in that context.

42. I am not able to relate the continual and inspired teachings she used to put to them, but I shall attempt to report a little about some of them. Her whole concern was to teach the sisters in every way about spiritual works and virtues, so that they could present the virginity of their souls and the spotlessness of their bodies to their heavenly Bridegroom and Master, Christ.

First she taught that it was necessary to stay vigilant during the night office, to oppose evil thoughts with sobriety, and not to let their attention wander, but to focus their minds on singing the Psalms. She would say, "Sisters, recall how the subjected stand before their mortal and worldly rulers with all fear and vigilance; so we, who stand before the fearsome and heavenly King, should perform our liturgy with much fear and trembling. Just keep in mind that neither the angels nor any intelligible and heavenly creature can worthily praise the Lord who needs nothing and is beyond praise. If then the incorporeal powers, who so much surpass our nature, fall short in worthily celebrating the God of all things, as we have already said, how much more ought we, useless servants, to sing Psalms in all fear and trembling, lest we bring judgment upon ourselves for our lack of care in glorifying our Master instead of reward and benefit.

43. "As for pure love to him and to each other, we are taught by the Holy Scriptures that we ought to guard it with all zeal, recognizing that without spiritual love all discipline and virtue is in vain. For the devil can copy all our good deeds that we seem to do, yet, in truth, he is conquered by love and by humility. I mean something of this sort: we fast, but he eats nothing at all; we keep vigil, but he never sleeps. Let us thus hate arrogance since it was through this fault that he fell from the heavens and by it he wishes to carry us down with him. Let us also flee the vainglory of this age that fades like a plant's flower. And before all else, let us guard the holy and orthodox faith without deviation, for this is the groundwork and the foundation of our whole life in the Lord. Let us love the holiness of our souls and bodies because apart from this, no one will see the Lord."

And since she feared that one of them might fall out of pride in excessive mortification, she said, "Of all the virtues, fasting is the least. Just as a bride, radiant in every kind of finery, cannot wear black shoes, but adorns even her feet along with the rest of her body, so does the soul also need fasting along with all the other virtues. If someone is eager to perform the good deed of fasting apart from the other virtues, she is like a bride who leaves her body unclothed and adorns only her feet."

44. . . . She used to tell them the story of an old holy man that concerned the necessity of submitting oneself to everyone, a situation that is likely to be the lot of a person who lives in the midst of humans: "Someone went to an aged holy man wanting to be instructed by him, and the holy man said to him, 'Can you obey me in everything for the sake of the Lord?' And he answered the father, 'I will do everything that you order me to do with great zeal.' The holy man said, 'Then take a scourge, go over to that place, and hit and kick that statue.' The man returned having

willingly done what he was commanded. The old man said to him, 'Did the statue protest or answer back while it was being struck or kicked?' And he replied, 'Not at all.' The father said, 'Then go again; hit it a second time and add insults as well.' When he had done this still a third time at the command of the father and the statue did not answer—for how could it, since it was stone?—then at last the old saint said to him, 'If you can become like that statue, insulted but not returning the insult, struck but not protesting, then you can also be saved and remain with me.' Thus let us, too, O children, imitate this statue and nobly submit to everything—to insult, reproach, contempt—in order that we may inherit the Kingdom of Heaven."

45. In regard to exerting oneself in fasting, Melania repeated the apostolic words, "Not from grief or from necessity, for God loves a joyful giver" [2 Cor 9:7], and left this matter of fasting to everybody's own personal decision. Concerning love, humility, gentleness, and the other virtues, in contrast, she said, "A person does not blame either his stomach or any other part of his body, but it is inexcusable for any human not to keep the Lord's commandments. Thus I exhort you to wage your contests in patience and longsuffering, for the saints enter into eternal life through the narrow gate. The labor is very small but the refreshment is grand and eternal. Just endure a little, that you may be crowned with the wreath of righteousness."

46. During the night hours she awakened the sisters for a service of praise, in accordance with the prophetic saying, "I have come so late and have cried," and again, "In the middle of the night I arose in order to confess to you" [Ps 119:62, 147–48]. She said, "It is not helpful to arise for the nightly liturgy after we have sated ourselves with sleep. Rather, we should force ourselves to rise, so that we may receive the reward for the force we have exerted in the age to come." After they had completed their customary office, Melania provided them with a little time to get some sleep, by which they might rest from the toil of the vigil and renew their bodies for the day's psalmody.

47. Their nightly office had three responses and three readings and near the hour of daybreak, fifteen antiphons. They chanted at the third hour, she said, "because at this hour the Paraclete descended on the

apostles [Acts 2:4, 14], and at the sixth, because at that hour the patriarch Abraham was deemed worthy to receive the Lord [Gen 18:1], and at the ninth, because according to the tradition of the holy apostles, at the ninth hour, Peter and John, while going up at the hour of prayer, healed the lame man [Acts 3:1]." She also listed other testimonies from Holy Scripture in accordance with the practice, for example, the most holy prophet Daniel who knelt to pray three times a day [Dan 6:10], and the parable in the holy Gospel that tells about the householder who went out at the third, the sixth, and the ninth hours to engage workers for his vineyard [Matt 20:3, 5].

"As for evening prayers," she said, "we ought to undertake them in all zeal, not only because we have passed the course of the day in peace, but also because in that hour Clophas and the one with him were deemed worthy to travel in the company of the Lord after his resurrection" [Luke 24:12–32]. She exhorted them to be especially zealous on Sundays and the other important feast days to give themselves to uninterrupted psalmody. She said, "If in the daily liturgy it is good not to be negligent, how much more ought we on Sundays and the remaining feasts to chant something beyond the customary office."

48. By thus saying these things, she affirmed the sisters' zeal through her teaching, so that when the blessed woman wished to spare them in their vigil, because of the great toil which they had had. . . . They would not agree and said, "Since you are ceaselessly concerned with our physical needs every day, thus we ought so much the more to be concerned with spiritual things, so that we leave nothing out from the customary office." And the blessed woman rejoiced mightily when she saw their good decision in the Lord.

3. Macrina

Macrina (ca. 327–379 C.E.) was the eldest child of a prominent Christian family in Cappadocia (in modern-day Turkey, north of Syria). This family produced three of the most important figures in the ascetic movement of the fourth century: St. Basil, St. Gregory of Nyssa, and St. Macrina herself. Macrina established a monastery for women on the family estate and was noted both for her ascetic discipline as well as for the power of her ascetic teaching; indeed, in his biography of his sister, Gregory of Nyssa credits Macrina with persuading Basil to devote himself to the ascetic cause rather than to a career in rhetoric and likens her ability as a philosophical teacher to that of Socrates.

Gregory of Nyssa, *On the Soul and the Resurrection* (selections)

Gregory presents this treatise as the conversation that he and his sister had when she was on her deathbed. I have added section titles to indicate major themes. See Section III, "Biographies of Ascetic Leaders," 1: "Macrina," below, for Gregory's mention of this conversation in his hagiographic portrait of Macrina.

Dialogue about grief and death

At the time that Basil, great among the saints, left the life of man [379 C.E.] and went to God, and a common onset of grief descended upon the Churches, my sister and teacher was still alive and I hurried to her to tell her the sad news about our brother. My soul was sorrowful as I suffered the pain of this affliction and I was seeking someone to share my tears, someone whose burden of pain was equal to my own. As we met each other, the sight of my teacher reawakened the grief within me for she was already ill and close to death. She, however, like those who are skilled in the equestrian art, first, allowed me to be swept along for a little while by the violence of my grief and, after this, tried to restrain me, guiding the disorder of my soul with her own ideas as if with a bridle. She quoted the following apostolic saying:

Macrina. "It is not right to grieve for those who are asleep, since we are told that sorrow belongs only to those who have no hope."

Gregory. And I, with my heart still seething with pain, asked: "How is it possible for me to achieve this attitude, since there is a natural aversion to death in each person and no one can endure the sight of others dying and those who are dying themselves flee from it as much as they can? Also, since among the sentences for wrongdoing the most extreme penalty decreed by the laws is death, how can we come to think that the departure from this life is nothing even in the case of strangers, not to mention the case of the death of our close friends?" . . .

Macrina. My teacher asked: "What is it about death itself which seems especially fearful to you? Surely, the unanimity of the foolish is not enough to make you condemn it."

[Note: Having established that grief in the face of death stems from uncertainty about the nature of the soul and its fate after death, Gregory and Macrina discuss and reject materialist definitions of the soul. Macrina then discusses the relation between the soul and the body, as well as the soul's relation to love and evil, as follows.]

Relation between the soul and the body

Gregory. "But," said I, "how does the belief in the existence of God prove that there is a human soul? For the soul is not the same thing as God, so that if a person accepts the one he must altogether accept the other."

Macrina. She answered: "It is said by the wise that man is a microcosm, encompassing in himself the elements by which he is made complete. If this is true, it is likely that we do not need any other support to strengthen our assumption about the soul. We assume that it exists by itself in a separate and particular nature within the bodily complex. For, as we know the whole world through sensual perception, we are led by this very activity of our senses to the notion of a thing and to a design beyond the senses and our eye becomes the interpreter of the all-powerful wisdom which is seen in everything and which, by itself, reveals that which encompasses everything in accordance with itself. Thus, looking at the cosmos within us, we have no small starting point for conjecturing as to what is hidden through those things that appear. But that is hidden which, being intelligible and invisible, escapes the observation of our senses."

Gregory. I said: "Yes, it is possible to consider the wisdom which underlies everything through the wise and skillful logic seen in nature in this harmonious universe. But what knowledge of the soul can be derived from what the body reveals to those who are looking for the invisible in the visible phenomena?"

Macrina. The virgin replied: "The soul itself is an especially suitable teacher of opinions about the soul for those who desire to know themselves according to that wise precept, because it is immaterial and incorporeal, acting and moving according to its own nature and indicating its own movements through the bodily organs. There is no less equipment in those who have become corpses through death; but, since the psychic power is not in them, it remains without movement and activity. There is movement when there is perception in the organs and the intelligible power goes through the body by perception as it seems best to it."

Gregory. "What then," said I, "is the soul, if it is possible for its nature to be outlined with some reason so that some observation of what lies underneath may come to us through this delineation?"

Macrina. My teacher answered: . . . "The soul is a substance which is begotten, alive, intelligible, and, by itself, it puts into an organic perceptive body a life-giving power as long as the nature capable of receiving these things endures. . . . But, you ask, isn't there some intelligible power present in each of the senses? What could the hand, by itself, teach us if the faculty of thought did not bring touch to an understanding of the object touched? What assistance could hearing separated from intelligence give us for a knowledge of what we seek, or the eye, or the nose, if each of these relied entirely on itself? This is the truest thing and well said: that the mind sees and the mind hears." . . .

The soul, beauty, and love

Gregory. But I, holding back a little and returning to an earlier part of our conversation, said: "It seems to me that there is a certain conflict between what we are saying and what we investigated before in connection with the emotions. On the one hand, these movements of the soul were thought to be active in us because of our affinity to irrational animals—I mean the emotions we enumerated earlier in our discussion: anger and fear and desire and pleasure and such things. But it has also been said that the good use of these emotions is a virtue and that evil comes about because of their abuse. Furthermore, we pointed out how each of them contributes to the virtuous life and we stated, in particular, that we are led to God through desire, being drawn up to Him from below as if by a choir. Somehow, it seems to me that there is a conflict here."

Macrina. "What do you mean?"

Gregory. I said: "Since every irrational impulse in us is removed after purgation, the desiring faculty will no longer exist, but, if this is so, there will be no inclination towards what is better, since the soul will no longer have a desire for the good."

Macrina. She said: "To this, we reply that the faculty of contemplation and of making distinctions is characteristic of the godlike portion of the soul, since, by these, we comprehend even the divine. When, either because of our effort here on earth or because of our purgation afterwards, our soul is freed from its association with the emotions, we shall in no way be impeded in our contemplation of the beautiful. The beautiful, by its very nature, is somehow attractive to everyone looking at it. If the soul is freed from all evil, it will exist entirely in the realm of the beautiful.

"But beautiful is the divine to which the soul will be joined on account of its purity, uniting with what is proper to it. If this occurs, there will no longer be a need for any movement based on desire to lead us to the beautiful. The one who lives in darkness has a desire for the light. If he comes into the light, the enjoyment of it follows upon the desire and the power of enjoying makes the desire useless and foolish. Nor, as far as our own participation in the good is concerned, will there be any penalty if the soul, freed from such impulses, turns back upon itself and sees itself clearly (that is, what its nature is) and looks towards the archetype because of its own beauty as if looking into a mirror and image. . . .

"For this is what love is: a state of mind directed towards what is pleasing to the mind. When the soul, having become simple and uncomplex and entirely god-like, discovers the good that is truly simple and incorporeal, the only thing in existence which is absolutely delectable and lovable, it clings to it and mingles itself with it through its affectionate movement and activity. It conforms itself to that which is always comprehended and discovered and, once it has become, through its similarity to the good, identical with the nature of what it participates in, desire is no longer present in it because there is no need of any of the goods. Consequently, the soul in this state of abundance expels from itself the desiring motion and disposition which existed only when what was desired was not present. . . .

"On this account, love is first among all the activities connected with virtue and all the commandments of the law. If, therefore, the soul ever attains this goal, it will need none of the others, having reached the fullness of its being, and it seems that it alone preserves in itself the character of the divine blessedness. And knowledge becomes love because what is known is, by nature, beautiful. Wanton satiety does not touch the truly beautiful. And, since the habit of loving the beautiful is never broken by satiety, the divine life, which is beautiful by nature and has from its nature a love for the beautiful, will always be activated by love. Nor does it have a limit of its activity of love, since we assume that beauty has no limit which would cause love to cease when beauty comes to an end. The beautiful comes to an end only through its opposite. Its nature is not to accept anything inferior and it continues to an unending and boundless good.

"Since all nature is attracted to what is related to it and a human being is somehow related to God, containing within himself imitations of the archetype, the soul is necessarily attracted to the divine and related to it. It is entirely and in every way necessary for what is related to God to be preserved. If the soul happens to be light and simple, with no material heaviness pressing it down, its approach to what is attracting it is pleasant and easy. However, if it is held down by the nails of a passionate attachment to material habits, it is likely to have the experience of bodies crushed in the ruins of earthquakes. Let us assume, for the sake of discussion, that not only are they oppressed by the ruins, but that they are also pierced by nails and pieces of wood embedded in the mass of ruins. It is likely that bodies lying like this until they are rescued by their relatives will be mangled and torn apart and they will suffer every kind of grave injury. The ruins and nails will crush them because of their power to drag them along." . . .

The soul, pain, and evil

Gregory. I said: "It seems, then, that the divine judgment does not inflict punishment upon those who have sinned, but, as your argument proves, only acts in separating good from evil and in drawing them to a share of blessedness. And it is the tearing off of the evil attached to the good which causes the pain to the one being drawn up to God."

Macrina. My teacher replied: "Thus it is my opinion that the pain is measured by the amount of evil in each person. For it is unlikely that the person deeply involved in forbidden evils and the person who has fallen into minor transgressions will undergo the same pain in the process of being purified of their bad habits. That painful flame will be applied to a greater or lesser degree in proportion to the amount of matter adhering to each one and as long as that which nourishes it is in existence.

"If a person has much earthy stuff clinging to him, his purging flame will necessarily be of long duration; but, if the flame is applied to someone with a smaller amount, there will be a remission of its more violent and fierce activity proportionate to the lesser evil. It is altogether necessary for evil to be removed entirely from that which exists and, as we said before, that which does not exist in being does not exist at all. Furthermore, since it is the nature of evil not to exist apart from choice, when all choice resides in God, evil will disappear completely because there will be nothing left to contain it."

Gregory. "But," said I, "of what use is this good hope to anyone thinking of how terrible it is to endure pain even for one year? Also, if the intolerable pain is extended over an endless period of time, what consolation is there in a hope to come for one whose punishment is measured throughout all eternity?"

Macrina. My teacher said: "It means that we must take thought ahead of time either to safeguard our soul so that it is entirely unmixed with and free from the defilements of evil, or, if that is impossible because of the weakness of our nature, we must see to it that, as far as possible, our deviations be in minor matters and ones easily remedied. For the teaching of the Gospel [see Matt 18:23–35] tells us of a debtor who owed ten thousand talents and one who owed five hundred denarii and one who owed fifty and one who owed a pence, which is the smallest coin.

"And it tells us that the just judgment of God pertains to all and the necessary repayment corresponds to the amount of the debt so that not even the smallest is overlooked. However, the Gospel says that the payment is not made in money, but that the debtor is 'delivered to the torturers until he pays all the debt,' which is nothing else than saying that the payment must be made through torture. The debt owed is participation in the troubles of life since he foolishly chose pleasure unmixed with pain. Once he has put aside everything that is alien to him, namely sin, and is relieved of the shame of being in debt, he becomes free and is at liberty.

"Freedom means being independent and without a master. It was given to us in the beginning by God, but it was obscured by the shame of our debts. All freedom is essentially the same and identical with itself. Consequently, everything that is free is in harmony with whatever is similar to itself. But virtue knows no master. Therefore, all freedom, being without a master, consists in virtue, and since the divine nature is the source of all virtue, those who are free from vice will exist in it, in order, as the apostle says: 'that God may be all in all' [1 Cor 15:28]. . . .

"This is clear from sacred pronouncements which tell us that God becomes a place to those who are worthy and a home and a garment and nourishment and drink and light and wealth and a kingdom and every idea and name we have for what makes up the good life. But the one who becomes everything exists in everything. Here, Scripture seems to me to be describing the complete disappearance of evil. For if God will exist in all being, clearly evil will not exist in it. If anyone supposes that evil also exists, how can we maintain that God exists in everything? For the removal of evil limits the idea of the inclusion of everything. But the one who is in everything will not be in that which is not."

4. Women, the Church, and Teaching

Presented here are comments from two prominent writers that typify the Fathers' view of women and teaching, followed by a selection from the *Didascalia apostolorum,* a collection of materials composed in early third-century Syria on ecclesiastical regulations whose strictures against women as teachers were included virtually word-for-word in the *Apostolic Constitutions* of the late fourth century.

Origen of Alexandria, *Commentary on 1 Corinthians,* fragment 74

"It is shameful for a woman to speak in church" [1 Cor 14:35], whatever she says, even if she says something excellent or holy, because it comes from the mouth of a woman.

John Chrysostom, *Discourse 4 on Genesis 1*

1. . . . After the sin came the words, "Your inclination shall be for your husband and he shall rule over you" [Gen 3:16]. God said in effect to Eve, "I made you equal in honor. You did not use your authority well, so consign yourself to a state of subordination. You have not borne your liberty, so accept servitude. Since you do not know how to rule—as you showed in your experiment with the business of life—henceforth be among the governed and acknowledge your husband as a lord." Note God's kindness here. For lest when she heard the words, "He shall rule over you," she might imagine them to mean a burdensome tyranny, God puts the words of caring first. He did this by saying, "Your inclination shall be for your husband," that is, "He is your refuge, your haven, and your security: he shall be these things to you. Amid all life's daily terrors, I give you the right to turn to him, to take refuge in him." . . . You see how sin introduced woman's subjection, but how God, so ingenious and wise, used the results of sin for our benefit.

Listen to how Paul speaks of this subjection, so that you may again be instructed on the agreement of the Old and the New Testaments. Paul says, "Let the woman learn in silence, in all subjection" [1 Tim 2:11]. Do you see how he, too, submits the woman to the man? Hold on, and you will hear the reason. Why does Paul say, "in all subjection"? He asserts, "I do not permit a woman to teach a man" [1 Tim 2:12]. Why not? Because she taught Adam once and for all, and taught him badly. "Nor should she have authority over the man" [1 Tim 2:12]. What in the world is he getting at? She exerted her authority once and exerted it badly. And she should be "in silence." Tell the reason for this as well. Paul says, "Adam was not deceived, but the woman was deceived and sinned" [1 Tim 2:14]. Therefore let her descend from the professor's chair! Those who know not how to teach, let them learn, he says. If they don't want to learn but rather want to teach, they destroy both themselves and those who learn from them. This is the very thing that occurred through the woman's agency. So here it is evident that she is subjected to the man and that the subjection is because of sin. I want you to heed that verse, "Your inclination shall be for your husband and he shall rule over you."

Didascalia apostolorum 3.6

It is neither right nor necessary therefore that women should be teachers, and especially concerning the name of Christ and the redemption of his passion. For you have not been appointed to this, O women, and especially widows, that you should teach, but that you should pray and entreat the Lord God. For he the Lord God, Jesus Christ our teacher, sent us the Twelve to instruct the people and the gentiles; and there were with us women disciples, Mary Magdalene and Mary the daughter of James and the other Mary; but he did not send them to instruct the people with us. For if it were required that women should teach, our Master himself would have commanded these to give instruction with us.

Prophets

Women were prophets in some very early Christian communities—most notably, the group of female prophets in the community in Corinth in the mid-first century—and they appear again in prophetic roles in two movements of the second century. Because both of these movements were ultimately declared heretical (in part, it would seem, due to the leadership roles undertaken by women), the information that remains comes largely from sources hostile to these forms of Christianity.

1. Disciples of Marcus

Marcus, after whom this movement is called, was a Christian teacher and theologian active in the mid-second century, probably in Alexandria, Egypt. He was a follower of the teachings of Valentinus, one of the most original philosophical interpreters of Christianity in the second century. Although both Valentinus and Marcus were condemned as "gnostic" by their opponents, their understanding of Christianity gained many adherents. The details of Marcus's theological system are reported by the heresiologist Irenaeus in *Against Heresies* 1.13.6–21.5. In the present context it should be noted that Marcus taught that there was a feminine dimension of God and he had seen a vision of God in the form of a woman. Also, women in this movement both functioned as prophets and performed the priestly office of consecration. The followers of Marcus were active in the Rhone Valley of Gaul, where the wife of one of the deacons in Bishop Irenaeus's church in Lyon adopted their understanding of Christianity. The apparent popularity, in his own congregation, of this form of Christian belief and worship, which was different from Irenaeus's, may explain in part his opposition to it.

Irenaeus, *Against Heresies* 1.13.1–3

1.13.1 Another of them [i.e., Valentinians], who prides himself on having corrected the master, is named Marcus. He is extraordinarily skilled in magical deceptions, by which he seduces many men and not a few women to devote themselves to him as to a man of the greatest knowledge and perfection and as to one who holds the greatest power that comes from invisible and indescribable places. He seems truly to be the precursor of the Antichrist, for, combining the games of Anaxilaus with the trickery of those who are called magi [magicians], he is thus considered a miracle-worker by those who have no sense and by those who have lost their minds.

1.13.2 Feigning to consecrate a cup [for the Eucharist] with mixed wine and prolonging greatly the prayer of invocation, he makes it appear purple and red, so that Grace [Charis], who is one of those who are above all things, is believed to drip her blood into that cup as a result of Marcus's invocation. Those present desire very strongly to take a drink from the cup, so that the Grace invoked by the magician might be infused in them also. Again, giving the mixed cups to some women, he commands them to consecrate the cups in his presence. And when this is done, he brings out another, much larger cup than the one which was consecrated by the seduced woman. He pours from the smaller cup which the woman had consecrated into the much larger cup which he has brought, and he speaks at once, as follows: "May she who is before all things, the Grace who is beyond knowledge and speech, fill your inner person and multiply her knowledge in you, sowing a grain of mustard seed in good soil." After saying such words and thus goading the unfortunate woman into a state of raving, he appears to be working wonders when the larger cup is filled by the smaller one to the point of overflowing. And by doing other similar things, he has led many astray and dragged them away after him [as his followers].

1.13.3 It seems that he has a certain demon as his familiar spirit, by which he seems to prophesy, and he makes to prophesy as many women as he thinks are worthy to be participants in his Grace. For he spends his time most of all around women and, among them, those who are distinguished, whose robes have a band of purple, and who are very rich. These he often tries to seduce with flattering words like the following: "I want you to participate in my Grace, since the Father of all has your angel continually in his sight. Further, the place of your greatness is with us: it is necessary that we unite as one. Receive Grace first from me and through me. Prepare yourself like a bride waiting for her bridegroom, so that you be what I am, and I be what you are. Put your seed of light in the bridal chamber. Receive a bridegroom from me and receive him and be received by him. Behold, Grace has descended into you: Open your mouth and prophesy." However, when the woman responds, "I have never prophesied and I do not know how to prophesy," Marcus makes certain invocations a second time in order to amaze the one he is seducing, and says to her, "Open your mouth and say anything whatever and you will prophesy." Then the woman, puffed up and proud by these things that were promised, and with her soul on fire at the thought that she will prophesy and with her heart fluttering, is emboldened and utters any ravings that come to her, carelessly and audaciously, like one heated by a spirit. As a man better than us has noted about such prophets, the soul is audacious and shameless when heated with empty air. Thereafter, the woman thinks herself to be a prophet. She thanks Marcus for sharing his Grace with her and she desires eagerly to reward him, not only by giving him a gift from her possessions—whence he has amassed an abundance of riches—but also by giving him her body, since she desires to be completely united with him, so as to descend with him into one body.

2. Montanists

Montanism, named after its founder, Montanus, was an ecstatic prophetic movement that originated in the Christianity of Asia Minor (modern-day Turkey) in the late

150s or early 160s. Montanus was joined by two female prophets, Priscilla (sometimes called Prisca) and Maximilla (and sometimes a third, Quintilla, is mentioned). Central to the message of this movement was the conviction that the Holy Spirit could still speak directly to the Christian community through inspired individuals, whether male or female. Montanism was notable for the leadership roles that it accorded to women. Presented here are, first, the oracles by women that have been preserved, and second, testimonies from a variety of sources.

Oracles

Eusebius, *Ecclesiastical History* 5.16.17

And let not the spirit that speaks through Maximilla say . . . "I am driven away from the sheep like a wolf. I am not a wolf. I am word, and spirit, and power."

Epiphanius, *Panarion* 48.2.4

For the one they call Maximilla, the prophetess, declares: "After me there will no longer be a prophet, but the end."

Ibid., 48.12.4

For hear, O children of Christ, what this Maximilla who belongs to such as are thus called Cataphrygians says in a straightforward manner: "Hear not me, but hear Christ."

Ibid., 48.13.1

And again the same Maximilla, who claims to be the gnosis of persuasion and doctrine, to speak derisively, declares: "The Lord has sent me as partisan, revealer, and interpreter of this suffering, covenant, and promise. I am compelled to come to understand the knowledge of God whether I want to or not."

Ibid., 49.1

For these Quintillians, or Priscillians, say that in Pepuza [in Phrygia, Asia Minor] either Quintilla or Priscilla, I cannot say precisely, but one of them, as I said before, had been asleep in Pepuza and the Christ came to her and slept with her in the following manner, as that deluded woman described it. "Having assumed the form of a woman," she says, "Christ came to me in a bright robe and put wisdom in me, and revealed to me that this place is holy, and that it is here that Jerusalem will descend from heaven."

Testimonies

Hippolytus, *Refutation of All Heresies* 8.19

But there are others who themselves are even more heretical in nature, Phrygians by race. Having been prejudiced by women named Priscilla and Maximilla, whom they take to be prophetesses, they have been deceived in that they say the Spirit, as the Paraclete, has gone forth in these women. And likewise they magnify a certain Montanus before them as a prophet. Since they have countless books of these people they go astray, because they neither apply the critique of reason to what they have said nor do they pay attention to those who can apply such a critique, but are swept away by their uncritical faith in them. They say that they have learned something more through them than from the Law and the Prophets and the Gospels. And they magnify these weak females above the apostles and every divine gift, so that some of them dare say that something greater has occurred in them than in Christ. They, like the Church, confess that God is the Father of the universe and the creator of all things, and they accept all that the gospel testifies about Christ. But they devise new fasts, feasts, and the eating of dry food and cabbage, declaring that these things have been taught by those females. But some of them, agreeing with the heresy of the Noetians, say that the Father himself is the Son, and that he has experienced birth, suffering, and death. I will present a more detailed treatment of these matters later, for their heresy has become an occasion of evil to many. [Note: Noetus was an early third-century theologian in Asia Minor whose view of the Trinity was modalist; since each person of the Trinity was a "mode" of God, this meant that God himself had suffered and died on the Cross.]

Origen, *Comm. on 1 Corinthians,* fragment 74

For insofar as all speak and can speak if a revelation should come to them [see 1 Cor 14:30–31], he [Paul] says: "Let the women be silent in the churches" [1 Cor 14:34]. But the disciples of the women, who were instructed by Priscilla and Maximilla, not by Christ the husband of the bride [see John 3:29], were not obedient to this command. But nevertheless let us be reasonable also as we reply to the arguments they find plausible. "Philip the evangelist had four daughters," they say, "and they prophesied [see Acts 21:9]. And if they prophesied, why is it strange that our prophetesses also prophesy?" as they say. But we shall put an end to these arguments. First, when you say that your prophetesses have prophesied, demonstrate the signs of prophecy among them. And second, even if Philip's daughters prophesied, they did not speak in the churches, for we do not have this in the Acts of the Apostles; nor do we find it even in the Old Testament. It is attested that Deborah was a prophetess [see Judg 4:4]. And Mariam, the sister of Aaron, took the timbrel and led the women [see Exod 15:20]. But you would not find that Deborah addressed the assembly of the people as Jeremiah and Isaiah did. You would not find that Huldah spoke to the people, although she was a prophetess; she spoke to a certain individual who came to her [see 2 Kgs 22:14]. And Anna, a prophetess, the daughter of Phanuel of the tribe of Asher, has been mentioned in the Gospel [see Luke 2:26], but she did not speak in the church. Therefore, even though a woman be granted to be a prophetess by a prophetic sign, nevertheless she is not permitted to speak in church. When Mariam the prophetess spoke, she was leading some women. "For it is shameful for a woman to speak in church" [1 Cor 14:35], and: "I do not permit a woman to teach in general, nor to have authority over a man" [cf. 1 Tim 2:12].

Debate of a Montanist and an Orthodox Christian (selections, author unknown)

The Montanist said: "And why do you also repudiate the saints Maximilla and Priscilla, and say that it is not permissible for a woman to prophesy? Did not Philip have four daughters who prophesied, and was not Deborah a prophetess (cf. Acts 21:9; Judg 4:4)? And does not the apostle say: 'Every woman who prays or prophesies with uncovered head . . .' (1 Cor 11:5)? If it is not possible for a woman to prophesy, neither can she pray. But if they can pray, let them also prophesy."

The Orthodox replied: "We do not repudiate the prophecies of women. Even the holy Mary prophesied and said: 'Henceforth all generations will call me blessed' (Luke 1:48). And as even you yourself said, the holy Philip had four daughters who prophesied, and Mary the sister of Aaron prophesied. But we do not permit them to speak in churches nor to have authority over men (cf. 1 Tim 2:12), with the result that books too are written under their names. For this is what it means for women to pray and prophesy without a veil, and this, then, has brought shame on her head (1 Cor 11:5), that is her husband. For could not the holy Mary, mother of God, have written books under her own name? But she did not, so that she might not bring shame on her head by exercising authority over men."

The Montanist: "Is not writing books the meaning of the statement about praying or prophesying with uncovered head?"

The Orthodox: "It certainly is."

The Montanist: "Then if the holy Mary says, 'Henceforth all generations will call me blessed' (Luke 1:48), is she being outspoken and speaking in an unveiled manner or not?"

The Orthodox: "She has the evangelist as her veil. For the Gospel has not been written under her name."

The Montanist: "Don't take allegories as though they were doctrines with me."

The Orthodox: "Saint Paul especially, then, also took allegories for the confirmation of dogmas when he said: 'Abraham had two wives' (cf. Gal 4:22), 'which things are allegories. For they are two covenants' (cf. Gal 4:24). But let us grant that the covering of the head does not have reference to an allegory. Put a stop to the allegorical meaning for me in the presence of everyone: Suppose there is a poor woman and she does not have the means to veil herself. Must she neither pray nor prophesy?"

The Montanist: "Is it possible for a woman to be so poor that she does not have the means to cover herself?"

The Orthodox: "We have frequently seen women so poor that they did not have the means to cover themselves. But since you yourself are not willing to admit that there are women so poor that they do not have the means to cover themselves, what do you do in the case of those who are baptized? Is it not necessary that the women themselves pray when they are baptized? And what do you say also in the case of men who often cover their head on account of distress? Do you also prevent them from praying or prophesying?"

The Montanist: "He uncovers himself at the time he prays or prophesies."

The Orthodox: "It is not necessary, then, for him to pray without ceasing, but he must disregard the teaching of the apostle who says: 'Pray without ceasing' (1 Thess 5:17). And you also counsel a woman not to pray when she is baptized."

The Montanist: "Is it because Priscilla and Maximilla composed books that you do not receive them?"

The Orthodox: "It is not only for this, but also because they were false prophetesses with their leader Montanus."

The Montanist: "Why do you say they were false prophetesses?"

The Orthodox: "Did they not say the same things as Montanus?"

The Montanist: "Yes."

The Orthodox: "Montanus has been refuted as having said things contrary to the divine Scriptures. Therefore, these women too will be cast out along with him."

Epiphanius, *Panarion* 48.1–49.2 (selections)

48.1, 3 These Phrygians too, as we call them, accept every scripture of the Old and the New Testaments and affirm the resurrection of the dead as well. But they boast of having Montanus for a prophet, and Priscilla and Maximilla for prophetesses, and have lost their wits by paying heed to them. (4) They agree with the holy catholic church about the Father, the Son, and the Holy Spirit, but have separated themselves by "giving heed to seducing spirits and doctrines of devils" [1 Tim 4:1] and saying, "We must receive the gifts of grace as well. . . ."

2, 1 For look here, their religion itself is proof that they cannot keep their contentiously made promises. If we must receive gifts of grace, and if there must be gifts of grace in the church, why do they have no more prophets after Montanus, Priscilla, and Maximilla? Has grace stopped working, then? Never fear, the grace in the holy church does not stop working! (2) But if the prophets prophesied up to a certain time, and no more <after that>, then neither Priscilla, nor Maximilla prophesied; <they delivered their prophecies after> the ones which were tried by the holy apostles, in the holy church.

2, 3 Their stupidity will be exposed in two ways, then. Either they should show that there are prophets after Maximilla, so that their so-called "grace" will not be inoperative. Or Maximilla will be proved a false prophet, since she dared to receive inspiration after the end of the prophetic gifts—not from the Holy Spirit but from devils' imposture—and delude her audience.

2, 4 And see how they can be refuted from the very things they say! Their so-called prophetess, Maximilla, says, "After me will be no prophet more, but the consummation." (5) Look here, the Holy Spirit and the spirits of error are perfectly recognizable! Everything the prophets have said, they also said rationally and with understanding; and the things they said have come true and are still coming true. (6) But Maximilla said that the consummation would come after her, and no consummation has come yet—even after so many emperors, and such a lapse of time! . . .

12, 3 And in turn, you introduce us to—Maximilla! Even your names are different and scary, with nothing pleasant and melodious about them, but with a certain wildness and savagery. (4) At once this Maximilla, who belongs to these so-called Phrygians—listen to what she says, children of Christ! "Hearken not unto me, but hearken unto Christ!"

12, 9 And don't tell me that she was in a rational state! A rational person doesn't condemn himself in his own teaching. If she said anything like, "Don't listen to me," what sort of spirit was speaking in her? (10) For if she spoke humanly, then she was not in the Holy Spirit—for it is plain that in saying, "Do not listen to me," she was speaking humanly, and was not in the Holy Spirit. But if she was not in the Holy Spirit from on high but was thinking humanly, she knew nothing and was no prophetess. For she did not have the Holy Spirit, but spoke and delivered her oracles with human intelligence. . . .

49.2, 3 In their church seven virgins with lamps often come in, if you please, dressed in white, to prophesy to the people. (4) They deceive the congregation with a show of some sort of inspiration and make them all weep by shedding tears and pretending to mourn for humankind, as though to encourage them to the mourning of penitence.

(5) They have woman bishops, presbyters, and the rest; they say that none of this makes any difference because "In Christ Jesus there is neither male nor female" [Gal 3:28]. (6) This is what I have learned [about them]. However, they call them Artotyrites [from *artotyros*, "bread and cheese"] because they set bread and cheese on the altar in their mysteries and celebrate their mysteries with them.

Martyrs

By the end of the first century C.E., being a Christian was a capital offense, since Christianity was not recognized as a legal religion under Roman law. Sporadic persecutions of Christians occurred until 313 C.E., when the emperor Constantine issued an edict of toleration. The worst, government-initiated persecutions were the Decian persecution of ca. 250 C.E. and the so-called Great Persecution of 303–313 C.E. Many women were martyrs for the faith, and their stories were preserved in the *acta martyrum,* a genre of literature that varied widely from court records of trials to narration of the martyrs' bravery and death. Female as well as male martyrs were highly venerated in the early church and were credited with being able to forgive sins and enter Paradise immediately upon death. A cult of the martyrs developed in the fourth century.

1. Blandina

Blandina, a slave, was killed along with several others in an anti-Christian uprising in Gaul in 177 C.E. Her story is told in the *Letter of the Churches of Lyons and Vienne,* which was addressed to the churches of Asia and Phrygia and is preserved in Eusebius's *Ecclesiastical History.*

Eusebius, *Ecclesiastical History* 5.1.3–54 (selections)

5.1.3 The servants of Christ who dwell in Vienne and Lyons in Gaul, to our brothers in Asia and Phrygia who have the same faith and hope in the redemption: peace, grace, and glory from God the Father and from Jesus Christ our Lord. . . .

(4) The intensity of our afflictions here, the deep hatred of the pagans for the saints, and the magnitude of the blessed martyrs' sufferings, we are incapable of describing in detail; indeed, it would be impossible to put it down in writing. (5) The Adversary swooped down with full force, in this way anticipating his final coming which is sure to come. He went to all lengths to train and prepare his minions against God's servants: the result was that we were not only shut out of our houses, the baths, and the public square, but they forbade any of us to be seen in any place whatsoever.

(6) Arrayed against him was God's grace, which protected the weak, and raised up sturdy pillars that could by their endurance take on themselves all the attacks of the Evil One. These then charged into battle, holding up under every sort of abuse and torment; indeed, they made light of their great burden as they sped on to Christ, proving without question "that the sufferings of the present time are not to be compared with the glory that shall be revealed in us" [Rom 8:18]. . . .

(17) All the wrath of the mob, the prefect, and the soldiers fell with overwhelming force on the deacon Sanctus of Vienne, on Maturus who was, though newly baptized, a noble athlete, on Attalus whose family came from Pergamum . . . and on Blandina, through whom Christ proved that the things that men think cheap, ugly, and contemptuous are deemed worthy of glory before God, by reason of her love for him which was not merely vaunted in appearance but demonstrated in achievement.

(18) All of us were in terror; and Blandina's earthly mistress, who was herself among the martyrs in the conflict, was in agony lest because of her bodily weakness she would not be able to make a bold confession of her faith. Yet Blandina was filled with such power that even those who were taking turns to torture her in every way from dawn to dusk were

weary and exhausted. They themselves admitted that they were beaten, that there was nothing further they could do to her, and they were surprised that she was still breathing, for her entire body was broken and torn. They testified that even one kind of torture was enough to release her soul, let alone the many they applied with such intensity. (19) Instead, this blessed woman like a noble athlete got renewed strength with her confession of faith: her admission, "I am a Christian; we do nothing to be ashamed of," brought her refreshment, rest, and insensibility to her present pain. . . .

(37) Maturus, then, Sanctus, Blandina, and Attalus were led into the amphitheater to be exposed to the beasts and to give a public spectacle of the pagans' inhumanity, for a day of gladiatorial games was expressly arranged for our sake. (38) Once again in the amphitheater Maturus and Sanctus went through the whole gamut of suffering as though they had never experienced it at all before — or rather as though they had defeated their opponent in many contests and were now fighting for the victor's crown. Once again they ran the gauntlet of whips (according to the local custom), the mauling by animals, and anything else that the mad mob from different places shouted for and demanded. And to crown all they were put in the iron seat, from which their roasted flesh filled the audience with its savor. (39) But that was not enough for them, and they continued to rage in their desire to break down the martyrs' resistance. But from Sanctus all they would hear was what he had repeated from the beginning, his confession of faith.

(40) Though their spirits endured much throughout the long contest, they were in the end sacrificed, after being made all the day long a spectacle to the world to replace the varied entertainment of the gladiatorial combat. (41) Blandina was hung on a post and exposed as bait for the wild animals that were let loose on her. She seemed to hang there in the form of a cross, and by her fervent prayer she aroused intense enthusiasm in those who were undergoing their ordeal, for in their torment with their physical eyes they saw in the person of their sister him who was crucified for them, that he might convince all who believe in him that all who suffer for Christ's glory will have eternal fellowship in the living God. (42) But none of the animals touched her, and so she was taken

down from the post and brought back to the jail to be preserved for another ordeal: and thus for her victory in further contests she would make irreversible the condemnation of the "crooked serpent" [Isa 27:1], and tiny, weak, and insignificant as she was, she would give inspiration to her brothers, for she had put on Christ, that mighty and invincible athlete, and had overcome the Adversary in many contests, and through her conflict had won the crown of immortality.

(53) Finally, on the last day of the gladiatorial games, they brought back Blandina again, this time with a boy of fifteen named Ponticus. Every day they had been brought in to watch the torture of the others, while attempts were made to force them to swear by pagan idols. And because they persevered and contemned their persecutors, the crowd grew angry with them, so that they had little pity for the child's age and no respect for the woman. Instead, they subjected them to every atrocity and led them through every torture in turn, constantly trying to force them to swear, but to no avail.

(54) Ponticus, after being encouraged by his sister in Christ so that even the pagans realized that she was urging him on and strengthening him, and after nobly enduring every torment, gave up his spirit. (55) The blessed Blandina was last of all: like a noble mother encouraging her children, she sent them before her in triumph to the King, and then, after duplicating in her own body all her children's sufferings, she hastened to rejoin them, rejoicing and glorifying in her death as though she had been invited to a bridal banquet instead of being a victim of the beasts. (56) After the scourges, the animals, and the hot griddle, she was at last tossed into a net and exposed to a bull. After being tossed a good deal by the animal, she no longer perceived what was happening because of the hope and possession of all she believed in and because of her intimacy with Christ. Thus she too was offered in sacrifice, while the pagans themselves admitted that no woman had ever suffered so much in their experience.

2. Agathonicê

Agathonicê was martyred along with two men, Carpus and Papylus, either in the second century C.E. during the reign of the emperor Marcus Aurelius (161–180 C.E.)

or in the mid-third century during the Decian persecution. The *acta* take the form of a trial held before the proconsul in Pergamum in Asia Minor. The selection presented here begins with the questioning of Papylus and ends with the story of Agathonicê.

The Martyrdom of Saints Carpus, Papylus, and Agathonicê (author unknown)

The proconsul then left Carpus and turned to Papylus and said to him: "Are you a senator?"

"I am a citizen," he replied.

"Of what city?" asked the proconsul.

Papylus said: "Of Thyatira."

The proconsul said: "Do you have any children?"

Papylus said: "Yes, many, by God's grace."

But one of the crowd shouted out: "He means he has children in virtue of the faith which the Christians repose in him."

The proconsul said: "Why do you lie saying that you have children?"

Papylus said: "Would you like to understand that I do not lie but that I am telling the truth? I have children in the Lord in every province and city."

"Will you sacrifice?" said the proconsul, "or what have you to say?"

Papylus said: "I have served God from my youth and I have never offered sacrifice to idols. I am a Christian, and you cannot hear any more from me than this; for there is nothing greater or nobler that I can say."

He too was hung up and scraped and endured three pairs [of torturers], but did not utter a sound; like a noble athlete he received the angry onslaught of his adversary.

When the proconsul observed their extraordinary patience he ordered them to be burnt alive, and going down they both hastened to the amphitheater that they might all the more quickly depart from the world. First of all Papylus was nailed to a stake and lifted up, and after the fire was brought near he prayed in peace and gave up his soul. After him Carpus smiled as he was nailed down. And the bystanders were amazed and said to him: "What are you laughing at?"

And the blessed one said: "I saw the glory of the Lord and I was happy. Besides I am now rid of you and have no share in your sins."

A soldier piled up wood and lit it, and the saintly Carpus said to him as he was hanging: "We too were born of the same mother, Eve, and we have the same flesh. Let us endure all things looking forward to the judgment seat of truth." After he had said this, as the fire came close he prayed aloud saying, "Blessed are you, Lord Jesus Christ, Son of God, because you thought me, a sinner, worthy of having this share in you." And with these words he gave up his spirit.

There was a woman named Agathonicê standing there who saw the glory of the Lord, as Carpus said he had seen it; realizing that this was a call from heaven, she raised her voice at once: "Here is a meal that has been prepared for me. I must partake and eat of this glorious repast!"

The mob shouted out: "Have pity on your son!"

And the blessed Agathonicê said: "He has God who can take pity on him; for he has providence over all. Let me do what I've come for!" And taking off her cloak, she threw herself joyfully upon the stake.

Those who witnessed this lamented it, saying: "It is a terrible sentence; these are unjust decrees!"

Then she was raised up and as soon as she was touched by the fire she shouted aloud three times: "Lord, Lord, Lord, assist me! For you are my refuge." And thus she gave up her spirit and died together with the saints. And the Christians secretly collected their remains and protected them for the glory of Christ and the praise of his martyrs; for to him belong glory and power, to the Father, the Son, and the Holy Spirit, now and forever and for all the ages to come. Amen.

3. Potamiaena

Potamiaena, from Alexandria, Egypt, was probably martyred sometime during the reign of the emperor Septimius Severus (193–211 C.E.). According to Eusebius, she was one of a group of followers of the Alexandrian theologian and exegete Origen of Alexandria.

Eusebius, *Ecclesiastical History* 6.5.1–7

(1) Seventh among these [disciples of Origen] should be numbered Basilides, who had led the famous Potamiaena to execution. Even today

she is much in honor among her own people. Boundless was the struggle she endured against her lovers in defense of her bodily purity and chastity (in which she was pre-eminent), for the perfection of her body as well as her soul was in full flower. Boundless too were her sufferings, until at last after tortures terrible and horrifying to describe she was consumed by fire with her mother Marcella.

(2) The story goes that her judge, a man named Aquila [prefect of Egypt, 205/6–210 C.E.], subjected her entire body to cruel torments, and then threatened to hand her over to his gladiators to assault her physically. For a moment the girl reflected, and then when asked what her decision was, she gave some answer which impressed them as being contrary to their religion.

(3) No sooner had she uttered the word and received the sentence of condemnation, when a man named Basilides, who was one of those in the armed services, seized the condemned girl and led her off to execution. The crowd then tried to annoy her and to insult her with vulgar remarks; but Basilides, showing her the utmost pity and kindness, prevented them and drove them off. The girl welcomed the sympathy shown her and urged the man to be of good heart: when she went to her Lord she would pray for him, and it would not be long before she would pay him back for all he had done for her.

(4) After she had said this she nobly endured the end: boiling pitch was slowly poured drop by drop over different parts of her body, from her toes to the top of her head.

(5) Such was the struggle that this magnificent young woman endured. Not long afterwards Basilides for one reason or another was asked by his fellow soldiers to take an oath; but he insisted that he was not at all allowed to do so, since he was a Christian and made no secret of it. For a while they thought at first that he was joking; but then when he persistently assured them it was so, he was brought before the magistrate, and when he admitted the situation he was put into prison.

(6) His brothers in the Lord came to visit him, and when they questioned him about this strange and sudden turn, he is said to have replied that three days after her martyrdom Potamiaena appeared to him at night and put a crown on his head; she said that she had requested his

grace from the Lord and had obtained her prayer, and that she would welcome him before long. At this his brothers shared with him the seal of the Lord, and on the next day he was beheaded, eminent in his witness for the Lord. (7) Indeed, in accordance with what has been said many others in Alexandria are reported to have gone over to the word of Christ in a body, after Potamiaena had appeared to them in sleep and called their names. But this must now suffice.

Catechumens

In the early centuries, men and women who wanted to join the church went through a period of training prior to baptism. Called catechumens, these people were instructed in the creedal and ritual practices of Christianity. There were a few special regulations for female catechumens preparing for a life as Christians, as the following excerpts from an ecclesiastical rule show.

Hippolytus, *The Apostolic Tradition* 17–21

17. Let catechumens spend three years as hearers of the word. But if a man is zealous and perseveres well in the work, it is not the time but his character that is decisive.

18. When the teacher finishes his instruction, the catechumens shall pray by themselves, apart from the believers. And [all] women, whether believers or catechumens, shall stand for their prayers by themselves in a separate part of the church. And when [the catechumens] finish their prayers, they must not give the kiss of peace, for their kiss is not yet pure. Only believers shall salute one another, but men with men and women with women; a man shall not salute a woman. And let all the women have their heads covered with an opaque cloth, not with a veil of thin linen, for this is not a true covering. . . .

20. They who are to be set apart for baptism shall be chosen after their lives have been examined: whether they have lived soberly, whether they have honored the widows, whether they have visited the sick, whether they have been active in well-doing. When their sponsors

have testified that they have done these things, then let them hear the gospel. Then from the time that they are separated from the other cate-chumens, hands shall be laid upon them daily in exorcism and, as the day of their baptism draws near, the bishop himself shall exorcise each one of them that he may be personally assured of their purity. Then, if there is any of them who is not good or pure, he shall be put aside as not having heard the word in faith; for it is never possible for the alien to be concealed. Then those who are set apart for baptism shall be instructed to bathe and free themselves from impurity and wash themselves on Thursday. If a woman is menstruous, she shall be set aside and baptized on some other day.

They who are to be baptized shall fast on Friday, and on Saturday the bishop shall assemble them and command them to kneel in prayer. And, laying his hand upon them, he shall exorcise all evil spirits to flee away and never to return; when he has done this he shall breathe in their faces, seal their foreheads, ears and noses, and then raise them up. They shall spend all that night in vigil, listening to reading and instruction. They who are to be baptized shall bring with them no other vessels than the one each will bring for the eucharist; for it is fitting that he who is counted worthy of baptism should bring his offering at that time.

21. At cockcrow prayer shall be made over the water. The stream shall flow through the baptismal tank or pour into it from above when there is no scarcity of water; but if there is a scarcity, whether constant or sudden, then use whatever water you can find. They shall remove their clothing. And first baptize the little ones; if they can speak for them-selves, they shall do so; if not, their parents or other relatives shall speak for them. Then baptize the men, and last of all the women; they must first loosen their hair and put aside any gold or silver ornaments that they were wearing: let no one take any alien thing down to the water with them. . . .

Widows

It is clear from the Pastoral Epistles of the New Testament that, by the beginning of the second century C.E., there was an order of widows in the church that was large and active enough to require official specifications for membership and duties. This order not only provided financial assistance and social support for older women but also assigned them the duty of charitable works. Eventually the order of deaconesses supplanted that of the widows in terms of such duties as instructing women prior to baptism. Some scholars have argued that the order of widows, with its emphasis on continence, provided the model for monastic orders for women.

1. New Testament

1 Timothy 5:3–16, RSV

This pastoral text from the New Testament is the foundational document for the development of the order of widows in the early church. Its concern to distinguish between "real" widows and others may reflect a concern for ecclesiastical finances as well as a concern about the propagation of false teachings. Prayer, charitable activities, and perhaps house calls are listed as features of the office of widow.

3 Honor widows who are real widows. 4 If a widow has children or grandchildren, let them first learn their religious duty to their own family and make some return to their parents; for this is acceptable in the sight of God. 5 She who is a real widow, and is left all alone, has set her hope on God and continues in supplications and prayers night and day; 6 whereas she who is self-indulgent is dead even while she lives. 7 Command this, so that they may be without reproach. 8 If anyone does not provide for his relatives, and especially for his own family, he has disowned the faith and is worse than an unbeliever. 9 Let no one be enrolled as a widow who is under sixty years of age, or who has been married more than once; 10 and she must be well attested for her good deeds, as one who has brought up children, shown hospitality, washed the feet of the saints, relieved the afflicted, and devoted herself to doing good in every way. 11 But refuse to enroll younger widows; for when they grow wanton against Christ they desire to marry, 12 and so they incur

condemnation for having violated their first pledge. 13 Besides that, they learn to be idlers, gadding about from house to house, and not only idlers but gossips and busybodies, saying what they should not. 14 So I would have younger widows marry, bear children, rule their households, and give the enemy no occasion to revile us. 15 For some have already strayed after Satan. 16 If any believing woman has relatives who are widows, let her assist them; let the church not be burdened, so that it may assist those who are real widows.

2. Second-century Correspondence

The following two brief texts are passages from letters written to various churches by the post-apostolic writers Ignatius of Antioch and Polycarp of Smyrna. These passages are examples of the kind of material that contemporary scholars have used in order to construct an understanding of the office of widow.

Ignatius, *To the Smyrneans* 13.1

Greetings to the families of my brothers, along with their wives and children, and to the virgins enrolled with the widows.

Polycarp, *To the Philippians* 4.3; 6.1

4.3 And the widows should be discreet in their faith pledged to the Lord, praying unceasingly on behalf of all, refraining from all slander, gossip, false witness, love of money—in fact, from evil of any kind— knowing that they are God's altar, that everything is examined for blemishes, and nothing escapes him whether of thoughts or sentiments, or any of "the secrets of the heart" [1 Cor 14:25].

6.1 Also the presbyters must be compassionate, merciful to all, turning back those who have gone astray, looking after the sick, not neglecting the widow or orphan or one that is poor. . . .

3. Third-century Church Rules

Hippolytus, *The Apostolic Tradition* 11; 25; 27

As the following excerpts from this ecclesiastical rule, composed in Rome, demonstrate, by the early third century the office of widow was well established, and qualification for the office as well as its duties were clearly spelled out.

11. When a widow is appointed, she shall not be ordained but she shall be appointed by the name. If her husband has been long dead, she may be appointed [without delay]. But if her husband has died recently, she shall not be trusted; even if she is aged she must be tested by time, for often the passions grow old in those who yield to them. The widow shall be appointed by the word alone, and [so] she shall be associated with the other widows; hands shall not be laid upon her because she does not offer the oblation nor has she a sacred ministry. Ordination is for the clergy on account of their ministry, but the widow is appointed for prayer, and prayer is the duty of all.

25. Widows and virgins shall fast frequently and shall pray for the church; presbyters, if they wish, and laymen may fast likewise. But the bishop may fast only when all the people fast.

27. If anyone wishes to give a meal to widows of mature years, let him dismiss them before evening. But if, on account of existing conditions, he cannot [feed them in his house], let him send them away, and they may eat of his food at their homes in any way they please.

Didascalia apostolorum 3.1–11; 4.5–8

By the third century, when this document from Syria was composed, the office of widow was a fully developed ecclesiastical institution, as this collection of regulations for church organization and practice shows. These passages on the widows were incorporated into the *Apostolic Constitutions* of the fourth century. [Note: I have revised this translation to reflect twenty-first-century usage, e.g., changing "thou" to "you" and using lower-case letters for pronouns referring to God and Christ.]

3.1 Appoint as a widow one who is not under fifty years old, who in some way, by reason of her years, shall be remote from the suspicion of taking a second husband. But if you appoint one who is young to the widows' order, and she cannot endure widowhood because of her youth, and marries, she will bring a reproach upon the glory of widowhood; and she shall render an account to God, first, because she has married a second husband; and again, because she promised to be a widow unto God, and was receiving (alms) as a widow, but did not continue in widowhood. But if there is one who is young, who has been a short time with her husband, and her husband dies, or for any other cause there is a separation, and she continues by herself alone, having the honor of widowhood, she shall be blessed before God; for she is like the widow of Sarepta of Sidon with whom rested the holy angel, the prophet of God [see 1 Kgs 17:9–24]. Or again, she shall be like Anna, who hailed the coming of Christ and received a (good) testimony [see Luke 2:36–38]; and she shall be honored for her virtue, winning honor on earth from people, and praise from God in heaven.

3.2 But do not let young widows be appointed to the widows' order, yet let them be taken care of and helped, lest by reason of their being in want they be inclined to marry a second time, and some harmful matter ensue. For this you know, that she who marries one husband may lawfully marry also a second [see 1 Cor 7:39]; but she who goes beyond this is a harlot.

3.3 Therefore, assist those who are young, that they may persevere in chastity unto God. And do you accordingly, O bishop, bestow care upon these. And be mindful also of the poor, and assist and support them, (3.4) even though there are among them those who are not widowers or widows, yet are in need of help through want or sickness or the rearing of children, and are in distress. It is necessary for you to be careful of all and heedful of all. Hence it is that they who give gifts do not themselves with their own hands give them to the widows, but bring them to you, so that you who are well acquainted with those who are in distress may, like a good steward, make distribution to them of those things which are given to you, for God knows who it is that gives, even though he does not happen to be present. And when you make distribution, tell them the name of him who gave, so that they may pray for him by name. For in all the Scriptures the Lord makes mention of the poor, and gives commands concerning them; . . . and even if they are married persons. And he adds further by Isaiah and says: "Break your bread to the hungry, and the poor man, that has no roof, bring into your house; and when you see the naked, cover him; and you shall not despise one that is of your own flesh" [Isa 58:7]. By all means therefore be careful of the poor.

3.5 Every widow therefore ought to be meek and quiet and gentle. And let her also be without malice and without anger; and let her not be talkative or clamorous, or forward in tongue, or quarrelsome. When she sees anything unseemly done, or hears it, let her be as though she saw and heard it not. For a widow should have no other care except to be praying for those who give, and for the whole Church. When she is asked a question by anyone, let her not immediately give an answer, except only concerning righteousness and faith in God; but let her send those that desire to be instructed to the rulers. And to those who question them let them (the widows) give answer only in refutation of idols and concerning the unity of God. But concerning punishment and reward, and the kingdom of the name of Christ, and his dispensation, neither a widow nor a layman ought to speak; for when they speak without the knowledge of doctrine, they will bring blasphemy upon the word. For our Lord likened the word of his tidings to mustard; but mustard, unless it is skillfully tempered, is bitter and sharp to those who use it. Thus our Lord said in the Gospel, to widows and to all the laity: "Cast not your pearls before swine, lest they trample upon them and turn against you and rend you" [Matt 7:6]. For when the Gentiles who are being instructed hear the word of God not properly spoken, as it ought to be, for edification of eternal life — and all the more in that it is spoken to them by a woman — concerning how our Lord clothed himself in a body, and concerning the passion of Christ, they will mock and scoff, instead of applauding the word of doctrine; and she shall incur a heavy judgment for sin.

3.6 It is neither right nor necessary therefore that women should be teachers, and especially concerning the name of Christ and the redemption of his passion. For you have not been appointed to this, O women, and especially widows, that you should teach, but that you should pray and entreat the Lord God. For he the Lord God, Jesus Christ our Teacher, sent us the Twelve to instruct the people and the Gentiles; and there were with us women disciples, Mary Magdalene and Mary the daughter of James and the other Mary; but he did not send them to instruct the people with us. For if it were required that women should teach, our Master himself would have commanded these to give instruction with us. But let a widow know that she is the altar of God; and let her sit always at home, and not stray or run about among the houses of the faithful to receive. For the altar of God never strays or runs about anywhere, but is fixed in one place.

A widow must not therefore stray or run about among the houses. For those who are gadabouts and without shame cannot be still even in their houses [see 1 Tim 5:13]; for they are no widows, but wallets, and they care for nothing else but to be making ready to receive. And because they are gossips and chatterers and murmurers, they stir up quarrels; and they are bold and shameless. Now they that are like this are unworthy of him who called them; for neither in the common assembly of rest of the Sunday, when they have come, are such women or men watchful, but they either fall asleep or prate about some other matter, so that through them others also are taken captive by the enemy Satan, who suffers not such persons to be watchful of the Lord. And they who are such, coming in empty to the Church, go out more empty still, since they do not listen to that which is spoken or read to receive it with the ears of their hearts. Such persons, then, are like those of whom Isaiah said: "Hearing you shall hear, and shall not understand; and seeing you shall see, and shall not see. For the heart of this people has become fat, and with their ears they hear heavily, and their eyes they have shut: lest at any time they should see with their eyes, and hear with their ears" [see Isa 6:9–10].

3.7 So in like manner the ears of such widows' hearts are stopped, because they will not sit beneath the roof of their houses and pray and entreat the Lord, but are impatient to be running after gain; and by their chattering they execute the desires of the Enemy. Now such a widow does not conform to the altar of Christ; for it is written in the Gospel: "If two shall agree together, and shall ask concerning anything whatsoever, it shall be given them. And if they shall say to a mountain that it move and fall into the sea, it shall so be done" [see Matt 18:19; 17:20; 21:21].

Now we see that there are widows who esteem the matter as one of traffic, and receive greedily; and instead of doing good (works) and giving to the bishop for the entertainment of strangers and the refreshment

of those in distress, they lend out on bitter usury; and they care only for
Mammon, whose god is their purse and their belly: "for where their
treasure is, there is their heart also" [Matt 6.21]. For she who is in the
habit of roaming abroad and running about to receive takes no thought
for good works, but serves Mammon and ministers to dishonest gain.
And she cannot please God, nor is she obedient to his ministry, so as to be
constantly praying and making intercession, because her mind is quite
taken captive by the greed of avarice. And when she stands up to pray,
she remembers where she may go to receive something; or else that she
has forgotten to tell some matter to her friends. And when she stands (in
prayer), her mind is not on her prayer, but on that thought which has occurred to her mind. Now the prayer of such a person is not heard in regard to anything. But she soon interrupts her prayer by reason of the dis-
traction of her mind; for she does not offer prayer to God with all her
heart, but goes off with the thought suggested by the Enemy, and talks
with her friends about some unprofitable matter. For she does not know
how she has believed, or of what order she has been accounted worthy.

But a widow who wishes to please God sits at home and meditates on
the Lord day and night, and without ceasing at all times offers intercession and prays with purity before the Lord. And she receives whatever
she asks, because her whole mind is set on this. For her mind is not
greedy to receive, nor has she much desire to make large expenses; nor
does her eye wander, so that she should see something and desire it, and
her mind be withdrawn; nor does she hear evil words to give heed to
them, because she does not go forth and run about abroad. Therefore her
prayer suffers no hindrance from anything; and thus her quietness and
tranquility and modesty are acceptable before God, and whatsoever she
asks of God, she presently receives her request. For such a widow, not
loving money or dishonest gain, and not greedy, but constant in prayer,
and meek and unperturbed, and modest and reverent, sits at home and
works at (her) wool, so that she may provide something for those who
are in distress, or so that she may make a return to others, in order that
she receive nothing from them. For she reminds herself of that widow of
whom our Lord gave testimony in the Gospel, who "came and cast into
the treasury two mites, which is one dinar," whom when our Lord and

Teacher, the tester of hearts, saw, he said to us: O my disciples, "this poor widow has cast in more alms than anyone; for everyone has cast in from that which was superfluous to him; but this, of all that she possessed she has laid her up treasure" [see Mark 12:41–44].

3.8 Widows ought then to be modest, and obedient to the bishops and deacons, and to reverence and respect and fear the bishop as God. And let them not act after their own will, nor desire to do anything apart from that which is commanded them, or without counsel to speak with anyone by way of making answer, or to go to anyone to eat or drink, or to fast with anyone, or to receive anything of anyone, or to lay hand on and pray over anyone without the command of the bishop or the deacon. But if she does anything that is not commanded her, let her be rebuked for having acted without discipline. For how do you know, O woman, from whom you receive, or from what ministry you are nourished, or for whom you fast, or upon whom you lay your hand? For do you not know that concerning every one of these you shall render an account to the Lord in the day of judgment, seeing that you share in their works?

But you, O widow who are without discipline, see your fellow widows or your brothers in sickness, and you have no care to fast and pray over your members, and to lay hands upon them and visit them, but you pretend to be in ill health, or busy; but to others, who are sinful or have gone forth from the Church, because they give much, you are ready and glad to go and visit them. You then who are like this ought to be ashamed; for you wish to be wiser and to know better, not only than the men, but even than the presbyters and the bishops. Know then, sisters, that whatsoever the pastors with the deacons command you, and you obey them, you obey God; and with whomsoever you communicate by the command of the bishop, you are without blame before God; and so is every brother of the laity who obeys the bishop and submits to him, for they (the bishops) are to render an account for all. But if you do not obey the mind of the bishops and deacons, they indeed will not be responsible for your offenses, but you shall render an account of all that you do of your own will, whether men or women.

Now whoever prays or communicates with one who has been expelled from the Church must rightly be counted as one of the same; for these things lead to the undoing and destruction of souls. If someone communicates and prays with a man who has been expelled from the Church, and does not obey the bishop, he does not obey God and is defiled along with the one who has been expelled. Moreover, he does not allow that man to repent. For if no one communicates [with the expelled person], he will feel compunction and weep, and will ask and plead to be received (again), and will repent of what he has done, and will be saved.

[For *Did. apost.* 3.9, see below in the section on "Writings Opposed to Women's Ecclesiastical Duties."]

3.10 Concerning envy or jealousy, or slander and fault-finding, or contention and ill-will, and carping or rivalry, we have already told you that these things ought not to be found in a Christian; but among widows it is not fitting that any of these things should so much as be named. Yet because the author of evil has many wiles and devices, he enters into those who are no widows and acts through them. For there are some indeed who profess themselves widows, but do not do works worthy of their name. For widows are found worthy to enter into the kingdom not because of the name of widowhood but for faith and works. If one practices good works, she shall be praised and accepted; but if she practices evil works and does the works of the Evil One, she shall be blamed and cast out of the everlasting kingdom, because she has left the eternal things and desired and loved those that are temporal.

Now we see and hear that there are widows who envy each other. For when your fellow aged woman has been clothed, or has received something from someone, you ought, O widow, when you see your sister refreshed—if you are a widow of God—to say, "Blessed be God, who has refreshed my fellow aged woman," and to praise God. Afterwards you ought to praise the man that ministered, and say, "May his work be acceptable in truth," and, "Remember him, Lord, for good in the day of your recompense, and my bishop who has ministered well before you and has dispensed the alms fairly; for my fellow aged woman was naked, and has been provided; and add glory to him, and give him also a crown of glory in the day of the manifestation of your coming." Likewise also the widow who has received alms from the Lord, let her pray for the man who provided this ministration, suppressing his name like a wise woman, so that his righteousness may be with God and not with men—as he said in the Gospel: "When you do an alms, let not your left hand know what your right hand does" [Matt 6:3]—lest, when you pronounce and reveal his name in praying for him who gave, his name should be disclosed and come to the ears of a pagan, and the pagan, being a man of the left hand, know it. Or it may even happen that one of the faithful, hearing you, will go out and talk. It is not expedient that those things which are done or spoken in Church should be revealed in public; for he who divulges and speaks of them disobeys God, and becomes a betrayer of the Church. But when you are praying for him, suppress his name, and thus you will fulfill that which is written, you and the widows who are like you; for you are the holy altar of God, (even of) Jesus Christ.

But now we hear that there are widows who do not behave according to the commandment, but care only for this, that they may stray and run about asking questions. Moreover, she who has received alms from the Lord—being without sense, in that she discloses (the matter) to her that asks her—has revealed and declared the name of the giver; and the other, hearing it, murmurs and finds fault with the bishop who has dispensed, or with the deacon, or with him who has made a gift, saying: "Didn't you know that I was nearer to you and in more distress than she?" And she does not know that it was not by man's will that this was done, but by the command of God. For if you protest and say to him, "I was nearer to you, and you knew that I was more naked than she," you need to know who it was that commanded, and to be silent and not find fault with him who ministered, but to go into your house and fall on your face and give thanks to God for your fellow widow; and to pray likewise for him who gave and for him who ministered, and to beseech the Lord that he might open to you also the door of his favor. And the Lord would soon have heard your prayer bountifully, and have sent you more favor than your fellow widow, whence you never thought to receive a ministry; and (such) proof of your patience would have been praiseworthy. Or do you not know that it is written in the Gospel: "When you do alms, do not sound the trumpet so as to be seen by others, as the hypocrites do. For truly I say to you, they have received their reward" [Matt 6:2]?

Now if God has commanded that a ministry be ministered in secret, and he who ministered did minister in this way, why then do you, who have received in secret, proclaim it openly? Or again, you who have not received, why do you question it? For you not only find fault and murmur, as one who is no widow, but you even utter a curse like the pagans. Or have you not heard what the Scripture says, "Everyone that blesses, is blessed; and everyone that curses, is cursed" [see Gen 27:29; Num 24:9]? And again in the Gospel he says, "Bless them that curse you" [Luke 6:28], and again, "When you enter into a house, say, 'Peace be in this house.' And if that house is worthy of peace, your peace shall come upon it; but if it is not worthy, your peace shall return to you" [Matt 10:12–13].

3.11 If, then, peace returns to those who send it, much more will a curse return against those who utter it idly, because the man against whom it was sent does not deserve to receive a curse. For everyone who curses a man idly, curses himself, since it is written in Proverbs, "As birds and fowl fly, so do idle curses return" [Prov 26:2]. And again he says, "They who utter curses are void of understanding" [Prov 10:18]. For we are shown in a parable by the example of a bee, as the Lord says, "Go to the bee, and learn how she works. For she performs her work in wisdom; and her labor produces food for rich and poor. Although she is little in strength, she is beloved and praiseworthy" [Prov 6:8 LXX]. As then the bee is "little in strength," and when she has stung a man she loses her sting, and becomes barren and soon dies, so also we the faithful: whatever evil we do to another, we do it to ourselves. For "whatever you hate to have done to you, do not do to another" [see Tob 4:15]. Thus, "everyone who blesses is blessed" [Num 24:9].

Therefore, admonish and rebuke those (widows) who are undisciplined and likewise exhort and encourage and help those who conduct themselves rightly. And let widows keep themselves from cursing, for they have been appointed to bless. Let not the bishop, nor a presbyter, nor a deacon, nor a widow utter a curse out of their mouths, that they may not inherit a curse but a blessing. And let this also be your care, O bishop, that not even one of the laity utter a curse from his mouth, for you have the care of all.

4.5 You bishops and deacons must be constant in the ministry of the altar of Christ—we mean the widows and orphans—so that with all care and with all diligence you make it your endeavor to investigate concerning the things that are given, (and to learn) the kind of conversation engaged in by him or her who gives for the nourishment—we say again—of "the altar." For when widows are nourished from (the fruits of) righteous labor, they will offer a holy and acceptable ministry before almighty God through his beloved Son and his Holy Spirit, to whom be glory and honor for ever more.

Make it your care and endeavor therefore to minister to widows out of the ministry of a clean conscience, so that what they ask and request may be granted them at once upon their praying for it. But if there should be bishops who are careless and give no heed to these matters, through respect of persons, or for the sake of dishonest gain, or because they neglect to make inquiry, they shall render no ordinary account.

4.6 For in fact, to administer for the nourishment of orphans and widows, they receive from rich persons who keep men shut up in prison, or ill-treat their slaves, or behave with cruelty in their cities, or oppress the poor; or from the lewd, and those who abuse their bodies; or from evildoers; or from forgers; or from dishonest advocates, or false accusers; or from hypocritical lawyers; or from painters of pictures; or from makers of idols; or from workers of gold and silver and bronze (who are) thieves; or from dishonest tax-gatherers; or from spectators of shows; or from those who alter weights or measure deceitfully; or from inn-keepers who mingle water (with their wine); or from soldiers who act lawlessly; or from murderers; or from spies who procure condemnations; or from any Roman officials, who are defiled with wars and have shed innocent blood without trial—perverters of judgment who, in order to rob them, deal unjustly and deceitfully with the peasantry and all the poor; and from idolaters; or from the unclean; or from those who practice usury, and extortioners.

Now they who nourish widows from these (sources) shall be found guilty in judgment in the day of the Lord; for the Scripture has said, "Better is a supper of herbs with love and amity than the slaughter of fatted oxen with hatred" [Prov 15:17]. For if a widow is nourished with bread only from the labor of righteousness, it shall even be abundant for her; but if much is given her from (the proceeds) of iniquity it shall be insuffi-

cient for her. But again, if she is nourished from (the proceeds) of iniquity, she cannot offer her ministry and her intercession with purity before
God. And even though she is righteous and prays for the wicked, her intercession for them will not be heard, but that for herself alone; for God
makes trial of the hearts in judgment, and receives intercessions with
discernment. But if they pray for those who have sinned and repent, their
prayers will be heard. But those who are in sin, and do not repent, not
only are they not heard when they pray, but they even call to remem-
brance their transgression before the Lord.

4.7 Therefore, O bishops, fly and avoid such ministrations; for it is
written, "There shall not go up upon the altar of the Lord (that which
comes) from the price of a dog or from the hire of a harlot" [Deut 23:18].
For if widows pray for fornicators and transgressors through your blind-
ness, and are not heard, not receiving their requests, you will necessarily
bring blasphemy upon the word through your evil management, as
though God were not good and ready to give. Take good heed therefore
that you do not minister to the altar of God out of the ministrations of
transgression. You have no pretext to say, "We do not know"; for you have
heard what the Scripture says: "Depart from an evil man, and you shall
not fear; and trembling shall not come close to you [Isa 54:14].

4.8 But if you say, "These are the only ones who give alms; and if we
do not receive from them, from what source shall the orphans and widows and those in distress be provided?" God will say to you, "To this end
did you receive the gifts of the Levites, the firstfruits and offerings of your
people, that you might be sustained and even have more than enough, so
that you might not be constrained to receive from evil persons." But if the
Churches are so poor that those in want must be supported by such, it
would be better for you rather to be wasted with famine than to receive
from evil persons. . . .

Deaconesses

The office of deaconess is well attested by the third century C.E. in the *Didascalia apostolorum* and is further specified in the *Apostolic Constitutions* of the fourth century C.E. Duties of this office included assisting at the baptism of women and giving them ethical instruction following baptism. In the fifth century, canon 15 of the Council of Chalcedon (451 C.E.) required that deaconesses be at least forty years of age and that they not marry after appointment to this office. These texts, and indeed the office of deaconess, were indigenous to the eastern parts of the early Christian world.

Didascalia apostolorum 2.26; 3.12

2.26 . . . Let [the bishop] be honored by you as God, for the bishop sits for you in the place of God almighty. But the deacon stands in the place of Christ; and you must love him. The deaconess shall be honored by you in the place of the Holy Spirit; and the presbyters shall be to you in the likeness of the Apostles; and the orphans and widows shall be reckoned by you in the likeness of the altar. . . .

3.12 Therefore, O bishop, appoint for yourself workers of righteousness as helpers who will cooperate with you for salvation. Those that please you out of all the people you shall choose and appoint as deacons: a man for the performance of most of the things that are required, but a woman for the ministry of women. For there are houses where you cannot send a deacon to the women, on account of the pagans, but you may send a deaconess. Also, because in many other matters the office of a woman deacon is required. In the first place, when women go down into the water, those who go down into the water ought to be anointed by a deaconess with the oil of anointing; and where there is no woman at hand, and especially no deaconess, he who baptizes must of necessity anoint the woman who is being baptized. But where there is a woman, and especially a deaconess, it is not fitting that women should be seen by men, but with the imposition of the hand you must anoint the head only. As of old the priests and kings were anointed in Israel, likewise, with the imposition of the hand, anoint the head of those who receive baptism, whether of men or of women. Afterwards—whether you yourself baptize, or whether you command the deacons or presbyters to baptize—let a woman deacon, as we have already said, anoint the women. But let a man pronounce over them the invocation of the divine Names in the water.

And when a woman who is being baptized has come up from the water, let the deaconess receive her, and teach and instruct her how the seal of baptism ought to be (kept) unbroken in purity and holiness. For this reason we say that the ministry of a woman deacon is especially needed and important. For our Lord and Savior was ministered to by women ministers, "Mary Magdalene, and Mary the daughter of James and mother of Jose, and the mother of the sons of Zebedee" [Matt 27:56], and other women besides. And you also need the ministry of a deaconess for many things. For a deaconess is required to go into the houses of the pagans where there are believing women, and to visit those who are sick, and to minister to them according to what they need, and to bathe those who have begun to recover from sickness.

Apostolic Constitutions, selections

This text is a compilation of previously existing material pertaining to a variety of topics, from ecclesiastical hierarchy and discipline to questions of morality and theology. Compiled toward the end of the fourth century, its author and place of composition are unknown.

2.26.6 You should honor the deaconess as an image of the Holy Spirit. She should not do or say anything without the deacon, just as the Comforter does not create or speak on its own, but awaits the will of Christ while glorifying him [see John 16:7, 13–14]. And as it is not possible to believe in Christ without being instructed by the Spirit, so do not let a woman approach a deacon or a bishop without the deaconess.

2.57.2–4 When you [the bishop] gather the church of God together [for worship], command, like the pilot of a large ship, that the assemblies be organized with great skill, directing the deacons, like sailors, to assign places to the brothers as to passengers with all care and solemnity. And first, let the house be oblong, oriented toward the east, with the priestly chambers on both sides, also turned to the east. Thus it will be like a ship. The bishop's throne will be placed in the middle, with the presbyterate seated on either side; the deacons will stand near at hand, watchful and well-clothed, for they are like sailors and managers of the crew.

2.57.10–13 Let the door-keepers stand at the entries of the men in order to observe them, and let the deaconesses stand at the entries of the women, like sailors who steer a ship. . . . If anyone is found sitting out of place, let the deacon, like a commanding officer, reprimand the person and take him to the proper place. For the church is not only like a ship but also like an animal pen. The shepherds place each of the animals—I refer to goats and sheep—according to species and age, and each of them gathers together with its own kind. Likewise in the church: the young men will sit by themselves, if there is room; otherwise let them stand. Old people will sit in their place, and as for the children that stand, let their fathers and mothers take charge of them. The young women will also sit by themselves, if there is room; otherwise, let them stand behind the adult women. Let the married women with children have their own place. Virgins, widows, and old women will stand or sit in front of all the others. The deacon thus will attend to the seating, so that each one who comes in finds his proper place and so that no one sits near the entrance. Likewise let the deacon watch over the people to make sure that no one whispers, dozes, laughs, or makes gestures. For in church it is necessary to be wise, sober, and attentive, lending the ear to the word of the Lord.

3.16.1–2 Ordain also a deaconess, faithful and holy, for the service to women, because it sometimes happens that a male deacon cannot be sent to the houses of certain women because of the unbelievers. You shall therefore send a woman deacon, because of the suspicion of evil-minded people. Actually we need a woman as deacon for many services. In the first place, in the baptizing of women, the deacon shall anoint only their foreheads with the holy oil; following this the deaconess shall anoint them; for it is not necessary that the women be observed by men.

8.19.1–20.1–2 Concerning [the ordination of] a deaconess, I, Bartholomew, declare the following. O bishop, you will lay your hands on her, in the presence of the presbyterate, the deacons, and the deaconesses, you will say: "O eternal God, the Father of our Lord Jesus Christ, the creator of man and woman, who filled with the Spirit Miriam, Deborah, Anna, and Huldah [see Exod 15:20–21; Judg 4:4; Luke 2:36–38; 2 Kgs 22:14–20], who did not judge it unworthy that your only-begotten Son should be born of a woman, who also in the tent of witness and in the temple appointed women as guardians for your holy gates; look now upon this woman, your servant, who has been chosen for the diaconate, and give her the Holy Spirit, and 'purify her from every defilement of the flesh and spirit' [2 Cor 7:1] so that she may worthily accomplish the work with which she has been entrusted, for your glory and the praise of your Christ, through whom be glory and adoration to you in the Holy Spirit forever. Amen."

Writings Opposed to Women's Ecclesiastical Duties

Presented here are representative examples of strictures against the performance of ecclesiastical functions by women, mainly functions pertaining to the priesthood.

Didascalia apostolorum 3.9

That a woman should baptize, or that one should be baptized by a woman, we do not recommend, for it is a transgression of the commandment, and a great danger to the woman who baptizes and to him who is baptized. For if it were lawful to be baptized by a woman, our Lord and Teacher himself would have been baptized by Mary his mother, whereas he was baptized by John, like others of the people. Do not therefore imperil yourselves, brethren and sisters, by acting contrary to the law of the Gospel.

Apostolic Constitutions 3.9.1–4

(1) And about a woman's baptizing, we are informing you that there is no small danger to the women who attempt it. Therefore we do not advise it. For it is dangerous, or rather, it is illegal and impious. (2) For if "the man is the head of the woman" (1 Cor 11:3), he was chosen for

priesthood; it is not right to set aside the order of creation and leave what is chief to descend to the lowest part of the body. For woman is the body of the man, being from his side and subjected to him, from whom also she was separated for the sake of the production of children. He said, "For he shall rule over you" (Gen 3:16). For the man is the ruler of the woman, since he is also her head. (3) And if in what came earlier we did not allow women to teach, how can we assent to their being priests, which is contrary to nature? For this is an error of Gentile atheism to ordain women as priests to the goddesses; it is not in the dispensation of Christ. (4) And also, had it been necessary for women to baptize, certainly the Lord would have also been baptized by his own mother, not by John, or when he sent us to baptize, he would have sent women with us as well for this purpose. But now, nowhere, neither by command nor in writing did he transmit this, since he knew the order of nature and the fittingness of things, being the Creator of nature and the Legislator of the arrangement.

Epiphanius, *Panarion* 79.2,3–4,1

In this passage, Epiphanius uses an attack on a group of women who were making offerings to the Virgin Mary as the occasion to discuss at length why women cannot be priests. For information on the specific group under attack, the Kollyridians, see Section V, "Marian Cult," below.

2,3 For to begin with, to whom is it not immediately obvious, <if he will> investigate the whole scope of the past, that their [i.e., the Kollyridians'] teaching and behavior are devilish, and their undertaking a deviation? Never at any time has a woman been a priest— (4) Eve herself, though she had fallen into transgression, still did not dare to undertake anything so impious. Not one of her daughters did, though Abel sacrificed to God at once, and, even though they were not accepted, Cain offered sacrifices before the Lord. Enoch pleased God and was translated. Noah made thank offerings to the Lord, as a token of gratitude, with the extra animals in the ark, in thanksgiving to the One who had preserved him. (5) The righteous Abraham offered God sacrifice, and Melchizedek the priest of God Most High. Isaac was pleasing to God, and Jacob made the best offering he could on the stone, by pouring oil from his flask. . . .

(6) And why name the throngs of those who sacrificed to God in the Old Testament? We find Ahitub sacrificing, and the sons of Korah, and the Gershonites and the Merarites, to whom the levitical order was entrusted. And the house of Eli, and his kinsmen after him in the household of Abimelech and Abiathar, Helkiah and Buzi, down to the high priest Joshua, and Ezra the priest, and the rest. And nowhere was a woman a priest.

3,1 But I shall go on to the New Testament. If it were ordained by God that women should be priests or have any canonical function in the church, Mary herself, if anyone, should have functioned as a priest in the New Testament. She was counted worthy to bear the king of all in her own womb, the heavenly God, the Son of God. Her womb became a temple, and by God's kindness and an awesome mystery was prepared to be the dwelling place of the Lord's human nature. But it was not God's pleasure [that she be a priest]. (2) She was not even entrusted with the administration of baptism—for Christ could have been baptized by her rather than by John. But John the son of Zacharias dwelt in the wilderness entrusted with baptism for the remission of sins, while his father served God as a priest and saw a vision at the time of the offering of incense.

3,3 Peter and Andrew, James and John, Philip and Bartholomew, Thomas, Thaddaeus, James the son of Alphaeus, Judas the son of James and Simon the Zealot, and Matthias who was chosen to make up the number of the Twelve—all these were chosen to be apostles and "offer the gospel" [Rom 15:16] <throughout> the world, together with Paul, Barnabas and the rest. And with James, the Lord's brother and the bishop of Jerusalem, [they were chosen] to preside over mysteries.

3,4 Successors to the episcopate and presbyterate in the household of God were appointed by this bishop and these apostles, and nowhere was a woman appointed. (5) Scripture says, "Philip the evangelist had four daughters which did prophesy" [Acts 21:9], but they were certainly not priests. And "Anna the daughter of Phanuel was a prophetess" [Luke 2:36], but not entrusted with the priesthood. For the words, "Your sons shall prophesy, and your daughters shall dream dreams, and your young men shall see visions" [Joel 3:1; Acts 2:17], required fulfillment.

3,6 <It is plain> too that there is an order of deaconesses in the church. But this is not allowed for the practice of priesthood or any liturgical function, but for the sake of female modesty, at either the time of baptism or of the examination of some condition or trouble, and when a woman's body may be bared, so that she will be seen not by the male priests but by the assisting female who is appointed by the priest for the occasion, to take care of the woman who is in need of it when her body is uncovered. For the ordinance of discipline and good order in the church has been protected with understanding and care, in proportion to our rule. For the same reason the word of God does not allow a woman "to speak" [1 Cor 14:34] in church either, or "bear rule over a man" [1 Tim 2:12]. And there is a great deal that can be said about this.

4,1 But it must be observed that the ordinance of the church required no more than deaconesses. It mentioned widows too, and called those of them who were still older, "elder," but nowhere did it prescribe "eldresses" or "priestesses." Indeed, not even the deacons in the hierarchy of the church have been commissioned to celebrate any mystery, but only to administer mysteries already celebrated.

SECTION II

WOMEN AND VIRGINITY

Female Comportment

Much of what Christian men wrote about Christian women focused specifically on the behavior of virgins and of wives. The author presented in this selection was concerned with describing the comportment of women as a group. Clement of Alexandria (ca. 160–215 C.E.), a man of culture and wide learning as well as a theological writer, did not expound the ascetic vision as it was later elaborated in the fourth century. However, much of what he wrote concerning women's behavior and self-control can be seen as a harbinger of later ascetic ideals for women's lives; for the rest, one sees in Clement's advice a portrait of how Christian women should act in society.

Clement of Alexandria, *The Pedagogue* (selections)

On Table Manners

2.2.31 We ought also to give special thought here to proper decorum. . . . We should drink without turning our head about, without swallowing all we can hold, without feeling compelled to roll our eyes around in the presence of the drink, and without draining the cup in one gulp with utter lack of self-control; thus we will not wet our chin or our clothes as we tip the cup all at once, practically washing or bathing our face in it. It is certainly a disgusting and undignified spectacle of self-indulgence to see a person greedily swallowing a drink with noisy intake of air.

2.2.33 As for women, who are especially trained in good manners, if only they would not keep their lips wide open as they drink from big cups, with their mouths distorted out of shape! And if only they would not lean their heads back when they drain vessels narrow of neck, thereby exposing their throats with—or so it seems to me—such immodesty!

They hold their chins high as they pour the drink down, as if they were trying to reveal as much of themselves as they can to their companions at table; then they belch like men, or, rather, like slaves, and at their carousals begin to play the coquette. There is no fault that can be excused in a man of reason, and much less so in a woman to whom notoriety, whoever she is, brings only disgrace. "A drunken woman," in the words of Scripture, "is a great wrath" [Eccl 26:11], as if to say that a woman become dissolute from wine is the wrath of God. Why? Because "her shameless conduct shall not be hid." A woman is quickly drawn into immorality even by only giving consent to pleasure. . . . Women are not at all to be allowed to expose or lay bare any part of their bodies, lest both men and women fall: the one by being aroused to steal glances, the other by attracting the eyes of men to themselves. We must always behave with good manners, realizing that the Lord is present, so that he may never say to us reproachfully what the apostle said to the Corinthians: "When you meet together, it is no longer to eat the Lord's supper" [1 Cor 11:20].

On Toiletry and Dress

2.8.64 The words of Aristippus the Cyrenian [a fifth-century B.C.E. rhetorician], who loved ease and comfort, come to mind. He devised this sophistic argument: "A horse, when it is anointed with perfume, does not lose any of its excellence as a horse, nor does a dog, when it is anointed, lose any of its excellence as a dog." Then he went on to draw the conclusion: "neither, then, does man." But the horse and the dog do not have any understanding of what perfume is; those whose perception is intellectual are more to be blamed for their indulgence when they make use of such effeminate sweet odors. . . . Habitually, some people use both the oil of lilies and that of cypress; they prize the oil of roses highly, and so many other kinds which women still use, some liquid, others dry, some in the form of salves, others only for scenting. Day after day they plan ways of procuring them, with an insatiable desire for this sweet fragrance. There are women who always exude extreme vulgarity; they keep scenting and sprinkling their bed covers and their houses, and, in their daintiness, stop short only of making their chamber-pots fragrant with myrrh. (65) . . . Men of our way of life should be redolent, not of perfume, but of perfection, and women should be fragrant with the odor of Christ, the royal chrism, not that of powders and perfumes. Let her be ever anointed with the heavenly oil of chastity, taking her delight in holy myrrh, that is, the Spirit. Christ provides this oil of good odor for his followers, compounding his myrrh from sweet heavenly herbs.

2.8.66 Yet, let us not develop a fear of perfume, like vultures and scarabs who are said to die if anointed with the oil of roses. Let the women make use of a little of these perfumes, but not so much as to nauseate their husbands, for too much fragrance suggests a funeral, not married life.

2.10.105 . . . I admire the ancient city of the Lacedemonians [Sparta] for allowing only courtesans to wear brightly colored garments and gold ornaments; in this way, restricting such showy finery to that type of woman, they bred into their good women a reluctance to adorn themselves. On the other hand, in Athens, even the archons utterly forgot their manhood in their lust for the finer delicacies of life; they used to put on flowing tunics and load themselves with gold. . . . (106) . . . I maintain that man needs clothing only for bodily covering, as a protection against excessive cold or intense heat, so that the inclemency of the weather may not harm him in any way. If that is the purpose of clothes, then one kind of garment surely should not be provided for men and another for women. The need for clothing, like the need for food and drink, is common to both. . . .

2.10.107 Both [men and women] have the same need of being protected; therefore, what they use as protection should be very similar, except, perhaps, that women ought to use a type of garment that will cover their eyes. If the female sex is rightly allowed more clothing out of deference to its weakness, then the practice of a degenerate way of life must be censured which accustoms men to unworthy customs that so often make them more womanish than the women. But we do not feel free to relax our strictness in any way. If we need to make any concessions, we might allow women to use softer garments, provided they give up fancy weaves, symptoms of vanity, and fabrics too elaborate in weave, or with gold thread, Indian silks and all products of the silk-worm. . . . These flimsy and luxurious things are proof of a shallow character, for, with the scanty protection they afford, they do nothing more than disgrace the body, inviting prostitution. An overly soft garment is no longer covering, since it cannot conceal the bare outline of the figure; the folds of such a garment clinging to the body and following its contours very flexibly take its shape and outline the woman's form so that even one not trying to stare can see plainly the woman's entire figure.

2.10.111 But we must moderate our severity for the sake of the women. We say, then, that their garment may be woven smooth and soft to the touch, but not adorned with gaudy colors, like a painting, just to dazzle the eye. For, just like a picture which fades with time, so the constant rinsing and steeping of these woolen robes in plant juices serving as dyes deteriorates the garments, wears them out, weakens the weave, and is definitely opposed to economy. It is the height of vanity to let oneself be fascinated by the flowing robes and gowns and cloaks and mantles and tunics "that cover nakedness," as Homer says [Iliad 2.262]. . . .

2.10.114 We must also guard against all waywardness in our use of [garments]. For instance, it is not right for a woman to wear her dress up over her knees, as the Laconian maidens [in southern Greece] are said to do, because a woman should not expose any part of her body. Of course, when someone tells her: "Your arm is shapely," she can always cleverly make the witty reply: "But it is not public property"; to "Your legs are beautiful," this reply: "But they belong to my husband"; or if he says, "Your face is lovely," she can answer: "But only for him to whom I am married"; still, I am unwilling that a chaste woman even give occasion for such praise from men with sinful intent. I should like, too, not only that it be forbidden them to expose their ankle, but also that it be made obligatory for them to wear a veil over their face and a covering on their head. It is not becoming, either, for a woman to make a show of herself by wearing a purple veil. If I could but wring the purple out of all the veils, that passersby might not turn to catch a glimpse of the face behind it! Yet, such women, who weave almost the whole ensemble of their wardrobe, make everything purple to inflame lusts. . . . A covering, it seems to me, should make what it covers more conspicuous than itself, as the temple does the statue, the body the soul, and the clothing the body. Now, everything is just the opposite. If these women sold their bodies, they would get scarcely a thousand Attic pieces, yet they pay ten thousand talents for one garment, proving that they are less valuable and profitable than their clothes. . . .

2.11.116 There are women who manifest a very similar vanity in their footwear, thereby revealing considerable shallowness of character. It is a matter for shame to have sandals plated with the costliest gold, and even worse to decide, as some do, to have nails hammered into the soles in a circular pattern. Many even engrave love messages on them so that they mark the earth in recurring pattern as they walk, and stamp the eroticism of their own hearts upon it with their footprints. . . . (117) We permit women the use of white sandals, unless they are traveling, when they should use sandals anointed with oil. They also need footwear that has soles nailed on, for their traveling. Otherwise, they should always use sandals, because it is unbecoming for women to expose their bare foot, and also because they are more easily hurt.

On Gems and Cosmetics

2.12.118 It is pure childishness to let ourselves become fascinated by gems, whether they are green or dark red, and by the stones disgorged by the sea, and by metals dug up out of the earth. To set one's heart on shining pebbles and peculiar colors and iridescent glass is simply to play the part of a man without intelligence, easily spell-bound by gaudy appearances. . . . The precious pearl has become an all too common item in the apparel of our women. This stone is formed in the oyster, a bivalve very similar to the pinna [a type of mussel], in size about the shape of the eye of a large fish. These bewitched women are not ashamed to center all their interests on this small oyster. Yet they could adorn themselves instead with that holy stone, the Word of God, called somewhere in Scripture "a pearl" [see Matt 13:46], that is, Jesus in all his splendor and purity, the mysterious eye of the divine vision in human form, the glorious Word through whom human nature is born again and receives a great new value. . . .

2.12.119 Tradition assures us that the heavenly Jerusalem that is above is built up of holy gems and we know that the twelve gates of the heavenly city, which signify the wonderful beauty of the apostolic teaching, are compared to precious jewels [see Rev 21:18–21]. . . . But these women, not understanding that the Scriptures speak only metaphorically, totally blinded by their passion for jewels, offer this remarkable excuse: "Why may we not make use of what God has manifested? I already possess them, so why may I not enjoy them? For whom have they been made if not for us?" Such words can come only from those who are completely ignorant of the will of God. He supplies us, first of all, with the necessities such as water and the open air, but other things that are not necessary he has hidden in the earth and sea. . . .

2.12.121 . . . As a general rule, ornaments should not be desired, as they are mere childish toys, and women should eschew the very thought of embellishment. A woman should be adorned, assuredly, but interiorly; there she should be beautiful indeed. Beauty or ugliness is found only in the soul. . . . (127) Therefore, let them leave these playthings for the sophists who trifle with the truth; let them not take part in such gaudy embellishment nor worship images under a fair veil. The blessed Peter says eloquently: "In like manner, women adorning themselves not with plaited hair or gold, or pearls or costly attire, but as it becomes women professing godliness, with good works" [see 1 Tim 2:9–10; cf. 1 Pet 3:3]. As a matter of fact, there is sound reasoning in his command that such adornments be left alone, for either a woman is already beautiful, and then nature is sufficient (and let not art contend with nature, that is, let deception not vie with the truth), or else she is naturally ugly, and then she proves what she does not have by attiring herself with all these things. (128) Those who worship Christ ought to accept plainness. Indeed, plainness promotes the growth of holiness because it moderates avarice and ministers to real need from what is ready at hand. . . .

2.12.129 Wear, then, as a holy ornament of good fruits on your arms, the generous giving of your possessions and the faithful fulfillment of your household duties. . . . Let there appear upon your feet the ornament of unhesitating readiness for good deeds and steadiness in the path of justice. Modesty and temperance are the true neck-bands and necklaces, for they are chains God forges out of gold. . . . The ears of women should not be pierced, either, to enable them to suspend earrings and ear pen-

dants from them. It is contrary to nature. It is wrong to do violence to nature in a way nature does not intend. Surely, there is no better ornament
for the ears than learning the truth, nor is there any that enters the ears
in as natural a way. Eyes anointed by the Word and ears pierced to hear
are ready to contemplate holy things and to hear divine things. It is only
the Word who reveals true beauty "which eye has never seen before, nor
has ear heard" [1 Cor 2:9].

3.2.4 It is not the appearance of the outer person that should be made
beautiful, but the soul, with the ornament of true virtue. It should be possible, too, to speak of an ornament for the body, the ornament of self-control. But women, busy in making their appearances beautiful, allowing
the interior to lie uncultivated, are in reality decorating themselves,
without realizing it, like [elaborately ornamented] Egyptian temples. . . . (5)
Women who are loaded down with gold seem to me much like that temple. They carefully curl their locks, paint their cheeks, stencil under their
eyes, anxiously dye their hair, and practice perversely all the other
senseless arts. . . . But if anyone draw back the veil of this temple, I mean
the hair net and the dye and the garments and gold and rouge and cosmetics—or the cloth woven of all these things, which is a veil—if he
draws back this veil to discover the true beauty that is within, I am sure
he will be disgusted. He will not find dwelling within any worthy image
of God, but, instead, a harlot and adulteress who has usurped the inner
sanctuary of the soul. The beauty within will turn out to be nothing more
than a beast, "an ape painted up with powder"; as a deceitful serpent, it
will devour the person's intellect with love of ornaments and make the
soul its den. . . . Such women have little care for managing household
expenses for their husbands. Rather, they unloose the strings of their
husbands' purses and waste their fortunes on their own desires. . . .

3.2.6 . . . By day, they stay closeted up, devoting themselves to their
toilet, lest they be caught dyeing their hair blonde; then at night, this arti-
ficial beauty comes creeping out into candle light, as if from her lair, and
both the dimness of the light and the bleary-eyed vision of drunkenness
aid her in her deception. . . . These deluded souls are actually destroying
their natural beauty, without being aware of it, when they add all this ar-
tificial beauty. As soon as day breaks, they massage their skin and rub it

down, then coat it with lotions—but this only dries the skin; while the many preparations make the flesh flabby, and excessive use of soaps robs it of its natural healthy bloom. Women acquire a paleness of face from all these lotions, and their bodies, made delicate from all their beautifying cosmetics, become very susceptible to diseases. Besides, they insult the Creator of mankind, implying that he has not given them the beauty they deserve. . . .

Major Treatises on Virginity

As a form of ascetic practice, voluntary continence was practiced by both men and women in Christianity as early as the second century C.E.; indeed, the apostle Paul already in the mid-first century had described the celibate life as an ideal in 1 Corinthians 7 (see Section IV for this text). Virginal asceticism as a lifestyle for women emerged most fully in the fourth century, when several theologians wrote major treatises on virginity and when virginal women, as well as women who adopted continence during or after marriage, became the subjects of biographies. Virginity for women was constructed as a form of liberation not only from the strictures of marriage and childbearing but also from physical passion and materiality.

1. Methodius, *The Symposium* (selections)

Little is known of the life of Methodius, bishop of Olympus in Lycia (southwest Asia Minor), who was probably martyred ca. 311 C.E. during the persecution of Diocletian. He was learned in Platonic philosophy, quoting from it frequently, and modeled the present work after Plato's *Symposium*. Here, however, the speakers are not male but female, and the topic is not *eros* but asceticism: ten virgins at a banquet give discourses on the importance of chastity and virginity. Although the major treatises on virginity were written during the latter part of the fourth century, this one, written a century earlier, is included because of its unusual form as well as its allegorical appropriation of Scripture for the ascetic cause.

1.1 Marcella, if I remember correctly, immediately began her discourse as follows:

"Virginity is something marvelously great, wonderful, and glorious. Speaking straightforwardly in agreement with the Scriptures, this best and most beautiful way of life is the church's breast, her flower, her first fruits. For this reason also the Lord promises that all who have preserved themselves as virgins will enter the kingdom of heaven; he teaches this in that passage in the gospels in which he speaks about the different ways in which men have become eunuchs [Matt 19:12]. Chastity is rare and difficult for people to maintain; its loftiness and magnificence are matched by the risks it entails. Thus it needs powerful and noble natures which, completely diverting the stream of sensuality, guide upward the vehicle of their soul, never relinquishing their goal, until, nimbly leaping over the world with the eager flight of their intelligence, and placed upon the very vault of heaven, they gaze directly upon incorruptibility itself as it wells up from the undefiled breast of the Almighty. A drink like this cannot be produced on earth; heaven alone is the source of this spring.

"For while Virginity walks on earth, her head touches the heavens. And there are some who have desired her, but saw in her only a goal to be attained. Vulgar as they are and uninitiated, they approached her with unwashed feet and have had to turn back from the middle of the road; they were incapable of the thought worthy of this way of life. For it is not enough simply to guard bodies from corruption, just as one should not show off temples as though they were more important than the statues in them; but it is souls—the images housed in bodies—that must be cared for by adorning them with righteousness. This care and cleansing are constituted for souls above all by the degree to which they strive to hear the divine words and do not give up until they come to the gates of the wise and reach what is true.

"Just as the bloody fluids of meat and all the elements which make for putrefaction are drawn off by salting it, so too for the virgin: all the irrational desires of the body are dried up by sacred teachings. For the soul that has not been salted with Christ's words necessarily begins to smell and breed worms. Surely it was this that King David tearfully confessed when he cried out on the mountains, 'My sores are putrefied and corrupted' [Ps 37:6 LXX; 38:5], because he had not salted and cured himself by self-discipline, but being careless he was dragged down to frenzied pas-

sion and smelled of adultery. This is why it is forbidden in Leviticus to offer any gift to the Lord God as a burnt offering which has not first been
seasoned with salt [Lev 2:13]. Actually we have been given a salt whose
sting dries us up to our advantage: this salt is the spiritual study of the
Scriptures, and without it no soul can approach the Almighty through the
word. 'You are the salt of the earth,' said the Lord to his apostles [Matt
5:13].

"It is necessary, therefore, that the virgin should always love what is
beautiful and distinguish herself among those who excel in wisdom. She
must keep herself from laziness and softness. She must gain the highest
distinction, with thoughts worthy of her virginity. With the Word she must
always wipe clean the putrid juices of sensuality, lest somehow a small
spot of decay, escaping her notice, breed the worm of incontinence.

"Thus, as blessed Paul says, 'the unmarried woman thinks about the
things of the Lord, how she may please the Lord, so that she may be holy
in both body and spirit' [see 1 Cor 7:32–34]. However, there are many
women who think that listening to instruction is of no great importance
and think they are doing a great favor if they lend their ears for even a
short time. These must be excluded. For one must not share the divine
teachings with one who has a petty, mean nature and pretends to be
wise. Would it not be ridiculous to go on talking to such women, who ex-
ert themselves over trifles, without even a thought for the meticulous
care which is necessary if the love of continence is to grow in them?

1.2 "It was indeed a most extraordinary disposition that the plant of
virginity was sent down to humankind from heaven. Hence too, it was
not revealed to the first generations: for in those days there were but few
people, and it was necessary that their numbers be first increased in order to fulfill a goal. Thus men of old did not bring disgrace upon themselves if they married their own sisters, until the Law came and separated them, forbidding and denouncing as sinful what had previously been
thought to be virtuous, and calling him cursed who should uncover the
nakedness of his sister [see Lev 18:9; 20:17]. In such a way did God in his
goodness bring assistance to the human race in due season as do fathers
to their sons. For they do not at once put their sons in charge of peda-
gogues, but they allow them during their early years to frisk about like

little calves. First they send them to teachers who take them through their stammering period. Then, after their minds have shed their downy puerility, they are introduced to the study of more serious subjects, and from there to still more important ones. In this way we should imagine that God the father of all acted towards our forefathers. For the world while still unpopulated was in its infancy, as it were, and had first to be taken from this condition and grow to adulthood.

"But when later it had become populated from end to end overflowing with countless numbers, God did not suffer humankind to continue in its old ways any longer. He took thought how people might make progress and advance farther on the road to heaven, until at last they might become perfect by attaining to the most sublime goal of all, the science of virginity. To begin with, they were to advance from brother-sister unions to marriage with wives from other families. Then they were to give up practicing, like brute beasts, multiple marriage (as though men were born merely for intercourse!). The next step was to take them from adultery; and the next, to advance them to continence, and from continence to virginity, in which state they train themselves to despise the flesh and come to anchor unafraid in the peaceful haven of immortality.

1.3 "Now someone may have the hardihood to attack this account on the grounds that it has no Scriptural foundation. Very well, let us also bring forward the writings of the prophets and so demonstrate the truth of what has already been said. Surely Abraham, in being the first to receive the covenant of circumcision and in circumcising a member of his body [see Gen 17:10–14], symbolizes nothing less than this: that one was no longer to procreate children with an offspring of the same parent. He teaches us that a man must cut off the pleasure of intercourse with his own sister, as with his own flesh. Hence from the time of Abraham men ceased the practice of living in marriage with their sisters. Next, marriage with more than one wife is disallowed by the time of the prophets. 'Go not after your lusts,' we read, 'but turn away from your own will' [Sir 18:30]; for 'wine and women make wise men fall off' [Eccl 19:2]. And in another passage, 'Let your fountain of water be your own and rejoice with the wife of your youth' [Prov 5:18], obviously forbidding multiple marriage. Jeremiah, too, frankly calls men who lust after different women 'amorous stallions' [5:8]. Indeed we read: 'The multiplied brood of the wicked shall not thrive, and bastard slips shall not take deep root' [Wis 4:3].

"But, not to spend too long a time citing the testimony of the prophets, let us further show how monogamy was succeeded by continence, and how continence little by little destroyed the sensuality of the flesh until it completely removed the habitual inclination to intercourse. For presently we are introduced to one who clearly deprecates henceforth this same distracting emotion. He says: 'O Lord, father, and sovereign ruler of my life, leave me not to their counsel. . . . Take from me haughtiness of eyes. . . . Let not the greediness of the heart and lust of the flesh take hold of me' [Eccl 23:1, 4, 6]. And in the book of Wisdom, that model of all virtue, the Holy Spirit clearly tries to draw those who hear him to moderation and continence, singing as follows: 'Better it is to have no children and to have virtue, for the memory thereof is immortal, because it is known both with God and with men. When it is present, they honor it, and they desire it when it has withdrawn itself. And it triumphs crowned forever, winning the reward of undefiled conflicts' [Wis 4:1–2].

1.4 "So much then for the ages of the human race, and how men advanced from brother-sister marriages to the practice of continence. Finally we must consider virginity, and I shall make every effort to speak of it as well as I can. The first question to be answered is this: how is it that of the many prophets and righteous men who spoke and taught so many noble things, not one of them praised or embraced the state of virginity? The answer is that it was reserved for the Lord alone to be the first to exalt this doctrine, just as he alone taught humankind how to draw near to God by detachment from human beings. It was only fitting that he who was archpriest, archprophet, and archangel should also be called archvirgin.

"Again, in antiquity human beings were not yet perfect and thus did not have the capacity to comprehend the perfect, that is, virginity. For being made in the image of God, human beings had yet to receive that which was according to his likeness [see Gen 1:26]. And this was precisely what the Word was sent into the world to accomplish. He took upon himself our form, spotted and stained as it was by our many sins, in order that we, for whom he bore it, might be able to receive in turn the divine form. For then it is possible for us truly to fashion ourselves in the likeness of God when like skilled portrait-painters we express his features in ourselves, and thus possess them in innocence, learning to follow the path he showed us. This was why, although he was God, he chose to put on human flesh, that, by looking upon God's representation of our life as in a painting, we might be able to imitate him who painted it. Thus there is no discrepancy between his thoughts and his actions, nor between what he thought to be good and what he actually taught us. He both taught and did those things that were truly both good and useful.

1.5 "What then did the Lord, the truth and the light, accomplish in coming down to the world? He preserved his flesh incorrupt in virginity with which he had adorned it. And so let us too, if we are to come to the likeness of God, endeavor to aspire to the virginity of Christ. For becoming like God means to banish corruptibility. Now we are told that the Word incarnate became the archvirgin as well as archshepherd and archprophet of his church, by John in the book of the Apocalypse where, filled with Christ, he says: 'And I beheld, and, lo, the Lamb stood upon Mount Sion, and with him a hundred forty-four thousand, having his name, and the name of his Father, written on their foreheads. And I heard a voice from heaven, as the noise of many waters and as the voice of great thunder; and the voice which I heard was as the voice of harp-players harping on their harps. And they were singing as it were a new song, before the throne, and before the four living creatures, and the elders; and no man could understand the song, but those hundred forty-four thousand, who were purchased from the earth. These are they who were not defiled with women; for they are virgins. These follow the Lamb wherever he goes'— thus showing that the Lord is the leader of the choir of virgins. And notice, again, how excellent is the dignity of virginity in God's sight. 'These were purchased from among men, the first fruits to God and to the Lamb; and in their mouth was found no lie; they are without spot; these follow,' he says, 'the Lamb wherever he goes' [Rev 14:1–5].

"Here it is also clear that he wishes to teach us that the virgins were restricted to this number, that is, 144,000, from above, whereas the multitude of the rest of the saints is beyond counting. Note what he teaches us as he considers the others: 'I also saw a great multitude which no one could number, of every tongue and tribe and of every nation' [Rev 7:9]. Obviously, then, as I have said, he introduces an untold number in the case of the other saints, but only a very small number in the case of the virgins, as though he deliberately intended a contrast with the larger, uncounted number.

"There, my dear Arete, is my discourse on virginity," said Marcella. "If I have left anything out, Theophila, who comes after me, can supply the omission." . . .

6.1 When Thallusa had finished speaking, Theopatra said that Arete touched Agathe with her staff, and that when she felt it, she immediately arose and replied as follows. . . .

"All of us, my dear maidens, come into this world with an extraordinary beauty which has a relationship and kinship with wisdom. And then it is that human souls most clearly resemble the one who begot and formed them, when they continue to reflect the pure image of his likeness and the lineaments of that vision which God saw when he fashioned them and gave them an imperishable and immortal form.

"For the unbegotten and incorporeal beauty, that knows neither beginning nor decay, but is unchangeable and ageless and without need, he who abides in himself and is light itself in secret and unapproachable places, embracing all things in the orbit of his power, creating and arranging them—he it was who made the soul in the image of his likeness. This is why it is endowed with reason and immortality; for, fashioned, as I have said, in the image of the only-begotten, it has an unsurpassed loveliness. It is for just this reason that the spirits of wickedness become enamored of it and lie in wait for it; they would force it to defile that godlike and lovely image which it possesses. Thus also the prophet Jeremiah [3:3] tells us in reproaching Jerusalem: 'You had a harlot's forehead, you would not blush' before your lovers, where he is speaking of Jerusalem as having submitted herself to the enemy forces for her profanation. Her 'lovers,' understand, are the devil and his angels, who scheme to dirty and defile, by their sinful contact, the spiritual and translucent beauty of our minds, and lust to commit adultery with every soul that is espoused to the Lord.

6.2 "If anyone, therefore, will keep this beauty spotless and intact and just as it was when the creator artist himself fashioned it according to type, in imitation of that eternal and intelligible nature of which the human being is the image and expression, then, becoming like some beautiful sacred statue transported from this world to the city of the blessed in the heavens, he will dwell there as within a temple. Now this beauty of ours is then best preserved intact when, shielded by virginity, it is not blackened by the heat of corruption from without, but, remaining within itself, it adorns itself with justice and is led as a bride to the Son of God. And this indeed is his own teaching, when he inculcates the duty of kindling the unquenchable light of chastity in one's own flesh as in so many lamps [for this and what follows, see the parable of the ten virgins in Matt 25:1–13]. For the number of the ten virgins stands for the number of souls who believe in Jesus, the number 'ten' symbolizing by means of its corresponding letter, the letter 'I,' the only direct road to heaven [in ancient number symbolism, the number 'ten' symbolizes totality or completion, and each letter of the alphabet was assigned a number]. Five of them were prudent and wise, and five were stupid and foolish; they did not have the foresight to fill their vessels with oil, thus remaining empty of justice. And so by the foolish ones he symbolizes those who make strenuous efforts to reach the confines of virginity and do everything properly and prudently in their striving to bring this love to fruition, and they solemnly profess that this is their purpose; yet they become careless and are overcome by the vicissitudes of the changing world. They are like those artists who paint with shadows, portraying a mere image of virtue instead of the truth itself.

6.3 "Certainly, when it is said that 'the kingdom of heaven is like ten virgins who took their lamps and went out to meet the bridegroom' [Matt 25:1], the meaning is that all of them took on the same course of conduct, for this is signified by the letter 'I' ['iota' in Greek signifying the number 'ten']. They all set out with a similar dedication; this is why they are designated jointly as 'ten,' because, as I have said, they chose the same course. But the similarity did not extend to the way in which they went out to meet the bridegroom. Some had taken with them fuel in abundance so that they were able to replenish their oil lamps later, but others had been negligent, thinking only of the present. Thus they are divided into two equal groups, five and five, since the first group protected their five senses (generally called the gates of wisdom) from sin, keeping them pure and virginal, while the second group, on the contrary, dishonored their senses with a multitude of sins, mixing them with evil. They exercised self-control and kept themselves pure but opposed these activities to justice and preferred to bear sinful fruits. Accordingly it happened that they were shut out and excluded from the precinct of divine things. For whether we act correctly or sinfully, it is through the senses that brave deeds and failures are strengthened.

"As Thallusa has said that there is a chastity of the eyes, ears, tongue, and all the other senses, so also in the present instance, the five [prudent] virgins designate the woman who faithfully guards inviolate the five pathways of virtue—sight, taste, smell, touch, and hearing—because she has restored to Christ the five kinds of sensory perception and through each of these her holiness shines like a radiant lamp. For our flesh is truly like a lamp with five flames which the soul carries like a torch to stand before her bridegroom Christ on the day of the resurrection, demonstrating her faith which leaps up brightly through all her senses. Christ himself has also taught this, saying, 'I have come to cast fire upon the earth, and what do I wish but that it already be kindled?' [Luke 12:49]. [In this verse] 'earth' designates our temples [i.e., our bodies], in which he desired the swift and fiery practice of his teaching to be kindled quickly. The oil can be compared to wisdom and righteousness; for if the soul pours these forth plentifully and anoints the body, then the inextinguishable light of virtue flares up before all people, showing [the soul's] good works in all their radiance in order to glorify 'the Father who is in the heavens' [see Matt 5:16].

6.4 "This was indeed the oil that they offered according to Leviticus: 'clarified oil, pure, beaten to burn in the lamp outside the veil [of the Tent of Meeting], before the Lord' [see Lev 24:2; Exod 27:20]. But they were ordered to maintain the flame for only a very short time, 'from evening until morning.' Their light seems to represent figuratively the prophetic word, shining outspokenly in favor of temperance and nourished by the actions and faith of the people. The sanctuary represents the 'allotment of their inheritance' [see Deut 32:9; Ps 104 (105):11], since a light can shine only in one house. This lamp thus was to be kept burning until morning, for the text says, 'They shall burn it until morning,' [see Lev 27:2–3; Exod 27:20–21], that is to say, until the coming of Christ, because when 'the sun' of chastity and 'of righteousness' had risen, there was no need of a lamp [see Mal 4:2].

"For as long as that people kept a reserve of nourishment for the lamp, supplying the oil by their deeds, the lamp of temperance did not go out among them but was always shining and illuminating 'the allotment of their inheritance'; but when the oil ran out because they wandered away from faith toward licentiousness, then the lamp was utterly extinguished. Thus the virgins once again have to make their lamps flash as with lightning by passing the light from one to the other, so that from above incorruption might blaze in the world.

"Today also it is necessary to furnish abundantly the pure oil of good works and sagacity, an oil strained free of all the impurities that weigh it down, so that 'if the Bridegroom is delayed' our lamps will not go out in the same way. For the delay is the interval before the coming of Christ; the drowsiness and sleep of the ten virgins is the departure from life, and midnight represents the reign of the Antichrist, when the destroying angel passes over the houses. And the cry that went forth, 'Behold, the Bridegroom is coming; go out to meet him' [Matt 25:6], is the voice from the heavens and the trumpet, [which sound] when, all having been resurrected, the saints with their bodies will dwell in the clouds, ravished by 'meeting the Lord' [see 1 Thess 4:15–17].

"One must notice that the Word says that after the cry, all the virgins awakened, which means that after the cry comes from the heavens, the dead will rise. Paul also teaches this somewhere, when he says, 'The Lord himself, with a word of command, with the voice of an archangel and a trumpet of God, will descend from heaven, and the dead in Christ will rise first' [see 1 Thess 4:15–17]—that is to say, the bodies which died when they were stripped of their souls.

"'Then we the living will be snatched up together with them'—I mean the souls [see 1 Thess 4:15–17]. For 'we the living' are in the proper sense called souls which, with the bodies that they have recovered, will go to meet [Christ] in the clouds, carrying lamps adorned not with some alien and worldly decoration but with self-control and temperance, like stars brilliantly reflecting the brightness of a heavenly splendor.

6.5 "O beautiful virgins, these are the secret rites of our mysteries; such are the rites of initiation into virginity. These are the rewards 'of the undefiled struggles' of self-control [see Wis 4:2]. I am betrothed to the Word and I receive as a dowry the everlasting crown of incorruption and riches from the Father. 'I walk in a procession crowned for all eternity,' with unfading and bright flowers of wisdom [ibid.]. I am in the same chorus in heaven with Christ who acts as judge, whose reign is without beginning and indestructible. I am the torch-bearer of unapproachable lights [see 1 Tim 6:16], and with the company of archangels I sing a completely new song in order to announce the new grace of the church. For the Scripture says that the assembly of virgins accompanies the Lord forever and forms his company wherever he may be. This also is what John hints at when he mentions the hundred forty-four thousand [Rev 14:3].

"Go, therefore, youth of the new ages, go fill your vessels with righteousness; for it is now time to awaken and go to meet the Bridegroom. Go, and with a light heart leave behind the spells and charms of life which beguile the soul and spin it like a top. For you will receive what was promised, 'I swear it in the name of the one who has shown us the path of life' [fragment of a Pythagorean poem]. I offer you, Arete, this wreathed crown, decorated from the meadows of the prophets." . . .

8, prologue: When Procilla had spoken, Thecla said, "Now it falls to me to take my turn and enter the contest, and I am pleased to have as my companion wisdom in my words; for I sense that she has tuned me inwardly like a cithara and has prepared me to speak carefully and with grace and dignity."

Arete replied, "Well said, Thecla; I approve of your eagerness and I have faith that you will speak gracefully in a manner consonant with your ability. No one surpasses you in philosophy and in general education, and is it necessary to mention your knowledge of things evangelical and divine?—for you were instructed by Paul."

8.1 "Very well," [said Thecla], "let us speak right from the beginning by reflecting on the name 'virgin' itself—the reason why this most excellent and blessed way of life has been so designated, what sort of life it happens to be, what its power is, and finally what fruits it produces. For almost all people run the risk of being ignorant of it, and the countless advantages it conveys over all the others offered by virtue, which we cultivate for the purification and beautification of the soul. The word 'virginity' [parthenia] becomes the word 'near-the-divine' [partheia] by dropping just one letter, just as virginity alone makes like God those who have been initiated into her pure rites. It would be impossible to find a greater good than this, from which both pain and pleasure have been banished. And the wings of the soul, having truly been watered, grow light and increase in strength [see Plato, Phaedrus 246, 248], becoming accustomed daily to flying away from human concerns.

"Wise men have said that our life is a festal assembly, and that we have come as though into a theater to show the drama of truth, that is, of righteousness, and our adversaries and rivals are the devil and demons. Thus it is necessary for us to look upwards and take wing, flying away from the charms of their beautiful voices and appearances, which seem at first glance to be continent but really are not; they are even more dangerous than the sirens of Homer [Odyssey 12.44–60]. Many who have adopted our way of life have been bewitched and weighed down by the pleasures of error, and they lose their wings, because the sinews whose nature is to strengthen the wings of continence and protect them from the seduction of the body have become weak and loose.

"For this reason, Arete ['virtue' in Greek], whether you are so named because [you are innately virtuous] or because you take souls and lift them up to heaven, always walking in the midst of the purest minds, come and help me with my speech, which you yourself commanded me to deliver.

8.2 "Those who have thus lost their wings and fallen into pleasure will not see the end of grief and sufferings until, because of the longing of their passion, they satisfy the needs of their unspeakably great incontinence. Thus they remain outside, uninitiated into the drama of truth. Instead of begetting children in a spirit of sobriety and temperance, they rave madly in the wild pleasures of passionate desires. But those whose wings are strong and light, flying up to the supramundane place beyond this life, see from afar what no other human has gazed upon, the very meadows of immortality, which are filled with flowers of extraordinary beauty. They forever meditate on the wonders of that place and because of this they have little regard for those things that are considered good in this world—wealth, reputation, class, and marriages. There is nothing that they value more highly than the things of that place.

"Furthermore, if they should wish that their bodies be handed over and punished by wild beasts or fire [i.e., martyred], they willingly pay no attention to the pain on account of their longing and passion for the things of that higher place, such that they seem to be in the world and yet not in the world, having already, in their thoughts and intense desire, joined the assembly of those who are in the heavens. For according to its own nature, the wing of virginity is not weighed down toward earth but rather carries [the soul] upward into the pure ether [i.e., heaven] and to the life near to the angels. Thus, after the call and the departure from this life to the other, those who have lived genuinely and faithfully as virgins in Christ will, before all the others, be awarded the victory prizes for their struggles, crowned by Christ with the flowers of incorruptibility. For as soon as their souls depart from the world, it is said that angels come to meet the virgins with solemn rejoicing, and they escort them to the aforementioned meadows, into which they had longed to enter before when they had imagined them from afar, since they were able to picture the things of the divine world even while they were still embodied.

8.3 "When they arrive there, they see beauties that are marvelous, shining and blessed, so much so that they are difficult to describe to human beings. For in that place there is righteousness itself and continence itself, as well as love itself, truth, and prudence, and in like manner appear all the other flowers and plants of wisdom, which we here below see only as shadows and phantoms as in dreams, when we think they arise from human actions. This is because here in this world there is no clear image of them [that is, of the beauties just listed] but only indistinct copies, and even these we often perceive obscurely when we imagine them. For no one has ever yet seen with the eyes the form, greatness, and beauty of righteousness itself or sagacity itself or peace. But there they can be seen as they really are, in their wholeness and perfection. . . .

8.4 "So, virgins, daughters of undefiled continence, our zeal should at present be aimed at the abundant life of the kingdom of the heavens. . . . Let faith be victorious everywhere, and let its light chase away the phantoms which the Evil One sends to surround the heart. . . . For the clouds sent by the Evil One will be driven away by the Spirit, if only you, like your mother, the virgin who gave birth to a male child in heaven, will not be afraid of the serpent that lies in wait to assault you. It is she that I wish to describe to you as clearly as possible, and now is the right time.

"In the book of Revelation, John explains, 'A great sign appeared in heaven: a woman clothed with the sun, with the moon under her feet, and on her head a crown of twelve stars. She was with child, and she cried out in anguish and strained to give birth. And another sign was seen in heaven: behold, a great red dragon with seven heads and ten horns, and on its heads seven diadems; and its tail dragged down a third of the stars of heaven and cast them on the earth. The dragon stood in front of the woman who was about to give birth so that, when she had given birth, he could devour her child. And she gave birth to a son, who is destined to govern all the nations with a rod of iron; but her child was snatched up to God and to his throne, and the woman fled into the wilderness, where she has a place prepared by God and will be nourished there for one thousand two hundred and sixty days' [Rev 12:1–6]. This, then, is a brief account of the woman and the dragon. . . .

8.5 "The woman who appeared in heaven clothed with the sun, wearing a crown of twelve stars and with the moon beneath her feet, crying out and laboring to give birth: she is, precisely and according to the exact sense of the word, our mother, O virgins, and she has a power that is distinctly her own, different from that of her children. She is the one whom the prophets, while sharing a general perspective, have sometimes called Jerusalem, sometimes bride, sometimes Mount Sion, and sometimes the temple and tabernacle of God. She is the power that, in [the book of] the prophet, was urged to be enlightened when the Spirit cried to her: 'Be enlightened, be enlightened, Jerusalem; for your light has come, and the glory of the Lord has risen upon you. Behold, darkness and storm-clouds will cover the earth, they will cover the nations; but to you the Lord will be revealed, and the glory of the Lord will be seen upon you. Kings will walk in your light and the nations in your brilliance. Lift up your eyes around you and see your children gathered together. All of your sons have come from far away, and your daughters shall be carried on their shoulders' [Isa 60:1–4]. [This power] is the church, whose children, born in baptism, will come running to her from every direction after the resurrection. She is the one who takes delight in receiving the light that never sets and in wearing the brilliance of the Word as though it were a robe. . . .

"Let us proceed, then, and see clearly in the Word that this great woman is like virgins preparing for marriage; her beauty is pure, completely undefiled and enduring, and her bright shining is not inferior to the brilliance of the [celestial] lights. For in place of a robe she clothes herself with light, and in place of precious stones she adorns her head with shining stars. What for us is clothing is for her light, and what for us is gold or glowing stones is for her the stars, but these stars are not those that are situated in the celestial space but better and brighter stars, such that the stars we see are to be considered images and representations of those others.

8.6 "When the text says, 'she stands on the moon,' I think 'moon' refers figuratively to the faith of those who have cleansed themselves from corruption by baptism, because the light of the moon resembles tepid water, and all moist substance depends upon the moon. Thus the Church stands upon our faith and our adoption—following this way of interpreting the moon—and until 'the full number of the Gentiles has come in' [Rom 11:25] she is in labor and conceives spiritual people out of natural people [see 1 Cor 2:14]; according to this way of reasoning she is indeed their mother. For just as a woman receives the unformed seed of her husband and after a period of time gives birth to a fully formed human being, so too one might say that the Church always conceives those who have fled for refuge in the Word, and she shapes them in the likeness and form of Christ to make them, after a period of time, citizens of blessed eternity. . . .

8.7 [On the identity of the woman's male child] . . . "The mystery of the incarnation of the Word was completed long before the book of Revelation [was written]; John's prophecies pertain to the present and the future. And

Christ, who was conceived long before, was not the one who was taken up to the throne of God for fear that he would be attacked by the serpent. Rather, he was begotten and in his very person came down from the throne of the Father for this reason, that he might, standing firm, subdue the dragon's assaults on the flesh. Thus you are forced to agree that it is the Church that is in labor, and she gives birth to those who are washed in baptism. . . .

8.8 ". . . I think that the Church is said to have produced a male child because those who have been enlightened receive, without qualification, the form, characteristics, and masculinity of Jesus; the likeness of the form of the Word is stamped on them and produced in them by genuine knowledge and faith, and so in each of them Christ is born spiritually. . . .

8.10 "The 'dragon,' 'great' and 'red,' wily and complex, with its seven heads and its horns, the one that drags down 'a third of the stars' and lies in wait in order to 'devour the child' of the woman in labor: this is the Devil, who lies in ambush to harm both the Christ-accepting mind of those who have been enlightened and the clear imprint of the Word begotten in them. But he is foiled and fails to catch his prey because those who have been born again are snatched up 'to the throne of God' on high. That is to say, the thought of those who have been renewed is taken up near the divine seat and the unshakable foundation of truth and is taught to see and imagine the things there in order not to be seduced by the serpent's downward pull. For he is not allowed to destroy those who direct their gaze upwards. . . .

8.12 "Coming, then, into 'the wilderness,' which signifies a place devoid of evils, as we have said earlier, the Church is nourished and takes flight on wings of virginity that take her on heavenly pathways; Scripture calls these wings 'the wings of a great eagle' [Ezek 17:3]. Thus she has defeated the serpent and driven the stormy clouds away from her own full moon. Everything that has been said up until now has been for the sake of bringing us to this point: to teach you, O beautiful virgins, to imitate our mother with all your strength and not be troubled by the burdens, the [unexpected] turns, and the afflictions of life, so that, rejoicing, you may enter with her into the bridal chamber, with your lamps lighting the way. . . .

8.13 "Therefore, with sober and manly courage take up arms and set them against the swollen beast; don't retreat at all, and don't be thrown into confusion by his audacity. For you will have glory beyond measure if, conquering him, you take away his seven crowns, which are set before us as the prize for our contest and battle, as our teacher Paul has said [see Rev 12:3 and Eph 6:12–17]. For she who first prevails against the devil and kills the seven heads gains possession of the seven crowns of virtue, since she has struggled through the seven great contests of chastity. One of the heads of the dragon is incontinence and luxury, and whoever crushes this head receives the crown of temperance. Another head is cowardice and weakness, and whoever tramples on this one takes for herself the crown of martyrdom. Yet another head is lack of both faith and understanding, and so on through all the other excesses of evil. Whoever overpowers these and destroys them receives the appropriate honors, and so in many ways the dragon's power is uprooted and destroyed."

2. Gregory of Nyssa, *On Virginity* (selections)

A prolific writer well educated in philosophy, rhetoric, and theology, Gregory of Nyssa (331/40–ca. 395 C.E.) was one of the most prominent churchmen and theologians of the fourth century. *On Virginity,* probably written in the early 370s, was one of his earliest works, and in it Gregory explains the philosophical and theological foundations of virginity as the highest form of Christian life. Part of Gregory's argument for virginity depends upon a demonstration of the miseries of marriage; some of those passages are included here as well, and can be read in conjunction with material on marriage in Section IV below.

2.1 We need a good deal of intelligence to recognize the superiority of this grace which is perceived in connection with the incorruptible Father. Indeed, it is a paradox to find virginity in a Father who has a Son whom he has begotten without passion, and virginity is comprehended together with the only-begotten God who is the giver of incorruptibility, since it shone forth with the purity and absence of passion in his begetting. And again, the Son, conceived through virginity, is an equal paradox. In the same way, one perceives it in the natural and incorruptible purity of the Holy Spirit. For when you speak of the pure and incorruptible, you are using another name for virginity. Since, by reason of its lack of passion it exists with the whole of other-worldly nature and associates with the superior powers, it neither separates itself from things divine nor does it attach itself to their opposites. For whatever inclines towards virtue by nature and by choice is rendered quite beautiful by the purity of the incorruptible, and whatever rejects virtue for its opposite is referred to as such because of its lack of purity. What power of words can equal such a grace? . . .

2.2 Virginity is exceptional and peculiar to the incorporeal nature, and, through the kindness of God, it has been granted to those whose life has been allotted through flesh and blood, in order that it may set human nature upright once more after it has been cast down by its passionate disposition, and guide it, as if by the hand, to a contemplation of the things on high. It is for this reason, I think, that our Lord Jesus Christ, the source of incorruptibility, did not come into the world through marriage. He wanted to demonstrate through the manner of his becoming human this great mystery, that purity alone is sufficient for receiving the presence and entrance of God, a purity that cannot be otherwise achieved fully, unless one alienates himself entirely from the passions of the flesh. For what happened corporeally in the case of the immaculate Mary, when the fullness of the divinity shone forth in Christ through her virginity, takes place also in every soul spiritually giving birth to Christ, although the Lord no longer effects a bodily presence. For Scripture says, "We no longer know Christ according to the flesh" [see 2 Cor 5:16], but, as the gospel says somewhere, he dwells with us spiritually and the Father along with him [see John 14:23].

2.3 Therefore, since the power of virginity is such that it resides in heaven with the Father of spiritual beings, and takes part in the chorus of the supramundane powers, and attains to human salvation, and since, by itself, it brings God down to a sharing in human life and lifts man up to a desire of heavenly things, becoming a kind of binding force in man's affinity to God, and since it brings into harmony by mediation things so opposed to each other by nature, what power of words could be found to equal the grandeur of this marvel? . . .

3.2 Where can one begin in decking out in tragic phrase this burdensome way of life [i.e., marriage]? . . . Do you want us to begin with the most delightful features of married life? Truly, what is chiefly sought after in marriage is the joy of living with someone. Grant this is so, and let the marriage be described as blessed in every respect: good family, sufficient wealth, harmony in age, the very flower of youth, much affection, and, what is divined in each by the other, that sweet rivalry in subduing one's own will in love. Let there be added to these glory, power, renown, and whatever else you wish, but see the smoldering grief necessarily attendant upon the advantages enumerated. I do not mean the envy which is directed against the prosperous, and the treachery which apparent happiness arouses in people. . . .

3.3 But, you will say, what grief will there be if not even envy touches them in their happiness? I say that the very sweetness of their life is the fomenting of their grief. For as long as people, these mortal and perishable creatures, exist and look upon the tombs of those from whom they came into being, they have grief inseparably joined to their lives even if they take little notice of it. For the continuous expectation of death is not known through spoken symbols, but because of the uncertainty of the future, inherently frightening, it dissipates our present joy and disturbs our well-being with the fear of what is to come. If only it were possible to know the things of experience before we experience them! If only it were possible to examine things ahead of time, how frequent would be the race of deserters from marriage to virginity! What care and forethought there would be never to be in the power of inescapable snares, the discomfort of which one cannot know accurately if one has never been caught in the net. For you would see, if one could see without taking a risk, a constant mingling of opposites: laughter moistened by tears, grief mingled with joy, death, everywhere present, fastening itself upon each of our pleasures. When the bridegroom looks upon the face of his beloved, the fear of separation immediately comes over him; while he listens to her sweet voice, he is aware that sometime he will not hear it; when he is delighted by the sight of her beauty, then, especially, does he shudder at the expectation of misfortune. . . . 3.4 Can anyone live happily when such thoughts are in his mind? Will he believe that his present joys will continue forever, or is it not clear from this that he will be at a loss like one in the fantasy of dreams?. . .

3.5 . . . Assume that the moment of childbirth is at hand; it is not the birth of the child, but the presence of death that is thought of, and the death of the mother anticipated. Often, the sad prophecy is fulfilled and before the birth is celebrated, before any of the anticipated goods are tasted, joy is exchanged for lamentation. Still burning with affection, still at the peak of desire, without having experienced the sweetest things of life, one is all at once bereft of everything as if in a nightmare. . . .

3.6 But perhaps this is not the case. Let us assume that conditions are more favorable, that the mother survives the pains of childbirth and a child is born, the very image of the springtime of his parents; what then? Is the supposition of grief lessened because of this, or is it not rather increased? In addition to their earlier fears, they have added those in behalf of the child lest he encounter something unpleasant, lest some disagreeable chance befall him with regard to his upbringing, some unwished-for casualty or suffering or mutilation or danger. These are shared by both parents. But who could enumerate the special worries of the wife? I pass over the ordinary factors known to all, the discomfort of pregnancy, the risk of childbirth, the toil of educating the child, and the special heartbreak caused by a child. And if she becomes the mother of more than one, her soul is divided into as many parts as the number of her children, since she experiences in her own being whatever happens to them. . . .

And since, according to the divine plan, the wife does not govern herself, but has her place of refuge in the one who has power over her through marriage, if she is separated from him for even a short time, it is as if she has been deprived of her head. She cannot endure the separation and has a premonition of the life of widowhood and of her husband's departure from the world in a little while. Suddenly, fear makes her despair of her dearest hopes. For this reason, she keeps her eyes glued on the door, full of worry and fright. She pays too much attention to gossip. Her heart, scourged by fear, tortures itself even before any news is brought back. . . . Such is the life of the happy pair! Truly a fine one! Certainly, it cannot be measured against the freedom of virginity.

4.7 Since . . . human life is overflowing with disturbances and anom-
alies and is always pouring forth from the precipitousness of its nature
and never restrains itself and is never sated, but contaminates everything
it happens upon and runs over everything it touches . . . it would, for this
reason, be advantageous to keep oneself away from such a stream in order not to slight what is established forever because of our being involved with what has no substance. For how is it possible for anyone passionately in love with anything in this life finally to achieve what he longs
for? Which of the special objects of our interests remain what they are?
What is the acme of youth? What is the good fortune of power or beauty?
What is wealth? What is glory? Power? Do not all such things blossom for
a short time and then fade away and turn into their opposites? Who has
lived an entire life of youthfulness? For whom did power persist until the
end? What flower of beauty has nature not made more short-lived than
those which come forth in the spring? . . .

4.8 Since, then, such changes, occurring according to the necessity
of nature, distress the human being with this obsession, there is only one
escape from this evil, that is, not to attach oneself to anything change-
able. Since it is possible to be separated from any association with the life
of passion and the flesh, most assuredly it is also possible to be beyond
any sympathy with one's own body, in order not to be subject to the evils
of the flesh. But this means living for the soul alone and imitating, as far
as possible, the regimen of the incorporeal powers, among whom there
is neither marriage nor giving in marriage [see Luke 20:34–35]. Their work
and zeal and success consist in the contemplation of the Father of incorruptibility and in beautifying their own form through imitation of the ar-
chetypal beauty.

4.9 We say that virginity is given to man as an ally and an aid in this
thought and lofty desire, as Scripture suggests [see Gen 2:18]. And just as
in other pursuits certain skills are devised for the perfection of each of
the things sought after, it seems to me that the pursuit of virginity is a
certain art and faculty of the more divine life, teaching those living in the
flesh how to be like the incorporeal nature.

5 In such a life, every effort is made to insure that the loftiness of the
soul is not brought low by the insurrection of pleasures, for then the soul

turns down towards the passions of flesh and blood instead of occupying itself with lofty things and looking upwards. For how is it possible for the soul, nailed down by the pleasure of the flesh and indulging in a desire for human passions, to look up with a free eye to the natural and intelligible light, when it is inclined toward the material through some sorry and coarse misconception? For just as the eyes of pigs are by nature trained on the ground and have no experience of the wonders of the sky, so the soul pulled down by the body can no longer look towards the heaven and the beauties on high, being bent towards what is low and brutish in nature. Whereas if the soul, quite free and relaxed, looks up to the divine and blessed pleasures, it will never turn itself back to any of the earthly things, nor will it exchange them for what are commonly considered pleasures, but it will transfer its power to love from the body to the intelligible and immaterial contemplation of the beautiful. It was for such a disposition of the soul that the virginity of the body was intended, to make the soul forget and become unmindful of the passionate movements of its nature, affording it no necessity to descend to the lowly guilt of the flesh. For once freed from such needs, it no longer runs the risk of turning away from and ignoring the divine and unmixed pleasure which only purity of heart naturally seeks after. . . .

12.3 The human effort extends only to this: the removal of the filth which has accumulated through evil and the bringing to light again of the beauty in the soul which we had covered over. It is such a dogma that I think the Lord is teaching in the gospel to those who are able to hear wisdom when it is mysteriously spoken: "The kingdom of God is within you" [Luke 17:21]. This saying shows, I believe, that the goodness of God is not separated from our nature, or far away from those who choose to seek it, but it is ever present in each individual, unknown and forgotten when one is choked by the cares and pleasures of life, but discovered again when we turn our attention back to it. If there is need for further support of the argument, I think this is what the Lord was suggesting in the search for the lost drachma [Luke 15:8–10]. The rest of the virtues which the Lord refers to as drachmas are of no use, even if they all be present in the soul, if the soul is bereft of the one that is lost. Consequently, he bids us, first of all, to light a lamp, and by this he means perhaps the word which brings to light that which is hidden. Then, he tells us to look for the lost drachma in our own house, i.e., in ourselves. Through this parable, he suggests that the image of the King is not entirely lost, but that it is hidden under the dirt. We must, I think, interpret the word "dirt" as the filth of the flesh. Once this is swept away and cleaned off by our caring for our life, that which is being looked for becomes visible, and then the soul can rejoice and bring together the neighbors to share her joy. For in reality, all the faculties of the soul, which is what the Lord means by neighbors, do live together, and when the great image of the King which the Creator implanted in our hearts from the beginning is uncovered and brought to light, then, these faculties turn towards that divine joy and merriment, gazing upon the unspeakable beauty of what has been recovered. For it says, "Rejoice with me, for I have found the drachma that I had lost" [Luke 15:9]. . . .

12.4 This concern, then, for the finding of what is lost is the restoration to the original state of the divine image which is now covered by the filth of the flesh. Let us become what the first being was during the first period of his existence. But what was he? Liberated from the threat of death, looking freely upon the face of God, not yet judging the beautiful by taste and sight, but only enjoying the Lord and using the helpmate given to him for this purpose, as Holy Scripture tells us, because he did not know her earlier, before he was driven out of paradise, and before she was condemned to the punishment of the pains of childbirth for the sin which she committed, having been deceived [see Gen 3.16–24]. Through this sequence of events, we, together with our first father, were excluded from paradise, and now, through the same sequence, it is possible for us to retrace the steps and return to the original blessedness. What was the sequence? It was pleasure brought about through deceit which initiated the fall. Shame and fear followed upon the experience of pleasure and they no longer dared to be in the sight of God. They hid themselves in leaves and shadows and, after that, they covered themselves with skins. And in this way, they came as colonists to this place, which is full of disease and toil, where marriage was contrived as a consolation for death.

13.1 If, then, we are going to return thence and be with Christ, we

must begin at the point of deviation, just as those who have become separated from their own group on a journey, after they have retraced their
steps, talk, first of all, to those who are just leaving the spot at which they
went astray. Since the point of departure from the life in paradise was the
married state, reason suggests to those returning to Christ that they, first,
give this up as a kind of early stage of the journey. Next, they must withdraw from the earthly wretchedness in which man became involved after the fall; in addition, they must put off the coverings of the flesh, the
garments made of skin [Gen 3:21], that is, they must put aside the thought
of the flesh, and, after they have rejected the concealments of their
shame, they must no longer stand in the shade of the fig tree of the bitter
life; they must cast aside the coverings of these ephemeral leaves of life
and be once more under the eyes of the Creator; they must disdain the
deceptions of taste and sight; they must no longer have as their guide the
poisonous serpent, but only the commandment of God. . . .

13.2 But since paradise is a dwelling place of living beings which
does not admit those who are dead because of sin, and we are "carnal
and mortal, sold into the power of sin" [Rom 7:14], how is it possible for
one who is ruled by the power of death to dwell in the land of the living?
What means and plan could anyone devise to be beyond this power? The
advice of the gospel is altogether sufficient for this. We have heard the
Lord telling Nicodemus: "That which is born of the flesh is flesh; and that
which is born of the spirit is spirit" [John 3:6], and we know that the flesh
because of sin is subject to death, whereas the spirit is of God, incorruptible, life-giving, and immortal.

13.3 Therefore, just as the power which destroys what is born is begotten along with physical birth, so it is clear that the Spirit bestows a
life-giving power upon those born through it. What, then, can be de-
duced from what we have said? That separating ourselves from life in the
flesh which death normally follows upon, we must seek a kind of life
which does not have death as its consequence. This is the life of virginity.
That this is true will be clearer if we explain a little further. Everyone
knows that the function of bodily union is the creation of mortal bodies,
but that life and incorruptibility are born, instead of children, to those
who are united in their participation in the Spirit. Excellent is the apos-

tolic saying about this, that the mother blessed with such children "will be saved by child-bearing" [1 Tim 2:15], just as the psalmist utters in the divine hymns: "He establishes in her home the barren wife as the joyful mother of children" [Ps 112:9 LXX; 113:9]. The virgin mother who begets immortal children through the Spirit truly rejoices and she is called barren by the prophet because of her moderation.

14.4 What place does death still have in such births? In them, mortality is truly conquered by life and the life of virginity seems to be an image of the blessedness that is to come, bringing with it many tokens of the goods that are stored up through hope. It is possible for those examining this argument to see the truth of what has been said. First of all, once one is dead to sin, he lives the rest of the time for God. Death is no longer his harvest. Having put an end to carnal life, as far as this is within his power, he awaits the blessed hope and the epiphany of the great God, putting no distance between himself and the presence of God because of the generations in between. Secondly, he reaps the choicest goods in the resurrection and in the present life. For if the life which is promised to the just by the Lord after the resurrection is similar to that of the angels— and release from marriage is a peculiar characteristic of the angelic nature—he has already received some of the beauties of the promise, having mingled with the splendor of the saints and having imitated the purity of the incorporeal beings in the undefiled character of their lives. If virginity is the sponsor of such experience, what word can sufficiently extol this grace? What other goods of the soul will appear so great and honorable, that they can be compared with the grandeur of this gift?

19 . . . The prophetess Mariam, immediately after the crossing of the sea, took a dry, tuneful "tambourine in her hand" [Exod 15:20] and led a chorus of women. Perhaps by the tambourine Scripture means to suggest the virginity achieved by the first Mary, who was, I think, the prototype of Mary the Mother of God. For, as the tambourine produces a loud sound, having no moisture in it and being quite dry, so also virginity is clear and noised abroad and has nothing in itself of the life-preserving moisture of this life. If it was a tambourine, a dead body, which Mariam used, then virginity is the deadening of the body, and it is perhaps not unlikely that it was being a virgin which set her apart. We suggest from conjecture and

assumption and not from proof that the prophetess, Mariam, led a chorus of maidens. Many of the learned affirm clearly that she was unmarried from the fact that there is no mention in Scripture of her marriage or of her children. Also, she would not have been referred to or been known as the sister of Aaron if she were married, since it is the husband who is the head of the woman and not her brother, and it is her husband's name that she is called by. And so if the grace of virginity appeared precious among a people who considered childbearing desirable and lawful, let us, who hear the divine injunctions, not according to the flesh, but according to the spirit, cling to it all the more. . . .

20.3 The desiring element in us does not by nature serve bodily pleasures and, at the same time, participate in a spiritual marriage. It is not possible to attain each of these goals through similar activities. Self-control and the mortification of the body and a disdain for everything connected with the flesh are the sponsors of the latter, and the opposites of these are the sponsors of the physical union. . . . So, when we have the choice of two marriages, since a person cannot participate, at the same time, in both ("for he who is unmarried is concerned about the things of the Lord, and he who is married about the things of the world" [1 Cor. 7:32–33]), it will be wise for us not to make the wrong selection or to be ignorant of the road that leads to the better one, and this we can learn only through some such analogy.

20.4 Just as in a physical marriage a person who is eager not to be rejected makes an effort to have a fine appearance, fitting adornment, and sufficient wealth, and takes much care not to be a burden because of his way of life or his family background . . . in the same way, the person planning a spiritual marriage will want to present himself as being youthful and intellectually rejuvenated, and he will indicate that he is from a family that is rich in the way that is most desirable, a family not respected because of its earthly possessions, but because of the abundance of its heavenly treasures. That person will not pride himself on having a family that is looked up to because of the good fortune which comes automatically to many, even to the foolish, but the good fortune that is present because of the toil and effort of one's own accomplishments, which only those achieve who are sons of the light and children of

God and called well-born "from the risings of the sun" [see Isa 41.25] through their enlightened deeds. He will not busy himself with his bodily strength or his appearance or with exercising his body or fattening his flesh, but quite the opposite; he will perfect the power of the spirit in the weakness of the body. I know that the dowry in this wedding does not consist of corruptible things, but of what is given us as a gift from the special wealth of the soul. Do you want to know the names of these gifts? Let anyone who introduces himself as a man of wealth listen to Paul, the fair escort of the bride. Listing many other important qualities, he also mentions "innocence" [2 Cor 6:6]. And, again, wherever the fruits of the spirit are enumerated [see Gal 5:22], they are the gifts of this marriage. If anyone is going to obey Solomon and take true wisdom as the companion and sharer of his life, concerning which he says: "Love her, and she will safeguard you" [Prov 4:6], and: "Honor her, in order that she may embrace you" [see Prov 4:8], he will worthily prepare himself for this longing, keeping festival in a pure garment, rejoicing with those in this marriage, in order not to be rejected because of being clothed as a married person.

It is clear that the eagerness for this kind of marriage is common to men and women alike, for since, as the apostle says, "There is neither male nor female" [Gal 3:28], and Christ is all things for all human beings, the true lover of wisdom has as his goal the divine one, who is true wisdom, and the soul, clinging to its incorruptible Bridegroom, has a love of true wisdom which is God. . . .

21.1 Since it is impossible for anyone to draw near to the purity of God who has not become pure himself, it is necessary for a person to separate himself from pleasures with a large and strong partition, so that the purity of the heart will in no way be defiled by coming near them. A safe protective wall is the complete estrangement from everything involving passion. For if one pleasure exists (as we learn from the philosophers), it is like the stream of water from one source which, when it is divided into different streams, spreads to each of the pleasure-loving organs of the senses. Therefore, the one who is weakened by any one of the sensual pleasures, damages his heart, as the voice of the Lord teaches, when he says that the one who has fulfilled the desire of his eyes has already received the wound in his heart [see Matt 5:28]. I think that the Lord is speaking of all the senses in this one example, so that those of us who follow his words should add that the one who has heard or touched or employed any faculty in the service of pleasure has sinned in his heart. . . .

23.1 . . . Great is the power to teach this divine regimen through deeds, both on the part of those who are silent and those who speak out, since every word seen apart from deeds, even if it is beautifully decked out, is like a lifeless icon which portrays a form blooming with paint and color, but "he that shall do and teach," as the gospel says somewhere [see Matt 5:19], this person is truly alive and outstandingly beautiful and effective.

23.2 Indeed, the novice who is going to acquire the habit of virginity in accordance with convincing logic must have this kind of teacher. For just as one eager to learn the language of a certain people cannot teach himself, but is taught by those who know it, and thus comes to speak the foreign tongue, in the same way, I think, one's nature does not make progress in this life automatically, since it is foreign to the novelty of the regimen, unless the person is taken in hand and learns the details from someone who has succeeded in it. . . .

23.3 Therefore, since the majority of persons who intend to lead a life of virginity are still young and immature, they must concern themselves with this before all, the finding of a good guide and teacher on this path, lest, on account of their ignorance, they enter upon trackless places and wander away from the straight road. . . .

3. John Chrysostom, *On Virginity* (selections)

Like his contemporary Gregory of Nyssa, John Chrysostom (ca. 347–407 C.E.) was a well-educated theologian and churchman; he served as bishop of Constantinople from 398 until 404. Among his many writings on ascetic topics is the present treatise, written some twenty years after Gregory's treatise on virginity. The two share many themes, notably those of the burdens and anxieties produced by the married life and the contrasting joys of the virginal life. John's treatise is particularly interesting for its exegesis of Paul's First Letter to the Corinthians, as well as for its view of the command in Gen 1:28 to "reproduce and multiply" in the context of ascetic ideals.

10.3 Is virginity a good? Yes, I fully agree. But is it better than marriage? I agree with this, too. If you wish, I will illustrate the difference like this: virginity is as much superior to marriage as heaven is to earth, as the angels are to men, and, to use far stronger language, it is more superior still. For the angels, if they do not marry and are not given in marriage [see Matt 22:30; Luke 20:36], are not a mixture of flesh and blood. They do not pass time on earth and endure trouble from passions. They require neither food nor drink. Sweet song cannot appease them, nor can a radiant face win them over, nor any other such thing. Their natures of necessity remain transparent and brilliant, with no passion troubling them, like the heavens at high noon clear and undisturbed by any cloud.

11.1 But mankind, inferior in its nature to blessed spirits, strains beyond its capacity and, in so far as it can, vies eagerly to equal the angels. How does it do that? Angels neither marry nor are given in marriage; this is true of the virgin. The angels have stood continuously by God and serve him; so does the virgin. Accordingly, Paul has removed all cares from virgins "to promote what is good, what will help you to devote yourselves entirely [to God]" [1 Cor 1:35]. If they are unable for a time to ascend to heaven as the angels can because their flesh holds them back, even in this world they have much consolation since they receive the Master of the heavens, if they are holy in body and spirit. 11.2 Do you grasp the value of virginity? That it makes those who spend time on earth live like the angels dwelling in heaven? It does not allow those endowed with bodies to be inferior to the incorporeal powers and spurs all men to rival the angels. . . .

12.6 What, then, does Paul say under the inspiration of the Lord? "Now for the matters you wrote about. A man is better off having no relations with woman" [1 Cor 7:1]. Here one could congratulate the Corinthians for questioning Paul before he brought the subject up, since they never received any counsel from their master about virginity. In this way, they indicated the progress they already made thanks to grace. For from the time of the ancient covenant there was no question about marriage. Not only did all the people but even the Levites, the priests, and the chief priest himself treated marriage with great respect.

13.1 How, then, did the Corinthians arrive at this question? They quickly and quite rightly perceived that they needed more virtue since they were deemed worthy of a greater gift. It is appropriate to inquire why the apostle had never instructed them in this, for, if they had learned of any such counsel, they would not have written again asking the question anew. In fact, here we can observe the depth of Paul's wisdom. He did not omit giving advice on so important a matter without a reason. Instead, he waited for them to first desire counsel and have some perception of the nature of the problem, so that finding their souls already receptive to the idea of virginity, he might profitably sow his words among them; for the right attitude of one's listeners provides the appropriate frame of mind for receiving one's counsel. In addition, he underscores the loftiness and majesty of the matter.

13.2 He would not have waited for an indication of their readiness if it were not so; rather he would have introduced the subject himself previously, if not as an injunction or precept, at least as a recommendation and counsel. By refusing to act first, he has clearly established that virginity requires much effort and a great struggle. Even in this he has imitated our common Master, for he too did not discuss virginity when his disciples asked him. 13.3 When his disciples said: "If that is the case between man and wife, it is better not to marry" [Matt 19:10], Christ replied: "There are some men who have castrated themselves for the kingdom of heaven" [Matt 19:12]. For when it is a matter of a magnificent act of virtue (which is therefore not obligatory), it is necessary to wait for the willingness of those intending to act rightly and in some other unsuspected way to instill in them the will and the desire, just as Christ did. He did not implant a desire for virginity in their minds by talking about it. No, by discussing marriage alone and by pointing out its burdensome character, and then saying no more, he managed the subject wisely. The result was that his listeners, hearing nothing about not marrying, declared on their own: "It is better not to marry."

13.4 Accordingly, Paul, the imitator of Christ, said: "Now for the matters you wrote about," not only to explain his silence but even to indicate this: I did not dare lead you to this lofty peak because of the difficulty of obtaining it. Since you have written me first, with confidence I advise that a man is better off having no relations with a woman. Why did he nowhere add this counsel when they wrote to him about many questions? For no other reason than what I have just stated. . . .

14.1 Someone would object perhaps: if it is better to have no relations with a woman, why has marriage been introduced into life? What
use, then, will woman be to us, if she is of help neither in marriage nor in
the procreation of children? What will prevent the complete disappearance of the human race since each day death encroaches upon it and
strikes people down, and if one follows this program, there is no repro-
duction of others to replace the stricken? If all of us should strive after
this virtue and have no relations with a woman, everything—cities,
households, cultivated fields, crafts, animals, plants—everything would
vanish. For just as when a general dies, the discipline of the army inevitably is thrown entirely into confusion, so if the ruler of all on earth, if
mankind disappears because of not marrying, nothing left behind will
preserve the security and good order of the world, and this fine precept
will fill the world with a thousand woes.

14.2 If these words had been merely those of our enemies and the
unbelievers, I would have hardly considered them. However, many of
those who appear to belong to the Church say this. They fail to make an
effort on behalf of virginity because of their weakness of purpose. By
denigrating it and representing it as superfluous, they want to conceal
their own apathy, so that they seem to fail in these contexts not through
their own neglect of duty but rather through their correct estimation of
the matter. Come then, having dismissed our enemies—for "the natural
man does not accept what is taught by the spirit of God. For him, that is
absurdity" [1 Cor 2:14]—let us teach two lessons to those who claim to be
with us: that virginity is not superfluous but extremely useful and necessary; and that such a charge is not made with impunity but will endanger
the detractors in the same way that right actions will earn wages and
praise for the virtuous.

14.3 When the whole world had been completed and all had been
readied for our repose and use, God fashioned man for whom he made
the world. After being fashioned, man remained in paradise and there
was no reason for marriage. Man did need a helper, and she came into
being; not even then did marriage seem necessary. It did not yet appear
anywhere but they remained as they were without it. They lived in paradise as in heaven and they enjoyed God's company. Desire for sexual in-

tercourse, conception, labor, childbirth, and every form of corruption had been banished from their souls. As a clear river shooting forth from a pure source, so were they in that place adorned by virginity.

14.4 And all the earth was without humanity. This is what is now feared by those who are anxious about the world. They are very anxious about the affairs of others but they cannot tolerate considering their own. They fear the eclipse of mankind but individually neglect their own souls as though they were another's. They do this when they will have demanded of them an exact accounting for this and the smallest of sins, yet for the scarcity of mankind they will not have to furnish even the slightest excuse.

14.5 At that time there were no cities, crafts, or houses—since you care so very much for these things—they did not exist. Nevertheless, nothing either thwarted or hindered that happy life, which was far better than this. But when they did not obey God and became earth and dust, they destroyed along with that blessed way of life the beauty of virginity, which together with God abandoned them and withdrew. As long as they were uncorrupted by the devil and stood in awe of their master, virginity abided with them. It adorned them more than the diadem and golden raiment do kings. However, when they shed the princely raiment of virginity and laid aside their heavenly attire, they accepted the decay of death, ruin, pain, and a toilsome life. In their wake came marriage; marriage, a garment befitting mortals and slaves.

14.6 "But the married man is busy with this world's demands" [1 Cor 7:33]. Do you perceive the origin of marriage? Why it seems to be necessary? It springs from disobedience, from a curse, from death. For where death is, there is marriage. When one does not exist, the other is not about. But virginity does not have this companion. It is always useful, always beautiful and blessed, both before and after death, before and after marriage. Tell me, what sort of marriage produced Adam? What kind of birth pains produced Eve? You could not say. Therefore why have groundless fears? Why tremble at the thought of the end of marriage, and thus the end of the human race? An infinite number of angels are at the service of God, thousands upon thousands of archangels are beside him, and none of them have come into being from the succession of generations, none from childbirth, labor pains, and conceptions. Could he not, then, have created many more people without marriage? Just as he created the first two from whom all human beings descend.

15.1 And today our race is not increased by the authority of marriage but by the word of our Lord, who said at the beginning: "Be fertile and multiply; fill the earth" [Gen 1:28]. How did marriage help Abraham in the procreation of children? After participating in it for so many years, did he not finally cry out: "Master, what will you give me? Am I to die childless?" [Gen 15:2]. Even as God at that time had provided from lifeless bodies the foundation and roots for so many thousands of descendants, so at the beginning too, if those about Adam had obeyed his commands and overcome their desire for the forbidden tree, they would not have needed a means of increasing the race of humankind. For marriage will not be able to produce many people if God is unwilling, nor will virginity destroy their number if he wishes there to be many of them. But he wanted it to be so, Scripture says, because of us and our disobedience.

15.2 Why did marriage not appear before the treachery? Why was there no intercourse in paradise? Why not the pains of childbirth before the curse? Because at that time these things were superfluous. The necessity arose later because of our weakness, as did cities, crafts, the wearing of clothes, and all our other numerous needs. Death introduced them in its wake. Moreover, do not prefer this, a concession to your own weakness, to virginity; or rather, do not assign marriage to an equal rank. If you follow this reasoning, you will say it is better to have two wives instead of being content with only one since this had been allowed under the law of Moses. In the same way, you will also prefer wealth to voluntary poverty, luxury to a moderate way of life, and revenge to a noble endurance of injustice.

16.1 Someone objects: You are denigrating these ancient laws. Not at all, for God has permitted them, and they were useful in their time. Yet, I say that they are of little value and are the virtues of children, not adults. For this reason, Christ, desiring to make us perfect, has ordered us to lay them aside as though they were children's garments that cannot encompass the complete person nor adorn that perfect man who is Christ come to full stature [see Eph 4:13]. He asks us to put on clothes more fitting and perfect than these. He has not contradicted himself. Indeed he is very consistent.

16.2 Although the new commandments are superior to the old, the aim of the lawgiver is the same. What is it? To reduce the baseness of our soul and to lead it to perfect virtue. Therefore, if God had been anxious not to dictate obligations greater than the former ones but to leave things eternally the same and never to release people from that inferior state, he completely contradicted himself. If at the beginning, in fact, when the human race was more childlike, God had prescribed this regimented way of life, we would never have accepted it with moderation but would have completely jeopardized our salvation through immoderation. Similarly, if after a long period of training under the old law when the time called us to this heavenly philosophy, if then he had permitted us to remain on earth, we would have gained nothing much from his concession since we had no part in that perfection on account of which his indulgence arose.

17.3 Let us not think, therefore, that the power to marry, which arose in the beginning, is binding upon us for the future and keeps us from withdrawing from marriage. God wants us to leave it behind. Hear his words: "Let him accept this teaching who can" [Matt 19:12]. Do not be surprised that he had not ordered this at the beginning. A doctor for example does not prescribe everything all at once to his patients. When they are seized by a fever, he keeps them from solid food; but when the fever and accompanying physical weakness subside, he bans disagreeable foods from that point on and returns the patients to their customary regime. In the body, when the elementary principles quarrel with each other, they cause illness by their excesses or deficiencies; in the soul, the unruliness of the emotions ruins its health. It is also necessary above all else to have at the right moment the appropriate precept for the emotions in question, since without both of these conditions the law by itself would be powerless to correct the disorder in the soul. Just as the essence of drugs could not by itself heal a wound, the same is true of laws in general: for what drugs are to injuries, laws are to sins.

17.4 You do not meddle with the physician when he lances a wound or when he cauterizes it or when he does neither. Yet he often fails. Do you, a man, interfere with God who never fails, who manages everything in a manner worthy of his wisdom? Will you demand of him an accounting of his commandments? Will you not defer to his boundless wisdom? Is this not the height of madness? He said: "Be fertile and multiply," which the times required since human nature raved and was unable to contain its violent passions and had no other haven amid that storm.

17.5 But what commandment was necessary? To live in continence and virginity? That would have produced a more disastrous result and a more violent fire of passion. Indeed, if children who need only milk were removed from the nurture proper for human beings and were forced to alter their diet, nothing would keep them from dying at once; so grievous is the untimeliness of that action. For this reason, virginity was not granted from the beginning. No, rather, virginity did appear at the beginning and was prior to marriage. Marriage was introduced later for the reasons cited and was thought necessary. Adam would not have needed it if he had remained obedient. You will ask if all people were to be created in this manner. Yes, either in this way or in another that I cannot say. The point is that God did not need marriage for the creation of a multitude of human beings upon the earth.

19.1 So marriage was granted for the sake of procreation, but an even greater reason was to quench the fiery passion of our nature. Paul attests to this when he says: "But to avoid immorality, every man should have his own wife" [1 Cor 7:2]. He does not say: for the sake of procreation. Again, he asks us to engage in marriage not to father many children, but why? so "that Satan may not tempt you," he says [1 Cor 7:5]. Later he does not say: if they desire children, but "if they cannot exercise self-control, they should marry." At the beginning, as I said, marriage had these two purposes, but now, after the earth and sea and all the world has been inhabited, only one reason remains for it: the suppression of licentiousness and debauchery.

27.1 I know the violence attendant upon this state [of virginity]. I know the strain of these deeds. I know the burden of the fight. You need a soul fond of strife, one forceful and reckless against the passions. You must walk over coals without being burned [see Prov 6:28], and walk over swords without being slashed. The power of passion is as great as that of

fire and sword. If the soul happens not to have been prepared in this way
to be indifferent to its suffering, it will quickly destroy itself. We need
iron will, eyes always open, much patience, strong defenses, external
walls and barriers, watchful and high-minded guards, and in addition to
all of these, divine help. For "unless the Lord guard the city, in vain does
the guard keep vigil" [Ps 126 (127):1].

27.2 How will we obtain this help? By giving all of ourselves: by reasoning soundly, by enduring the strain of fasting and sleeplessness, by
adhering strictly to the rules of conduct and observing precepts, and
above all, by not being overconfident in ourselves. If we happen to have
been very successful, we must say to ourselves constantly: "Unless the
Lord build the house, they labor in vain who build it" [Ps 126 (127):1]. For
"our battle is not against human forces but against the principalities and
the powers, the rulers of this world of darkness, the evil spirits in regions
above" [Eph 6:12]. Day and night we must stand armed with arguments
and appear formidable to these shameful passions. When they arouse us
just a little, the devil stands by with fire in hand ready to burn down the
temple of God. Therefore, we must be fortified on all sides. Our battle is
against natural compulsions. We emulate the life of the angels. Our race
is with the incorporeal powers. Earth and dust compete eagerly to equal
the life of those in heaven, and corruption has undertaken battle with incorruption [see 1 Cor 15:54].

27.3 Tell me, who will still dare to compare the pleasure of marriage
with so magnificent a state? Is it not too simple-minded? Aware of all this,
Paul said: "Every man should have his own wife." This is why he hesitated, this is why he feared discussing virginity with them from the start. He
continued to speak about marriage with the desire of turning them gradually away from it; then, keeping his discussion of continence brief, he
interspersed in it many words on marriage, thereby not allowing them to
be struck by the harshness of his exhortations. . . . 27.4 For after he says,
"A man is better off having no relations with a woman," he straightway
takes up marriage and says: "Every man should have his own wife."
While he pronounces virginity alone blessed, he passes over it with the
words: "A man is better off having no relations with a woman." But with
respect to marriage, he advises and orders it, and he adds his reason: "To

avoid immorality." Thus he seems to account for his acquiescence to marriage. In fact, although the audience is unaware of it, he praises continence while giving pretexts for marriage. He does not reveal this thought clearly in his speech but leaves it behind in the consciousness of his listeners. For the man who learns that marriage is advised not because it is the height of virtue but because Paul has condemned him for having so much lust that without marriage he is incapable of restraining it, this man blushing with shame will hastily pursue virginity and be anxious to divest himself of such ill repute.

28.1 What does he say next? "The husband should fulfill his conjugal obligations toward his wife, the wife hers toward her husband" [1 Cor 7:3]. Then, to explain and clarify this, he adds: "A wife does not belong to herself but to her husband; a husband does not belong to himself but to his wife" [1 Cor 7:4]. This seems to be said in defense of marriage; but, in fact, he is wrapping the hook with familiar bait, and coaxing his disciples to his way of thinking. He desires by these very words about marriage to lead them from it. For when you hear that you will not be your own master after marriage but be subject to the will of your wife, you will quickly aspire not to pass under the yoke at all, since once you have entered into this state, you must be a slave henceforth, so long as it pleases your wife.

28.2 It is easy to learn from the disciples that I am not simply conjecturing about Paul's opinion. They did not think at first that marriage was burdensome or oppressive until they heard the Lord forcing them to the conclusion that the Corinthians were led to by Paul. The statements: "Everyone who divorces his wife—lewd conduct is a separate case—forces her to commit adultery" [Matt 5:33], and "a husband does not belong to himself" [1 Cor 7:4] express the same idea in different words. . . .

59 The virgin need not make inquiries about her bridegroom, nor fear any deception. For he is God not man, a master not a fellow-slave. The difference between the bridegrooms is vast; but observe too the conditions of their marriage bonds. The wedding gifts of this bride are not bondage, parcels of land, and just so many talents of gold, but the heavens and its advantages. In addition, the married woman shudders at the thought of death, among other reasons because it separates her from her companion. The virgin, however, both yearns for death and is oppressed

by life, anxious as she is to see her groom face to face and to enjoy that glory.

60.1 Living in a state of poverty could not, as with marriage, be disadvantageous for the virgin. Instead it makes her, if she willingly endures it, more desirable to the bridegroom. Likewise, a humble birth, a lack of beauty, and other such traits, they too are not prejudicial to her. Why mention this? Even if she is not free, even this status does not spoil her betrothal. It is enough to display a beautiful soul and to attain the first rank. There is no fear of jealousy there, or distressing envy of another woman who has been united with a more brilliant spouse. No one is similar or equal to him; no one approaches him even a little. But in the case of marriage, although a woman has a very wealthy and powerful husband, nevertheless she could discover another woman having far more.

60.2 In an extraordinary way, the superiority of those surpassing us diminishes our own pleasure in surpassing people inferior to us, and the great luxury of money, clothes, a rich table, and other excesses is able to entice and attract the soul. And how many women enjoy these luxuries? Most people live in poverty, misery, and toil. If some women have such advantages, they are very few and far between, and they are in conflict with the will of God, for no one is permitted to luxuriate in these things, as we have pointed out earlier.

61 However, let us assume once again that this life of luxury is permitted and that neither the prophet nor Paul speak out against jewelry for women [see Isa 3:16–26; 1 Tim 2:9]. What advantage is there in much golden jewelry? None whatsoever, except envy, worry and extraordinary fear. For the owners are troubled not only when it is stowed away in a box and when night has fallen, but also when they wear it. During the day they live with the same—no, actually, greater anxiety. Indeed, in the baths and churches there are women standing about who are capable of mischief. Oftentimes, besides these thieves, women wearing golden ornaments when pushed and squeezed by a crowd do not realize that some of their jewelry has fallen off. So, in any case, many women lose not only this but, in addition, far more valuable necklaces made from high-priced gems when they are pulled off and fall to the ground. But enough of this fear; let even this anxiety be laid to rest.

62.1 —Another man has noticed me, you say, and has been impressed. —But he admires the ornaments, not the woman wearing them; she is often reproached because of them, as if she were adorned by them contrary to her true worth. If she is beautiful, they violate her natural beauty, for many ornaments do not allow beauty to appear unadorned and detract from the greater part of it. However, if a woman is misshapen and ugly, it sets off her unattractiveness even more. Ugliness, however extreme, if it appears entirely by itself, seems only what it is; but when the splendor of gems or the beauty of any other material exposes it, its unsightliness is greatly increased.

63.1 But the ornament of virginity is not like this. It does not detract from the one wearing it because it is not corporeal but wholly spiritual. Therefore, if the virgin is unattractive, virginity immediately transforms her ugliness by surrounding it with an irresistible beauty. If she is in the bloom of youth and radiant, virginity makes her brighter still. Gems and gold and costly garments and lavish, embroidered flowers of various colors and anything else perishable in nature in no way adorn souls. But the following do: fasts, holy vigils, gentleness, reasonableness, poverty, courage, humility, patience—in a word, disdain for everything in this life.

63.2 For the eye of the virgin is so beautiful and comely that it has as a lover not men but the incorporeal powers and their master. It is so pure and clear it can contemplate incorporeal instead of physical beauty, so gentle and calm that it stands aloof. It is not angered by unfair people who continually cause annoyance; it even considers such persons with kindness and graciousness. So great is the decorum surrounding the virgin that the intemperate, ashamed and blushing, check their frenzy when they attentively look at her. As a handmaid waiting on a discreet mistress must follow her example, even if she does not wish to, so the body of a soul so practiced in virtue must harmonize its own impulses with the movement of that soul. For her glance, her language, her demeanor, her walk, in short, everything is defined by the discipline within. It is like a costly perfume: although enclosed in a vial, it penetrates the air with its own sweet smell and suffuses with pleasure those inside and nearby, and even all those outside.

63.3 So the fragrance of the virginal soul flowing round the senses gives proof of the excellence stored within. The virgin, applying the golden reins of good behavior to everything, keeps each of the horses in perfect rhythm. She forbids her tongue to utter anything discordant or unsuitable, her glance to stray impudently or suspiciously, her ears to hear any improper song. She cares too that her feet not walk in a provocative or pampered fashion. She has an unaffected and artless gait. She cuts away the decoration from her clothes and continually exhorts her countenance not to dissolve into laughter, not to even smile quietly, but always to exhibit a serious and austere visage, one prepared always for tears, never for laughter.

77 —What is his response when the virgin busies herself with human affairs and cares greatly for them? Come now, does he drag her out of the chorus of virgins? —It is not enough to be unmarried to be a virgin. There must be spiritual chastity, and I mean by chastity not only the absence of wicked and shameful desire, the absence of ornaments and superfluous cares, but also being unsoiled by life's cares. Without that, what good is there in physical purity? Virgins are like soldiers: nothing could be more disgraceful for a soldier than to throw aside his arms and spend his time in taverns; and nothing could be more indecorous for a virgin than to be embroiled in earthly affairs. For truly, those five maidens held their torches and practiced virginity but they enjoyed nothing in return. They remained outside the closed doors and perished [see Matt 25:10]. Therefore, virginity is beautiful because it removes every pretext for unnecessary care and affords complete leisure for works of God. If this is not so, it is much inferior to marriage, since it surrounds the soul with thorns and suffocates the pure and heavenly seed.

The Subintroductae

Beginning at least as early as the second century, some Christian ascetics adopted a form of cohabitation called "spiritual marriage" (*syneisaktism*), in which a man and woman who had both taken vows of sexual continence lived together in a chaste but non-legalized partnership. The women who engaged in spiritual marriage were called *virgines subintroductae* in Latin (literally, "those brought in covertly," suggesting the illicit nature of the relationship) and *agapetae* (beloved ones) or *syneisaktoi* (those brought into [the house] together) in Greek. Although spiritual marriage was repeatedly condemned by church councils and by various theologians, it was a widespread and popular practice. For the female partners, in particular, this living arrangement provided a way to live an ascetic life before monasteries for women were widely available; in addition to protection, companionship, and help with the routines of daily life, spiritual marriage may also have been understood by those who practiced it as an anticipation of the eschatological "angelic life."

1. Athanasius of Alexandria, *Second Letter to Virgins* (selections)

One of the most prominent churchmen of the fourth century, Athanasius (ca. 298–373 C.E.) was bishop of Alexandria, Egypt, from 328 until his death, although he spent several periods during his bishopric in exile due to political and theological disputes. He is best known for his defense of Nicene Christianity against Arianism and for his championing of the ascetic lifestyle, particularly in his influential *Life of Saint Antony,* a biography of one of the first desert monks that became a model for subsequent hagiographic writing. He also wrote extensively on female virginity, likening virgins to "brides of Christ" and promoting the virginity of Mary as a model for Christian women to imitate. In his first letter to virgins, Athanasius presents virginity as a state of being superior to that of marriage; as the most virtuous way of life, virginity is, in his words, "the image of angelic purity" (sec. 19). Whereas in the first letter he situates virginity theologically as an imitation of the Virgin Mary's lifestyle, here in the second letter he writes to a group of virgins who had just returned from a pilgrimage to the Holy Land, consoling them for their separation from the spiritual place they had visited; he also offers practical advice for continuing their ascetic discipline (for example, on how to converse with men), including the following section on spiritual marriage, which concludes with an image of the true virgin as the "enclosed garden" of the Song of Songs.

20. But consider some among the virgins, as I have heard; they do not merely confuse and fail to distinguish good from evil by speaking (to men), but they dare even to live and mix with men, not considering such a great danger or how easy it is to fall in this life. Others of this (ascetic

life) employ aids and strategies so that, through fasts and dried-up ascetic practices, they extinguish the flame of passion that burns within them. But as for these (virgins who live with men), because of regular conversation with men and toilsome custom, the flame burns greatly within them, just as when someone, by giving a lot of fuel to a small fire, will change a flame into a great roaring blaze.

21. But you will say to me that such a living arrangement is one of "fellowship" and "spiritual love," as if it were without harm or injury, although it bears danger in its bosom and walks on fire. "For does a person tie up a fire in his bosom and not burn his clothes? Or does a man walk on a fire's burning coals and not burn his feet? So, too, no one who goes in to his neighbor's wife will be pardoned, nor any who touch her" (Prov 6:27–29). So, if he who goes in to his neighbor's wife is not pardoned, what will he who goes in to and touches the bride of Christ endure from the heavenly King? Hence, "it is good for a man not to touch a woman" (1 Cor 7:1)—even more, the bride of Christ! Or are you ignorant of how jealous a bridegroom he is, both avenging sins swiftly and establishing tortures for a great variety of crimes?

22. All of you have promised God to stand at the King's right hand; offer up to your Lord all the wealth of your virginity, lest, by keeping back a portion, you suffer the fate of Ananias and Sapphira (Acts 5:1–11). And if they kept back things from the fleshly offering of their wealth and so awaited these (sufferings), what will you endure, you who neglect the valuable wealth of your virginity? For she who greets a man in order to be seen by him, or to have fun with him, or to speak with him in a fleshly way—what else has she done except taken from that offering pledged by her to God and given it to a man? For fittingly it is said to her: "As long as it remained, did it not remain yours? And when it was sold, was it at your disposal? Why has Satan filled your heart so that you cheat the Holy Spirit and hold back some from the field's proceeds?" (Acts 5:4)

23. For by your own will you became a virgin: you presented a willing sacrifice. Rejoicing, you offered (yourself) and wrote that you would strive. By your own will you were brought to the arena: he did not bring you by force, but persuaded you with the promise. He did not use a threat, but he was earnest with counsels. He did not require you by law,

but led you by your will. You did not fear some punishment stored up, but you were encouraged by the glory stored up. You were not compelled by a torture made ready, but you were emboldened by the crown reserved. Shouts did not force you, rather "the crown of the upward call" (Phil 3:14). The chains of force did not compel you, but the liberty of Christ attracted you. You have not yielded to the deception of human beauty, but to the love of him who is more beautiful in his appearance than human beings (Ps 44 [45]:3). You have not been enticed by numerous marriage gifts, but you have hoped in heavenly treasures. You did not desire the noble birth of a man, but you relied upon divine chastity.

24. Therefore, this kind of sin is unforgivable; this offense, without excuse; this lifestyle, unacceptable. "It is better not to make a vow than to make a vow and not to accomplish it" (Eccl 5:4). For it is better not to promise virginity than, when you have promised, not to accomplish it perfectly. For just as it is impossible for two men in the world to have one wife, so too one soul cannot perfectly be with God and with humanity. For "no person can serve two masters, for either he will hate one and love the other, or he will love one and treat the other with contempt" (Matt 6:24). Therefore, O virgin, abandon such a love, one which separates you from the divine love. Break your bond of goodwill toward a man, lest you break your covenant with the heavenly bridegroom. Do not, when you consider a small pleasure or gift, fall away from the true one. Therefore, if you are oppressed by poverty, receive, but do not give that which is great. Do not, for the sake of a corruptible garment, lose the name of him who is incorruptible. Do not, for the sake of nourishment, remain outside the banquet of Paradise, lest by fearing to leave an (earthly) house you fall from the heavenly mansion.

25. But perhaps you will say, "I guard my virginity and holiness." But it is fitting for the perfect virgin to be "holy in body and soul" (1 Cor 7:34), to escape from the defilement of spirit and flesh, and—for the sake of him who came to collect human thoughts, for the sake of him who knew the secrets of the heart—to be undistracted and undividedly attentive (1 Cor 7:35). Therefore, see whether you are (holy) in spirit, for if he who looks at a woman—as he (Jesus) says—so as to desire her has sinned (Matt 5:28), what about him who is constantly with her? So see whether

you are able to be undividedly attentive, whether you are permitted also to be undistracted, or whether you serve and are subject to a man. For in this way in body and mind you will be anxious, so that you are engaged in human affairs (see 1 Cor 7:35). But you say, "On every side I guard myself with fasts and vigils, prayers and complete continence, lest I fall from this position." But what need is there for you to walk beside a fire so that you require lots of cool, quenching water?

26. But if you are not injured, consider him who is with you. Are you not killing him? His soul is sought in your hands. Do not strike him all the time, lest his mind be conquered, lest he become a captive instead of a conqueror, lest he become subject to a woman rather than (her) head (1 Cor 11:3), a slave instead of lord of the house. Therefore, it is not expedient to be a virgin with a man, lest she in his view be lacking in her soul. "The one who cleaves to the Lord," it says, "becomes one spirit (with him)" (1 Cor 6:17). But the one who cleaves to flesh is flesh. "Are you bound to a wife? Do not seek to be free. Are you free from a wife? Do not seek a wife" (1 Cor 7:25).

27. What do you, O monk, seek with a virgin, with another man's bride? You will not dare to approach a man's wife because of her husband's jealousy, lest you fall into his hands. But you do not fear to approach the bride of Christ although you know his fearful jealousy: "It is a fearful thing to fall into the hands of the living God" (Heb 10:31). Why do you catch God's dove with a few grains? Why do you capture an innocent bird? For she sees only what is given by you, but does not see what is taken by you. For she receives from you fleshly things, but she forsakes spiritual things. By a few (earthly) gifts she loses heavenly gifts. Why do you draw away the virgin's mind, which it is fitting for her to place always before God?

28. But you say, "I am doing a noble thing, for God's sake, for the name of the virgin" (see Matt 10:41–42). You are doing good if you are giving without approaching (her), without staying with her, without being served (by her), if you are not giving "favor" in exchange for "favor." If (you do this) on account of God's command, you will have a reward; but if on account of your own desire, you have received your reward. Give necessary things if she requests something for food or clothing, but

not for fleshly decoration. For these are the desires of the flesh and not spiritual gifts. Therefore, be distant from other men's wives; do not embrace a woman who is not yours. Make a covenant with your eyes not to gaze upon a virgin, as Job said (Job 31:1). And again: "Do not gaze upon a virgin. Avert your eyes, and do not gaze upon another's beauty" (Sir 9:5, 8). You are called a solitary in name; be one in deed. But if you live with another person, you are not a solitary; rather, you are a second person.

29. "The queen of the south will rise and condemn this generation" (Matt 12:42). The married women who have separated from their husbands for the sake of the pure life condemn those "virgins" who live with men, and they receive their glory. Virgins like these will be rejected from their honor, but those who have kept themselves will receive the virginal honor. Be ashamed, O virgin of this kind! Even she who has not promised to lead a life pure and solitary lives diligently, but you who have so promised cheat the true one and take another man. Therefore, put on adornment, and strip off virginity, for the adorned class claims you. Therefore, occupy yourself with baths and myrrh, and take care of yourself with cleansings, so that you might please him who is with you. For she who is like this is anxious about how to please men, and she is divided. But she who is dedicated to God alone thinks night and day about how to please the Lord (1 Cor 7:32–34).

30. Therefore, it behooves you to be enshrouded, separated, set apart, and withdrawn in every way, with a steadfast will, and to be sealed up, just as you were sealed by the Lord at the beginning as a servant:

> An enclosed garden is my sister, the bride,
> an enclosed garden, a sealed fountain,
> a paradise of pomegranates with fruits of the trees:
> cyprus with nard, nard and saffron, cane and cinnamon,
> with all the cedar-wood of Lebanon. (Song 4:12–14)

Thus it is fitting for her to be guarded and withdrawn and sealed who is all fruit and goodness. Virginity is like an enclosed garden that is not trodden upon by anyone, except its gardener alone. Be careful that no merciless stranger spoils the manifold seedlings and beautiful blossoms of the garden; that no one mars the injured vine; that no ferocious foxes from some place or other destroy the beautiful clusters of grapes (Song

2:15); that no one disturbs the sealed fountain or muddies the bright and shining waters of virginity; that no one fills the paradise of sweet fragrance with a foul odor.

31. Therefore, remove yourself from fleshly and human love, O virgin! Rather, turn and seek him whom your soul loved, where he grazes, where he lies down at midday, until you find him whom your soul loved, and he shows you his face and makes you hear his voice. For his face is beautiful and his speaking sweet. When you have found him, hold on to him, and do not leave him until he brings you into his bedroom (Song 3:2; 1:7; 2:14; 3:4). He is your bridegroom. He is the one who will crown you. It is he who is preparing the wedding garment for you. It is he who is revealing to you the treasures. It is he who is preparing the Father's table for you and from the torrent of delight gives you to drink (Ps 35 [36]:9). Wait for him; gaze on him with your mind; speak to him; rejoice with him; take everything from him. For when you are fed by the Lord, you will lack nothing, and you will enjoy eternal life. Amen.

2. John Chrysostom, *Instruction and Refutation Directed Against Those Men Cohabiting with Virgins* (selections)

Chrysostom wrote this and the following treatise, *On the Necessity of Guarding Virginity,* late in the fourth century, probably while he was a priest in Antioch prior to his ordination as bishop of Constantinople in 398 C.E. Both treatises attack the practice of spiritual marriage, but from different points of view. *Instruction and Refutation* is addressed to the male partners in the relationship and employs a rhetoric of satire and parody to shame these men. *On the Necessity of Guarding Virginity* is addressed to the female partners and emphasizes the tragic spiritual consequences of what Chrysostom views as their "prostitution." Ancient understandings of gender—the social construction of sexuality—undergird the charges in these treatises, which should not be read as literal portrayals of what spiritual marriage was like but rather as reflections of Chrysostom's understanding of the proper locus of power as well as a Scripturally-based sexual hierarchy, which he felt spiritual marriage threatened. Overall, both essays attempt to expose as a sham the claims to holiness of those practicing spiritual marriage.

1. In our ancestors' era, two justifications were given for men and

women living together. The first, marriage, was ancient, licit, and sensible, since God was its legislator. "For this reason," he said, "a man shall leave his father and mother and cleave to his wife, and the two shall be one flesh" [Gen 2:24; Eph 5:31]. And the other, prostitution, of more recent origin than marriage, was unjust and illegitimate, since it was introduced by evil demons. But in our time, a third way of life has been dreamed up, something new and incredible which greatly perplexes those who wish to discover its rationale. There are certain men who apart from marriage and sexual intercourse take girls inexperienced with matrimony, establish them permanently in their homes, and keep them sequestered until ripe old age, not for the purpose of bearing children (for they deny that they have sexual relations with the women), nor out of licentiousness (for they claim that they preserve them inviolate). If anybody asks the reason for their practice, they have plenty and start rehearsing them; however, I myself think that they have not found a single decent, plausible excuse.

But let us not dwell on these matters any longer nor address ourselves for the time being to their excuses. Instead let us make public the one reason which we suspect is primary. . . . It seems to me that living with a woman entails a certain pleasure, not only in the lawful state of marriage, but also in cases which do not involve marriage and sexual intercourse. Whether or not I judge correctly, I cannot say; I am only setting forth my own point of view. But perhaps it is not just my opinion but yours too? That it does seem to be yours as well the following argument makes clear: they would not enjoy such a despicable reputation nor would there be so many scandals, if a violent and tyrannical pleasure were not found in their cohabitation. . . .

Since sexual intercourse is not hindered in a relationship with a legitimate wife, it serves to still passion and often leads the man to satiation, greatly reducing his desire. And besides this, the birth pangs, parturition, the bearing and rearing of children, and prolonged sicknesses with their aftereffects besiege the body, cause the bloom of youth to fade, and produce a diminution of the sting of pleasure. But with a virgin, nothing of this sort happens, for there is no intercourse which can restrain and relax the frenzy of nature, nor do labor pains and child-rearing dry up her flesh; to the contrary, these virgins stay in their prime for a long time, since they remain untouched. After the birth and care of children, the bodies of married women become feeble, but these women retain their beauty until they are forty, rivaling the virgins being led to the nuptial chamber! Thus the men who live with them are stirred by a double desire: they are not permitted to satisfy their passion through sexual intercourse, yet the basis for their desire remains intensely potent for a long time. I suppose this is the pretext for their living under the same roof.

3. If anyone should reproach us as intemperate for these words about the fine gentlemen who live with a woman without anything too terrible happening to them, I congratulate such men as these and wish that I also would receive similar strength. Probably I can even convince myself that it is possible there *are* such men! But I do wish our accusers could also persuade us on this point: that a young man bursting with vigor can cohabit with a girl, sit side by side with her, eat with her, talk with her all day long (not to mention all the rest: untimely laughter, merriment, sweet talk, and so forth, which is perhaps not nice to speak about), have the house, the table, the salt in common, share everything very frankly, and yet not be seized by any human sentiment, but remain pure of evil desire and pleasure. About these things I would like to be able to convince those who censure us, but they do not wish to be won over. Instead, when we present our side of the story concerning these matters, they cry out against us that we are shameless, that we are sick with the same malady and are covering up our own immorality.

"And how does that concern us?" one of the men interjects. "We are not responsible for the ignorance of others and if anyone should take offense without reason, I should not deserve to take the penalty for his lack of knowledge." But Paul did not talk in this fashion; rather, if somebody were scandalized without just motivation because of weakness, he commanded us to help him. We are freed from the penalty set for the offense we cause only when greater profit than harm results from it. When this is not the case, but there is only scandal occasioned for others, whether they take offense for good reason, irrationally, or through weakness, their blood is on our head and God will demand an account of such souls from our hands. Therefore, lest we neither despise nor scorn in any way those who are affronted, Christ has set limits and rules for us, so that we do this or that thing at the opportune time.

When he discussed the nature of food, proving that it was clean and liberating it from Jewish observances, Peter approached him and said, "They have taken offense." Christ replied, "Let them alone." Not only did he scorn them, he also condemned them. "For every planting which my heavenly Father has not planted will be uprooted" [Mark 7:14–23 = Matt 15:10–20]. Thus did he abrogate the law concerning food. But when those who demanded the double drachma came up to Peter and asked, "Does not your master pay the double drachma?" Christ acted differently than he did in the first case. He noticed that they had taken exception, and replied, "Lest we offend them, throw the fish-line into the sea, catch the first fish which rises up, and you will find in its mouth a stater; take it and give it on behalf of both of us" [Matt 17:24–27].

Do you see how he considers people's scruples at times and not at others? In the latter case, it was unimportant to reveal the glory of the Only-begotten. Why? Did he not seek to conceal it, did he not command many not to reveal that he was the Christ? Thus there was no harm in paying the drachma, though from not paying it great evils might have arisen. Christ would have seemed like a tyrant, an agitator, an enemy of the whole state, throwing it into extreme danger, with the result that they would have turned away from him. This is why he fled far away from those who wished to seize him and make him king, repudiating the opinion held by the crowd around him. In this circumstance, setting things in correct perspective was necessary. He condemned the offense in a helpful way and at the right time through his astute handling of the situation. For it was the appropriate time not to hold back those about to ascend to the highest philosophy by sparing the Jews, but to free them for the future hour which summons them to purify the soul and not hinder them with physical observances, but permit them to be delivered from that lowly business.

Thus Paul also, following his teacher, both condemned those who took offense and refrained from condemning them, when he said, "I please all men in all things, not seeking my own advantage but that of the

multitude, in order that they may be saved" [1 Cor 10:33]. And if Paul overlooked his own benefit in order to seek that of his brothers, what punishment may we not deserve when we do not even have to choose to stand
aloof from an injury to ourselves for the sake of promoting the advantage
of others; rather, we joyfully destroy others along with ourselves, when
we could save both them and us. Therefore when Paul sees a greater
gain, greater than the harm arising from the offense, he scorns those
who are affronted, but when there is no gain and the offense is the only
result, he chooses to do and suffer everything lest that occur. He does not
philosophize in the manner we do nor does he inquire, "Why are they
weak? Why do they act foolishly?" Instead, he spares them for this very
reason, that they *are* senseless, that they *are* weak.

4. For tell me, what plausible reason can the person give who is offended at the eating of meat and the drinking of wine? God at the beginning gave this law to us [Gen 1:29]. But still, if someone were scandalized
by these things, Paul refrained from doing them. "For I will not eat
meat," he said, "nor drink wine, lest my brother be offended" [1 Cor 8:13;
Rom 14:21]. He did not respond in the way we do: "Do I have to be responsible for someone else's foolishness? If it suits someone to be offended in
such a simpleminded fashion, do I deserve the punishment?" Yet even if
Paul had uttered such words, he would have had far more right to pronounce them than you do, for the person who is scandalized by these
matters could list many fitting and sensible explanations for his views.
Nevertheless, he would have had more just reasons than you if he had
wished to voice them, but he did not do so. To the contrary, he looked to
only one goal, the salvation of his neighbor. . . .

Note again with me the wisdom of the teacher: leaving the weak
alone, he corrects the strong man instead, for the strong man is the cause
of the other's weakness and he has the authority to amend feebleness,
not to produce it. . . . The stronger you claim you are and assert that you
are in no way harmed by this cohabitation, the more you are obliged to
sever that bond. For the more stalwart you are, the more justly you ought
to bear with the weaker person. . . .

And if you claim to be strong yet do not heed the weakness of another, you will be given a double punishment, because you did not spare the

weak when you had considerable power to do so. For each of us is responsible for the salvation of our neighbor [1 Cor 10:24; Rom 15:2; Sir
17:14]; therefore we are commanded to look not to our own interests but
to those of our neighbor. "For we have been purchased at a price" [1 Cor
6:20], and the one who bought us gave this order for the common profit of
us all. For the gain which results is not just that we save our own members but that we establish enormous security for ourselves [see 1 Cor 12].

As much as you may philosophize, you are refuted by your deeds, for
you do not admit that any harm comes to you from this cohabitation.
Whenever I see you having great difficulty in tearing yourself away from
the relationship, ignoring the innumerable dangers, not repenting even
when many people reproach you but dashing your own reputation to the
ground; whenever I see you prompting many accusations about the
church community, giving unbelievers the opportunity to gossip, and
bringing everyone into bad repute; when so many evils, and nothing
good, arise from this cohabitation, but all these are annulled by your separation and in addition you come into possession of many other benefits;
how can I convince your accusers that you have removed yourself from
all desire, that you are untainted by evil passion, since this argument
does not encourage you to turn away from the practice? . . .

5. [Note: At the end of the preceding section, Chrysostom offered Job as a model of behavior, referring to Job 31:1: "I have made a covenant with my eyes; how
then could I look upon a virgin?" He then continues as follows.] But if it is too trivial a matter for you to contest with Job (although we are not worthy even
of his dung heap), unless you consider that his example is too far beneath your greatness of soul, think of Paul, the strong-voiced herald of
truth, who having wandered throughout the whole world was able to
pronounce these words so laden with wisdom, that he no longer lived for
himself but for Christ in him [Gal 2:20], that he crucified himself to the
world and the world to himself [Gal 6:14], and that he would die daily [1
Cor 15:31]. After such spiritual grace, after such an exhibition of contests,
after untold dangers [2 Cor 11:25–27], after the perfecting of wisdom, he
shows and demonstrates to us that as long as we breathe and are clothed
in this fleshly covering, the labors of the palaestra [place of gymnastic exer-
cises] are necessary for us, and that temperance is never correctly prac-

ticed without difficulty; it is rather necessary to prepare for this trophy with quantities of sweat and weariness. Thus he says, "I mortify my body and keep it in subjection, lest in preaching to others I myself be rejected as counterfeit coin" [1 Cor 9:27].

He made these remarks to indicate the rebelliousness of the flesh and the madness which stems from desire, to show that the battle was a constant one and his own life a contest. For this reason Christ also made clear the magnitude of the problem. He did not permit a man even to look into the eyes of a woman, but threatened those who did with the penalty laid on adulterers [Matt 5:28]. When Peter commented, "It is better not to marry," Christ did not make a law prohibiting marriage but replied, indicating the importance of the subject, "He that is able to receive it, let him receive it" [Matt 19:10–12]. . . . You say, however, that if you were to see a man living with a virgin, a man who is bound to her and delights in her, who would give up his life rather than his roommate and would choose to suffer and do everything than to part from his beloved, you should not believe anything evil nor view the situation as one involving lust, but rather piety. O wondrous man! This opinion is appropriate to a person who lives among stones, but not to anyone who resides among flesh-and-blood humans. . . . But you probably are unconvinced because of your great virtue! I myself, however, have heard tell that there are some who have become emotionally affected by statues and stones. And if a hard, rigid model all by itself has such power, what madness is not elicited when a tender body, in contrast to the model, is lying there? Will not the accusers appear to speak with greater probability than we the defenders? . . .

Tell me, why do you live with a virgin? This cohabitation is not based on law but on love and lust. For if this reason is taken away, the need for the practice also disappears. What man, if he were free from the compulsion to have a woman, would choose to put up with the delicacy, wantonness, and all the other faults of that sex? Thus even from the beginning God endowed woman with this strength, knowing that she would be totally despicable unless she were provided with this power, that no man would choose to live with her if he were innocent of desire. For if such a necessity also presses upon us now, in addition to her many other uses (indeed we could also mention the bearing of children, taking care of the house, and the rendering of other services even loftier than these), and if even now women performing such chores for men are often easy to despise and are expelled from their homes, how would you love them if it were not for desire, especially since they cast so much reproach upon you? Now either tell us the reason for cohabitation or we will necessarily suspect that there is no other one than wanton desire and the most shameful pleasure.

6. What next? Our opponent asks, "If we are able to give a sensible and legitimate reason for the practice, will we have wasted our breath in speaking on our own behalf?" Certainly you will not be able to present any reasons of this sort! All the same, I would like to learn whether you have even the shadow of a plausible pretext to offer. "The virgin," he replies, "is unprotected, without a husband or inlaws; often she does not have even a father or a brother. She needs someone to lend her a hand, to comfort her solitude, to come to her defense on all occasions, and to establish her in a haven of considerable security." What sort of security, tell me? What sort of a haven? For I do not see a bulwark which shuts out the waves but rather one which stirs them up; I do not see a haven which repulses the winter storms but one which produces huge waves not present before. Are you not ashamed, do you not hide your face, when you present such a defense? For if neither condemnation, harm, nor scandal were generated by this service, but it were possible to do this same thing with honor, would you not be more deserving of pity than anyone, you who increase her riches, you who excite her to avarice, you who thrust her into business, you who train her for worldly offices, and whose role you exchange for that of a manager, a governor, a lawyer? By all means that would be the case!

For you cannot talk about poverty and convince anyone to scorn wealth, all those of you who do everything imaginable to retain and increase the women's possessions, adding treasure to treasure; you have become peddlers and petty businessmen for their sakes! How high-minded and noble your hopes are, are they not! Men who have been commanded to carry the cross and follow Christ have discarded it [Mark 8:34 = Matt 16:24 = Luke 9:23], resembling effeminate soldiers who throw away their shields and sit down with a spindle and a basket; they have opened the door to the present life through another more disgraceful entrance.

It is not so shameful for married people to attend to the management of these domestic matters as it is for you, you who pretend to have turned away from present realities but slip them back in under another disguise. This is why we have won the reputation everywhere for ourselves of being gluttons, flatterers, and above all slaves of women, because we have dashed to the ground all the nobility given us from above and exchanged it for earthly servility and shabbiness. . . .

"What then?" our opponent asks. "Shall we look on indifferently while all the virgin's belongings are stolen, removed, carried off by her relatives and servants, by strangers as well as by the members of her household? It is admirable, is it not, how we shall provide the virgin with compensation for not having married or being enamoured with the present world but for choosing Christ above all else when we leave her open prey to those who wish to steal her goods!"

How much better it would have been for her to marry and live with a man who could attend to the management of these matters than to have remained unwed, yet trampled upon the compact she made with God, treated an exceedingly dignified and formidable matter with insolence, and in addition drawn others along into the shipwreck of her own sins. How can you claim that she has chosen Christ above all else when Christ cries out, "You cannot serve God and mammon" [Matt 6:24 = Luke 6:13]? And how can you profess to hate the world and present realities when you convince her to become passionately excited by worldly desires? How can you exhort a married woman to scorn wealth when you help establish a virgin in riches? And will you allow her to be constantly and undistractedly in attendance on the Lord if you are devoting all your life and energy to her affairs? How will the virgin ever be able to philosophize if she observes you, a man, becoming angry when her assets are demolished? How will she be able to overlook the loss when she sees you doing and suffering everything in order to increase her present wealth? God does not wish us to free ourselves from practical concerns in this manner; instead he wants us to despise possessions, to be detached from all the things of this life. You, however, do not permit this nor do you concede that God's law should prevail.

7. "But what," the man asks, "if she needs another's protection, if she

is subjected to many indignities? Now are not these things unworthy of the virgin?" Nothing is so unworthy as to become rich and be thrust into a multitude of business matters. What if she insists on engaging in other activities besides these, such as lending money at interest? What if next she summoned us to make a contract and did not convince us to do so; when she failed to persuade us and seized upon other persons, would we be blamed? What then? If she established certain other low-class, disreputable taverns and since we did not wish to join the enterprise she found it necessary to seek out others, would we be liable to accusations brought against us? Certainly not; rather we should be praised. Quite to the contrary, we would be deserving of blame and condemnation if we contributed to such pursuits and assisted in them.

Do you wish that her wealth not be taken away or carried off? Advise her to deposit it where a man will not be required to guard it and where it will remain forever undiminished. If she wants to have business to attend to, why does she play with things which are not to be trifled with? For when a virgin does such things, the game she plays does not give pleasure but results in death. Whenever she undertakes such combats, she does everything unworthy of her promise and she is accountable. Her punishment will be heavier, her chastisement more severe. Have you not heard what sort of law Paul gave her, or rather Christ who spoke through him, that the wife and the virgin are to be differentiated? "The unmarried woman cares for the things of the Lord, in order that she may be holy both in body and in spirit" [1 Cor 7:34]. But you do not allow that, since you yield to all their desires more readily than do slaves purchased with silver.

"Yes," he says, "but what if she wrestles with extreme poverty? As far as the rich virgins went, your points were well-taken. But what sort of crime is it to raise up those sunk in grievous poverty and neglect?" Oh, if only you did not cast them down nor push them to the abyss of destruction, it would be an act of Christian love! Indeed if you do these things out of obedience to the one who commanded that we assist the poor, then you have thousands of brothers. Demonstrate this good work in an area where scandal cannot be secretly anchored. But here, alms of this sort are worse than any inhumanity, any cruelty. For of what use is it to nourish the body but cast down the spirit, to give a cloak but arouse a suspicion more disgraceful than nakedness, to provide aid with bodily goods but destroy all the spiritual ones, to facilitate her earthly affairs but cast her out of heaven? . . .

9. . . . "And who will manage our household?" our opponent continues. "Who will keep an eye on our possessions? Who will direct the operation when we are spending time elsewhere, if we don't have a woman at home?" To be sure, they utter sentiments like this, the very opposite of what they expressed earlier, ones even more disgraceful than their former argument. They care nothing about these contradictions nor are they embarrassed, but resemble drunken men who say everything which comes into their heads. But let us not therefore grow weary of answering them, of gently disputing with them, until we have rescued them from this drunkenness as far as that is in our power. For I am ashamed and blush to undertake the refutation of these points which they set forth in opposition to us without even blushing. Nevertheless, one must bear the disgrace for the sake of the advantage it may bring to those who are not ashamed. Indeed, it would be foolish if those who accused them of disdaining their scandalized brethren should themselves despise serving these men because of shame.

For what, tell me, do they say these household matters are for which they deem it necessary to utilize the virgin's managerial skills? Do you have a crowd of recently purchased foreign maids who need to be trained in wool-working and in other duties? Do you have a storeroom for your tremendous treasures and expensive garments? Is it necessary for a guard to sit at home all the time, for the virgin's eyes to serve as a fortress against the wickedness of the servants? Or do you continually prepare feasts and banquets and require the house to be decorated? Do you have cooks and waiters who receive the benefit of the virgin's advance planning? Or are there a variety of frequent expenses, and is it necessary for someone always to be in charge, carefully guarding things, so that items do not disappear at random from the house?

"For none of these reasons," he replies. "Rather I need a woman so that she can oversee my chest of drawers, my cloak, and my other poor needs, such as setting the table, making the bed, lighting the fire, washing my feet, and providing for every other comfort. Surely on account of these rather trivial and dreary forms of relaxation we will not fear such condemnation and be subject to such censure, will we?"

Yet how much better, how much more easily a brother will serve in these matters, for a man is by nature stronger than a woman, more like us in his needs, and not so extravagant. For the woman, since she is more delicate, requires a softer bed, finer clothes, and perhaps a maid to wait on her; she does not provide us with as much service as we must give her. But a brother is aloof from all these problems. If he has needs, they will be the same as ours. It is no small advantage for housemates not to differ in their requirements but to have identical ones—the very thing which is not the case with the virgin.

In the first place, if she needs to bathe or if she becomes physically ill, surely a brother should not attend her in these circumstances, even if he might opt for such dreadful self-disgrace, nor will she be able to make do on her own. But if it is brothers who are living together, they will render each other this service. Furthermore, when sleep calls, if there is a virgin in the house you need two beds, two carpets and sets of covers, and if you are thinking clearly, also two bedrooms. But if the two are brothers, then the need is reduced, since they are more alike; indeed, one house, one pillow, one bed, and the same covers suffice for both of them. In short, if anyone should make a list of all these requirements, he will find it very easy to supply them if two men are living together, but very difficult if it is a woman and a man who are housemates—and I pass over the disgrace occasioned by the household.

For what shall we think when we enter a monk's house and see women's shoes hanging up, and girdles, headbands, baskets, a distaff, various items of weaving equipment, and all the other things women have, too numerous to be counted? And if you review the situation of a virgin who is well-provided for, the laughter increases. First of all, the monk twists and turns in the midst of so many serving girls, a veritable herd of them, as if he were the dancer in the orchestra of a theater accompanied by the singing of the women's chorus. Could anything be more disgraceful, more dishonorable? Then he is bursting with irritation at the domestics all day long because of incidents pertaining to the woman; either he has to keep quiet, disregard everything which concerns her and take the blame, or speak out in rebuke and disgrace himself.

Just see what happens. He who has been forbidden even to approach worldly affairs not only immerses himself in them, but also in those which concern women. Indeed, these men will not refuse to devote themselves to matters concerning women's paraphernalia; instead, they will constantly be stopping in at the silversmith's to inquire if the mistress's mirror is ready yet, if he has finished the urn, if he has delivered the perfume flask. For things are in such a state of corruption that the majority of these virgins has greater need of such items than women in secular life do.

10. From there he runs again to the perfume maker to discuss aromatics for his mistress and often he will not hesitate in his abundant zeal to insult the poor fellow. (Yes indeed, even virgins use a variety of expensive perfumes!) From the perfumer he goes on to the linen merchant and from him to the umbrella maker. Nor are the women ashamed to command these trifles, since they see how completely obedient the men are, how they thank the women who order them about rather than the other men who serve them. Then again, when it is necessary to have that umbrella repaired, the men linger on until evening without food, riveted to the workshops. . . . They expose themselves to ridicule both at home and in the market and even more.

(Migne 10) In church they bring unspeakable disgrace upon themselves, as if no place should remain ignorant of their arrogance and ignoble slavery. Even in this holy and formidable spot, they proclaim their lack of self-restraint to everyone, and what is still worse, they show off about things which ought to make them blush. The men receive the women at the door, strutting as if they had been transformed into eunuchs, and when everyone is looking, they guide them in with enormous pride. Nor do they slink away, but go so far as to glory in their performance. Even at that most awesome hour of the mysteries, they are much occupied with waiting on the virgins' pleasure, providing many of the spectators with an occasion for offense.

But these pitiful and unfortunate women, who ought to prevent the men from showing such signs of favor, are conceited and exceedingly presumptuous. Yet if anyone intended to put a curse on these men and women, could he invent anything more difficult to bear than their having innumerable witnesses to their licentiousness and their disgracing themselves in everybody's eyes? . . .

Christ wants us to be stalwart soldiers and athletes. He has not furnished us with spiritual weapons so that we take upon ourselves the service of girls worth only three obols, that we turn our attention to matters which concern wool and weaving and other such tasks, that we sit alongside women as they spin and weave, that we spend all day having our souls stamped with women's habits and speech. We have rather been so armed in order that we might cast down the invisible powers which assault us, wound their leader, the devil, drive out the fierce phalanx of demons, raze their fortifications to the ground, bind in chains the powers of the world ruler of darkness, rout the evil spirits, breathe fire, and prepare and equip ourselves to brave death daily. For this reason he has clothed us in the armor of righteousness, encircled us with the girdle of truth, placed the helmet of salvation on our heads, shod us with zeal for the gospel of peace, handed us the sword of the spirit, and kindled a fire in our souls [Eph 6:11–17].

11. . . . . Let us not diminish our strength nor frazzle our nerves by keeping such company, for through doing so an enormous and unspeakable evil streams into our souls. How can we help ourselves if we are not even conscious of our intoxication with this friendship? This very aspect is the most terrifying one of all: we do not realize how we are being unnerved and made softer than wax. Just as someone captures a proud and fiercely-glaring lion, then shears his mane, breaks his teeth, clips his claws, and renders him a disgraceful and ridiculous specimen, so that this fearsome and unassailable creature whose very roaring causes everyone to tremble is easily conquered even by children, so these women make all the men they capture easy for the devil to overcome. They render them softer, more hot-headed, shameful, mindless, irascible, insolent, importunate, ignoble, crude, servile, niggardly, reckless, nonsensical, and, to sum it up, the women take all their corrupting feminine customs and stamp them into the souls of these men.

(Migne 11) To tell the truth, if a man lives with women in such intimacy and is reared in their company, he is at a loss to escape being some kind of vagabond, the dregs of the earth, one of the rabble. If he says anything, his talk will entirely concern weaving and wool; his language will be tainted with the characteristics of women's speech. And anything he may do, he will carry out with great servility (the freedom appropriate to a Christian is like a far-distant colony to him); he becomes unfit for any of the splendid deeds of virtue. In fact, if such a man is useless for matters of daily living and civic affairs, how much more so is he for the magnitude of spiritual matters, which to so great an extent require men of a nobler type that those intending to pursue these goals are not able to attain them unless they be transformed from humans into angels?

For not only do the men welcome such vice, they also become the causes of corruption to the virgins' morals. Just as the men who wish to please the virgins recklessly abandon the way of life to which they have pledged themselves, so also the women fall from their proper modesty on account of the men, exhibiting to them this wicked and dangerous exchange of proclivities. Indeed, the women even deck themselves out with special care, lavishing much attention on appearance and a coquettish gait, and they babble all day long about unsuitable topics. Since they see the men are delighted by these dissolute customs and conversation, they invent all sorts of means through which they will be able to keep them captive. But if we wish to come to our senses a bit and master ourselves, we will win the women, ourselves, and all the others as well. Just as at present we are accountable for the destruction of the multitude, so then we will reap the reward of everyone's salvation, and those whom we now enjoy shamefully, we will then enjoy with much honor. . . .

(Migne 12) Having thoroughly discussed all these points, let us at least reconcile ourselves somewhat belatedly to the salvation of our souls. If it seems difficult to be torn away from a long-standing habit, let us turn everything over to the power of reason, after the grace of God, and convince ourselves that if we will just make a start, no longer will we find it vexing, and in this way we shall boldly attack the custom. For if you refrain from the practice for ten days, twenty will seem easier, and double the time again. Then as you progress along the way, you will not find the sensation you receive later on as unpleasant as the one in the be-

ginning; instead, you will see that which was so terribly hard to sur-
mount becoming quite simple and you will in turn form a different habit
for yourself. You will find the change easy not only on account of the custom but also because of your good hopes. Thus those women will admire
you more, God will accept you before them, all men will crown you, and
you will live a life which is full of freedom, full of delight.

For what could be more pleasant than to be delivered from a bad
conscience, to end the constant war with desire, to plait the beautiful
crown of self-control with much ease, to look toward heaven with free
eyes, and to call upon the Lord of all with a pure voice and heart? . . .

13. . . . Let us turn away, even belatedly, from this severe and destructive sickness, that we may depart from this present state with shining crowns, that we may be able to confess freely with our lips to Christ,
"For you and your honor we have despised intimacy, triumphed over
pleasure, and troubled our souls as well. We have put aside every friendship and preference and have chosen you and our desire for you before
everything else." In this way we shall win ourselves, those wretched
women, and those who are scandalized. We shall place ourselves among
the very martyrs and shall receive the first rank. For those who contend
in that greatest of contests and bear suffering in patience, I do not place
below the man held fast by a former passion, overpowered by a very tender old relationship, who then breaks the chains out of fear of God and
hastens back toward that which pleases God. Truly it is much more difficult to cast off a sympathy and affection of long standing, break through
the intricate circumstances, spread wings, and fly up to the vault of heav-
en. . . .

For when bodily passions are henceforth undone and tyrannical desire has been quenched, there will be no hindrance in the next world to
prevent man and woman from being together, for every evil suspicion is
removed and all who have entered the Kingdom of Heaven can maintain
the way of life of those angels and intellectual powers.

3. John Chrysostom, *On the Necessity of Guarding Virginity* (selections)

1. Alas, my soul! Now is the time for me to repeat this with the prophet, once, twice, many times: alas, my soul! [Jer 15:10?] A matter so important and full of such wisdom as virginity is despitefully treated, the veil which separates it from marriage has been destroyed, torn asunder by shameless hands, the holy of holies is trod underfoot, and that which is august and full of terror has become impure, exposed to all. This state which is more honorable than marriage has been degraded and dashed to the ground so that those women who are married are considered more fortunate. As compared with marriage, virginity was assigned the first place, the front row seat, we might say. Now it cannot even retain the second rank but probably is further down, banished to the last place. And what is more bitter, it is not those who are enemies or opponents who have treated it in this fashion, but those who appear to serve virginity the most. Those women who more than all the rest allowed us to speak openly before the unbelievers have above all others stitched up our mouths and poured much dishonor on us. . . .

For the cause of all the evil is that virginity remains in name only and that everything is defined by the bodily condition—the very thing which is the least part of virginity—but that which is more necessary and is its greater proof is neglected. . . . Tell me, how in the future shall we be able to single out such a virgin from the ranks and society of those prostitutes when she behaves the same as they do, inflaming the hearts of young men, when she is flighty and debauched, when she grinds the same poisons, mixes the same cups, prepares the same hemlock? But she does not say, "Come! Let us roll ourselves up together in love!" nor does she say, "I have perfumed my couch with crocus and my bed with cinnamon" [Prov 7:17]. . . . Granted you have not engaged in conversations, you have not spoken the words of a harlot, "Come! Let us roll up together in love!" You have not pronounced them with your tongue, but you have spoken them with your demeanor; you have not uttered them with your lips, but with your gait you have loudly proclaimed them; you have not called with your voice, but you have spoken them more clearly with your eyes than with your voice. But after you called, you did not give yourself.

Not in this way were you delivered from sin; indeed, this is also another kind of prostitution. You remained free from wantonness—but in body, not in soul. You carry out the sinful deed, if not by intercourse, then by the eyes. . . . Indeed, you have wrought a perfect adultery for the man conquered by your scheme. How then is it possible not to be an adulteress when your action is condemned as adultery [Matt 5:28]? That man's madness is your work. It is plain to anyone anywhere that the woman who makes a man an adulterer can never escape the punishment for adultery. . . .

(Migne 2) . . .[T]hese women fasten upon certain men who are in no way related to them, shut them in, and live perpetually with them, as though they were trying to prove by these deeds and by the ones already discussed that they had been dragged into virginity against their wills, had been subjected to the utmost violence, and were consoling themselves in this manner for the violence and the compulsion. What else can we think? When these events occur, will not everyone, both friends and relatives, say things still worse? Don't these women live? Don't they, to put it bluntly, breathe? Surely they have not been cut asunder through the middle, or buried alive with these men, have they? Indeed, everyone says things of this sort and much more.

Further, there is the daily running of midwives to the virgins' houses, as if they were rushing to women in the throes of labor, not to deliver the one giving birth (although even this has occurred on some occasions), but in order to discern who is violated and who is untouched, just as people do with the slaves they purchase. One virgin readily consents to the examination but another resists it and by her very refusal goes out disgraced even if she has not been deflowered. The one was convicted, the other not, but she for her part is shamed no less than the first, insofar as she was unable to demonstrate her trustworthiness by her character but required the testimony afforded by minute examination. . . .

(Migne 3) . . .[T]ime in its entirety would not suffice for us to lament in accordance with the worth of the soul which suffers such things. For in the first place, about what should a person weep? Is it not that the honorable, great, and holy name of God is blasphemed among the heathen because of you, and that his glory is profaned, that such a dignified and important matter is slandered, that many souls fall because of these scandals, that even the healthy section of the virginal choir is infected by the blemish of your reputation, that an unquenchable fire is kindled both for yourselves and for those who live with you?

"But how is that necessarily so," the virgin asks, "when we can show that our body has not been deflowered or prostituted?" It is precisely this proof which is not manifest at the present but will be clear on that future day of judgment. For the wisdom and skill of the midwife can see only such things as whether the body has experienced intercourse with a man. But whether it has also fled the rude touch, the adultery of kisses and embraces and their defilement, that day will then reveal, when the living Word of God, who is aware of what happens in secret, sets their lives naked and exposed before the eyes of men and brings the hidden thoughts of human hearts into the open [Heb 4:12–13]; then we will know well whether your body is pure of these sins and is in every way untainted.

4. . . . For the time being, let it be assumed that the body has eluded all these snares, is pure in all respects and free from any damage: let the virgin remain a virgin! What has this got to do with what we previously said? Certainly this is the most terrible part of all, one laden with countless tears, that she has sustained so much effort carefully to preserve her body's purity in every way, then empties out all her labor and pours off her toils by blaspheming Christ. . . .

"And how have I done this?" she asks. By shutting men in the house with you and making them sit by you constantly. If you want to have men live with you, then you ought not to choose virginity but proceed on into matrimony, for it is far better to marry in that fashion than to be a virgin in this. God does not condemn such a marriage nor do men disparage it, for it is a matter worthy of honor in which no one is injured, no one is wounded. On the other hand, this "virginity in the company of men" is more severely slandered among all than is prostitution; having lost its own proper place, it has rolled headlong down into the abyss of harlotry. . . .

For when the virgins invade the marketplace or when a conversation takes place about them at home, the people who discuss this strange coupling, if they wish to signify the female companion of such a man, do not call her his mother (for she has not given birth to him), nor his sister (for she did not unloose the same birth pangs), nor his spouse (for she does not dwell with him according to the law of marriage), nor any other relation's name upon which we can agree and which is legitimate; instead, they call her by a term which is shameful and ludicrous [*syneisaktos*]. For my part, I will not even suffer to pronounce it, so much do I despise and spurn the very name. Even the expression "living together" offends me.

You, of course, have not given birth or suffered labor pains. What is more disgraceful than such a defense? What is more wretched than a virgin who wants to appear as a virgin by these excuses in which many prostitutes can also take refuge? "But prostitutes," she argues, "reveal their licentiousness in another manner." What other manner, tell me? "By their form, their glance, their walk, by the lovers they capture with these traits." You have very nicely depicted for us the characteristics of the harlot, but watch out lest you yourself rather than they be convicted by these proofs and arguments. Certainly you also provide many such lovers for yourself, just as she does, and lay the same nets for them. Even if you do not station yourself in the doorway to lure the passersby but have sequestered the men inside forever, this is far more serious. The practice exists for no other reason than to satisfy an unnatural pleasure, both his and yours. I am not talking about sexual intercourse, for what would be its advantage when even the communion of the eyes accomplishes the very same thing? If this is not the case, if you do not commit adultery, why do you keep this man at home? . . .

"Why are you meddling with other people's business," one of the virgins asks, "when our housemates do not sleep with us, nor have relations with us, as those men do with those women?" Most certainly, people say that as well! "So what?" she replies. "The blame falls on their own head." Whether it is only on their own head we will investigate later on. Already it has been plainly proved when we discoursed with the men that it is not only the people who indulge in evil talk but also those who rashly provide the occasion for it who pay the penalty which the accusation carries. . . .

If meanwhile I ask you the pretext for this joint homesteading, what can you say? The virgin answers, "I am just a weak woman and am not capable of satisfying my own needs by myself." But when we summoned your housemates, we heard them claim the opposite, that *they* kept *you* because of *your* service to *them*! How come, then, if out of your abundant energy you can give relief to the men, you are not able to help yourselves, since you are women, but need others? For just as a man can live together easily and contentedly with a man, so also can a woman with a woman, and if you are fit for the service of men, how much more so for aiding yourselves? Tell me, how could the company of a man be beneficial and necessary? What kind of service will this man render which could be impossible for a woman to provide for one of her own sex? Can he weave at the loom and spin thread and cloth with you more ably than a woman? Just the opposite is so! For even if a man wanted to, he would not know how to put his hand to any of these tasks, not unless you have just now taught him the skill; this is the work of woman alone.

5. But to launder a cloak, kindle a fire, boil a pot—is not a woman able to manage these things not less proficiently, but even more so, than a man? In what ways, then, is the man an advantage to you, tell me? Perhaps whenever it is necessary to buy or sell something? But the woman is not inferior to the man here, as the marketplace might also testify: all who wish to buy clothes, buy most of them from women. But if it is disgraceful for a virgin to stand in the marketplace for business dealings of such a kind (and it is in truth shameful), certainly it is much more disgraceful for her to live with men. Besides, you can escape this rather minor problem more easily than that one by entrusting everything to a serving girl to minister to your needs or to older women who are useful for these purposes. . . .

6. (Migne 5) . . . For what, O unfortunate woman, can this dreary cohabitation profit you, as much as it casts you out from enjoying your treasure? Just look: it leads you down from the heavens, bars you from the spiritual wedding chamber, separates you from your celestial Bridegroom, procures eternal punishment and torture without end. Instead, even if the man living with you supplied you with thousands of gold talents, if he were more submissive before you than slaves purchased with

silver, if he established you in greater honor and comfort than the empress herself, would it not still be necessary to hate and avoid him as a corrupter and an enemy who takes away more than he gives? Although the Word has set forth for you instruction concerning the heavenly goods, the Kingdom above, eternal life, and ineffable glory, you call to mind earthly matters and serve him who appears to be useful in those affairs as if he were a lord. And you do not slink away, do you, nor do you pray that the earth engulf you, that in this manner you might depart the world?

7. Instead, you present to me as a defense the weakness of woman's nature, the provision in the household for human needs, and comfort in the home; you formulate and devise excuses which are not genuine. Even so, you will not deceive intelligent people. For there can be no comfort, no, none, which compels us to disgrace ourselves in such a way. The woman if she chooses is sufficient not only for her own service but also for that of many others, since even from the beginning the man was assigned to civic affairs and it was her lot to guard the house and manage all its arrangements.

It is not, then, because you need comfort that you drag the men inside. . . . "Then what is the reason which makes the practice agreeable to us?" The love of vanity. Just as the men were motivated by a bleak and wretched pleasure, so also for these women this household companionship is inspired by a desire for esteem. For as it is said, the whole human race is vain, but especially the female sex. Since these women are not in need of relaxation, as has been shown, nor are they corrupted by their sexual involvement with the men, it is apparent that this reason alone remains for us to suspect.

(Migne 6) Since, then, we have found the root of the evil, well, in the future let us abandon this accusation. Let us exhort and persuade them that just as their male living companions seem to reap pleasure, but are encompassed by a greater torture (indeed, the only pleasure which would be enduring and innocent would be that which arises from a separation), so also it appears to these women that a certain glory and celebrity are born from this practice, as they themselves believe. But if a person should examine the subject more closely, he would see that they are covered with laughter, disgrace, reproach, and the utmost ill-repute. At the beginning these matters were briefly mentioned to you, but now we will develop the theme. . . .

Perhaps these women themselves think this very thing, their overpowering men, is laudable. To the contrary, it is completely ridiculous; certainly only courtesans take pride in it. For it is not characteristic of free and virtuous women to be conceited about such snares. This is also another reason for dishonor; to the degree that they dominate the men and become harsher in their commandeering, to this extent they rather disgrace themselves in addition to the males. It is not the woman who brings men under her rule who is esteemed and considered remarkable by everyone, but the woman who respects them. But if they cannot endure these words of ours, the law of God will be able to bridle their mouths when it says, "Your refuge is with your husband, and he will rule over you [Gen 3:16], for the head of the woman is the man" [1 Cor 11:3]. . . .

It is a great disgrace when the upper assumes the position of the lower so that the head is below, the body is above. If this dislocation is shameful in marriage, how much more so in the union of which we are speaking, in which it is something dreadful not only insofar as it is a transgression of the divine law, but because it creates an extremely bad reputation for both the woman and the man. If cohabitation is shameful, it is doubtless much more so when the man living with the woman is enslaved. Dominion does not always bring praise; rather, it is also possible to be esteemed without holding sway and for the one who rules to be disgraced. . . .

9. Since here among humans, even if they do not talk openly about the matter but rather bring charges at home when they are among themselves, dishonor follows and such grief arises from the practice, what will be the case when we depart for the offended Bridegroom himself, when that which is unknown is brought into public view, when even hearts, words, attitudes, looks, and thoughts are open for reading (I leave aside things more disgraceful than these). When, in a word, everything will appear naked, laid open [Heb 4:13] before the whole world, to what disgrace, punishment, and retribution will we be subjected? For if our soul then does not appear shining in the manner reasonable to expect of one

betrothed to that Bridegroom, if it is not pure of every spot, uncleanness, and wrinkle [Eph 5:27], it will perish and suffer the utmost punishment. Indeed, the first reproach we encounter is sufficient to cast out the soul, and if the first one casts it out, who will rescue it from that punishment, that retribution, when there is so much filth, such ill stench, and innumerable ulcers everywhere?

For if the present life of such a woman emits such a foul and disagreeable odor amidst people that all, friends and foes alike, turn away from it, how will she be able to arrive at the royal doors when she is stained with such mire? . . . If those virgins who had no oil were shut out from the wedding chamber [Matt 25:1–13], how do you expect to arrive at that innermost sanctuary? Indeed this sin of yours is much more serious than theirs. You are guilty not just of their fault: there is no equivalence between not distributing bodily nourishment and destroying many souls. For those virgins did not harm the poor in any way, yet because they did not share their own goods with them nor delivered them from their poverty, they suffered these penalties. You, in contrast, have injured souls and have thrust them out; not only have you not purchased goods for them, you have also harmed them enormously. And if those women who had been of no use were delivered up to such a penalty, even when their virginity remained inviolate, those who have not benefited others and who have greatly wronged themselves, those living with them, and those they have offended, and above all else have dishonored the name of the Bridegroom, to what retribution will they be subjected? . . .

(Migne 8) But let us not just talk about cohabitation, let us also unfold the subject, if you will, so that the practice may appear even more shameful. . . . [L]et us first closely examine what goes on inside the house. Let us grant that they are separated by walls and sleep in separate rooms, for no man, I think, even if he chose to behave in an extremely disgraceful fashion, would go so far in making an example of himself as to sleep in the same room with a virgin. Then let them be separated by walls—so what? That concession is not sufficient to free them of suspicion! However, let us not talk about suspicion at the present, not even if a thousand maidens were living with him, but rather examine meanwhile the other form of disgrace.

Perchance they arise at the same time, not to observe the night vigils (for no reverence can ever come from souls such as these), and pass by each other as they are lying down, conversing with one another at night. Could there be anything more disgraceful? And if it happened that the woman suddenly took ill, the walls would not henceforth serve as any protection, but the man, having arisen before the others, comes in beside the recumbent virgin and uses her sickness as his excuse. Since servant girls are often disposed to be quite sluggish, he sits down next to her and takes charge of all her needs, needs which usually only women ought to serve. She is not ashamed, either, but even feels proud, nor does he blush, but rejoices mightily, and the more shameful the servitude he displays, the more mightily he rejoices. That apostolic verse which goes, "The glory is in their shame" [Phil 3:19], is here manifested through their deeds. And when the maids have arisen, the disgrace is greater. For they run into his presence with uncovered head, bare-armed, wearing only a tunic, since they were thrown into confusion by being roused at night; or rather, picture him shuffling and scurrying in their midst, while they are required to perform all the tasks. What could be more disgraceful? Even if a nurse is in attendance he is not ashamed; far from it, he is full of conceit when the maidens from outside the household arrive. For he sees only one thing, how he can demonstrate his service to the sick woman, unaware that the more he evidences this concern, the more he rather disgraces both himself and her. What wonder if he does not blush in the presence of the nurse? For often in the middle of the night these men do not hesitate to do the work of common maids, running to the nurse's dwelling. But now after she arrives, they drive him out, even if he, truly shameless, is unwilling to go; at the next moment she permits him to come back in and sit beside her. Even if someone invented a thousand ways to disgrace him, what could he devise which would be as shameful as the things these men construct for themselves?

11. When day breaks and both must arise from bed, watch out! Be on guard! She cannot set foot into the outer room without trepidation, for often when she enters she runs the risk of rushing headlong into the naked body of the man. And he himself, anticipating this, sometimes comes in after he has announced himself beforehand, yet sometimes he enters in-

cautiously and becomes the butt of uproarious laughter. I do not wish to say any more. These things, even if they are trivial, are likely to furnish the tinder for a smoldering licentiousness. These incidents and even worse than these take place in the household.

But when he must return home after he has hurried to the market-place, here again we meet with even greater unseemliness. For inasmuch as he is entering his own house, he is not obliged to give previous announcement; he finds the virgin sitting with women and is put to shame and often she experiences the same sentiment as well. The woman considers it a disgrace to receive women, the man, to receive men, but they do not refuse to live with one another although they refuse each other the privilege of entertaining guests of the same sex. What could be worse than this? It is when they find him seated beside a woman who is weaving and grasping the distaff.

Why should anyone speak of the outrages, the daily battles? For even if there is firm friendship between them, it is still probable that such upsets occur. I for my part have heard that some of them even give way to jealousy, for where there is no spiritual love, this result necessarily comes to pass as well. Hence there are continual calamities, hence there are corruptions, hence the virgins become vile and impudent; even if their bodies are not damaged, their morals are. When a virgin learns to discuss things frankly with a man, to sit by him, to look at him, to laugh in his presence, to disgrace herself in many other ways, and does not think this is dreadful, the veil of virginity is destroyed, the flower trampled underfoot. Hence they shrink from nothing, there is nothing they avoid. To the contrary, they become the bulwarks of marriage and peddlers in shoddy merchandise; they hinder many women who wish to be part of the order of widows, imagining that they have found this defense for their own shortcomings.

Hence they are despised by everyone. Hence even married women are not shamed by these virgins, inasmuch as the former comport themselves better in all respects than the latter do. For it is far preferable to unite in a single marriage or even in a second one than to behave in such an unseemly fashion and have everybody suspect them of prostitution and procurement.

Why, when you stand aloof from the pleasures of marriage, do you subject yourself to its burdens? For what is more burdensome than having a husband and being anxious about his affairs? God has freed you from this encumbrance. The saying, "Your refuge is your husband and he will rule over you" [Gen 3:16], has been brought to naught for you by virginity. Why do you welcome slavery anew? Christ has made you free, but you stitch together annoyances for yourself. He has released you from anxiety, but you contrive cares for yourself.

12. . . . . "Hear, O daughter, and see, and incline your ear; forget your own people and your father's house and the king will desire your beauty" [Ps 45:10–11], David said to a world which was then in a sorry state. We sing this too as an incantation to you now, changing the prophet's word just a bit. We will say with him, "Hear, O daughter, and see, and incline your ear; forget this immoral relationship and those who live with you in a depraved manner and the King will desire your beauty." What could be more splendid for you than this, what could equal our words, than that when you receive the Lord of heaven and earth as a lover, the Lord of both angels and archangels and the powers above, you are delivered from these base companions in slavery who dishonor even your nobility?

Thus it is appropriate to end our speech here for we can say nothing equal to this honor. If the woman receiving the king of those on earth as a bridegroom is herself considered to be happier than all women, you who do not have a bridegroom here on earth or a companion in slavery, but a Bridegroom in the heavens, who is above every principality, authority, power, and every name which is named [Eph 1:21], who sits above the cherubim [Ps 99:1], who shakes the earth, who stretches out the heavens [Ps 104:2; Isa 40:22], who is dreadful to the cherubim, inaccessible to the seraphim—and you have him not only as a Bridegroom but also as a lover, a lover more ardent than any man, how will you not give up everything here below and if it were necessary life itself? Since this word alone then suffices to set aright even the heavier lumps of lead and furnishes them with wings for the way of life above, let us also stop here and exhort you. We chant this incantation as a divine refrain both at home and in the market, by day and by night, on the road and in the chamber, with our voice and in our thoughts, and repeat to our soul constantly,

"Hear, my soul, and see, and incline your ear; forget your immoral relationship and the King will desire your beauty." And if you rehearse the words constantly, you will render your soul purer than all gold, since it inspires the considerations of your thought more ardently than fire, cleansing you from all your defilements.

Transvestism

Canons of the Council of Gangra (selections)

In the mid-fourth century a group of bishops from Asia Minor and Armenia met in the city of Gangra in the province of Paphlagonia in northern Asia Minor. A major concern was the extreme asceticism of Eustathius, bishop of Sebaste in Armenia, whose ideas were gaining in popularity. The canons of this council attempted to control the definition and practice of asceticism by rejecting the rigorist Eustathian position, in which sexual intercourse was rejected, marriage was condemned, and monastic clothing was adopted by women as well as men. The conduct of women was of special concern. This selection begins with part of the opening statement of the Council and then gives the canons that apply specifically to women. (For other materials concerning transvestism, see *The Acts of Paul and Thecla* and *Life of Saint Pelagia the Harlot* in Section III.)

Inasmuch as the most holy synod of bishops, having convened in the church at Gangra on account of certain pressing matters of ecclesiastical business, when the affairs concerning Eustathius were also investigated, discovered that many things were being done unlawfully by Eustathius's followers, it has out of necessity established guidelines [concerning these things] and has hastened to make [them] known to all in order to put an end to the things being done evilly by him.

For as a result of their condemnation of marriage and their enjoining that no one who is married has hope before God, many married women, being deceived, have withdrawn from their own husbands, and men from their own wives. Then afterwards, not being able to control themselves, the women have committed adultery. And for this reason, they have fallen into reproach.

Moreover, they were found to be promoting withdrawal from the houses of God and the church, [and] disposed contemptuously against the church and the things [done] in the church, and have established their own assemblies, churches, different teachings, and other things in opposition to the churches and the things [done] in the church. They wear strange dress to the downfall of the common mode of dress. . . . Contrary to custom, women put on male dress in place of women's, thinking they are justified by this; and many [women], under pretext of piety, cut off the natural growth of feminine hair. . . . They do not wish to make prayers in the homes of married persons and despise such prayers when they are made; frequently they do not participate in the oblations taking place in the very houses of married persons; they condemn married presbyters; they do not engage in the liturgies when performed by married presbyters. . . .

Because of these things, the holy synod convened in Gangra was compelled to vote in condemnation of them and to set forth definitions, to the effect that they are outside the church. . . .

Canon 1: If anyone censures marriage, and loathes or censures the faithful and pious woman who sleeps with her husband, claiming she is not able to enter the kingdom, let such a one be anathema.

Canon 9: If anyone practices virginity or self-control, withdrawing from marriage as if it were a loathsome thing and not because of the inherent beauty and sanctity of virginity, let such a one be anathema.

Canon 10: If any of those who practice virginity for the Lord's sake acts arrogantly toward those who are married, let such a one be anathema.

Canon 13: If, because of presumed asceticism, any woman change her clothing, and in place of the clothing customary for women adopt that of men, let her be anathema.

Canon 14: If any woman abandons her husband and wishes to withdraw from marriage because she loathes it, let her be anathema.

Canon 17: If, because of presumed asceticism, any woman cuts her hair, which God gave as a reminder of [her] subjection, under the impression that this annuls the ordinance of subjection, let her be anathema.

SECTION III

PORTRAITS OF
ASCETIC WOMEN

Ascetic Heroines in Literature

Novelistic literature designated by scholars as "Apocryphal Acts" proliferated in the second and third centuries C.E. Instructive as well as entertaining, this literature narrates teachings and events ascribed to such apostolic figures as John, Peter, Thomas, and Paul, and provides important information about early Christian theological developments as well as views of the relation of Christians to their social and political contexts in the Roman world. A remarkable feature of these narratives is their stories about women, who are credited with such a degree of autonomy and authority that some have suggested that this literature was written for a female audience and possibly even written by women (although the authors remain anonymous in all cases). The female characters in the Apocryphal Acts are notable for advocating chastity and abstinence as defining characteristics of Christian practice and self-identity; also notable is the theme of the rejection of traditional definitions of women's roles as wives, daughters, and mothers. These popular narratives of bold female discipleship in the context of an ascetic form of Christianity may well have developed as an alternative to the more traditional views of women's roles in the Pastoral Epistles of the New Testament.

1. Thecla

Foremost among the female characters of the Apocryphal Acts is Thecla. She was immensely popular throughout the early Christian centuries, first as a model for women's leadership roles in the church (teaching and baptizing) and as an image of the virginal woman, and later as a saint with a widespread cult that focused particularly on healing.

The Acts of Paul and Thecla

1. As Paul was going to Iconium after his flight from Antioch, his fellow-travelers were Demas and Hermogenes, the coppersmith, who were full of hypocrisy and flattered Paul as if they loved him. Paul, looking only to the goodness of Christ, did them no harm but loved them exceedingly so that he made sweet to them all the words of the Lord and the interpretation of the gospel concerning the birth and resurrection of the Beloved; and he gave them an account, word for word, of the great deeds of Christ as they were revealed to him.

2. And a certain man, by name Onesiphorus, hearing that Paul was to come to Iconium [a city in southern Galatia], went out to meet him with his children Simmias and Zeno and his wife Lectra, in order that he might entertain him. Titus had informed him what Paul looked like, for he had not seen him in the flesh, but only in the spirit.

3. And he went along the royal road to Lystra [just south of Iconium] and kept looking at the passersby according to the description of Titus. And he saw Paul coming, a man small in size, bald-headed, bandy-legged, of noble mien, with eyebrows meeting, rather hook-nosed, full of grace. Sometimes he seemed like a man, and sometimes he had the face of an angel.

4. And Paul, seeing Onesiphorus, smiled; and Onesiphorus said, "Hail, O servant of the blessed God." And he said, "Grace be with you and your house." And Demas and Hermogenes were jealous and showed greater hypocrisy, so that Demas said, "Are we not of the blessed God that you have not thus saluted us?" And Onesiphorus said, "I do not see in you the fruit of righteousness, but if such you be, come also into my house and refresh yourselves."

5. And after Paul had gone into the house of Onesiphorus there was great joy and bowing of knees and breaking of bread and the word of God about abstinence and the resurrection. Paul said, "Blessed are the pure in heart, for they shall see God [Matt 5:8]; blessed are those who have kept the flesh chaste, for they shall become a temple of God; blessed are the continent, for God shall speak with them; blessed are those who have kept aloof from this world, for they shall be pleasing to God; blessed are

those who have wives as not having them, for they shall experience God
[1 Cor 7:29; Rom 8:17]; blessed are those who have fear of God, for they
shall become angels of God.

6. "Blessed are those who respect the word of God, for they shall be
comforted [Matt 5:4]; blessed are those who have received the wisdom of
Jesus Christ, for they shall be called the sons of the Most High [Matt 5:9];
blessed are those who have kept the baptism, for they shall be refreshed
by the Father and the Son; blessed are those who have come to a knowledge of Jesus Christ, for they shall be in the light; blessed are those who
through love of God no longer conform to the world [see Rom 12:2], for
they shall judge angels [see 1 Cor 6:3], and shall be blessed at the right
hand of the Father; blessed are the merciful, for they shall obtain mercy
[Matt 5:7] and shall not see the bitter day of judgment; blessed are the
bodies of the virgins, for they shall be well pleasing to God and shall not
lose the reward of their chastity. For the word of the Father shall become
to them a work of salvation in the day of the Son, and they shall have rest
for ever and ever."

7. And while Paul was speaking in the midst of the church in the
house of Onesiphorus a certain virgin named Thecla, the daughter of
Theoclia, betrothed to a man named Thamyris, was sitting at the window
close by and listened day and night to the discourse of virginity, as proclaimed by Paul. And she did not look away from the window, but was led
on by faith, rejoicing exceedingly. And when she saw many women and
virgins going in to Paul she also had an eager desire to be deemed worthy to stand in Paul's presence and hear the word of Christ. For she had
not yet seen Paul in person, but only heard his word.

8. As she did not move from the window her mother sent to
Thamyris. And he came gladly as if already receiving her in marriage.
And Thamyris said to Theoclia, "Where, then, is my Thecla (that I may
see her)?" And Theoclia answered, "I have a strange story to tell you,
Thamyris. For three days and three nights Thecla does not rise from the
window either to eat or to drink; but looking earnestly as if upon some
pleasant sight she is devoted to a foreigner teaching deceitful and artful
discourses, so that I wonder how a virgin of her great modesty exposes
herself to such extreme discomfort.

9. "Thamyris, this man will overturn the city of the Iconians and your Thecla too; for all the women and the young men go in to him to be taught by him. He says one must fear only one god and live in chastity. Moreover, my daughter, clinging to the window like a spider, lays hold of what is said by him with a strange eagerness and fearful emotion. For the virgin looks eagerly at what is said by him and has been captivated. But go near and speak to her, for she is betrothed to you."

10. Thamyris greeted her with a kiss, but at the same time being afraid of her overpowering emotion said, "Thecla, my betrothed, why do you sit thus? And what sort of feeling holds you distracted? Come back to your Thamyris and be ashamed." Moreover, her mother said the same, "Why do you sit thus looking down, my child, and answering nothing, like a sick woman?" And those who were in the house wept bitterly, Thamyris for the loss of a wife, Theoclia for that of a child, and the maidservants for that of a mistress. And there was a great outpouring of lamentation in the house. And while these things were going on Thecla did not turn away but kept attending to the word of Paul.

11. And Thamyris, jumping up, went into the street, and watched all who went in to Paul and came out. And he saw two men bitterly quarrelling with each other and he said to them, "Men, who are you and tell me who is this man among you, leading astray the souls of young men and deceiving virgins so that they should not marry but remain as they are? I promise you money enough if you tell me about him, for I am the chief man of this city."

12. And Demas and Hermogenes said to him, "Who he is we do not know. But he deprives the husbands of wives and maidens of husbands, saying, 'There is for you no resurrection unless you remain chaste and do not pollute the flesh.'"

13. And Thamyris said to them, "Come into my house and refresh yourselves." And they went to a sumptuous supper and much wine and great wealth and a splendid table. And Thamyris made them drink, for he loved Thecla and wished to take her as wife. And during the supper Thamyris said, "Men, tell me what is his teaching that I also may know it, for I am greatly distressed about Thecla, because she so loves the stranger and I am prevented from marrying."

14. And Demas and Hermogenes said, "Bring him before the Governor Castellius because he persuades the multitude to embrace the new teaching of the Christians, and he will destroy him and you shall have Thecla as your wife. And we shall teach you about the resurrection which he says is to come, that it has already taken place in the children [2 Tim. 2:18] and that we rise again, after having come to the knowledge of the true God."

15. And Thamyris standing before the tribunal said with a great shout, "O proconsul, this man—we do not know where he comes from—makes virgins averse to marriage. Let him say before you why he teaches this." But Demas and Hermogenes said to Thamyris, "Say that he is a Christian and he will die at once." But the governor kept his resolve and called Paul, saying, "Who are you and what do you teach? For they bring no small accusation against you."

17. And Paul, lifting up his voice, said, "If I today must tell any of my teachings then listen, O proconsul. The living God, the God of vengeance, the jealous God, the God who has need of nothing, who seeks the salvation of men, has sent me that I may rescue them from corruption and uncleanness and from all pleasure, and from death, that they may sin no more. On this account God sent his Son whose gospel I preach and teach, that in him men have hope, who alone has had compassion upon a world led astray, that men may be no longer under judgment but may have faith and fear of God and knowledge of honesty and love of truth. If then I teach the things revealed to me by God what harm do I do, O proconsul?" When the governor heard this he ordered Paul to be bound and sent to prison until he had time to hear him more attentively.

18. And Thecla, by night, took off her bracelets and gave them to the gatekeeper; and when the door was opened to her she went into the prison. To the jailer she gave a silver mirror and was thus enabled to go in to Paul and, sitting at his feet, she heard the great deeds of God. And Paul was afraid of nothing, but trusted in God. And her faith also increased and she kissed his hands.

19. And when Thecla was sought for by her family and Thamyris they were hunting through the streets as if she had been lost. One of the gatekeeper's fellow slaves informed them that she had gone out by night.

And they examined the gatekeeper who said to them, "She has gone to the foreigner in the prison." And they went and found her, so to say, chained to him by affection. And having gone out from there they incited the people and informed the governor what had happened.

20. And he ordered Paul to be brought before the tribunal, but Thecla was riveted to the place where Paul had sat while in prison. And the governor ordered her also to be brought to the tribunal, and she came with an exceedingly great joy. And when Paul had been led forth the crowd vehemently cried out, "He is a sorcerer. Away with him!" But the governor gladly heard Paul speak about the holy works of Christ. And having taken counsel, he summoned Thecla and said, "Why do you not marry Thamyris, according to the law of the Iconians?" But she stood looking earnestly at Paul. And when she gave no answer Theoclia, her mother, cried out saying, "Burn the wicked one; burn her who will not marry in the midst of the theater, that all the women who have been taught by this man may be afraid."

21. And the governor was greatly moved, and after scourging Paul he cast him out of the city. But Thecla he condemned to be burned. And immediately the governor arose and went away to the theater. And the whole multitude went out to witness the spectacle. But as a lamb in the wilderness looks around for the shepherd, so Thecla kept searching for Paul. And having looked into the crowd she saw the Lord sitting in the likeness of Paul and said, "As if I were unable to endure, Paul has come to look after me." And she gazed upon him with great earnestness, but he went up into heaven.

22. And the boys and girls brought wood and straw in order that Thecla might be burned. And when she came in naked the governor wept and admired the power that was in her. And the executioners arranged the wood and told her to go up on the pile. And having made the sign of the cross she went up on the pile. And they lighted the fire. And though a great fire was blazing it did not touch her. For God, having compassion upon her, made an underground rumbling, and a cloud full of water and hail overshadowed the theater from above, and all its contents were poured out so that many were in danger of death. And the fire was put out and Thecla saved.

23. And Paul was fasting with Onesiphorus and his wife and his children in a new tomb on the way which led from Iconium to Daphne. And after many days had been spent in fasting the children said to Paul, "We are hungry." And they had nothing with which to buy bread, for Onesiphorus had left the things of this world and followed Paul with all his house. And Paul, having taken off his cloak, said, "Go, my child, sell this and buy some loaves and bring them." And when the child was buying them he saw Thecla their neighbor and was astonished and said, "Thecla, where are you going?" And she said, "I have been saved from the fire and am following Paul." And the child said, "Come, I shall take you to him; for he has been mourning for you and praying and fasting six days already."

24. And when she had come to the tomb Paul was kneeling and praying, "Father of Christ, let not the fire touch Thecla but stand by her, for she is yours"; she, standing behind him, cried out, "O Father who made the heaven and the earth, the Father of your beloved Son Jesus Christ, I praise you that you have saved me from the fire that I may see Paul again." And Paul, rising up, saw her and said, "O God, who knows the heart, Father of our Lord Jesus Christ, I praise you because you have speedily heard my prayer."

25. And there was great love in the tomb as Paul and Onesiphorus and the others all rejoiced. And they had five loaves and vegetables and water, and they rejoiced in the holy works of Christ. And Thecla said to Paul, "I will cut my hair off and I shall follow you wherever you go." But he said, "Times are evil and you are beautiful. I am afraid lest another temptation come upon you worse than the first and that you do not withstand it but become mad after men." And Thecla said, "Only give me the seal in Christ, and no temptation shall touch me." And Paul said, "Thecla, be patient; you shall receive the water."

26. And Paul sent away Onesiphorus and all his family to Iconium and went into Antioch, taking Thecla with him. And as soon as they had arrived a certain Syrian, Alexander by name, an influential citizen of Antioch, seeing Thecla, became enamored of her and tried to bribe Paul with gifts and presents. But Paul said, "I know not the woman of whom you speak, nor is she mine." But he, being of great power, embraced her in the street. But she would not endure it and looked about for Paul. And

she cried out bitterly, saying, "Do not force the stranger; do not force the servant of God. I am one of the chief persons of the Iconians and because I would not marry Thamyris I have been cast out of the city." And taking hold of Alexander, she tore his cloak and pulled off his crown and made him a laughing-stock.

27. And he, although loving her, nevertheless felt ashamed of what had happened and led her before the governor, and as she confessed that she had done these things he condemned her to the wild beasts. The women of the city cried out before the tribunal, "Evil judgment! Impious judgment!" And Thecla asked the governor that she might remain pure until she was to fight with the wild beasts. And a rich woman named Queen Tryphaena, whose daughter was dead, took her under her protection and had her for a consolation.

28. And when the beasts were exhibited they bound her to a fierce lioness, and Queen Tryphaena followed her. And the lioness, with Thecla sitting upon her, licked her feet; and all the multitude was astonished. And the charge on her inscription was "Sacrilegious." And the women and children cried out again and again, "O God, outrageous things take place in this city." And after the exhibition Tryphaena received her again. For her dead daughter Falconilla had said to her in a dream, "Mother, receive this stranger, the forsaken Thecla, in my place, that she may pray for me and I may come to the place of the just."

29. And when, after the exhibition, Tryphaena had received her she was grieved because Thecla had to fight on the following day with the wild beasts, but on the other hand she loved her dearly like her daughter Falconilla and said, "Thecla, my second child, come, pray for my child that she may live in eternity, for this I saw in my sleep." And without hesitation she lifted up her voice and said, "My God, Son of the Most High, who are in heaven, grant her wish that her daughter Falconilla may live in eternity." And when Thecla had spoken Tryphaena grieved very much, considering that such beauty was to be thrown to the wild beasts.

30. And when it was dawn Alexander came to her, for it was he who arranged the exhibition of wild beasts, and said, "The governor has taken his seat and the crowd is clamoring for us; get ready, I will take her to fight with the wild beasts." And Tryphaena put him to flight with a loud

cry, saying, "A second mourning for my Falconilla has come upon my house, and there is no one to help, neither child for she is dead, nor kinsman for I am a widow. God of Thecla, my child, help Thecla."

31. And the governor sent soldiers to bring Thecla. Tryphaena did not leave her but took her by the hand and led her away saying, "My daughter Falconilla I took away to the tomb, but you, Thecla, I take to fight the wild beasts." And Thecla wept bitterly and sighed to the Lord, "O Lord God, in whom I trust, to whom I have fled for refuge, who did deliver me from the fire, reward Tryphaena who has had compassion on your servant and because she kept me pure."

32. And there arose a tumult: the wild beasts roared, the people and the women sitting together were crying, some saying, "Away with the sacrilegious person!" others saying, "O that the city would be destroyed on account of this iniquity! Kill us all, proconsul; miserable spectacle, evil judgment!"

33. And Thecla, having been taken from the hands of Tryphaena, was stripped and received a girdle and was thrown into the arena. And lions and bears were let loose upon her. And a fierce lioness ran up and lay down at her feet. And the multitude of the women cried aloud. And a bear ran upon her, but the lioness went to meet it and tore the bear to pieces. And again a lion that had been trained to fight against men, which belonged to Alexander, ran upon her. And the lioness, encountering the lion, was killed along with it. And the women cried the more since the lioness, her protector, was dead.

34. Then they sent in many beasts as she was standing and stretching forth her hands and praying. And when she had finished her prayer she turned around and saw a large pit full of water and said, "Now it is time to wash myself." And she threw herself in saying, "In the name of Jesus Christ I baptize myself on my last day." When the women and the multitude saw it they wept and said, "Do not throw yourself into the water!" Even the governor shed tears because the seals were to devour such beauty. She then threw herself into the water in the name of Jesus Christ, but the seals, having seen a flash of lightning, floated dead on the surface. And there was around her a cloud of fire so that the beasts could neither touch her nor could she be seen naked.

35. But the women lamented when other and fiercer animals were let loose; some threw petals, others nard, others cassia, others amomum, so that there was an abundance of perfumes. And all the wild beasts were hypnotized and did not touch her. And Alexander said to the governor, "I have some terrible bulls to which we will bind her." And the governor consented grudgingly, "Do what you will." And they bound her by the feet between the bulls and put red-hot irons under their genitals so that they, being rendered more furious, might kill her. They rushed forward but the burning flame around her consumed the ropes, and she was as if she had not been bound.

36. And Tryphaena fainted standing beside the arena, so that the servants said, "Queen Tryphaena is dead." And the governor put a stop to the games and the whole city was in dismay. And Alexander fell down at the feet of the governor and cried, "Have mercy upon me and upon the city and set the woman free, lest the city also be destroyed. For if Caesar hears of these things he will possibly destroy the city along with us because his kinswoman, Queen Tryphaena, has died at the theater gate."

37. And the governor summoned Thecla out of the midst of the beasts and said to her, "Who are you? And what is there about you that not one of the wild beasts touched you?" She answered, "I am a servant of the living God and, as to what there is about me, I have believed in the Son of God in whom he is well pleased; that is why not one of the beasts touched me. For he alone is the goal of salvation and the basis of immortal life. For he is a refuge to the tempest-tossed, a solace to the afflicted, a shelter to the despairing; in brief, whoever does not believe in him shall not live but be dead forever."

38. When the governor heard these things he ordered garments to be brought and to be put on her. And she said, "He who clothed me when I was naked among the beasts will in the day of judgment clothe me with salvation." And taking the garments she put them on. And the governor immediately issued an edict saying, "I release to you the pious Thecla, the servant of God." And the women shouted aloud and with one voice praised God, "One is the God, who saved Thecla," so that the whole city was shaken by their voices.

39. And Tryphaena, having received the good news, went with the

multitude to meet Thecla. After embracing her she said, "Now I believe that the dead are raised! Now I believe that my child lives. Come inside and all that is mine I shall assign to you." And Thecla went in with her and rested eight days, instructing her in the word of God, so that many of the maidservants believed. And there was great joy in the house.

40. And Thecla longed for Paul and sought him, looking in every direction. And she was told that he was in Myra [on the southern coast of Lycia, southwest of Iconium]. And wearing a mantle that she had altered so as to make a man's cloak, she came with a band of young men and maidens to Myra, where she found Paul speaking the word of God and went to him. And he was astonished at seeing her and her companions, thinking that some new temptation was coming upon her. And perceiving this, she said to him, "I have received baptism, O Paul; for he who worked with you for the gospel has worked with me also for baptism."

41. And Paul, taking her, led her to the house of Hermias and heard everything from her, so that he greatly wondered and those who heard were strengthened and prayed for Tryphaena. And Thecla rose up and said to Paul, "I am going to Iconium." Paul answered, "Go, and teach the word of God." And Tryphaena sent her much clothing and gold so that she could leave many things to Paul for the service of the poor.

42. And coming to Iconium she went into the house of Onesiphorus and fell upon the place where Paul had sat and taught the word of God, and she cried and said, "My God and God of this house where the light shone upon me, Jesus Christ, Son of God, my help in prison, my help before the governors, my help in the fire, my help among the wild beasts, you alone are God and to you be glory for ever. Amen."

43. And she found Thamyris dead but her mother alive. And calling her mother she said, "Theoclia, my mother, can you believe that the Lord lives in heaven? For if you desire wealth the Lord will give it to you through me; or if you desire your child, behold, I am standing beside you." And having thus testified, she went to Seleucia [possibly the city southwest of Iconium] and enlightened many by the word of God; then she rested in a glorious sleep.

[Note: For later citations of Thecla as a model of ascetic and virginal perfection, see Life of Saint Macrina 2, and The Life of Olympias 1, in "Biographies of Ascetic Leaders" later in this section; see also Methodius, *Symposium* 8, in Section II above, in which Thecla appears as a philosopher who gives the winning speech on the virginal life at the banquet.]

2. Xanthippe and Polyxena

The first part of the following text tells the story of Xanthippe; it is a conversion narrative, filled with prayers, that emphasizes the theme of baptism and the healing, both spiritual and physical, associated with it. The second part tells the story of Polyxena and takes the form of a typical Graeco-Roman adventure novel with numerous mishaps and characters. Note the themes of cross-dressing and helpful lions that this text shares with Thecla's story. [Note: I have altered this translation so that it conforms to twenty-first-century usage.]

The Acts of Xanthippe and Polyxena

1. When the blessed Paul was at Rome through the word of the Lord, a certain servant of a ruler of Spain came to Rome with letters of his master's, and heard the word of God from Paul, the truly golden and beautiful nightingale. Being greatly touched but unable to remain and be filled with the divine word, . . . the servant returned to Spain in great grief. Unable to show his desire to anyone because his master was an idolater, he was always pained at heart and sighing greatly. Now this servant was honored and faithful to his masters, and as time went by, the servant fell sick and grew lean of flesh, and his master, perceiving this, said to him, "What has happened to you that you are so downcast?" The servant said, "There is a great pain in my heart, and I cannot find rest." His master said to him, "And what is the pain that cannot be healed by my chief physician?" The servant said, "While I was still in Rome, this pain and its recurring misfortune made itself known to me." His master said, "And do you know of any who have had this disease and been healed?" The servant said, "Yes, but where that physician is, I don't know, for I left him in Rome. Many have been treated by that physician and have gone through the water in his hands and have received healing immediately." His master said, "I ought not to grudge to send you again to Rome, in case you might be healed."

2. And while they spoke, behold his wife, named Xanthippe, over-

heard these words and learned about the teaching of Paul. She said, "What is the name of that physician, and what is the healing to ward off such a disease?" The servant said to her, "The calling upon a new name, and anointing with oil and washing with water. By this treatment I have seen many that had incurable pains receive healing." As he said this, the images of the idols that stood in the house began to shake and fall down. And his wife beckoned to him, saying, "Look, brother, the images of the idols are shaken; they cannot endure the power of the word." And his master, named Probus, arose from his midday sleep with a very gloomy countenance, for the devil had greatly disturbed him because the knowledge of God had come into his house. And he questioned the servant about everything, and the servant, seized by sickness by the foreknowledge of God, disclosed to him the life of humanity, and Xanthippe was incurable in her soul concerning this teaching. So Probus too was grieved for Xanthippe, because from then on she was wasting away with vigils and abstinence and other austerities.

3. [The first part of this section recounts Xanthippe's earnest prayer to know the name of the teacher about whom her servant had spoken.] Probus, her husband, said to her, "Why do you trouble yourself so much, and not go to sleep?" Xanthippe said, "I cannot sleep, for there is an incurable pain in me." Probus said to her, "And what is your pain or grief, O lady, that I am not sufficient to comfort you? All that you have wished up to now I have given you, and now what is it that you are troubled by and don't tell me?" Xanthippe said to him, "I beg you for this thing only, my lord; permit me for a while and for this day only to sleep apart from you." And Probus said, "Let it be as you wish, lady; only cease your groaning."

4. Then entering her bedchamber alone, she spoke thus with tears, "In what way, my God, I shall act, or what counsel I shall take, I do not know. Shall I speak the thought I have had? I fear the madness and disorder of the city. Shall I flee from this impious city? I fear the ruse of the devil for seizing the sheep. Shall I await the mercy and swiftness of the Lord? Again, I fear the untimely snatching away of life, for the death of sinners has no warning. Shall I depart and escape to Rome? I fear the length of the journey, being unable to go by foot. But while I speculate about these things, bound by my desire (for I cannot speak with certain-

ty), may I find pardon with you, my God, and fulfill my desire with an excess of right words, and consider me worthy to hear your preacher, for if
I say, 'to see his face,' I ask a great thing. Blessed is he who is found in the
company of your preachers, and is satisfied with their precious faces.
Blessed are they who are yoked under the preaching of your commandments. Blessed are they who keep your commandments; but where now,
Lord, are your mercies to our fathers, that we also may be their successors in love toward you and heirs of faith. But behold now, Lord, I cannot
find anyone that has love for you with whom I might speak and refresh
my soul a little. Hurry, therefore, Lord, to bind me in desire for you, and
keep me under the shadow of your wings, for you alone are God, glorified to all eternity. Amen."

5. Saying these and other words like them, Xanthippe groaned continually all night long, and Probus heard her and was greatly distressed.
Arising from his couch when morning came he went in to her and, seeing her eyes swollen with tears, he said, "Why, lady, do you vex me so,
and will you not tell me your pain? Tell it to me, so that I may do whatever is pleasing to you, and do not distress me with your trouble." Xanthippe said to him, "Be of good cheer, my lord, and do not be vexed, for
my trouble will not harm you, but if I have found favor before you, go
now to the salutation, and allow me to indulge myself in it as I will, for it
is not possible for anyone to take from me this insatiable pain." And he
went out immediately to receive the salutations of the men of the city, for
he was the great man among them, and was also known to Nero, the Emperor. And sitting down, great grief appeared in his face, and when he
was asked the reason for his grief by the chief men of the city, he said to
them that he had fallen into many and unfounded charges.

6. [Xanthippe has again been praying in the first part of this section.] As she
said these things, Probus came up from the street to break his fast, and
when he saw her face stained by tears, he began to pull out the hairs of
his head, but he dared not speak to her then so as not to mingle other
trouble with her trouble. So he went and fell upon his couch, and said,
groaning, "Alas, that I had not even the consolation of a child from her,
but only acquire grief upon grief. Two years are not yet full since I was
married to her, and already she is thinking about divorce."

7. But Xanthippe was always keeping watch through the doors into the streets of the city, and the blessed Paul, the preacher and teacher and illuminator of the world, left Rome and came to Spain by the foreknowledge of God. And coming up to the gates of the city he stood and prayed, and crossing himself he entered the city. When Xanthippe saw the blessed Paul walking quietly and tranquilly, and adorned with all virtue and understanding, she was greatly delighted in him and her heart leaped continually, and possessed with an unexpected joy she said to herself, "Why does my heart beat vehemently at the sight of this man? . . . Why is his expression kindly, like that of one who tends the sick? Why does he look so lovingly here and there, like one who desires to assist those who are seeking to flee from the mouths of dragons? Who shall tell me that this is one from the flock of preachers? If it were possible for me, I should wish to touch the hem of his garments [Mark 5:28], so that I might behold his kindness and readiness to receive and sweet odor." For the servant had told her that the hems of his garments had the odor of precious perfumes.

8. Now Probus heard her words, and immediately ran out by himself into the street, and laying hold of Paul's hand said to him, "Man, I do not know who you are, but deign to enter my house; you might be a cause of salvation to me." Paul said to him, "It will be well with you because of your request!" And they went in together to Xanthippe. When Xanthippe saw the great Paul, the intellectual eyes of her heart were opened, and she read upon his forehead, which had as it were golden seals, these words: "Paul the Preacher of God." Then exulting and rejoicing she threw herself at his feet, and twisting her hair together she wiped his feet [Luke 7:38], saying, "Welcome, O man of God, among us humble ones who live like shadows among shadows. For you have looked upon those who were running into Hades as though into something beautiful and those who addressed the crooked serpent and destroyer as though it were a provider and protector; you have looked upon those who were running into dark Hades as though to their father and those who were created with a rational nature but have become like irrational creatures. You have sought me, a lowly one, having the sun of righteousness [Mal 4:2] in my heart. Now the poison is stopped, since I have seen your precious

face. Now he that troubled me has flown away, since your most beautiful counsel has appeared to me. Now I shall be considered worthy of repentance, when I have received the seal of the preacher of the Lord. Before now I have judged many to be happy who met with you, but I say boldly that from this time forward I myself shall be called happy by others, because I have touched your hem, because I have received your prayers, and because I have enjoyed your sweet and honeyed teaching. You have not hesitated to come to us, you that fish the dry land in your time, and gather the fish that fall in your way into the net of the kingdom of heaven."

9. The great Paul said to her, "Arise, daughter. . . . Christ, the provider of the world, the one who seeks out sinners and the lost, who has not only called to mind those upon the earth, but also by his own presence has redeemed those in Hades, he himself has pitied you and sent me here so that he might visit and pity many others together with you. For this mercy and visitation are not from me but are his commandment, even as I also have received mercy and have been saved by him." Listening to them, Probus was astonished at their words, for he was completely ignorant of these things. But Paul by force raised up Xanthippe from his feet, and she ran to set a new gilded chair for Paul to sit on. The great Paul said to her, "My daughter Xanthippe, do not do this, for you have not yet conformed to the faith of Christ; wait awhile, until the Lord sets in order what is necessary." Xanthippe said to Paul, "Are you saying this to test me, O preacher of God, or do you have some foreknowledge?" Paul said, "No, daughter, but the devil, who hates the servants of God, sows wickedness in the hearts of his own servants, to oppose those who labor for Christ in preaching, for his wickedness has extended to the apostles and even to the Lord himself. Therefore it is fitting to approach the unbelievers gently and kindly." Xanthippe said to Paul, "I beg you, if you love your servants, pray for Probus, and let me see if the one who is hated by you can work in him; let me see if he can stand even against your prayer." And Paul rejoiced greatly at the words of her faith. . . .

10. Now the report of his presence ran through the whole city and the surrounding country, for some people had been in Rome and had seen the signs and wonders that were done by the blessed Paul, and they

came to see if this was he. Thus many came to the house of Probus, and he began to be annoyed and to say, "I will not allow my house to be made into an inn." Xanthippe, knowing that Probus had become estranged, was greatly distressed and said, "Alas, wretched me, that we are not thought fully worthy to keep this man in our house; for if Paul goes away, the church will also be held somewhere else." Then Xanthippe, considering these matters, put her hand on Paul's foot, and taking dust she called Probus to her, and placing her hand on his breast said, "O Lord, my God, who has sought me out, lowly one and ignorant of you, send what is fitting into this heart." And Paul perceived her prayer and made the sign of the cross, and for several days the people entered unhindered, and the sick and those vexed by unclean spirits were brought and all were healed.

[Note: In sections 11–13, Xanthippe's husband, Probus, incited by the devil, orders Paul out of his house. Xanthippe, desiring to be baptized, prays to God to bring prolonged sleep upon Probus; she then bribes the porter and goes to the house of Philotheus, where Paul is staying.]

14. Thus the great Paul immediately took her hand and went into the house of Philotheus, and baptized her in the name of the Father and the Son and the Holy Ghost. Then, taking bread, he also gave her the eucharist, saying, "Let this be to you for a remission of sins and for a renewing of your soul." Then the blessed Xanthippe, receiving the divine grace of holy baptism, returned to her own house, rejoicing and praising the Lord. . . .

15. While she was speaking in this way, a cross appeared on the eastern wall, and immediately a beautiful youth entered through the wall; there were shimmering rays around him, and he walked on a beam of light. As he entered, all the foundations of the house shook and resounded with a great trembling. Seeing him, Xanthippe cried out and fell to the ground as if dead; but being compassionate and kind, the youth changed immediately into the shape of Paul and raised her up, saying, "Arise, Xanthippe, and fear not, for the servants of God are thus glorified." Then Xanthippe arose and gazed upon him, and thinking that he was Paul, she said, "How have you come in here, preacher of God, since I have given

five hundred pieces of gold to the porter, even though he is my slave, while you have no money?" The Lord said to her, "My servant Paul is richer than all wealth, for whatever treasure he acquires here he sends before him into the kingdom of heaven, so that when he goes there he may rest in the unending and eternal rest. This is the treasure of Paul, you and those like you." Then Xanthippe, gazing upon him and wanting to say something, saw his face shining like the light; being greatly amazed, she put both hands over her face and threw herself to the ground, saying, "Hide yourself, Lord, from my bodily eyes and enlighten my understanding, for I know now who you are. You are he whose precursor was the cross, the only begotten Son of the Father alone above, and the only son of the virgin alone below. You are he who was pierced in the hands and who rent the rocks. You are he whom only the bosom of the Father can carry."

16. As she spoke, the Lord was again hidden from her, and Xanthippe, coming to herself, said, "Woe is me, wretched one, that no one has told me what is the gratitude of slaves towards their master. If Paul the preacher of the Lord were here, how would he give praise? But perhaps in the presence of such favors and gifts they are silent, possessed only with tears, for it is not possible worthily to praise anyone according to his favor." Then she was seized with great faintness from lack of food, for having been strongly possessed with desire for Christ, she had forgotten to eat. Being thus exhausted by abstinence, the vision, lack of sleep, and other austerities, she was unable to rise from the ground.

17. And Probus arose from his couch with a very gloomy countenance, for in his sleep he had seen a dream, and was greatly troubled about it. But the porter, seeing him about to go to the marketplace with a troubled face, was greatly afraid, "Lest," he said, "he finds out what has happened and will miserably destroy me." Probus, however, conducted his business in the marketplace and returned quickly to the house and said to his servants, "Summon quickly the wise men Barandus and Gnosteas." When they arrived, he said to them, "I have seen a very terrible vision, and what appeared in it is difficult to interpret. But explain it to me when I tell it to you." Barandus said to him, "If the vision can be interpreted by our wisdom, we shall explain it to you, but if it is from the faith

that is now spoken about we cannot explain it to you, for it is from another wisdom and understanding. However, let our lord and master tell the dream, and let us see whether there is any explanation for it."

. . . Probus said, "I thought I was standing in a certain unknown and strange country, and that sitting there was an Ethiopian king who ruled over all the earth and seemed never to have any successor. Standing beside him were multitudes of servants, and all of them were destroyers and had mastery far and wide. And when the Ethiopian seemed to have succeeded in his goal, a raven came and stood above him croaking with a pitiful voice. And immediately an eagle came from the eastern parts and seized his kingdom, and the Ethiopian lost his power and those standing by him fled to the eagle. Then the king fought against those who fled to the eagle, but the eagle carried the kingdom up to heaven, and a helper came to those who fled to the eagle, and left his staff with them. They took the staff and were not overcome by the violence of the king. All who ran to those who had the staff were washed in pure water, and they had power over the kingdom. . . . And the king fought against them but had no power at all, but he hindered many from believing in the one who sent out men into the world to bear witness, and for that reason many were sorrowful. Nevertheless, that one did not persecute anyone like the Ethiopian king, for he himself was the ruler of all light. This was the end of the dream."

18. Then the wise Barandus said, "By the grace of God I shall tell the things sent into the world by the Lord. The king whom you saw is the devil, and the multitudes of his servants are the demons, and the throngs around him are those that worship the gods. Because he thought he had no successor, he did not anticipate the coming of Christ. The raven signified the weakness of his kingdom, for the raven did not obey the righteous Noah [Gen 8:7], but loved pitiful things. The eagle that arose and took away the kingdom and carried it up to heaven, and the protector of those that fled to the eagle who had a staff, that is the Lord Jesus Christ, who left them his staff, which is his precious cross. The fact that he washed those who fled to him signifies the invulnerable breastplate of baptism, and that is why they were not overcome. The capable men sent into the world with the cross are the preachers of God like Paul, who is

now with us, against whom that king has no power. This was made
known to you because even on those who do not believe, God has compassion in some way. See then whether you will be able to injure Paul,
even though you desire it, for the mighty power that shields him has
been shown to you by the Lord. Therefore, understand what I have said
to you, and do not serve that king of darkness, for as you saw his kingdom vanish away, so shall all his servants perish with him. Come now,
my lord, let us go to Paul and receive baptism from him, lest Satan have
mastery over us also." Probus said, "Let us first go to Xanthippe and see
whether she is still alive, for it has been twenty-nine days since she has
eaten anything; for I saw her face in the evening, and it was like that of
one prepared to depart."

19. As they went into the chamber, they heard her singing: "Praise
the Lord also you sinners, because he accepts your prayers also. Alleluia.
Praise the Lord you that have despaired like me, for many are his mercies. Alleluia. Praise him you ungodly ones, because for you he was crucified. Alleluia. Praise him you that strive for the salvation of sinners, because God loves you. Alleluia. Praise him you that rejoice at the calling of
sinners, because you are fellow-citizens with the saints. Alleluia." As she
said these words and more than these with tears, the wise men Barandus
and Gnosteas opened the door and fell at her feet, saying, "Pray for us
lowly ones, O servant of Christ, that he may bring us also into your number." But she said to them, "Brothers, I am not Paul who remits sins, but
neither is he far from you. Therefore do not fall at my knees, but go to
him; he is better able to help you." So they ran to the house of Philotheus
and found Paul teaching a great multitude. Probus also went to hear
Paul, and Xanthippe entered along with him to salute him, and going
near Paul she bent her knees and paid him reverence. Seeing this,
Probus marveled that her proud spirit had changed to such great humility, for she sat humbly on the ground beside the feet of Paul and as one of
the worthless. . . .

20. The great Paul was teaching the following: "Let those that burn
in the flesh observe lawful marriage, avoiding fornication, especially
with another's wife, and let those that are united keep to one another"
[see 1 Cor 7:9–11]. Probus heard this teaching with delight, and said, "O

Paul, how wisely you employ this teaching. Why then has Xanthippe withdrawn from me?" And Paul said, "My son Probus, those that foresee that the works of humanity shall be tried with fire, and always have in their minds the inexorableness of death, cast out all desire that cleaves to the flesh. But woe when the desire shall judge the one who desired; then he will gnash his teeth to no effect, for the time of repentance will have passed." Hearing this, Probus went up into his house marveling, and ate nothing that day, but went and lay down on his bed. And about the third hour of the night he arose and said, "Alas, how wretched was the day on which I was married to Xanthippe. If only I had died and not seen her! I shall pray to the God of Paul. Perhaps he will do to me also what is fitting, so that I may not become a reproach in the world, being rejected by her." And immediately he fell on the ground and said, "O God of Paul, if, as I have heard from Xanthippe, you seek after the ignorant and turn back those who are astray, do to me also what is fitting, for you are the king of life and death, as I have heard, and have dominion over things in heaven and on earth and under the earth, and over all the thoughts and desires of humanity, and to you alone belongs glory to all eternity. Amen."

21. Then Probus arose from the ground and fell again on the couch; arising early, he went to Paul and found him baptizing many in the name of the life-giving Trinity. He said, "My lord Paul, if only I were worthy to receive baptism, behold the hour." Paul said to him, "Son, behold the water is ready for the cleansing of those that come to Christ." Immediately Probus took off his garments, and Paul laying hold of him, he leaped into the water, saying, "Jesus Christ, son of God, and everlasting God, let all my sins be taken away by this water." And Paul said, "I baptize you in the name of the Father and Son and Holy Ghost." After this he administered the Eucharist of Christ to him. Then toward evening, Xanthippe, rejoicing greatly, began together with her husband to give good cheer to all those in the house and to prepare a feast with orders for the supper to be magnificent. When they all came, she herself went up to the chamber. And behold, on the stairs there was a demon coming in the likeness of one of the actors, and it stood in a dark corner desiring to frighten and terrify Xanthippe. But she thought it was the actor that she ordinarily employed [for entertainment at the meal], and said in anger, "Many times I

have said to him that I no longer care for playful behavior, and he despis-
es me because I am a woman." And immediately she took an iron lamp-
stand and hurled it at his face, crushing all his features. Then the demon
cried out, saying, "O violence, from this destroyer even women have received power to strike us." But Xanthippe was greatly afraid.

22. After supper Probus went out to hear the word, but Xanthippe sat
in her bedchamber reading the prophets. Her sister Polyxena was lying
on the couch. Xanthippe loved Polyxena dearly because she was younger
than herself and beautiful in appearance. Probus also loved her greatly.
And as Polyxena lay upon the couch she saw this dream: a dragon,
hideous in appearance, came and signaled her to come to him, and when
she did not obey, he ran up and swallowed her. Out of fear of the dream,
the girl leaped up trembling, and Xanthippe ran to her and said, "What
happened to you, dearest, that made you leap up so suddenly?" She was
unable to speak for a long time. When she came to herself, she said,
"Alas, my sister Xanthippe, I do not know what danger or tribulation
awaits me; for I saw in my dream that a hideous dragon came and signaled me to come to him, and when I would not go, he ran up and swallowed me, beginning at my feet. While I was terrified by this, suddenly a
beautiful youth spoke out of the air in the light of the sun, a youth whom
I thought to be the brother of Paul, saying, 'Truly, you have no power.' He
took me by the hand and drew me out of the dragon, which immediately
disappeared. The youth's hand was full of sweet odor like balsam or
some other fragrance." Xanthippe said to her, "Truly, you must be greatly
troubled, my sister Polyxena, but God holds you dear, seeing that he has
shown you strange and marvelous things. Therefore arise quickly in the
morning and receive the holy baptism, and ask in the baptism to be delivered from the snares of the dragon."

23. Saying this to Polyxena and having made a cross of wood, Xanthippe then went to Paul, but Polyxena remained alone in the bedchamber. . . . [Polyxena is now kidnapped by a powerful man and taken by ship to
Greece; she escapes and the action resumes as follows.]

26. Going out of the city and not knowing which way she should
walk, Polyxena found herself in desert places in the hills; she sat down
and said with tears, "Woe is me, outcast and captive; I cannot find even a

wild beast's den to rest in. . . . Alas for me who was formerly devoted to idols; for this now even the mercy of God has passed me by in silence. Whom, then, shall I call upon to help me? The God of Paul whom I have constantly offended? . . . Truly I shall implore him who sees the hidden things, for who is more compassionate and kind than he who always keeps watch over the oppressed? But because my mouth is unclean and defiled, I dare not ask him for help. . . . What then shall I do, for death has not come, and night has fallen, and there is no help anywhere." So she got up and began to walk on. . . . She came to a thick and large forest and, finding a hollow in a tree, which was the den of a lioness, she sat there, for the lioness had gone out for food. . . .

27. . . . Morning came and the lioness returned from her hunting. Seeing the wild beast, Polyxena trembled and said, "By the God of Paul, O wild beast, have compassion on me and do not tear me until I receive baptism. . . . The wild beast immediately went away and stood apart gazing at her. And she said; "Behold, the beast has obeyed me; I will leave its dwelling." And she immediately began to go towards the east, and the beast walked in front of her until she was out of the forest. Then Polyxena said, "What shall I give you in return, O beast? The God of Paul will repay you this kindness"; and the wild beast, hearing her prayer, immediately returned to its place. Then Polyxena found a public road and wept while standing there, since she did not know which direction to take. Though many people passed by, she turned to none of them but said, "Perhaps the God of Paul will remember me, and I will go with whoever has compassion on me."

28. As she said this, Andrew, the apostle of the Lord, came traveling to that place, and as he drew near Polyxena he felt some agitation in his heart. Standing to pray and folding his arms in the shape of the cross, he said, "Lord Jesus Christ, partaker of light and knower of things hidden, from whom nothing on earth is hidden, give me kindness and mercy, and make clear to me this agitation in my heart, and calm my reason, you who always make peace with those that love peace." Then Polyxena ran to him, and Andrew said to her, "Do not approach me, daughter, but tell me who you are and where you are from." Polyxena said, "My lord, I am a stranger here, but I see that your face is gracious, and your words like

the words of Paul, and I suppose you to be a worshipper of the same God." Andrew understood that she was referring to the apostle Paul and said to her, "And where did you know Paul?" She said, "In my own country, Spain." Andrew said to her, "And how do you happen to be here, in a country so far away?" She said, "Because it was thus appointed for me and came to pass; but I beg you and fall at your feet, seal me, as Paul seals, by the baptism of regeneration, so that even I, lowly one, may be known by our God, for the kind God, seeing my distress, sent you to have compassion on me." Andrew, the great apostle of the Lord, said to her, "Let us go, daughter, where there is water."

29. And when they had gone a short way, they came to a well with pure water. And as the blessed Andrew stood to pray beside the well, a certain young woman named Rebecca, of the tribe of Israel, who had been brought as a captive to that country, came to draw water at the well and recognized Andrew. Rebecca said, "He has the appearance of a prophet, and this is one of the apostles. She bowed down to him and said, "Have mercy on me, servant of the true God. I am captive and have been sold for the third time; I was once honored by prophets but am now insulted by idolaters. Recall me, lowly one, you who were sent to call back many sinners." Andrew said, "God will care for you also, daughter, as well as for this stranger. Therefore, receive baptism now and be as of one people, glorifying God always.". . .

31. And Andrew went his way rejoicing and glorifying God. Then Polyxena said, "Where shall we go, sister?" Rebecca said, "Let us go wherever you wish, lest my mistress send for me and separate us." Polyxena said, "Come, let us go up the mountain to the lioness." Rebecca said, "It is indeed better for us to live with wild beasts and perish of hunger than to be compelled by Greeks and idolaters to fall into the filth of marriage." So they began to travel. . . . [At this point, Polyxena and Rebecca meet up with a helpful ass-driver who is a disciple of the apostle Philip.]

33. As if commanded by the voice of God, the ass-driver eagerly accompanied the young women and went on his way rejoicing in the Lord. And he said to Polyxena, "Change your appearance to that of a man, so that no one will snatch you away from me because of your beauty." [The disguise does not work, and Polyxena is kidnapped by a Roman official and locked

up in a chamber, but Rebecca escapes. Polyxena avoids being raped by the prefect by appealing to his attendants for help; she is then visited by the prefect's son, who speaks to her as follows.]

36. . . . The youth said to her, "Do not be afraid, I do not seek to wed you as the bridegroom of destruction, for I know from your prayer that you are the bride of the God of heaven. I know this God who is never overcome by anyone, for a certain man of glorious countenance recently preached this God in Antioch, and a certain young woman, whose name was Thecla, believed in him and followed him, and encountered dangers on account of her beauty. . . . Therefore I continually gazed upon the man, and he observed me and said, "God observes you, my son." From that time onward, by the grace of Christ I have not gone to the sacrifices of idols." . . . Polyxena said, "And what is the name of that man?" The youth said, "Paul is his name." Polyxena said, "He is in my city." The youth said, "Come then, put on my appearance, and go down to the shore and wait for me there; I will get money and come quickly."

37. And one of the servants overheard them and told all this to the prefect, who was filled with anger and condemned them to be thrown to the wild beasts. And when they were thrown into the arena, a fierce lioness was let loose on them, but it ran and embraced the feet of Polyxena and licked the soles of her feet. Then the prefect and the whole city, seeing this fearful and wonderful sight, gave praise and glory to the merciful God, saying, "Truly you alone, the God named by Polyxena, are God, for the gods of the heathen are the works of human hands, unable to save or assist anyone. Let them perish now, them and their makers." And the prefect immediately took his son and Polyxena to the palace, and listened to them about the faith and religion in Christ, and he and the whole city believed, and there was great joy and glorifying of God. And Polyxena said to the prefect, "Be of good cheer, my lord, for the man of God will come quickly and he will teach, exhort, instruct, and enlighten you in the knowledge of Christ." But she prepared hurriedly to depart for Spain. [Prior to their departure, Polyxena and her companions convert thousands of people to Christianity, endure more adventures, and finally arrive home.]

40. Seeing us, Paul rejoiced greatly and said, "Welcome to you who have been troubled." And Polyxena, grasping his feet, said, "It may be

that this trouble came upon me because I would have blasphemed you, but now I beg that I may not be delivered again into such troubles and misfortunes." And Paul, weeping, said, "So we must be troubled, my daughter, so that we might know our defender, Jesus Christ."

41. And while we were giving the letters of the brothers to Paul, someone ran and told Xanthippe of Polyxena's arrival. And she hurried and came to us, and when she saw Polyxena she was overcome by an unspeakable joy and fell to the ground. But Polyxena embraced and caressed her for a long time and brought her back to life. Then Xanthippe said to her, "My true sister Polyxena, I did not go out for forty days, and I prayed much for you to the loving God that your virginity might not be taken away. And Paul, the preacher of God, said to me, "Her virginity will not be taken away, and she will come home quickly." And Probus said to me, "It was assigned to her by God to be afflicted like this." Xanthippe said, "Do you see by how many devices God saves many? But now, my beloved sister, since I have unexpectedly seen your face, now I will willingly die."

42. Then her captor came again and looked for Polyxena, but the great Paul persuaded him to stay away from her, and he also believed and was baptized by Paul, and the suitor of Polyxena also believed, and there was great joy in that city of Spain for the recovery of Polyxena. From that time on she did not leave Paul for fear of temptations. All rejoiced in the Lord, glorifying Father, Son, and Holy Ghost, one God, to whom is glory and power now and forever and to all eternity. Amen.

3. Maximilla

The setting of the following text is the praetorium (palace) of the praetor Aristocles in Patras, Greece. In sections 1–5, the apostle Andrew heals the slave of Stratocles, a philosopher and brother of the proconsul Aegeates, who is the husband of Maximilla. In sections 6–12, Andrew converts Stratocles. Maximilla's story begins with section 13.

The Acts of Andrew (selections)

13. There was great joy among the brethren as they gathered together night and day at the praetorium with Maximilla. On the Lord's day,

when the brethren were assembled in Aegeates' bedroom listening to Andrew, the proconsul [Aegeates, an unbeliever] arrived home. When her husband's arrival was announced to Maximilla she was troubled, anticipating the outcome, that he would find so many people inside.

When Andrew saw her perplexity, he said to the Lord, "Do not permit Aegeates to enter this bedroom, Lord Jesus, until your servants can leave here without fear, for they have come together for your sake, and Maximilla constantly pleads with us to meet and take our rest here. Inasmuch as you have judged her worthy to deserve your kingdom, may she be especially emboldened, and Stratocles too. Save us all by repelling that savage lion armed to attack us."

As the proconsul Aegeates came in, he had stomach pains, asked for a chamber pot, and spent a long time sitting, attending to himself. He did not notice all the brethren leave in front of him. For Andrew laid his hand on each one and said, "Jesus will screen your appearance from Aegeates, in order to secure your invisibility before him." Last of all, Andrew sealed himself and left.

14. When this grace of the Lord was completed, Stratocles, because he had been away from his brother for a long time, went out and embraced Aegeates, with a smile on his face but with no joy in his soul. The rest of his servants and freedmen greeted him in the same manner.

But Aegeates, out of passion for Maximilla, rushed into the bedroom assuming she was still asleep. She was at prayer. When she saw him, she looked away toward the ground. "First give me your right hand," he told her. "I will kiss the woman I will call no longer 'wife' but 'queen,' so that I may find relief in your chastity and love for me."

For when the wretch found her at prayer, he supposed she was praying for him and was delighted to hear his own name mentioned while she prayed. This is what Maximilla actually said: "Rescue me at last from Aegeates' filthy intercourse and keep me pure and chaste, giving service only to you, my God." When he approached her mouth intending to kiss it, she pushed him back and said, "Aegeates, after prayer a woman's mouth should never touch a man's." Taken aback by the sternness of her face, the proconsul left her. Because he had just completed a long journey, he took off his traveling clothes, relaxed, and lay down to sleep.

15. Maximilla then told Iphidama, "Sister, go to the blessed one so that he may come here to pray and lay his hand on me while Aegeates is sleeping. . . ."

16. Andrew laid his hand on Maximilla and prayed as follows: "I pray to you, my God, Lord Jesus Christ, who knows the future, and I entrust to you my child, the worthy Maximilla. May your word and power be mighty in her, and may the spirit that is in her struggle even against Aegeates, that insolent and hostile snake. O Lord, may her soul remain forever pure, sanctified by your name. In particular, protect her, O Master, from this disgusting pollution. With respect to our savage and unbearable enemy, cause her to sleep apart from her visible husband and wed her to her inner husband, whom you above all recognize, and for whose sake the entire mystery of your plan of salvation has been accomplished. If she has such a firm faith in you, may she obtain her own proper kinship through separation from those who masquerade as friends but are really enemies." When he had prayed thus and entrusted Maximilla to the Lord, he left with Stratocles once again.

17. Maximilla then planned the following. She summoned a comely, exceedingly wanton servant-girl named Euclia and told her something that delighted her and met her desires. "You will have me as a benefactor of all your needs, providing you scheme with me and carry out what I advise." Because she wanted to live chastely from that time on, Maximilla told Euclia what she wanted and got her word agreeing to it, and so for some time she employed the following subterfuge. Just as a woman customarily adorns herself to look like her rival, Maximilla groomed Euclia in just such finery and put her forward to sleep with Aegeates in her stead. Having used her as his lover, he let her get up and go to her own bedroom, just as Maximilla used to. By so doing, Maximilla escaped detection for some time, and thereby got relief, rejoiced in the Lord, and never left Andrew. [The slave Euclia begins to blackmail Maximilla, demanding her freedom, jewelry, money, and so on. Finally she tells her fellow slaves about Maximilla's trick, and they expose the ruse to Aegeates.]

23. Stricken by grief, Aegeates stayed in seclusion that day and ate nothing at all, baffled by the great change in Maximilla's attitude toward him. After crying for some time and reproaching his gods, he went to his

spouse, fell at her feet weeping, and said, "I cling to your feet, I who have been your husband now for twelve years, who always revered you as a goddess and still do because of your chastity and your refined character, even though it might have been tarnished, since even you are human. So if you are keeping some secret from me about another man—something I would never have suspected—I will make allowances and I myself will cover it up, just as you often put up with my follies. Or if there is something else even more serious than this that separates you from me, confess it and I will quickly remedy the situation, for I know it is entirely useless to contradict you."

While he persistently cajoled and begged, she told him, "I am in love, Aegeates. I am in love, and the object of my love is not of this world and therefore is imperceptible to you. Night and day it kindles and enflames me with love for it. You cannot see it for it is difficult to see, and you cannot separate me from it, for that is impossible. Let me have intercourse with it and take my rest with it alone."

24. The proconsul left her as if he were a maniac, not knowing what to do. . . .

25. [One of his servants] drew Aegeates aside and told him privately, "There is a certain stranger sojourning here who has become renowned not only in this city but throughout Achaea. He performs great miracles and cures which exceed human strength, as I in part can corroborate in that I was present and saw him revive corpses. And so that you may know the whole story, he proclaims a reverence for the divine and truly shows it to be shining forth into public view. My mistress, following Iphidama's lead, became acquainted with this stranger. She has so given way to desire for him that she loves no one more than him, including you I would say. Not only has she become intimately involved with the man, she has enchained your brother Stratocles with the same passion for him that has enchained her. They confess but one God, the one that that man disclosed to them, denying the existence of every other on earth. But listen to what your brother did that was the most insane thing of all. Even though he is of noble stock, the most honored man in Achaea, addressed as brother of the proconsul of Aegeates, he carries his own little oil flask to the gymnasium. Even though he owns many slaves, he appears in

public doing his own chores—buying his own vegetables, bread, and other necessities, and carrying them on foot through the center of the city—without shame in the sight of everybody."

26. While the youth was telling this to his master, who was taking a walk and staring at the ground all the time, he spotted Andrew from a distance and shouted out loud: "Look, master! There is the man responsible for the present disruption of your household." The entire crowd turned to see the cause of his shout. Without another word, the youth—who was as fearsome as Aegeates, as though he were his brother and not really his slave—ran away from the proconsul, seized Andrew, and forcibly brought him to Aegeates, wrapping around his neck the towel that the blessed one used to wear over his shoulder.

When the proconsul saw him, he recognized him and said, "You are the one who once cured my wife and who refused a considerable sum of money that I wanted to donate. Teach me too about your renown and what sort of power you have, such that you are praised, so I hear, by those who are rich and poor, including infants, even though you appear in this manner like a simple old man."

The entire crowd there dearly loved the apostle, and when they learned that the proconsul was speaking with him but not knowing why, they ran to the place where he was talking with Andrew. Without hesitation, Aegeates ordered him to be locked up, saying, "Corrupter! You will see my rewards to you for your benefactions to Maximilla."

[Learning that Andrew has been imprisoned, Maximilla and Iphidama are made invisible by Christ and visit Andrew in prison. He gives a speech of thanksgiving, and they return home.]

35. One day, while Aegeates sat as judge, he remembered the case of Andrew. Like a maniac, he left the case at hand, rose from the bench, and dashed to the praetorium seething with anger at Maximilla but flattering her all the same. . . .

36. When he went in to her, he said, "Maximilla, because your parents thought me worthy to be your husband, they pledged you to me in marriage without regard to wealth, heredity, or reputation, considering only the kindness of my soul. Just now I deliberately left the court and came here not to enumerate the many matters I had wanted to reproach

you with—such as the benefits I enjoyed from your parents, or the honors and favors you received from me during our lives together, such as your designation as my queen—but simply to learn from you this one thing. If you would be the woman you once were, living together with me as we are accustomed to—sleeping with me, having sexual relations with me, bearing my children—I would treat you well in every way. What is more, I will release the stranger whom I have in prison. But if you should not choose this course, I will do you no harm—I am unable to—but I will torment you indirectly through the one you love more than me. Answer me tomorrow, Maximilla, after you have considered which of the two options you want, for I am fully prepared to carry out this threat." Having said this, he left.

37. At the usual time, Maximilla again went with Iphidama to Andrew. Putting his hands on her eyes and then bringing them to her mouth, she kissed them and began to seek his advice about every aspect of Aegeates' ultimatum.

"O Maximilla my child," Andrew replied, "I know that you have been moved to resist any proposition of sexual intercourse and wish to be dissociated from a foul and filthy way of life. For a long time this conviction has dominated my thinking, but still you want me to give my opinion. I bear you witness, Maximilla: do not commit this act. Do not submit to Aegeates' threat. . . . Endure each of his tortures by looking to us for a while, and you will see him entirely numb and wasting away from you and from all of your kindred. . . . I rightly see in you Eve repenting and in me Adam converting. For what she suffered through ignorance, you—whose soul I seek—must now redress through conversion. The very thing suffered by the mind which was brought down with her and was estranged from itself, I make right with you, through your recognition that you are being raised up. You healed her deficiency by not experiencing the same passions, and I have perfected Adam's imperfection by fleeing to God for refuge. Where Eve disobeyed, you obeyed; what Adam agreed to, I flee from; the things that tripped them up, we have recognized. For it is ordained that each person should correct his or her own fall. . . ." [The next sections repeat these themes in Andrew's speech. He continues as follows.]

41. "Therefore, I beg you, wise man (*sic*), that your clear-sighted mind stand firm. I beg you, mind unseen, that you may be protected. I entreat you, love Jesus. Do not be overcome by the inferior. You [Maximilla] whom I entreat as a man, assist me in my becoming perfect. Help me too, so that you may recognize your true nature. . . ."

45. [In sections 42–44, Andrew gives encouragement to Stratocles, also present in this prison scene, and continues as follows.] "So that you all may know, tomorrow Aegeates will hand me over to be impaled on a stake. Maximilla, the Lord's servant, will trouble the enemy in him to whom he belongs, and will not consent with him to do anything alien to her. By turning against me he will presume to console himself."

46. Maximilla was not present when the apostle said this, for when she heard the words that applied to her and in some way was changed by them, she became what the words themselves had signified. She rushed out deliberately and resolutely and went to the praetorium. Because she had bidden farewell to her whole life as well as to wickedness, the mother of the flesh, and to things pertaining to the flesh, when Aegeates made the same severe demand which he had told her to ponder—namely, whether she would be willing to sleep with him—she rebuffed him. He turned attention at last to the destruction of Andrew and considered what kind of death he might impose on him. Of all the options crucifixion most preoccupied him. Then he went off with his friends and ate like an animal. [In sections 47–50, Andrew gives the first of several farewell speeches.]

51. . . . Early in the morning, Aegeates summoned Andrew from prison and said to him, "The time to complete my judgment against you has arrived, you stranger, alien to this present life, enemy of my home, and corrupter of my entire house. Why did you decide to burst into places alien to you and corrupt a wife who used to please me in every way and never slept with another man? She has convinced me that she now rejoices in you and your God. So enjoy my gifts!"

He commanded that Andrew be scourged with seven whips. Then he sent him off to be crucified and commanded the executioners not to impale him with nails but to stretch him out tied up with ropes, and to leave his knees uncut, supposing that by so doing he would punish Andrew even more cruelly. . . .

52. As the executioners led him to the place intending to carry out their orders, Stratocles, who had learned what was happening, arrived running and saw the executioners violently dragging off the blessed one like a criminal. Stratocles did not spare any of them but gave each a beating, ripped their clothing from top to bottom, tore Andrew away, and told them, "Thank the blessed one for educating me and teaching me to check my violent temper. Otherwise, I would have demonstrated for you what Stratocles and Aegeates the rogue are capable of. For we (believers) have learned to endure our afflictions." He grabbed the apostle's hand and went away with him to the seaside location where he was to be crucified.

53. The soldiers left and presented themselves to Aegeates explaining what had happened. "Change your clothes," the proconsul answered, "and go back there to perform your duties. When you rid yourselves of the convict's friends, then obey your orders. Avoid as best you can letting Stratocles see you, and do not argue if he should require from you anything at all. For I know the nobility of his soul, such that if provoked he probably would not even spare me." They did exactly as Aegeates told them.

Stratocles walked with the apostle to the designated spot, but he was perturbed, furious with Aegeates, now and then railing against him under his breath. "Stratocles my child," Andrew responded, "from now on I want you to keep your mind unwavering, and do not wait for advice from someone else, but take such advice from yourself—that you not be inwardly oriented toward seeming hardships nor attached to mere appearances—for it is fitting for a servant of Jesus to be worthy of Jesus. I will tell you and the brethren walking with me something else about people alien to us. As long as the demonic nature lacks its bloody food and cannot suck up nutrition because animals are not slain, it weakens and recedes to nothingness, becoming entirely dead. But if it has what it longs for, it strengthens, expands, and rises up, growing by means of those foods it enjoys. This situation, child, obtains to those outside who die when we do not attach ourselves to what they are attached to. But even that self within ourselves which is contrary (to our true nature), when it dares to do something and cannot find anyone to consent with it, is beaten and totally crushed to the earth, dead, because it did not complete what it undertook. Let us keep this image always before our eyes, children, so that we not grow drowsy and the opponent intrude and slaughter us. This is the end of my speech, for I think that while we were speaking we arrived at the appointed place. The cross planted there is a sign to me that this is the place."

54. He left everyone, approached the cross, and spoke to it in a loud voice: "Greetings, O cross! Greetings indeed! I know well that, though you have been weary for a long time, planted and awaiting me, now at last you can rest. I come to you, whom I have known. I recognize your mystery, why you were planted. So then, cross that is pure, radiant, full of life and light, receive me, I who have been weary for so long." [At this point the executioners tie Andrew to the cross.]

55. The brethren stood around, so many they were nearly innumerable. When they saw that the executioners had withdrawn and had carried out against the blessed one none of the usual procedures suffered by those who are hung, they expected to hear something more from him, for even while hanging he moved his head and smiled.

"Why do you smile, Andrew, servant of God?" asked Stratocles. "Should your laughter not make us mourn and weep because we are being deprived of you?" "Shall I not laugh, Stratocles, my child," Andrew answered, "at Aegeates' futile trap by which he intends to avenge himself on us? He has not yet been persuaded that we are alien to him and his designs. He is not able to hear, since if he were able, he would have heard that the person who belongs to Jesus and who has been recognized by him in the end cannot be punished."

56. When Andrew had said these things, he addressed a general speech to everyone, for even the pagans had hurried to the site, infuriated at Aegeates' unjust decision. "Men who are present with me, women, children, old, slaves, free, and any others who would hear: if you suppose this act of dying is the end of ephemeral life, leave this place at once. If you understand the conjunction of the soul with a body to be the soul itself, so that after the separation (of the two) nothing at all exists, you possess the intelligence of animals and one would have to list you among ferocious beasts. And if you love immediate pleasures and pursue them

above all, in order to enjoy their fruits exclusively, you are like thieves. And if you suppose that you are merely that which can be seen and nothing more, you are slaves of folly and ignorance. And if you perceive that only this nocturnal light exists and nothing in addition to it, you are kindred to this night. And if you think that your earthly food is capable of creating bodily mass and the blood's constitutive power, you yourselves are earthly. And if you suppose that you are happy even though you have an inequitable body, you are actually miserable. And if your external prosperity makes you happy, you truly are most wretched. And if the pleasure and intercourse of marriage please you, and if the corruption which is from them, full of pain, makes you sad, and if you are in need of sustenance for your many children, and if the irritating poverty they cause is known to you, it will upset you. And if the rest of your possessions draw you to themselves as though you belonged to them, may their impermanence reproach you. [Andrew's speech from the cross continues through the next two sections, expanding on the themes introduced here.]

59. When the crowds heard Andrew's speech, they were won over by him, so to say, and did not leave the spot. The blessed one proceeded to speak to them even longer than he had before, to such an extent that those who heard him took it as a sign. He spoke to them for three days and nights, and no one, no matter how weary, separated from him.

On the fourth day, when they observed his nobility, the adamancy of his thought, the sheer abundance of his words, the value of his exhortation, the stability of his soul, the prudence of his spirit, the firmness of his mind, and the precision of his reasoning, they were furious with Aegeates and together ran off to the tribunal. As he sat there they cried out, "What is this judgment of yours, O proconsul? You have judged wickedly! You have made an unjust decision! Your courts are a sacrilege! What crime did this man commit? What evil has he done? The city is in uproar! You are wronging us all! You are grieving us all! Do not betray the city of the emperor! Grant the Achaeans the just man! Grant us this God-fearing man! Do not kill this man possessed of God! Do not destroy this pious man! Even though he has been hanging for four days, he is still alive. Although he has eaten nothing, he has nourished us with his words. Bring the man down and we will all become philosophers! Untie the prudent one, and all Patras will be law-abiding! Release the wise man, and all Achaea will receive mercy!"

60. When Aegeates at first disregarded the crowd and gestured for them to leave the tribunal, they were enraged and were gaining courage to oppose him in some way; they numbered about two thousand. When the proconsul saw that they were in some way incensed he was terrified that he might suffer a revolution. He rose from the tribunal and went off with them, promising to release the blessed Andrew. Some ran ahead to disclose to the apostle this very fact as well as the reason for Aegeates' coming to the place. The crowd was jubilant because the blessed Andrew was about to be untied, and when the proconsul arrived, all the brethren were rejoicing, among them Maximilla.

61. When Andrew heard this, he said, "O the great lethargy of those I have taught! O the sudden fog engulfing us even after many mysteries! O, how much we have spoken up to the present, and we have not convinced our own! O, how much has happened so that we might flee the earthly! O, what strong statements have been spoken against carnal things, and yet they want more of the same! O, how many times I have prayed that I might lift them from these filthy habits, but instead they were encouraged to nothingness! Why this excessive fondness for the flesh? Why this great complicity with it? Do you again encourage me to be put back among things in flux? . . .

62. "But now that Aegeates is coming to me, I will keep quiet and embrace my children. Whatever I must resolve by speaking to him, these I will speak. Aegeates, why have you come to us again? . . . What do you want to attempt now? . . . Even if you really did change your mind, Aegeates, I would never accede to you. . . . Would you untie the one who has fled? Would you untie the one who was liberated? . . . I possess the one with whom I will always be. I possess the one with whom I will be a compatriot for countless ages. It is to him that I go. . . ." When the proconsul heard these things he stood there speechless and as if stunned. Andrew looked at him again and said, "Aegeates, enemy of us all, now you stand there watching. You stand there quiet and calm, unable to do anything you dare. My kindred and I speed on to things our own, leaving you to be what you are and what you fail to understand about yourself."

63. And when Aegeates again attempted to approach the wood to untie Andrew, the entire city was in an uproar at him. The apostle Andrew shouted: "O Master, do not permit Andrew, the one tied to your wood, to be untied again. O Jesus, do not give me to the shameless devil, I who am attached to your mystery. O Father, do not let your opponent untie me, I who am hanging upon your grace." . . . When he had said these things and further glorified the Lord, he handed over his spirit, so that we wept and everyone grieved his departure.

64. After the departure of the blessed apostle, Maximilla, accompanied by Stratocles, completely disregarding those standing around her, came forward, untied the corpse of the blessed one, and having provided it with the necessary attention, buried it at nightfall.

She separated from Aegeates because of his savage soul and lawless public life. Thereafter, though he simulated good behavior, she had nothing whatever to do with him. Choosing instead a life holy and quiet, provided for by the love of Christ, she spent her time happily with the brethren. Even though Aegeates often importuned her and offered her the opportunity to control his affairs, he was not able to persuade her. One night, undetected by anyone in his household, he threw himself from a great height and died. . . .

65. Here let me make an end of the blessed tales, acts, and mysteries difficult—or should I say impossible—to express. Let this stroke of the pen end it. I will pray first for myself, that I heard what was actually said, both the obvious and also the obscure, comprehensible only to the intellect. Then I will pray for all who are convinced by what was said, that they may have fellowship with each other, as God opens the ears of the listeners, in order to make comprehensible all his gifts in Christ Jesus our Lord, to whom, together with the Father, be glory, honor, and power with the all-holy and good and life-giving spirit, now and always, forever and ever, amen.

Biographies of Ascetic Leaders

Contemporary scholars have argued that an ascetic lifestyle, whether as a virgin or as a married woman living in a continent relationship with her husband, freed women to undertake more active leadership roles in the life of the church, especially when the ascetic movement began to flourish in the fourth century. For wealthy, aristocratic women in particular (about whom we know the most, thanks largely to the biographical literature that celebrated their achievements), an ascetic lifestyle offered possibilities for theological and Scriptural education, scholarship, reflection, and friendships with male ascetics. Freedom from domestic confinement and its attendant responsibilities meant that they could travel (as in pilgrimage), visit the holy men of the Egyptian desert, and establish centers of hospitality for various holy people. Such women used their wealth to support local churches as well as to found monasteries both for men and for women, and in the latter establishments they often took on roles as teachers and spiritual counselors as well.

1. Macrina

The older sister of the Cappadocian fathers Basil of Caesarea and Gregory of Nyssa, Macrina (sometimes called Macrina the Younger to distinguish her from her grandmother of the same name) was the daughter of a wealthy family in Pontus in Asia Minor. When her fiancé died (she was only twelve at the time), she pledged herself to a virginal life; as her brother notes in his biography, "Thecla" was her secret name and foreshadowed her life as an ascetic (see *The Acts of Paul and Thecla* in "Ascetic Heroines in Literature" above). Together with her mother Emmelia, she transformed the family compound at Annesi into a monastery for women and men, serving as superior in the convent. Her brother Gregory presents her as one living an "angelic" life, as a forceful personality who inspired her siblings in the ascetic life, and also as an astute philosopher-theologian (see "Teachers" in Section I, above; in the present text, "philosophy" connotes a form of Christian spirituality associated with liberation from the passions and with a contemplative life). Macrina lived from ca. 327–380 C.E.

Gregory of Nyssa, *Life of Saint Macrina* (selections)

[Note: I have added the conventional paragraph numbers to Corrigan's translation.]

1. This work appears from the general form of the heading, to be a

letter, but it exceeds the limits of a letter and stretches into a lengthy narrative. My excuse, however, is that the subject you [the unknown recipient of the letter] ordered me to write upon is too big to be treated within the proper bounds of a letter. You certainly cannot have forgotten our meeting when, on my way to visit Jerusalem in order to fulfill a vow to see the signs of the Lord's residence in the flesh in those places, I ran into you in the city of Antioch and we discussed all sorts of things. . . . In the course of our conversation we recalled the life of an honored person; it was a woman who prompted our narrative, if, that is, we may call her a woman, for I do not know if it is appropriate to apply a name drawn from nature to one who has risen above nature. . . . We had the same parents and she was, so to speak, a votive offering of the fruits to come, the first offshoot of our mother's womb. And so, since you were convinced that the story of her good deeds would be of some use because you thought that a life of this quality should not be forgotten for the future and that she who had raised herself through philosophy to the highest limit of human virtue should not pass along this way veiled and in silence, I thought it good to obey you and to tell her story, as briefly as I could, in a simple, unaffected narrative.

2. The maiden [parthenos] was called Macrina. Some time ago, there had been a celebrated Macrina in our family, our father's mother. At the time of the persecutions [303–313 C.E.] she had suffered bravely for her confession of faith in Christ and it was in honor of her that the child was given this name by her parents. But this was her public name used by her acquaintances; another name had been secretly given her as the result of a vision which had occurred during labor before she emerged into the light of day. . . . And when the time came when she [Emmelia] was to be freed from her labor pain by giving birth to the child, she fell asleep and seemed to be carrying in her arms the child still embraced by her womb, and someone in suprahuman majesty of form and shape appeared to address the little child by the name of Thekla, that Thekla of great fame among maidens. After doing this three times and calling upon her to witness it, the person disappeared from her sight and gave ease to her labor pains so that as soon as she woke up from her sleep she saw that the dream was reality. And so that was Macrina's secret name. In my view, however, the figure who appeared declared this not so much to guide the

mother in her choice of name as to foretell the life of the child and to point out, by the identity of name, a similarity in their choice of life.

3. And so the child grew. Although she also had her own nurse, for the most part her mother nursed her herself. When she had passed the age of infancy, she was quick to learn her children's lessons, and whatever lessons her parents decided to have the girl study, in those the nature of the little girl excelled. It was a matter of serious interest to her mother to instruct the child, but not in this pagan, secular course of studies where the students' early years are for the most part formed by the study of the poets. For she held that it was shameful and altogether unfitting to teach a tender and easily influenced nature either the passions of tragedy—those passions of women which have given the poets their sources of inspiration and their plots—or the indecent revels of comedy, or the causes of the evils which befell Troy, definitely spoiling the child's nature with the really rather irreverent tales about women. Instead, any passages of divinely inspired Scripture which seemed accessible to very young persons, were the child's study, and above all, the Wisdom of Solomon, and after this, whatever was conducive to the moral life. But also there was none of the psalms which she did not know since she recited each part of the Psalter at the proper times of the day, when she rose from her bed, performed or rested from her duties, sat down to eat or rose up from the table, when she went to bed or got up to pray, at all times she had the Psalter with her like a good traveling companion who never fails.

4. Growing up with these and similar occupations and having become especially skilled in the working of wool, she attained her twelfth year, the age in which the bloom of youth starts to radiate more than at any other time. Here it is indeed worth marveling how the beauty of the young girl, although concealed, did not remain unnoticed. There did not seem to be any such marvel in the whole of that country which could compare with her beauty and gracefulness, so that not even painters' hands could come close to her fresh beauty; and the art which engineers everything and which dares even to wrestle with the greatest subjects, going so far as to fashion in imitation images of the planets themselves, did not have the power to render a true likeness of her blessed beauty. Because of this a great swarm of suitors surrounded her parents. But her

father (for he was indeed wise and practiced in the discernment of what is noble) chose from the rest of the company a young kinsman of good repute . . . and decided to betroth his daughter to him when she came of age. Meanwhile the young man was among his brighter hopes and brought to the girl's father his reputation for oratory, like a pleasing wedding gift, demonstrating his rhetorical ability in lawsuits on behalf of people who had been wronged. But Envy cut short the bright promise by plucking him from life at a pitiable early age.

5. The young girl was not unaware of her father's resolution, but when the young man's death had broken off what had been decided for her, she called her father's decision a marriage, as if what had been decided upon had in fact really happened, and she determined to remain by herself [i.e., unmarried] for the rest of her life, a decision which was more firmly rooted than one might have expected in one of her age. Her parents brought up the subject of marriage to her on many occasions because of the many young men who as a result of her famed beauty, wanted to sue for her hand. . . . [But] she strongly insisted that the young man who had been joined to her in accordance with her parents' decision was not dead, but that, in her judgment, he who was living in God because of the hope of the resurrection was simply away from home on a journey and not a dead body; and it was improper not to keep faith with a husband who was away on a journey.

By arguments such as these she pushed aside those who were trying to persuade her and she hit upon one safeguard for her good decision, never to be separated from her mother even for a moment, so that her mother often said to her that she had been pregnant with the rest of her children for the prescribed term, but as for Macrina she bore her always and everywhere, embracing her, as it were, in her womb. But sharing her life with her daughter was not hard for the mother nor was it without benefit. For, instead of her many maidservants, there was now the attentive care of her daughter and a true exchange was realized between the two of them. The older woman cared for the young girl's soul, the young girl for her mother's bodily needs, fulfilling in all things the service that was needed, even frequently preparing bread with her own hands for her mother. . . .

6. And when her mother had arranged in a fair and fitting way the situations of her sisters with a view to what seemed best for each of them, the great Basil, brother of the girl we have been speaking about, came back from the school where he had been trained for a long time in the discipline of rhetoric. Although when she took him in hand he was monstrously conceited about his skill in rhetoric, contemptuous of every high reputation, and exalted beyond the leading lights of the province by his self-importance, so swiftly did she win him to the ideal of philosophy that he renounced worldly appearance, showed contempt for the admiration of rhetorical ability, and went over of his own accord to this active life of manual labor, preparing for himself by means of his complete poverty a way of life which would tend without impediment towards virtue. . . .

7. Since any reason for living a more materialistic way of life was now taken away, Macrina persuaded her mother to give up their accustomed way of life, their rather ostentatious lifestyle, and the services she had previously been accustomed to receive from her maids, and she also persuaded her to put herself on an equal footing with the many in spirit and to share a common life with all her maids, making them sisters and equals instead of slaves and servants. . . .

11. When the responsibility of bringing up the children and the worry of their education and establishment in life was over, and when most of the resources for the more material side of life were shared out among the children, then, as mentioned before, the life of the maiden became for her mother a guide towards the philosophical, immaterial way of life. Turning her away from all she was accustomed to, she led her to her own standard of humility, prepared her to put herself on an equal footing with the community of maidens, so as to share on equal terms with them one table, bed, and all the needs of life, with every difference of rank eliminated from their lives. And such was the order of their life, such was the high level of philosophy and the holy conduct of their living by day and by night that it exceeds the power of words to describe it. For just as souls are freed from their bodies by death and at the same time liberated from the cares of this life, so was their existence separated from these things, removed from all of life's vanity and fashioned in harmonious imitation of the life of the angels. In them no anger, envy, hate, arrogance,

nor any other such thing was seen; the desire for foolish things of no substance, for honor, glory, delusions of grandeur, the need to be superior to
others, and all such things had been eradicated. Self-control was their
pleasure, not to be known was their fame, their wealth was in possessing
nothing and in shaking off all material surplus, like dust from the body;
their work was none of the concerns of this life except in so far as it was
a subordinate task. Their only care was for divine realities, and there
was constant prayer and the unceasing singing of hymns, extended
equally throughout the entire day and night so that this was both work
and respite from work for them.

What human works could ever bring such a mode of existence before one's gaze—in a community whose way of life lay at the boundaries
between human nature and the nature which is without body? For to
have freed nature from human passions was a feat beyond human
strength, while to appear in body, to be encompassed by bodily shape and
to live with the organs of sense, was thereby to possess a nature inferior
to that of the angelic and the incorporeal. Perhaps one might even go so
far as to say that the difference was minimal, because, although they
lived in the flesh, by virtue of their affinity with the incorporeal powers
they were not weighed down by the attractive pull of the body, but their
lives were borne upwards, poised on high, and they took their souls'
flight in concert with the heavenly powers. The time spent in such a way
of life was not short and their accomplishments increased with time,
since philosophy always granted them an abundance of help in the dis-
covery of good things which led them on to greater purity.

12. Macrina had a brother who was of special assistance towards this
great goal of life. His name was Peter, and with him our mother's birth
pangs ceased; for he was the last, tender shoot of his parents, called both
son and orphan because at the moment he came into the light of this life,
his father departed from it. However, right at the time of his birth when
he had only been a few moments at the breast, his eldest sister, the subject of our story, snatched him straight up from the woman who was
nursing him and brought him up herself, and she led him to all the higher learning, exercising him from infancy in the sacred teachings so as
not to give his soul the leisure to incline to any profane pursuit. She be-

came everything for the child, father, teacher, guide, mother, counselor in every good, and she perfected him in such a way that before he left childhood, while he was still blossoming at the tender stage of adolescent youth, he was lifted up towards the sublime goal of philosophy; and by some happy, natural disposition he possessed a skillfulness for every kind of handicraft so that without having had anyone to teach him the art in all its specific details, he succeeded in mastering skills for which the majority of people require a long and laborious apprenticeship. . . . Once, when there was a severe famine and many people from all over, drawn by the fame of their generosity, came pouring into the remote country in which they lived, he provided such an abundance of provisions, thanks to his inventiveness, that because of the throng of visitors, the wilderness looked like a city. . . .

15. Nine months, or a little more, after this [the deaths of Emmelia and Basil, recounted in sections 13–14], a synod of bishops was convened in the city of Antioch, in which I also took part. And when we were free to return again, each to his own diocese, before the year went by, it was weighing heavy on my heart, I, Gregory, to go and visit [Macrina]. For it was a long time since our last meeting during which the critical circumstances of my trials had prevented our visiting each other, since I was constantly being exiled by the leaders of heresy. And when I counted up the intervening time in which my trials had precluded our seeing each other, no brief interval did it appear—it came to almost eight years. And so when I had finished most of the journey and was only one day's travel away from her, I had a vision in a dream which made me apprehensive for the future. I seemed to be holding in my hands the relics of martyrs, and there came from them a bright gleam of light, as from a flawless mirror which had been placed face to the sun, so that my eyes were blinded by the brilliance of the gleam. During that same night this vision occurred three times, and I was not able to interpret clearly the dream's hidden meaning, but I foresaw some distress for my soul and I awaited the outcome to make a judgment about what had appeared to me. And in fact when I did get close to the remote spot in which she spent her angelic, heavenly life, I asked one of her community first if my brother was there. He told me that he had set out about three days ago to meet me,

and I understood what had happened, that he had taken another road to meet us. Then I inquired of the great Macrina; and when he told me that she was sick, I was in an even greater hurry to finish the rest of the journey, for in truth a foreboding of what was to happen had come upon me and was troubling me deeply.

16. As I was arriving at the place itself (and the news of my presence had already been announced to the community), an entire contingent of men poured forth from the monastic enclosure—for it was customary for them to honor guests by coming out to greet them—and a group of maidens from the convent awaited our coming by the church in good order. When the prayers and blessing had been completed and the women had bowed their heads respectfully to receive the blessing and had retired to their own quarters, since none of them remained behind with me, I guessed correctly that their Superior was not among them. Someone guided me to the house where the great Macrina was, opened the door, and there I was inside that holy place. Macrina was already caught in the grip of a grievous sickness, but she was resting not on a bed or a couch, but on the ground, on a plank covered with sackcloth, with another plank supporting her head and designed to serve instead of a pillow, lying under her neck muscles at a raised angle and giving the right amount of support to her neck.

17. When she saw me standing by the door, she raised herself on her elbow, but she was unable to run up to me because her strength had already been undermined by the fever. But, planting her hands on the bare floor and stretching forward as far as she could reach from her bed, she managed to do me the honor of greeting me; and I ran up to her, and taking her bowed head in my hands, I lifted her up and put her back in her accustomed reclining position. And she stretched out her hand to God and said, "Even this favor you have fulfilled for me, my God, and you have not deprived me of my heart's desire in that you have inspired your servant to visit your handmaiden." And so that she might not bring any despondency to my soul, she tried to stifle her groans and forced herself somehow to hide her tortured gasping for breath. Throughout everything she was trying to create a more cheerful mood, and she initiated suitable topics of conversation and gave me the opportunity to speak by the ques-

tions she asked. But when in the course of our conversation we inadvertently made mention of the great Basil, then my heart sank, my face fell in sorrow, and the tears poured from my eyes. But she was so far from being downcast by our sorrow that she made our mention of the holy man a starting point for the higher philosophy, and she expounded arguments of such excellence, explaining the human situation in terms of natural causes, unveiling to reason the divine providence hidden in sad events, and recounting in detail events of the life to be hereafter as if she were inspired by the Holy Spirit, that my soul seemed to be almost outside of human nature, uplifted as it was by her words and set down inside the heavenly sanctuaries by the guidance of her discourse. . . . [Note: This is the conversation that Gregory purports to recount in "On the Soul and the Resurrection"; see "Teachers" in Section I, above.]

19. When our conversation was concluded, she said, "It's time, brother, for you to rest your body for a little while, as your journey must have tired you out," while for me it was really a complete relaxation just to look at her and to listen to her noble words; but since this was pleasing and important to her, in order that I might show obedience to my teacher in everything, I found ready for me in one of the nearby gardens a beautiful spot to rest in and I took my repose under the shade of the vine-girt trees. But it was not possible to savor the delightful surroundings when my soul within was awash with foreboding of unhappy events; for what I had seen seemed to unveil the hidden meaning of the vision in my dream. What I had seen before me was truly the remains of a holy martyr, one who had been dead to sin, but illumined by the indwelling grace of the Holy Spirit. And I explained this to one of those who had already heard my account of the dream. We were in the depths of despondency (as was only natural) in the anticipation of sad events, but Macrina guessed (I know not how) our state of mind and sent a message of better tidings to us, telling us to cheer up and to be of better hopes for her; for she perceived a turn for the better. This was not said to deceive us, but her communication was absolutely truthful, even if we did not recognize it at the time. . . . Macrina gave us to hope for greater things for her, since she was already looking towards the prize of her upward calling and all but applying the words of the apostle to herself when he says that

"all there is to come now is the crown of righteousness reserved for me, which the righteous judge will give to me" [2 Tim 4:8], since "I have fought the good fight, I have run the race to the end, and I have kept the faith" [2 Tim 4:7]. Reassured, then, by this good news, we started to enjoy the things that were put before us, and these were varied, the provision full of intent to give pleasure, since the great Macrina's thoughtfulness extended even to these things. . . .

22. When [the next] day came, it was clear to me from what I saw that this day was to mark her last in the life of the flesh, since the fever had totally spent all her natural, inbuilt strength. She saw our dispirited thinking and tried to bring us out of our despondency by again dispersing the pain of our souls with those beautiful words of hers, but from now on her breathing was shallow and tortured. It was at this moment above all that my soul was torn by what confronted it; on the one hand, my nature was heavy with sadness, as is understandable, in the anticipation that I would no longer hear that voice of hers; but, on the other hand, in so far as I did not yet grasp that the glory of our whole family was going to leave this human life, my soul was divinely inspired, as it were, by the things I saw and I suspected that she had transcended the common nature. For not even in her last breaths to feel anything strange in the expectation of death nor to fear separation from life, but with sublime thinking to philosophize upon what she had chosen for this life, right from the beginning up to her last breath, to me this seemed no longer to be a part of human realities. Instead, it was as if an angel had providentially assumed human form, an angel in whom there was no affinity for, nor attachment to, the life of the flesh, about whom it was not unreasonable that her thinking should remain impassible, since the flesh did not drag it down to its own passions. For this reason she seemed to me to be making manifest to those then present that pure, divine love of the unseen bridegroom, which she had nourished secretly in the most intimate depths of her soul, and she seemed to transmit the desire which was in her heart to rush to the one she longed for, so that freed from the fetters of the body, she might swiftly be with him. For it was really towards her beloved that she ran, and no other of life's pleasures ever turned her eye to itself away from her beloved. . . .

25. . . . Meanwhile, evening had come on and a light had been brought in. At once Macrina opened her eyes wide, directed their attention to the gleam of light, and made it clear that she also wished to say the evening prayer of thanksgiving; but as her voice failed her, she realized her desire in her heart and in the movement of her hands, her lips moving in time with her inward impulse. When she had completed the prayer of thanksgiving and, by bringing her hand to her face for the sign of the cross, had indicated that she had finished her prayer, she took a strong, deep breath, and with that she died.

When from then on she did not breathe or move, I remembered the instructions she had given me when I had first arrived. She had said that she wished my hands to be placed upon her eyes and that she wanted me to attend to the customary care of the body. So I put my hand, numbed by grief, to her holy face at least so as not to seem to disregard her instruction. For her eyes needed no arranging, since they were covered gracefully by her eyelids as if she were only asleep; and her lips were firmly closed and her hands rested naturally on her breast, and the whole position of her body was so spontaneously and beautifully harmonized that any hand to compose the features was superfluous. . . .

29. There was a deaconess, in charge of a group of the women, called Lampadion. She said that she knew exactly what Macrina had decided about her burial. And when I asked her about this, for she happened to be there when we were deciding what to do, she replied in tears and this is what she said: "The adornment of concern to the holy one was the pure life; this is for her both the ornament of her life and the shroud of her death. As to all those things which are for the ornamentation of the body, she neither had anything to do with them during her lifetime nor did she put any away for the present occasion, so that not even if we wanted to, would there be anything more than what we have here to dress her in." "But isn't it possible," I asked, "to find something in the store cupboards with which we can adorn the bier?" "In what store cupboards?" she replied. "You have in your hands everything she put away. Look at her cloak, look at the veil on her head, the worn sandals on her feet; this is her wealth, this her fortune! Apart from what you see there is nothing laid by in hidden chests or chambers in reserve. She knew only

one repository for her own wealth, the treasury of heaven. There she stored everything, and left nothing behind on earth." "In that case," I said to her, "what if I brought one of the things I had prepared for the funeral, would this be against her wishes?" She replied that she did not think that Macrina would have disapproved of this. . . .

30. When this had been decided and it was necessary for that holy body to be clothed in fine linen, we shared out our responsibility and we were each of us around her concentrating on a different task. I for my part told one of my own company to bring me the robe. Vetiana [an aristocratic widow in the convent] was arranging that holy head with her own hands when, putting her hand to Macrina's neck, she looked at me and said, "See what a necklace the holy woman wore for ornament." And as she said this, she untied the chain from behind Macrina's neck, reached out her hand and showed me a cross of iron and a ring of the same material, both of which were hung on a slender chain and had been always over her heart. And I said, "Let this be our common possession. You keep the cross for your protection; the ring will be sufficient inheritance for me." And in fact the cross was engraved on the seal of the ring. The woman looked intently at it and again spoke to me, "Your choice of this piece has not missed the mark; for the stone in the ring is hollow and in it is hidden a fragment of the wood of life; and so the seal with its own engraving reveals from above what is hidden below."

31. When it was finally time to wrap her pure body in the robe, and the great Macrina's command made it necessary for me to perform this office, the woman who had shared with me in that important inheritance of Macrina's possessions was there helping out with the work. "Do not let the greatest wonder accomplished by this holy lady," she said, "pass by unrecorded." "What is that?" I asked. She laid bare a part of Macrina's breast and asked, "Do you see this faint, tiny mark below the skin? It looks like a scar left by a small needle." And as she spoke she brought the lamp closer to the spot she was showing me. "What is so marvelous about that if the body has a tiny scar here?" "This is left on the body," she said, "as a reminder of God's great help. For at one time on this spot there was a painful growth, and it was just as dangerous to cut out the tumor as it was to let it take its own course entirely without treatment with

the risk that it would spread to the heart area. Her mother begged and entreated her many times to accept medical treatment, for she argued that this art too had been revealed by God for the saving protection of mankind. But Macrina had decided that to bare a part of her body to the eyes of strangers was worse than being sick, and one evening, when she had completed the tasks which she usually performed with her own hands for her mother, she went into the sanctuary and remained there all night long prostrate before the God of healing, weeping a flood of tears to moisten the earth, and she used the mud from her tears as a salve to put on the affected place. Her mother was at her wits' end and again tried to get her to see the doctor, but Macrina said that it would be enough to cure her disease if her mother would make the sign of the cross with her own hand on Macrina's breast. And when her mother put her hand inside Macrina's robe to make the sign of the cross on the affected spot, the sign of the cross worked and the affliction disappeared. But this little mark," she continued, "appeared also at the time in place of the horrible tumor and stayed there till the end to be a reminder, I think, of God's visitation, as an impetus and cause for constant thanksgiving to God."

32. When our task was finished and the body adorned with the means at our disposal, the deaconess again told me that it was not right for Macrina to be seen by the maidens dressed as a bride. "But I have a dark cloak of your mother's," she said, "which I think would be good to put over her so that this sacred beauty should not be made to shine in clothing brought in just for the occasion." Her view prevailed and the cloak was placed over the body. She shone even in the dark mantle; God's power, I think, added even such grace to her body that, exactly as in the vision I had while dreaming, rays of light seemed to shine out from her beauty. . . .

36. When we had completed all the customary funeral rites and it was necessary to go back, I fell upon the tomb and kissed the dust and then took my way back again, downcast and tearful at the thought of how my life had been deprived of such a good. Along the way, a distinguished military man who had command of a garrison in a little town of the district of Pontus, called Sebastopolis, and who lived there with his subordi-

nates, came with kindly intention to meet me when I arrived there. He had heard of our misfortune and he took it badly (for, in fact, he was related to our family by kinship and also by close friendship). He gave me an account of a miracle worked by Macrina; and this will be the last event I shall record in my story before concluding my narrative. When we had stopped weeping and were standing in conversation, he said to me, "Hear what a great good has departed from human life." And with this he started to tell his story.

37. "It happened that my wife and I once desired to visit that powerhouse of virtue; for that's what I think that place should be called in which the blessed soul spent her life. Our little daughter was also with us and she suffered from an eye ailment as a result of an infectious disease. And it was a hideous and pitiful sight, since the membrane around the pupil was swollen and because of the disease had taken on a whitish tinge. As we entered that divine place, we separated, my wife and I, to make our visit to those who lived a life of philosophy therein, I going to the monks' enclosure where your brother, Peter, was abbot, and my wife entering the convent to be with the holy one. After a suitable interval had passed, we decided it was time to leave the monastery retreat and we were already getting ready to go when the same, friendly invitation came to us from both quarters. Your brother asked me to stay and take part in the philosophic table, and the blessed Macrina would not permit my wife to leave, but she held our little daughter in her arms and said that she would not give her back until she had given them a meal and offered them the wealth of philosophy; and, as you might have expected, she kissed the little girl and was putting her lips to the girl's eyes, when she noticed the infection around the pupil and said, 'If you do me the favor of sharing our table with us, I will give you in return a reward to match your courtesy.' The little girl's mother asked what it might be and the great Macrina replied, 'It's an ointment I have which has the power to heal the eye infection.' When after this a message reached me from the women's quarters telling me of Macrina's promise, we gladly stayed, counting of little consequence the necessity which pressed us to make our way back home.

38. "Finally the feasting was over and our souls were full. The great

Peter with his own hands had entertained and cheered us royally, and the holy Macrina took leave of my wife with every courtesy one could wish for. And so, bright and joyful, we started back home along the same road, each of us telling the other what had happened to each as we went along. And I recounted all I had seen and heard in the men's enclosure, while she told me every little thing in detail, like a history book, and thought that she should omit nothing, not even the least significant details. On she went telling me about everything in order, as if in a narrative, and when she came to the part where a promise of a cure for the eye had been made, she interrupted the narrative to exclaim, 'What's the matter with us! How did we forget the promise she made us, the special eye ointment?' And I was angry at our negligence and summoned some one to run back quickly to ask for the medicine, when our baby, who was in her nurse's arms, looked, as it happened, towards her mother. And the mother gazed intently at the child's eyes and then loudly exclaimed with joy and surprise, 'Stop being angry at our negligence! Look! There's nothing missing of what she promised us, but the true medicine with which she heals diseases, the healing which comes from prayer, she has given us and it has already done its work, there's nothing whatsoever left of the eye disease, all healed by that divine medicine!' And as she was saying this, she picked the child up in her arms and put her down in mine. And then I too understood the incredible miracles of the gospel, which I had not believed in, and exclaimed: 'What a great thing it is when the hand of God restores sight to the blind, when today his servant heals such sicknesses by her faith in Him, an event no less impressive than those miracles!'" All the while he was saying this, his voice was choked with emotion and the tears flowed into his story. This then is what I heard from the soldier.

39. All the other similar miracles which we heard about from those who lived with her and who knew in detail what she had done I do not think it prudent to add to our narrative. For most people judge the credibility of what is told them by the yardstick of their own experience, and what goes beyond the power of the hearer, this they have no respect for, suspecting that it is false and outside of the truth. For this reason I pass over that incredible farming miracle at the time of the famine, how the

grain was distributed according to need and showed no sign of diminish-
ing, how the volume remained the same both before it was given out to
those who asked for it and after the distribution, and other miracles still
more extraordinary, the cure of sicknesses, the casting out of demons,
true prophecies of things to come; all of these are believed to be true by
those who knew the details of them, even if they are beyond belief. But
for those who are more bound to this world of flesh, they are considered
to be outside the realm of what can be accepted, that is by those who do
not know that the distribution of graces is in proportion to one's faith,
abundant for those who have in them a lot of room for faith. In order
therefore that those who have too little faith, and who do not believe in
the gifts of God, should come to no harm, for this reason I have declined
to make a complete record here of the greater miracles, since I think that
what I have already said is sufficient to complete Macrina's story.

2. Melania the Elder

A wealthy Roman aristocrat, Melania was widowed in her early twenties. After
her husband's death, she left Rome for Egypt in the early 370s to visit the famous ascetic monks living in the Nitrian desert; later in that decade, she went to Palestine,
where she founded monasteries for men and women on the Mount of Olives. Her
friend Rufinus, monk and translator especially of the works of Origen, oversaw the
monastery for men, and she oversaw the women's community. Her exemplary ascetic
lifestyle encouraged her granddaughter, Melania the Younger, to embrace asceticism.
She was born ca. 342 and died at her monastery in Jerusalem ca. 410 C.E.

Palladius, *Lausiac History* (selections)

46. The thrice-blessed Melania was of Spanish origin and later was a
Roman. She was a daughter of Marcellinus, one of the consuls, and wife
of a certain high-ranking man (I am not remembering well which one).
When she was widowed at twenty-two, she was deemed worthy of divine
love. She told no one her plan, because she would have been prohibited
at the time, since Valens held rule in the empire [364–78 C.E.; he was an Ar-
ian sympathizer]. She arranged to name a guardian for her son, and taking
all her movable property, she loaded it on a ship and sailed off at full

speed to Alexandria, along with illustrious women and children. There, having sold her things and turned possessions into money, she departed for the mountain of Nitria and met with the Fathers, with Pambo, Arsisius, Serapion the Great, Paphnutius of Scete, Isidore the Confessor, and Dioscorus, bishop of Hermopolis. And she spent up to half a year with them, going around the desert and seeking out all the holy men.

Later the Augustan prefect [governor of the province of Egypt] banished Isidore, Pisimius, Adelphius, Paphnutius, and Pambo, among whom also was Ammonius Parotes, and twelve bishops and priests, to Palestine, around Diocaesarea. She followed them and ministered to them from her private wealth. Since servants were prohibited, so it was reported (for I happened to meet the holy Pisimius, Isidore, Paphnutius, and Ammonius), she donned a slave's hood and in the evenings used to bring them the things they needed. When the consul of Palestine learned about this, he wished to fill his own pocket and thought he would blacken her reputation [a pun; melania means "blackness" in Greek]. He seized her and threw her into prison, unaware that she was a free woman. But she disclosed her identity to him in this way: "I am the daughter of thus-and-such a person, and so-and-so's wife — but I am the slave of Christ. Do not despise my vile appearance, for I can exalt myself if I so choose. You do not have the means to blacken me in this matter nor to take anything from me. I have thus made this clear to you lest you unknowingly become liable to charges." It is necessary in dealing with insensitive people to use conceit like a hawk! The judge then comprehended the situation; he apologized, revered her, and ordered that she might meet with the holy men unhindered.

After their recall, she built a monastery in Jerusalem and stayed there for twenty-seven years, having a group of fifty virgins. Near Melania lived the most noble, sturdy Rufinus, of similar habits to hers. He was from the city of Aquileia in Italy and later he was judged worthy of the priesthood. Among men there was not to be found a more reasonable and capable person. During the twenty-seven years, both of them received those who turned up in Jerusalem for the sake of a vow, bishops, monks, and virgins; at their own expense, they edified all those who passed through. They united the four hundred monks involved in the schism over Paulinus [from the 360s to the 380s in the church in Antioch, a schism involving rival bishops], and having convinced every heretic who fought against the divinity of the Holy Spirit, they led them back to the Church. They bestowed honors on the clergy of the area with gifts and food, and thus completed their lives without offending anyone.

54. I have reported above in a superficial way about the marvelous and holy Melania. Not less important, I shall now finish weaving into the story the remaining items. She lavished so much wealth in her godly zeal, as if she were ablaze with fire, that the residents of Persia, not I, should do the reporting. No one in either the east or the west, the north or the south, failed to benefit from her good works.

For twenty-seven years she offered hospitality; at her own expense, she assisted churches, monasteries, guests, and prisons. Her family, her son, and her own trustees supplied her with money. She persevered in her hospitality to such an extent that she did not keep a span of earth, nor pulled by longing for her son, did she separate herself from love of Christ. But through her prayers, the young man pressed on to a height of education and character, married, as was expected by worldly judgments, and became honored. He also had two children. Then after a long time, she heard about the situation of her granddaughter [Melania the Younger], that she had married and had decided to renounce the world. Fearing lest they be destroyed by evil teaching or by heresy or by evil living, she, although an old woman of sixty years, embarked on a boat and departed from Caesarea, arriving at Rome after twenty days.

There she met a very blessed and noteworthy man, Apronianus, a Greek; she taught him and made him a Christian, persuading him to practice sexual continence with his own wife, named Abita, who was Melania's niece. She strengthened her granddaughter Melania along with the latter's husband, Pinian, and taught her daughter-in-law, Albina, her son's wife. She got them ready to sell publicly all their possessions, led them out of Rome, and steered them to the harbor of a decent and calm life. Thus in reference to all these things, she was fighting the beasts—the senators and their wives, who would have prevented her from renouncing the remaining houses. But she said to them, "It was written four hundred years ago, 'Little children, it is the last hour' [1 John

2:18]. Why do you love the vain things of life, lest the days of the Antichrist overtake you and you not enjoy your wealth and your forefathers' property?"

And when she had freed all these relatives, she led them to a monastic life. She also taught the younger son of Publicola [her son] and led him to Sicily. She sold everything of hers that remained and went to Jerusalem, taking the proceeds. She distributed her money within forty days and fell asleep at a good old age, in the most profound gentleness, leaving also a monastery in Jerusalem and the funds for its upkeep.

And when all of them were far away from Rome, a barbarian hurricane of a kind that had long ago been predicted in prophecy fell on Rome [the sack of Rome by Goths, 410 C.E.]. Not even the bronze statues in the Forum were left intact, but everything was delivered up to destruction by the barbarian madness. Thus Rome, beautifully decorated for twelve hundred years, became a ruin. Then those whom Melania had instructed and those who had opposed her instruction praised God, who persuaded the unbelievers through the revolutionary events, because when all the others were taken captive, only those houses were saved that had become a burnt offering for the Lord through Melania's zeal.

3. Melania the Younger

A member of a wealthy Roman senatorial family, Melania the Younger was inspired by her grandmother Melania the Elder to pursue the ascetic life. She was married to another wealthy Roman, Pinian, and after bearing two children, both of whom died young, she persuaded her husband to live together in chastity when she was twenty and he was twenty-four. After selling many of their vast land holdings, they left Rome for North Africa and then for Jerusalem, founding monasteries in both places. Melania is celebrated by her biographer for her extreme ascetic practices (fasting, all-night vigils, regimens of reading and writing, and so on) and for her renunciation of her wealth. She lived from ca. 383–439 C.E. For a selection from this biography on Melania's teachings, see Section I, above.

Gerontius, *The Life of Melania the Younger* (selections)

Prologue

God be blessed, who has aroused your honored Reverence, holy priest, to seek an account from my lowly self concerning the life of our holy mother, Melania the Roman, who has her home with the angels. Since I spent not a little time with her, I know in an indistinct way the story of her senatorial family, and how she entered upon the angelic life, putting under foot all the pride of worldly glory. . . . It is not so amazing if I, an amateur author and slow of speech, lose heart at the undertaking of such a task, for by my reckoning not even the philosophers themselves have ventured too far on so great an assignment, so it seems. For who would be able to recount in a clear and worthy manner the manly deeds of this blessed woman? I mean of course her utter renunciation of worldly things, her ardor for the orthodox faith (an ardor hotter than fire), her unsurpassable beneficence, her intense vigils, her persistence in lying on the ground, her ill-treatment and ceaseless ascetic discipline of her soul as well as of her body, her gentleness and temperance that vie with the incorporeal powers, the cheapness of her clothing, and even more than these, her humility, the mother of all good things. Each one of this woman's virtues steers us to a boundless sea of thoughts and the composition of an entire book, a task which surpasses our ability by far. . . . I shall try to become like those who enter a garden, where they experience every kind of fragrance and pungent flower: even if they are not able to pick flowers from the entire meadow, they nonetheless leave only when they have selected a sufficient number. So using this comparison as well, and strengthened by the prayers of Your Holiness, I shall approach the spiritual meadow of our holy mother Melania's deeds, and gathering there what can be readily plucked, I shall offer those flowers to the ones who are fond of hearing recitations that inflame their virtue and to those who, wishing the greatest benefit, offer their souls to God, the savior of us all. . . .

Life

1. This blessed Melania, then, was foremost among the Romans of senatorial rank. Wounded by the divine love, she had from her earliest

youth yearned for Christ, had longed for bodily chastity. Her parents, because they were illustrious members of the Roman Senate and expected that through her they would have a succession of the family line, very forcibly united her in marriage with her blessed husband Pinian, who was from a consular family, when she was fourteen years old and her spouse was about seventeen. After she had had the experience of marriage and totally despised the world, she begged her husband with much piteous wailing, uttering these words: "If, my lord, you consent to practice chastity along with me and live with me according to the law of continence, I contract with you as the lord and master of my life. If, however, this seems burdensome to you, and if you do not have the strength to bear the burning passion of youth, just look: I place before you all my possessions; hereafter you are master of them and may use them as you wish, if only you will leave my body free so that I may present it spotless, with my soul, to Christ on that fearsome day. For it is in this way that I shall fulfill my desire for God."

At first, however, he neither accepted her proposal nor did he, on the other hand, completely rule out her plan. Rather, he replied to her in these words: "If and when by the ordinance of God we have two children to inherit our possessions, then both of us together shall renounce the world." Indeed, by the will of the Almighty, a daughter was born to them, whom they promptly dedicated to God for the virginal estate.

2. But Melania's heart burned even more strongly with the divine fire. If, as was the custom, she sometimes was sent to the baths by her parents, she went even though she did not want to. When she entered the hot air room, in order to show her obedience, she washed her eyes with warm water, and wiping them with her clothes, she bribed with gifts those who accompanied her so that they would not tell anybody what she had done. Thus the blessed woman constantly had the fear of God before her eyes.

3. The young man, however, was still desirous of worldly glory. Although she frequently asked him to keep bodily chastity, he would not agree, saying that he wanted to have another child.

4. Therefore the saint kept trying to flee and to leave him all her possessions. When this matter was brought to the attention of the holy men,

they advised her to wait a short while longer, so that through her patience she might fulfill the apostolic saying, "Wife, how do you know if you will save your husband?" [1 Cor 7:16] Under her silken clothing she began to wear a coarse woolen garment. Her aunt noticed this and pleaded with her not to be so rash as to clothe herself in such a garment. Melania, however, was exceedingly distressed that she had not escaped notice and begged her not to reveal to her parents what she had done.

5. Later on, when the prayers of the saint had taken effect and she was about to give birth to her second child, the feast of Saint Lawrence arrived. Without taking any rest and having spent the whole night kneeling in her chapel, keeping vigil, at dawn the next day she rose early and went with her mother to the Church of the martyr. With many tears she prayed to God that she might be freed from the world and spend the rest of her days in the solitary life, for this is what she had yearned for from the beginning. And when she returned from the martyr's shrine, she commenced a difficult labor and gave birth prematurely to a child. It was a boy, and after he was baptized, he departed for the Lord.

6. After this, when her blessed husband saw that she was exceedingly troubled and was giving up on life, he lost courage and was himself endangered. Running to the altar, he cried aloud with tears to the Lord for her life. And while he was sitting next to the altar, the saint declared to him: "If you want me to continue living, give your word before God that we will spend the rest of our lives in chastity, and then you will see the power of Christ." And since he was very fearful that he might never see her again alive in the flesh, he promised this joyfully. Because of grace from on high and the young man's promise, she was cheered; she got better and completely regained her health. She took the occasion of her child's death to renounce all her silk clothing.

At this time, their daughter who was devoted to virginity also died. Then both Melania and Pinian hastened to fulfill their promises to God. They would not consent to their parents' desires, and were so unhappy that they refused to eat unless their parents would agree with them and consent to release them so that they could abandon their frivolous and worldly mode of life and experience an angelic, heavenly purpose.

But their parents, whom we mentioned before, were wary of people's reproaches and would not agree to their children's wishes. Melania and Pinian suffered much pain since they were unable to take up the yoke of Christ freely because of their parents' compulsion. They planned with each other to go into seclusion and flee the city. As the blessed woman told us for our edification, while they were plotting these things, as evening was coming on, immediately and suddenly a heavenly perfume descended on them and changed the sadness of their grief to inexpressible joy. Thanking God, they were emboldened against the schemes of the Enemy [the devil].

7. After the passage of some time, her father's last illness finally came upon him. As he loved Christ greatly, he called the blessed ones and said, "Forgive me, my children. I have fallen into a great sin because of my enormous folly. Because I feared the abuses of blasphemous men, I have pained you, by keeping you from your heavenly calling. But now see that I am going to the Lord, and from now on you have the power to gratify your desire for God as you please. May you only intercede on my behalf with God, the ruler of all." They heard these words with much joy. Right away they felt free from fear; they left the great city of Rome and went to her suburban property where they devoted themselves to training in the practice of the virtues. They clearly recognized that it was impossible for them to offer pure worship to God unless they made themselves enemies to the confusions of secular life, just as it is written, "Hear, daughter, and see; turn your ear and forget your people and your father's house, and the king will desire your beauty" [Ps 45:11].

8. When they began the angelic way of life, the blessed Melania was twenty years old and Pinian, who was henceforth her brother in the Lord, was twenty-four years old. Although at the time they were not able to practice rigorous asceticism because of their pampered youth, they clothed themselves in cheap garb. Thus the blessed woman wore a garment that was exceedingly cheap in value and very old, trying in this way to extinguish the beauty of youth. As for Pinian, he then once and for all rejected the magnificent clothes and luxury of his recent life, and garbed himself in Cilician clothes [i.e., good but not fine linen]. The blessed woman was immeasurably saddened to see that he had not yet completely scorned the embellishments of dress. She feared to censure him openly,

however, because he was yet unproven in years and experienced the ardor of youth; she saw that he was still vigorous in body. She therefore changed her approach with him and said to him, "From the time when we began to carry out our promise to God, has your heart not been receptive to the thought of desiring me?" And the blessed man, who knew well the rectitude of his thoughts, affirmed in the Lord's presence, "From the time when we gave our word to God and entered the chaste life, I have looked on you in the same way as your holy mother Albina." Melania then exhorted him, saying, "Then be persuaded by me as your spiritual mother and sister, and give up the Cilician clothes; it is not fitting for a man who has left behind worldly frivolities for the sake of God to wear such things." And he saw that her exhortation was for his own good. Straightaway he obeyed her excellent advice, judging this to be advantageous for the salvation of them both. And changing his Cilician garments, he clothed himself in those of the Antiochene style that were natural-colored and were worth one coin. . . .

15. I shall report on their property by just skimming the surface of things I heard from the mouth of the blessed Pinian. He said that he had as an annual income 120,000 pieces of gold, more or less, not counting that derived from his wife's property. Their movable goods were such that they were too many to be counted. Immediately they began, with zeal, to distribute these, entrusting to the holy men the administration of alms. They sent money to different regions, through one man 40,000 coins, through another 30,000, by another 20,000, through another 10,000, and the rest they distributed as the Lord helped them do.

The saint herself said to her blessed husband and brother, "The burden of life is very heavy for us, and we are not competent in these circumstances to take on the light yoke of Christ. Therefore let us quickly lay aside our goods, so that we may gain Christ." Pinian received the admonition of the blessed woman as if it came from God, and with generous hands they distributed their goods.

16. Once, when we strongly urged her to tell how they could come from such great heights to such lowliness, Melania began by saying, "Not few were the problems and struggles we endured in the beginning from the Enemy who is hostile to good, until we could divest ourselves of the

burden of so much wealth. We were vexed and distressed because our battle was not against flesh and blood, but, as the apostle says, against the principalities, against the world rulers of this realm of darkness" [Eph 6:12].

"One night we went to sleep, greatly upset, and we saw ourselves, both of us, passing through a very narrow place in a wall. We were totally discomposed in the narrowness, so that all that remained was to give up our souls. When we came through that pain with great suffering," she said, "we found abundant great relief and ineffable joy. God manifested this to us, comforting our faintness of spirit, so that we might be brave concerning the future repose that we would receive after such suffering."

19. Furthermore, they fearlessly gave away the remainder of their possessions in Rome, as we have said before—possessions that were, so to speak, enough for the whole world. For what city or country did not have a share in their enormously good deeds? If we say Mesopotamia and the rest of Syria, all of Palestine, the regions of Egypt and the Pentapolis, would we say enough? But lest we continue on too long, all the West and all the East shared in their numerous good deeds. I myself, of course, when I traveled the road to Constantinople, heard many old men, especially lord Tigrius, the priest of Constantinople, give thanks to the holy ones. When they acquired several islands, they gave them to holy men. Likewise, they purchased monasteries of monks and virgins and gave them as a gift to those who lived there, furnishing each place with a sufficient amount of gold. They presented their numerous and expensive silk clothes at the altars of churches and monasteries. They broke up their silver, of which they had a great deal, and made altars and ecclesiastical treasures from it, and many other offerings to God.

When they had sold their properties around Rome, Italy, Spain, and Campania, they set sail for Africa. Just then Alaric [leader of the Goths who sacked Rome in 410 C.E.] set foot on the property the blessed ones had just sold. Everybody praised the Lord of all things, saying, "Lucky are the ones who anticipated what was to come and sold their possessions before the arrival of the barbarians!" And when they left Rome, the prefect of the city, who was a very ardent pagan, decided along with the entire Senate to have their property confiscated to the public treasury. He was eager to have this accomplished by the next morning. By God's providence, it happened that the people rebelled against him because of a bread shortage. Consequently he was dragged off and killed in the middle of the city. All the others were then afraid and held their peace.

They set sail from Sicily to the most holy bishop Paulinus, to whom even at the beginning they also bade farewell. By the dispensation of God, adverse winds prevented their ship from sailing; a great and sudden storm came upon them. Since there were many people on the boat, a water shortage developed, and for a brief while they were all in danger. When the sailors claimed that this had come about by the wrath of God, the blessed woman said to them, "It is certainly not God's will for us to go to the place we had intended. Therefore give the boat over to what carries it and do not struggle against the winds." They took the saint's advice, stretched the sail, and came to a certain island that the barbarians had blockaded after having carried off the most important men of the city with their wives and children. The barbarians had demanded from them a certain sum of gold which, if they gave it, they would be freed, but if they did not, they themselves would be murdered and the city would be burned by the barbarians. As the saints were disembarking from the ship, the bishop heard of their arrival. He came to them with others, fell on his knees, and said, "We have as much gold as the barbarians want except for 2500 coins." Melania and Pinian willingly presented them with this amount, freeing the whole city from the barbarians. They also gave them an extra 500 coins, and the bread and other provisions they were carrying with them, thus rescuing the suffering people from both famine and distress. And not only did they do this; they provided 500 coins to ransom one distinguished woman in their midst who had been captured by the barbarians.

20. Then they departed from the island and sailed toward Africa, as we mentioned before. When they arrived there, they immediately sold their property in Numidia, Mauretania, and in Africa [the province of Africa Proconsularis] itself. Some of the money they sent for the service of the poor and some for ransoming captives. Thus they distributed the money freely and rejoiced in the Lord and were gladdened, for they were fulfilling in

action what had been written, "He has given funds; he gave to the poor; his righteousness remains from age to age" [Ps 112:9].

When the blessed ones decided to sell all their property, the most saintly and important bishops of Africa (I mean the blessed Augustine, his brother Alypius, and Aurelius of Carthage) advised them, saying, "The money that you now furnish to monasteries will be used up in a short time. If you wish to have memorial forever in heaven and on earth, give both a house and an income to each monastery." Melania and Pinian eagerly accepted the excellent counsel of the holy men and did just as they had been advised by them. Henceforth, advancing toward perfection, they tried to accustom themselves to complete poverty in their living arrangements and in the food they ate.

21. The town of the very blessed bishop Alypius, named Thagaste, was small and exceedingly poor. The blessed ones chose this as their place to live, especially because this aforesaid holy man Alypius was present, for he was most skilled in the interpretation of the Holy Scriptures. Our blessed mother held him dear, for she was a friend of learning. Indeed, she herself was so trained in Scriptural interpretation that the Bible never left her holy hands. She adorned the church of this holy man with revenue as well as offerings of both gold and silver treasures, and valuable veils, so that this church which formerly had been so very poor now stirred up envy of Alypius on the part of the other bishops in that province.

22. They also constructed two large monasteries there, providing them with an independent income. One was inhabited by eighty holy men, and the other by 130 virgins. The holy woman made progress in the virtues. She saw herself become a little lighter from the burden of possessions. Fulfilling the work of Martha, she began henceforth to imitate Mary, who was extolled in the Gospel as having chosen the good part [Luke 10:38–42]. Indeed, in the beginning, Melania would just taste a little oil and take a bit of something to drink in the evening (she had never used wine during her worldly life, because the children of the Roman senatorial class were raised in this way). Then after that she began to mortify her body with strenuous fasting. At first she took food without oil every two days, then every three days, and then every five, so that it was

only on Saturday and Sunday that she ate some moldy bread. She was
zealous to surpass everyone in asceticism.

23. She was by nature gifted as a writer and wrote without mistakes
in notebooks. She decided for herself how much she ought to write every
day, and how much she should read in the canonical books, how much in
the collections of homilies. And after she was satisfied with this activity,
she would go through the *Lives* of the fathers as if she were eating
dessert. Then she slept for a period of about two hours. Straightaway after having gotten up, she roused the virgins who were leading the ascetic
life with her, and said, "Just as the blessed Abel and each of the holy ones
offered first-fruits to God, so we as well in this way should spend the
first-fruits of the night for God's glory. We ought to keep awake and pray
at every hour, for, just as it is written, we do not know at what hour the
thief comes" [Matt 24:42]. She gave strict rules to the sisters with her that
no idle word or reckless laughter should come forth from their mouths.
She also patiently inquired about their thoughts and refused to allow
filthy imaginations to dwell in them in any way.

24. As we said earlier, she fasted from the week of holy Pentecost until Easter, not taking oil at all. Many who knew her well testified that she
never slept outside her sackcloth nor ate on Saturday before she finished
the entire divine office.

25. After she had lived in this ascetic routine for many years, Melania
began to fast on the holy day of Christ's resurrection as well. Her blessed
mother, who imitated the holy women of old (her virtuous life requires
another person to write about it), was greatly grieved. It is enough for me
to say this about Albina, that from the fruit the tree is known, and a glorious fruit comes from a good root. Albina used to make such comments as
these to Melania: "It is not right for a Christian to fast on the day of our
Lord Jesus Christ's resurrection; rather, we should refresh our body just
as we also refresh our spirit." By saying these things, she scarcely persuaded her blessed daughter to take oil for the three days of the holiday
and then return once more to her usual ascetic discipline, just as the excellent farmer who owns a fertile field hastens to his own happy task.

26. The blessed woman read the Old and New Testaments three or
four times a year. She copied them herself and furnished copies to the

saints by her own hands. She performed the divine office in company
with the virgins with her, reciting by heart on her own the remaining
Psalms. So eagerly did she read the treatises of the saints that whatever
book she could locate did not escape her. To the contrary, she read
through the books that were bought, as well as those she chanced upon,
with such diligence that no word or thought remained unknown to her.
So overwhelming was her love of learning that when she read in Latin, it
seemed to everyone that she did not know Greek, and, on the other hand,
when she read in Greek, it was thought that she did not know Latin. . . .

29. Melania yearned so exceedingly for chastity that by money and
admonitions she persuaded many young men and women to stay clear of
licentiousness and an impure manner of life. Those whom she encountered, she taught with these words, "The present life is brief, like a
dream in every way. Why then do we corrupt our bodies that are temples
of the Lord, as the apostle of God states [see 1 Cor 6:19]? Why do we exchange the purity in which Christ teaches us to live for momentary corruption and filthy pleasures? Truly, the value of virginity is so great that
our Lord Jesus Christ deemed it worthy to be born of a virgin." Many
who heard these things were zealous for purity and leaped into the arena
of virtue. Only the Lord himself knows how many saints' feet she
washed, how many servants of God she served, some through money and
some through the exhortation of the word, how many Samaritans, pagans, and heretics she persuaded through money and exhortations to
come back to God! Through him she accomplished such great and numerous feats. . . .

32. Since she had been wounded by the divine love, she could not
bear to live the same life any longer, but prepared herself to contend in
even greater contests. She decided to shut herself up in a tiny cell and to
see no one at all, spending her time uninterruptedly in prayer and fasting. This was impossible to carry out because many profited from her inspired teaching and for this reason everyone bothered her. Thus she did
not carry out her plan, but rather set specific hours for herself when she
would help those who had come to her for good conversation. For the remaining hours, in contrast, she spoke to God in prayer and accomplished
her spiritual work. She had a wooden chest built for herself of such di-

mensions that when she was lying in it, she could turn neither to the
right nor to the left, nor was she free to extend her body. Although she
possessed such great and numerous virtues, she never became proud
about her own righteous deeds, but always made herself lowly, called
herself a useless servant.

33. And sometimes when her mother, full of compassion for her
daughter, went to enter Melania's little cell when she was writing or
reading, Melania would not even recognize her or speak to her until she
finished her usual office. Then she would speak to her as much as was
necessary. Albina, embracing Melania in such a manner, said amid tears,
"I trust that I, too, have a share in your sufferings, my child. For if the
mother of the seven Maccabean children, who in a single hour saw the
tortures of her sons, had eternal joy with them [2 Macc 7], how is it not that
I, who have been more tortured every day than she was, will have that
joy, when I see you thus wearing yourself out and never giving yourself
any pause from such labors?" And again Albina said, "I thank God that I
have received a daughter such as this from the Lord, unworthy as I am."

34. When they had remained in Africa for seven years and had renounced the whole burden of their riches, they at last started out for
Jerusalem, for they had a desire to worship at the Holy Places. They set
sail from Africa and headed eastward, arriving at Alexandria, where the
most holy bishop Cyril received them in a manner worthy of his holiness.
At that time, it just happened that the holy abba Nestoros, a man who
possessed prophetic gifts, was in the city. This holy man was accustomed
to come once a year to the city for the purpose of curing the sick. He also
possessed this gift from the Lord, that he could deliver from diverse diseases those who came to him, using oil that had been blessed. As soon as
the saintly ones, who were great friends of the holy men, heard about
him, they immediately set out to receive spiritual profit. Because of the
immense crowd of people who came to him, they got separated from one
another. The first to enter with the limitless crowd was Pinian, the most
blessed brother of the saint. He was eager to receive the blessing so that
he could leave. The holy man, however, looking intently at him with his
spiritual eyes, recognized the beauty of his soul, seized him, and made
him stand alongside him. Then Melania, the servant of Christ, also came

in with a great crowd. When Nestoros saw her, he recognized her with his spiritual eyes and made her stand with her brother. Thus when Melania's holy mother came in third, Nestoros stopped her and made her stand with the two. After he had dismissed the whole crowd, he began to tell them first with exhortation and prophetic speech what diverse troubles they had endured in their renunciation. He counseled them like his own children and exhorted them not to lose heart, since the goal of affliction is to have unutterable bliss. He said, "For the sufferings of the present time are not worthy to be compared to the coming glory that is to be revealed to us" [Rom 8:18].

35. Thus being much encouraged and praising God even more, they set sail for Jerusalem and hastened on to their destination. They stayed in the Church of the Holy Sepulcher. Since they themselves did not want to distribute with their own hands the gold left to them, they gave it to those who were entrusted with administering charity for the poor. They did not wish for people to see them doing good deeds. They were in such a state of poverty that the holy woman Melania assured us of this: "When we first arrived here, we thought of inscribing ourselves on the church's register and of being fed with the poor from alms." Thus they became extremely poor for the sake of the Lord, who himself became poor for our sakes and who took the form of a servant.

It happened that Melania was sick when we were first in Jerusalem and had nowhere to lie down except in her sackcloth. A certain well-born virgin presented her with a pillow as a gift. When she became healthy again, she spent her time in reading and prayer, sincerely serving the Lord.

36. Thus Melania and her mother lived together by themselves. Melania was not quick to see anyone except the holy and highly reputed bishops, especially those who stood out for their doctrine, so that she might spend the time of their conferences inquiring about the divine word. As we said before, she wrote in notebooks and fasted during the week. Every evening, after the Church of the Holy Sepulcher was closed, she remained at the cross until the psalm-singers arrived. Then she departed for her cell and slept for a short while. . . .

41. When the Lord called her holy mother, she departed to his saints

to receive the promised goods. When they had carried Albina's remains to the Mount of Olives with much honor and singing of Psalms, Melania straightaway remained there in a dark cell, no longer wishing to live in the city. She spent that year in great grief, ascetic discipline, and fasting, and at the end of it she had a monastery built for herself and decided to save other souls along with herself. She asked her brother to gather some virgins for her. So there arose a monastery of ninety virgins, more or less, whom she trained as a group from the first not to associate with a man. . . .

49. . . . After her brother, whom we have mentioned, fell asleep in the Lord, Melania remained in the Apostoleion that she had constructed a short time before and in which she had also deposited the remains of the blessed man. She remained here for about four years, very much wearing herself out in fasting, vigils, and constant sorrow. After these things occurred, aroused by divine zeal, she wished to build a monastery for holy men that they might carry out their nightly and daily psalmody without interruption at the place of the Ascension of the Lord and in the grotto where the Savior talked with his holy disciples about the end of time. Some people balked at her good proposal, however, alleging that she would not be able to complete such a great undertaking because of her extreme poverty. But the Lord, who is rich in everything, fulfilled the wishes of that holy soul by arranging for a certain man who loved Christ to offer her two hundred coins. Receiving them with great joy, she called the priest with her, whom she had taken from the world and presented to God as an offering—and that man was my own pitiable self—and said to him, "Since you believe that you will receive the compensation for this labor from the Lord in the ages to come, take these few coins and buy stones for us, so that we may begin the construction of the men's monastery, in the name of our Lord Jesus Christ. Thus while I am still in the flesh I may see both the divine service being offered without interruption in the church and the bones of my mother and my master find rest through their chanting."

And when, under God, she began this project, the Lord who worked with her in all things completed the vast undertaking in one year, so that everyone was astounded to learn that truly it was by a heavenly influence that the work had been accomplished. She lodged there holy men, lovers of God, who cheerfully performed the divine service in the Church of Christ's Ascension and in that of the Apostles, where the blessed ones were also buried. . . .

60. I shall try to recall a few of the many miracles that the Lord performed through her, for I am not capable of relating all of them, both because of their great number and because of my personal incapacity. Now one day a certain young woman was seized by a very evil demon. Her mouth and her lips were shut for many days. It was completely impossible for her either to talk or to take nourishment, so that quite soon she was in danger of starvation. Many doctors had lavished a number of drugs on her but were not able to make her move her lips even a bit. When medical skill had proven to be incapable of driving out the demon, then at last they carried her with an escort to the saint, with her parents following along. The blessed woman, who shunned the glory of men, said to them, "Since I am a sinner, I am incapable of doing this. Let us bring her to the holy martyrs and by their direct intercession, the God who loves humankind will cure her." As they arrived there, the saint earnestly called upon the Master of all things. She took the oil consecrated from the relics of the holy martyrs and with this she touched the mouth of the sick woman three times, saying in a clear voice, "In the name of our Lord Jesus Christ, open your mouth." And straightaway at the calling on the Lord, the demon, who was disgraced or rather frightened, fled, and the woman opened her mouth. The saint gave her something to eat and all who saw this glorified God. The woman who had been cured returned home with great joy, praising the Lord. Likewise another woman who had suffered from the same sickness was cured by Melania.

61. Once again, a woman had a very difficult labor and the fetus died in the mother's womb. The wretched woman could neither live nor die. When the true servant of the Lord heard about this, she was very sympathetically grieved. Pitying the woman, she said to the virgins with her, "Let us go to visit the sick woman, so that by seeing the suffering of those who live in the world, we can also thus understand from how many difficulties God has relieved us." When they arrived at the house where the woman was who was dangerously ill, they said a prayer. Immediately the

suffering woman, scarcely able to whisper in a weak voice, said to the saint, "Have pity on me." Melania stood there a long time supplicating God earnestly on the woman's behalf. She loosened her own belt which bound her around and placed it on the woman, announcing, "I have received this blessing from a great man, and I believe that his prayers will cure her speedily." Immediately the dead fetus emerged. . . . Melania said in humility, "The belt belongs to a saint, whose prayers cured the endangered woman." Thus she always attributed her virtuous deeds to the saints. . . .

63. After a certain time had passed, Melania, like an expert runner who having come round the stadium desires the trophy, was also eager to be released to be with Christ. For she groaned (in the apostle's phrase), desiring "to clothe herself in the garment of heaven" [2 Cor 5:2]. And when the holy Nativity of the Savior arrived, she said to her cousin, lady Paula, "Let us go to holy Bethlehem, for I do not know if I will hereafter see this festival in the flesh." Thus they went there and kept the whole vigil; at dawn they participated in the fearsome mysteries.

Finally the saint, as if she had received an answer from God, said the following to her cousin: "Pray on my behalf, for henceforth you will be celebrating the birth of the Lord alone. For me, the goal of bodily life is to be finished after a short while." When Paula heard this, she was greatly disturbed. After they returned from holy Bethlehem to the monastery, the saint, not reckoning at all the labor of the vigil and the journey, straightway went out into the grotto and prayed intensely.

64. On the next day we went to the martyrium of the holy protomartyr Stephen—for the memorial of his falling asleep had arrived—and after we had held a service there, we returned to the monastery. During the vigil, I read first, then three sisters read, and last of all Melania herself read from Acts about the death of the holy Stephen. When she had completed the extent of the reading, all the sisters said to the holy woman, "Be in good health for many years, and may you celebrate many memorials of the saints." But Melania, as if she had received complete assurance from on high, answered them, "You stay in good health, too, for you will no longer hear me read." At this word all the women were deeply moved, for they believed that she said these words as a prophecy. . . .

All were grieving greatly because they were about to lose such a good guide and divinely-inspired teacher. She left them and said to my own humble self, "Let us go to the martyrium of the men's monastery in order that we may pray, for there too are laid away the relics of Saint Stephen." With deep sorrow I did according to the command of the holy woman and followed her.

When we entered the martyrium, she, as if she were already in conversation with the holy martyrs, prayed with tears, saying, "God, the Lord of the holy martyrs, who knows all things before they come to pass, you know what I chose from the beginning, that I love you with all my heart, and from fear of you, my bone has been glued to my flesh. For I have given my soul and body to you, who formed me in my mother's womb, and you have taken my right hand to guide me in your counsel. . . . Purify me, your servant, so that in my coming to you, the steps of my soul may be unfettered and the evil demons of this air not hold me back, but that I may go to you spotless, guided by your holy angels. May I be deemed worthy of your heavenly bridal chamber." . . .

Next she entreated the holy martyrs, saying, "Athletes of the Lord who shed your honored blood in order to confess him, be compassionate to your humble servant who always reverenced your holy relics. Just as you have always listened to me, do so also now; you who speak openly, be my ambassadors to the God who loves mankind, so that he may receive my soul in peace and guard the monasteries up to the end in the fear of him."

She had scarcely finished her prayer when right away her slight frame began to shiver. When we returned to the monastery of the virgins, we came upon the sisters still celebrating the psalmody. And I, who was in anguish at being overwhelmed by distress, could not stand up any longer and went away to rest for a while, but Melania once again went to the divine office.

When the sisters saw that hence she had become weaker, they strongly begged her and said, "Rest yourself a bit, for you are not strong enough to stand." She did not agree to that and replied, "Not until we have completed the morning hymns." After the entire liturgy was completed, she departed and lay down. Gripped by a pain in the side, she became much weaker. She sent for my humble self and all the sisters, and began to speak to me: "Behold, I am going to the Lord. Therefore pray for me." And I was deeply pained in my heart when I heard this.

65. Once more she said to the virgins, "I beg you to pray for me, because I have never wished evil on any of you. Even if I at any time spoke a harsh word to one of you, I did it out of spiritual love. Therefore consider yourselves as true servants of Christ. Spend the remainder of your lifetimes in all knowledge, in order that you may have bright lamps on that day and be pleasing to the heavenly Bridegroom." . . . Having said these things, she desired to be placed in the oratory, and said, "Carry me close to the holy martyrs."

66. Then when her pains increased even more, she said to us, "The day has been fulfilled." All lamented bitterly, especially the virgins who mourned, since they were being deprived of a truly tender mother. When the saint saw that my heart as well was very pained, she said to me, on the fifth day of her illness, which was also the day she died, "My child, as much as you may pray and weep, it benefits nothing. For I have heard a voice saying in my heart that it is necessary that I be completely freed from the bonds of the body and go out to the Lord, according to his command." When the Lord's day was dawning, she said to me before sunrise, "Do me the honor of celebrating for us the holy offering." And while I was performing the offering, because of my great grief I was not able to speak up. When Melania did not hear the epiclesis [the calling down of the Holy Spirit on the Eucharistic elements], she, who was in total agony, indicated to me while I was standing at the altar, "Raise your voice so that I will hear the epiclesis." [In section 67 and the first part of 68, Melania bids farewell to her bishop and clergy as well as residents of her monasteries.]

68. And as she had given instructions to everybody in peace, she said, "Do pray." Thus she dismissed all of them, saying, "Leave me now to rest." About the ninth hour she began to lose consciousness. We assumed that she had died and tried to stretch her legs, but she recovered a little and whispered in a weak voice to my humble person, "My hour has not yet come." As for me, I was not able to bear the grief that overcame me, and answered her, "When the hour comes, will you tell us?" And she replied, "Yes." She said this, I think, to indicate that there was no need to

adjust her body after her death. And some holy men remained with me, for that had always been her prayer, to give over her spirit in the midst of holy men.

Again came the Christ-loving bishop, and the anchorites who lived around Eleutheropolis, most holy men, who said to the blessed woman, "You have fought the good fight on earth. Go with joy to the Lord, as all the angels rejoice. But we are greatly distressed that we will be separated from your beneficent presence." And she uttered to them her last word, "As the Lord has pleased, thus has it come to pass." And immediately she gave over her holy soul to her Master, gently and peaceably, in joy and exaltation, on the evening of the same holy Lord's day, in order that she might show in this her great love for the Lord and for his holy resurrection.

Her holy remains needed no further adornment, for her legs were found stretched, both her hands were folded on her chest, and her eyelids had naturally closed. As she had ordered, the holy fathers who had gathered from different places later buried her, after they passed the entire night in solemnly singing Psalms and readings.

69. Her burial garments were worthy of her holiness. I think it necessary for me to describe them for the benefit of those who may read this account. She had the tunic of a certain saint, the veil of another servant of God, another garment without sleeves, the belt of another which she had worn while she was alive, and the hood of another. Instead of a pillow she had a hood made from the hair of another saint, which we made into a cushion and placed under her honored head. For it was fitting that she be buried in the garments of those whose virtues she had acquired while she was living. She had no burial cloth, except the linen with which we wrapped her from without. . . .

4. Olympias

Granddaughter of Ablabius, who was elevated to senatorial rank by the Emperor Constantine, Olympias, born ca. 365, was married to Nebridius, a prefect of the city of Constantinople, in about 384 C.E. He died soon after the marriage. Thus widowed at the age of twenty, she refused to marry again, despite imperial pressure from the emperor Theodosius I, who eventually allowed her to dispose of her sizable wealth as she wished and to adopt the ascetic life. She was ordained deaconess by Nectarius, bishop of Constantinople, when she was not yet thirty years old, even though the official age for that office was sixty. When Nectarius died in 397, the monk and theologian John Chrysostom succeeded him; he and Olympias maintained a friendship that lasted through Chrysostom's exile. She used her wealth to support the ecclesiastical institution in Constantinople and founded a convent for women near the cathedral. She is especially noted for her charitable activities, especially those that benefited the clergy. She was exiled as a consequence of her support of Chrysostom; her date of death is uncertain (between 407–419 C.E.).

The Life of Olympias, Deaconess (selections)

1. The Kingdom of our Savior Jesus Christ, existing before the ages and shining forth to ages without end, confers immortality on those who have served as its shield-bearers, who have completed the race and kept their faith in God spotless and steadfast. There are those who have practiced hospitality, the crown of perfections, such as the holy forefather Abraham and his nephew Lot; others have fought for self-control, as the holy Joseph; others have contended with sufferings to win patience, as the blessed Job; others have delivered their bodies to the fire and to tortures in order to receive the crown of incorruptibility. Not fearing the outrages of tyrants, but as noble combatants they have trampled the devil under foot and have been received as inheritors of the Kingdom of God. Among them was Thecla, a citizen of heaven, a martyr who conquered in many contests, the holy one among women, who despised wealth, hated the sharp and transitory pleasures of this world, refused a pecunious marriage and confessed that she would present herself a chaste virgin to her true Bridegroom. . . . Olympias walked in the footsteps of this saint, Thecla, in every virtue of the divinely-inspired way of life. Olympias, most serious and zealous for the road leading to heaven, followed the intent of the divine Scriptures in everything and was perfected through these things.

2. She was daughter according to the flesh of Seleucus, one of the *comites* [holders of major civil and military offices], but according to the spirit, she was the true child of God. It is said that she was descended from

Ablabius, who was governor, and she was bride for a few days of Nebridius, the prefect of the city of Constantinople, but in truth she did not grace the bed of anyone. For it is said that she died an undefiled virgin, having become a partner of the divine Word, a consort of every true humility, a companion and servant of the holy, catholic, and apostolic church of God. . . .

3. Again she could have used the apostolic rule which says, "I wish young widows to marry, run a household" [1 Tim 5:14], but she did not agree to this, although she had birth, wealth, a very expensive education, a naturally good disposition, and was adorned with the bloom of youth; like a gazelle, she leapt over the insufferable snare of a second marriage. "For the law was not laid down for the righteous man, but for the unruly, the impure, and the insatiable" [1 Tim 1:9]. Through a certain demonic jealousy, it transpired that her untimely widowhood became the subject of mischief. She was falsely accused before the emperor Theodosius of having dispensed her goods in a disorderly fashion. Since indeed she was his relation, he took pains to unite her in marriage with a certain Elpidius, a Spaniard, one of his own relatives. He directed many persistent entreaties to her and when he failed to achieve his goal, he was annoyed. The pious Olympias, however, explained her position to the emperor Theodosius: "If my King, the Lord Jesus Christ, wanted me to be joined with a man, he would not have taken away my first husband immediately. Since he knew that I was unsuited for the conjugal life and was not able to please a man, he freed him, Nebridius, from the bond and delivered me of this very burdensome yoke and servitude to a husband, having placed upon my mind the happy yoke of continence."

4. She clarified these things to the emperor Theodosius in this manner, before the plot against the most holy John, patriarch of Constantinople. The emperor, when he had heard the testimony against the pious Olympias, commanded the man then prefect of the city, Clementius, to keep her possessions under guard until she reached her thirtieth year, that is, her physical prime. And the prefect, having received the guardianship from the emperor, oppressed her to such a degree at Elpidius' urging (she did not have the right either to meet with the notable bishops nor to come near the church) so that groaning under the strain,

she would meekly bear the option of marriage. But she, even more grateful to God, responded to these events by proclaiming, "You have shown toward my humble person, O sovereign master, a goodness befitting a king and suited to a bishop, when you commanded my very heavy burden to be put under careful guard, for the administration of it caused me anxiety. But you will do even better if you order that it be distributed to the poor and to the churches, for I prayed much to avoid the vainglory arising from the apportionment, lest I neglect true riches for those pertaining to material things."

5. The emperor, upon his return from the battle against Maximus [leader of an uprising in 388 C.E.], gave the order that she could exercise control over her own possessions, since he had heard of the intensity of her ascetic discipline. But she distributed all of her unlimited and immense wealth and assisted everyone, simply and without distinction. For the sake of many she surpassed that Samaritan of whom an account is given in the holy Gospels [Luke 10:29–37]. . . .

Then straightway after the distribution and sealing up of all her goods, there was rekindled in her the divine love and she took refuge in the haven of salvation, the great, catholic, and apostolic church of this royal city. She followed to the letter with intelligence the divinely-inspired teachings of the most holy archbishop of this sacred church, John, and gave to him for this holy church (imitating also in this act those ardent lovers and disciples of Christ who in the beginning of salvation's proclamation brought to the feet of the apostles their possessions [Acts 4:32–5:11]) ten thousand pounds of gold, twenty thousand of silver, and all of her real estate situated in the provinces of Thrace, Galatia, Cappadocia Prima, and Bithynia; and more, the houses belonging to her in the capital city, the one situated near the most holy cathedral, which is called "the house of Olympias"; together with the house of the tribune, complete with baths, and all the buildings near it; a mill; and a house which belonged to her in which she lived near the public baths of Constantinople; and another house of hers which was called the "house of Evander"; as well as all of her suburban properties.

6. Then by the divine will she was ordained deaconess of this holy cathedral of God and she built a monastery at an angle south of it. All the

houses lying near the holy church and all the shops which were at the
southern angle mentioned were torn down for the project. She constructed a path from the monastery up to the narthex of the holy church, and in
the first quarter she enclosed her own chambermaids, numbering fifty,
all of whom lived in purity and virginity. Next, Elisanthia, her relative
who had seen the good work pleasing to God, which God gave to her to
carry out, also herself a virgin, emulating the divine zeal, bade farewell to
the ephemeral and empty things of life with her sisters Martyria and Palladia, also virgins. Then the three entered with all the others, having
made over in advance all of their possessions to the same holy monastery.
Likewise also Olympia, the niece of the aforesaid holy Olympias, with
many other women of senatorial families, chose the Kingdom of Heaven
and disdained these lowly things below which drag us down, in accordance with the grace and good favor of God who wishes all to be saved
[see 1 Tim 2:4] and who fosters the divine love in them. They entered also
with the rest, so that all those who gathered together according to the
grace of God in that holy fold of Christ numbered two hundred and fifty,
all adorned with the crown of virginity and practicing the most exalted
life which befits the saints.

7. When these events had transpired in this manner by divine assistance, the noble servant of God Olympias again brought to the above-
mentioned hallowed church through the most holy patriarch John the
entire remainder of all her real estate, situated in all the provinces, and
her interest in the public bread supply. And he also ordained as deaconesses of the holy church her three relatives, Elisanthia, Martyria, and
Palladia, so that the four deaconesses would be able to be together without interruption in the most sacred monastery founded by her.

8. One was struck with amazement at seeing certain things in the
holy chorus and angelic institution of these holy women: their incessant
continence and sleeplessness, the constancy of their praise and thanksgiving to God, their "charity which is the bond of perfection" [Col 3:14],
their stillness. For no one from the outside, neither man nor woman, was
permitted to come upon them, the only exception being the most holy patriarch John, who visited continuously and sustained them with his most
wise teachings. Thus fortified each day by his divinely-inspired instruc-

tion, they kindled in themselves the divine love so that their great and holy love streamed forth to him. The pious and blessed Olympias (who in these matters too imitated the women disciples of Christ who served him from their possessions [Luke 8:1–3]) prepared for the holy John his daily provisions and sent them to the bishop, for there was not much separation between the episcopal residence and the monastery, only a wall. And she did this not only before the plots against him, but also after he was banished; up to the end of his life she provided for all his expenses as well as for those who were with him in his exile.

9. Then the devil could not bear the great and wondrous way of life of these pious women, the way of life, first of all, consistently made straight by God's grace, and secondly, a way made straight by the uninterrupted teaching of the most holy patriarch. Evil men who were hateful and had enmity to John among the holy men because he was no respecter of persons in his scrutiny of the unrighteous, the devil, the hater of good, suborned and struck with the arrow of calumny, and they contrived a diabolical machination against both him, i.e., John, and that holy woman. He was slandered by them not only in respect to her, but also concerning ecclesiastical affairs; according to their whim, they condemned and exiled him. The herald and teacher of truth, however, received the assaults of his antagonists like a noble athlete and carried off the prize of victory, departing the storm of the present life and being transposed to the calm above. And this pious woman after his exile did not give way but made a motion for his recall to every royal and priestly person. The opposition encompassed her with numerous evils; they stitched together slanders and untimely abuse against her until the occasion when they made her appear before the city prefect for interrogation by him.

10. When they saw her openness concerning the truth, they could not bear the nobility and immutability of her love for God. They wished to put a stop to the constant activity in which she was engaged on behalf of the holy John's recall and they sent her as well into exile in Nicomedia, the capital city of the province of Bithynia. But she, strengthened by the divine grace, nobly and courageously, for the sake of love of God, bore the storms of trials and diverse tribulations which came upon her. The whole rest of her life she passed in the capital city of Nicomedia, per-

forming every ascetic act and maintaining her rule of life unchanged
there. Victorious in the good fight, she crowned herself with the crown of
patience, having turned over her flock by the divine allotment to Marina,
among the blessed, who was her relative and spiritual daughter, whom
she had received from the undefiled and salvatory baptism; she prayed
that she receive in turn the souls unto herself and be preserved in tran-
quillity in all things. And Marina did this for Olympias, not only for the
remaining time which the holy Olympias passed in the metropolis of
Nicomedia, but also after her death. For when the pious woman was
about to join the holy fathers, both to be set free from the present life and
to be with Christ, again she decreed in writing that the aforesaid Marina
of divine choice exhibit much care and succor, and committed to her, after God, all the sisters and their care. Having done this, she escaped from
the storm of human woes and crossed over to the calm haven of our
souls, Christ the God.

11. But before her holy body was buried, she appeared in a dream to
the metropolitan of the same city of Nicomedia, saying, "Place my remains in a casket, put it on a boat, let the boat go adrift into the stream,
and at the place where the boat stops, disembark onto the ground and
place me there." The metropolitan did what had been told him in the vision concerning Olympias and put the casketed body in the boat and let
the boat loose into the stream. Toward the hour of midnight the boat
reached the shore in front of the gallery of the pure house of the holy
apostle Thomas which is in Brochthoi [a suburb of Constantinople] and there
it rested without advancing further. At the same hour an angel of the
Lord appeared in a dream to the superior and to the sacristan of the
same august house, saying, "Rise and put the casket which you have
found in the boat which has come to anchor on the shore in front of the
gallery in the sanctuary." When they heard this, they saw all the church
gates open by themselves, but since they were still asleep, they thought
that the event was an illusion. Having secured the gates again, there appeared to them once more the previous vision. Still a third time, the angel pressed them with much earnestness and said, "Go out and take the
casket of the holy Olympias, for she has suffered much for the sake of
God, and put the casket in the sanctuary." Then they arose, again saw the
gates of the church open, and no longer remained disbelieving. Taking

the holy Gospels, the cross, the candelabra with candles, along with the incense, they went out praying into the gallery and found her holy remains in the boat. They called together all the female and male ascetics, and holding the candles and making great praise and thanksgiving to God, they deposited her holy remains in the sanctuary of the aforementioned venerable house of the holy apostle Thomas in Brochthoi. People could see numerous cures taking place at her holy tomb; impure spirits were banished and many diverse illnesses departed from those afflicted with them. And the holy, pious blessed servant of God, Olympias, ended her life in the month of July, on the 25th, in the reign of Arcadius, the most divine and pious emperor. She is numbered in the choir of the pious confessors and reigns together with the immortal King, Christ our God, for ages without end. . . .

13. Let these things be said. I have deemed it necessary and entirely useful for the profit of many to run over in the narrative one by one the holy virtues of the noble servant of God, Olympias, who is among the saints. For no place, no country, no desert, no island, no distant setting, remained without a share in the benevolence of this famous woman; rather, she furnished the churches with liturgical offerings and helped the monasteries and convents, the beggars, the prisoners, and those in exile; quite simply, she distributed her alms over the entire inhabited world. And the blessed Olympias herself burst the supreme limit in her almsgiving and her humility, so that nothing can be found greater than what she did. She had a life without vanity, an appearance without pretense, character without affectation, a face without adornment; she kept watch without sleeping, she had an immaterial body, a mind without vainglory, intelligence without conceit, an untroubled heart, an artless spirit, charity without limits, unbounded generosity, contemptible clothing, immeasurable self-control, rectitude of thought, undying hope in God, ineffable almsgiving; she was the ornament of all the humble and was in addition worthily honored by the most holy patriarch John. For she abstained from eating meat and for the most part she went without bathing. And if a need for a bath arose through sickness (for she suffered constantly in her stomach), she came down to the waters with her shift on, out of modesty even for herself, so they said. . . .

15. . . . Engaging in much catechizing of unbelieving women and

making provision for all the necessary things of life, she left a reputation for goodness throughout her whole life which is ever to be remembered. Having called from slavery to freedom her myriad household servants, she proclaimed them to be of the same honor as her own nobility. Or rather, if it is necessary to speak truthfully, they appeared more noble in their way of dress than that holy woman. For there could be found nothing cheaper than her clothing; the most ragged items were coverings unworthy of her manly courage. And she cultivated in herself a gentleness so that she surpassed even the simplicity of children themselves. Never any blame, not even from her neighbors, was incurred by that image of Christ, but her whole intolerable life was spent in penitence and in a great flood of tears. One was more likely to see the fount run dry in the trenches than her eyes, lowered, always gazing on Christ, leave off crying for awhile. . . .

Women in Desert Asceticism

In the deserts of Egypt, Syria, and Palestine from the fourth century onward, solitary and communal forms of ascetic life and practice began to flourish. Although most of the solitary desert ascetics whose memory was preserved were men, a few women also practiced this extreme form of physical and spiritual discipline. Many more women lived in the nunneries established by Pachomius (ca. 292–346) in upper Egypt. The following passages present both solitary (anchorite) and communal (coenobitic) women.

1. The Nun who Feigned Madness

Palladius, monk and historian of monasticism (ca. 365–425), visited many of the desert ascetics as well as the monasteries in the Egyptian desert and recorded brief anecdotal stories about the figures he met. The following selection is included to represent women living the monastic life in the desert.

Palladius, *Lausiac History* 34

1. In this monastery [on the upper Nile in Egypt, close to the monastery of Pachomius in Tabennesi] there was another maiden who feigned madness and demon-possession. The others felt such contempt for her that they never ate with her, which pleased her entirely. Taking herself to the kitchen she used to perform every menial service and she was, as the saying goes, "the sponge of the monastery," really fulfulling the Scriptures, "If any man among you seem to be wise in this world, let him become a fool that he may be wise" [1 Cor 3:18]. She wore a rag around her head—all the others had their hair closely cropped and wore cowls. In this way she used to serve.

2. Not one of the four hundred ever saw her chewing all the years of her life. She never sat down at table or partook of a particle of bread, but she wiped up with a sponge the crumbs from the tables and was satisfied with scouring pots. She was never angry at anyone, nor did she grumble or talk, either little or much, although she was maltreated, insulted, cursed, and loathed.

3. Now an angel appeared to Saint Piteroum, the famous anchorite dwelling at Porphyrites [between the Nile River and the Red Sea], and said to him, "Why do you think so much of yourself for being pious and residing in such a place as this? Do you want to see someone more pious than yourself, a woman? Go to the women's monastery at Tabennisi and there you will find one with a band on her head. She is better than you are.

4. "While being cuffed about by such a crowd she has never taken her heart off God. But you dwell here and wander about cities in your mind." And he who had never gone away left that monastery and asked the prefects to allow him to enter the monastery of women. They admitted him, since he was well on in years and, moreover, had a great reputation.

5. So he went in and insisted upon seeing all of them. She did not appear. Finally he said to them: "Bring them all to me, for she is missing." They told him: "We have one inside in the kitchen who is touched"—that is what they call the afflicted ones. He told them: "Bring her to me. Let me see her." They went to call her; but she did not answer, either because she knew of the incident or because it was revealed to her. They

seized her forcibly and told her: "The holy Piteroum wishes to see you"—
for he was renowned.

6. When she came he saw the rag on her head and, falling down at
her feet, he said, "Bless me!" In similar manner she too fell down at his
feet and said, "Bless me, lord." All the women were amazed at this and
said, "Father, take no insults. She is touched." Piteroum then addressed
all the women: "You are the ones who are touched! This woman is spiritual mother"—or so they call them spiritually—"to both you and me, and
I pray that I may be deemed as worthy as she on the day of judgment."

7. Hearing this, they fell at his feet, confessing various things—one
how she had poured leavings of her plate over her; another had beaten
her with her fists; another had blistered her nose. So they confessed various and sundry outrages. After praying for them, he left. And after a few
days she was unable to bear the praise and honor of the sisters, and all
their apologizing was so burdensome to her that she left the monastery.
Where she went and where she disappeared to, and how she died, nobody knows.

2. Pelagia

The theme of the harlot who repents and undertakes monastic life, sometimes
even cross-dressing so as to escape detection, was a popular one from the fourth century onward. A sizable hagiographic literature was written about such figures as Saint
Mary Magdalene, a biblical model of repentance, and Saint Mary the Egyptian, famous
among the "saved prostitutes" for having lived alone in the desert. The story of Pelagia
is a classic story of conversion and repentance. Originally written in Greek, this text
was translated into many languages; the present translation is from the Latin version.

James the Deacon, *Life of Saint Pelagia the Harlot*

Preface

We should always have in mind the great mercy of our Lord who
does not will the death of sinners but rather that all should be converted
to repentance and live (1 Tim 2). So, listen to a wonder that happened in
our times. It has seemed good to me, James, to write this to you, holy
brothers, so that by hearing or reading it you may gain the greatest possi-

ble aid for your souls. For the merciful God, who wills that no one should perish, has given us these days for the forgiveness of our sins, since in the time to come He will judge justly and reward everyone according to his works. . . .

Life

1. The most holy bishop of the city of Antioch called together all the bishops nearby about a certain matter; and so eight bishops came, and among them was Nonnus, the most holy man of God, my bishop, a marvelous man and a most observant monk of the monastery called Tabennisis. Because of his incomparable life and most excellent conduct, he had been snatched away from the monastery and ordained bishop. When we had all assembled in the aforesaid city, the bishop of Antioch told us the meeting would be in the church of the most blessed martyr Julianus. So we went out and sat there before the door of the church with the other bishops who had come.

2. When we were seated, the bishops asked my lord Nonnus to speak to them, and at once the holy bishop began to speak words for the edification and salvation of all. Now while we were marveling at his holy teaching, lo, suddenly there came among us the chief actress of Antioch, the first in the chorus in the theater, sitting on a donkey. She was dressed in the height of fantasy, wearing nothing but gold, pearls, and precious stones; even her bare feet were covered with gold and pearls. With her went a great throng of boys and girls all dressed in cloth of gold with collars of gold on their necks, going before and following her. So great was her beauty that all the ages of mankind could never come to the end of it. So they passed through our company, filling all the air with traces of music and the most sweet smell of perfume. When the bishops saw her bare-headed and with all her limbs shamelessly exposed with such lavish display, there was not one who did not hide his face in his veil or his scapular, averting their eyes as if from a very great sin.

3. But the most blessed Nonnus gazed after her very intently for a long space of time. And after she had gone by, he turned around and still gazed after her. Then he turned towards the bishops sitting around him and said, "Were you not delighted by such great beauty?" When they did

not reply, he buried his face on his knees over the holy Bible which he held in his hands and all his emotion came out in tears; sighing deeply, he said again to the bishops, "Were you not delighted by her beauty?" Still they did not answer, so "Indeed," he said, "I was very greatly delighted and her beauty pleased me very much. See, God will place her before his awful and tremendous judgment seat and he will judge her on her gifts, just as he will judge us on our episcopal calling." And he went on to say to the bishops, "What do you think, beloved brothers, how many hours does this woman spend in her chamber giving all her mind and attention to adorning herself for the play, in order to lack nothing in beauty and adornment of the body; she wants to please all those who see her, lest those who are her lovers today find her ugly and do not come back tomorrow. Here are we, who have an almighty Father in heaven offering us heavenly gifts and rewards, our immortal Bridegroom, who promises good things to his watchmen, things that cannot be valued, 'which eye has not seen, nor ear heard, nor has it entered into the heart of man to know what things God has prepared for those who love him' (1 Cor 2:9). What else can I say? When we have such promises, when we are going to see the great and glorious face of our Bridegroom which has a beauty beyond compare, 'upon which the cherubim do not dare to gaze' (1 Pet 1:12), why do we not adorn ourselves and wash the dirt from our unhappy souls, why do we let ourselves lie so neglected?"

4. When he had said all this, Bishop Nonnus took me, his sinful deacon, with him, and we went to the rooms we had been given for our lodging. Going into his bedchamber, the bishop threw himself on the ground with his face to the floor, and beating his breast he wept, saying, "Lord Jesus Christ. I know I am a sinner and unworthy, for today the ornaments of a harlot have shone more brightly than the ornaments of my soul. How can I turn my face towards you? What words can justify me in your sight? I will not hide my heart from you, for you know all its secrets. Alas, I am a sinner and unworthy, for I stand before your altar and I do not offer you a soul adorned with the beauty you want to see in me. She promises to please men; I have promised to please you; and my filthiness makes me a liar. I am naked before earth and heaven, because I do not keep your commandments. I cannot put my hope in anything good that I do, but I

place my trust in your mercy which saves." He said this kind of thing and wept for many hours; that day was a great festival of tears for us.

5. When day came, it was Sunday and after we had completed our night prayers, the holy bishop Nonnus said to me, "I tell you, brother deacon, when I was asleep I was deeply disturbed and I do not understand it." Then he told me the dream he had had: "At the corner of the altar was a black dove, covered with soot, which flew around me, and I could not bear the stench and filth of it. It stood by me until the prayer for the dismissal of the catechumens, and when the deacon announced to the catechumens, 'Depart,' no more was seen of it. After the prayer of the faithful, and the complete oblation had been offered and everyone had been dismissed, I came to the threshold of the house of God, and there I saw the dove again, covered grievously with filth, and again it fluttered around me. Then I held out my hands and drew it to me, and plunged it into the font which was in the antechamber of the holy church and washed off all the dirt with which it was covered and it came out of the water as white as snow. It flew up into the highest heaven and was lost to my sight." When the holy man of God, bishop Nonnus, had recounted his dream, he took me with him and brought me to the cathedral with the rest of the bishops and there we greeted the bishop of Antioch.

6. He went in and preached to the people who came and sat around his throne and when he had read the canon of the holy Gospel, the same bishop of that city held the Gospel book towards the most blessed Nonnus and asked him to speak to the people. Nonnus then opened his mouth and spoke by the wisdom of God, without any set speech or philosophy and with no indiscretion. Filled with the Holy Spirit, he exhorted and urged the people, speaking very earnestly about the future judgment and the good gifts in store in eternity. All the people were moved with compunction by his words, and the floor of the church was awash with the tears of the hearers.

7. Now by the guiding hand of the mercy of God it happened that there came into the church that very harlot about whom I am speaking. What was even more marvelous was that she who was outside the church and had never before entered the house of God and had never before considered her sins, was now suddenly pierced by the fear of the Lord when

she heard Bishop Nonnus preaching to the people. She was so struck that she despaired of herself, and her tears flowed in such a flood that she could not control them. At once she gave orders to two of her servants: "Stay in this place and when holy Nonnus the bishop comes out follow him, find out where he is lodging and come and tell me." The servants did as their mistress ordered them, and followed us as far as the basilica of Saint Julianus which was near the place where we were lodging. They returned home and told their mistress, "He is in the church of the most blessed Julianus." When she heard this at once she sent the same servants for the *dyptiches* [writing tablets] and on them she wrote: "To the holy disciple of Christ, greetings from a sinner and disciple of the devil. I have heard of your God, how he bent the heavens and came down to earth not for the righteous but for the salvation of sinners. So greatly did he humble himself that he came near to publicans, and he whom the cherubim do not dare to look upon (1 Pet 1:12) spoke with sinful people. My lord, you are very holy, and so, just as your lord Jesus showed himself to the harlot in Samaria at the well (John 4:7) will you look upon me, as he did whose follower you are, as I have heard Christians say? If you are a true disciple of Christ, do not reject me, for through you I may deserve to see his face." The holy bishop Nonnus wrote in reply, "Whoever you are, show yourself to God and you will be saved. But I tell you, I am a man, a sinner, and a servant of God, and you would tempt my humanity. But if you really do desire God, have strength and faith and come to me among the other bishops, for I cannot let you see me alone." When the harlot read this, filled with joy she came running to the church of the blessed martyr Julianus, and we were told that she was there. When Nonnus heard this, he called all the bishops around him, and ordered that she should be brought to him. When she came in where the bishops were gathered, she threw herself on the floor and seized the feet of the holy bishop Nonnus saying, "I beg you, my lord, imitate your master the Lord Jesus Christ and pour out on me your goodness and make me a Christian. My lord, I am an ocean of sin, a deep pit of iniquity, and I ask to be baptized."

8. Bishop Nonnus could hardly persuade her to get up, but when she did, he said, "The holy canons say that a harlot may not be baptized unless she has sponsors who will guarantee that she will not return to her old

way of life." When she heard this ruling of the bishops she threw herself on the floor again and seized the feet of Nonnus, washing them with her tears and wiping them with the hair of her head (Luke 7:38) saying: "You will give account for my soul and to you I will confess all the sins I have committed; and you will wash away by baptism all my great sins and wickednesses. You will not now find a place with the saints before God unless you put away from me my evil deeds. Unless you give me rebirth as a bride of Christ and present me to God, you are no more than an apostate and idolater." Then all the bishops and clergy which were there, when they saw how greatly this sinner desired God, were amazed and said they had never before seen such faith and such desire for salvation as in this harlot; and at once they sent me, the sinful deacon, to the bishop of Antioch to tell him all about it and to ask him to send one of his deaconesses back with me. When he heard about it, he rejoiced with great joy saying, "It is right, Bishop Nonnus, that this great work should have waited for you. I know that you will speak for me in this matter." At once he sent back with me the lady Romana, the first of the deaconesses. When we got back, we found the harlot still at the feet of the holy bishop Nonnus, who was with difficulty urging her to get up, saying, "Get up, my daughter, so that I may exorcise you." Then he said to her, "Do you confess all your sins?" To which she replied, "I have looked so closely into my heart that I cannot find there any single good action. I know my sins and they are more than the sand upon the seashore; water like the sea is little compared to the extent of my sins. But I trust in your God that he will forgive me the whole extent of my sinfulness and look upon me again." Then the holy bishop Nonnus said, "Tell me, what is your name?" and she replied, "I was called Pelagia by my parents but the people of Antioch have called me Margaret (pearl) because of the amount of jewelry with which my sins have adorned me; for I am decked out as a slave for the devil." Nonnus said to her, "Your natural name is Pelagia?" To which she replied, "Yes, my lord." Then Nonnus exorcised her and baptized her, placing on her the sign of the cross, and he gave her the body of Christ. And with the lady Romana he was godparent to her and the deaconess received her and took her to the place of the catechumens while we remained where we were. Then the bishop said to me, "I tell you, brother deacon, today we are rejoicing with the angels of God, with the bread and wine of spiritual joy beyond measure, because of the salvation of this girl."

9. While we were eating some food, we suddenly heard sounds as of a man suffering violence and the devil cried out, saying, "Alas, alas, what am I suffering from this decrepit old man? It was not enough for you to snatch from me three thousand Saracens and baptize them, and obtain them for your God. It was not enough for you that you took over Heliopolis and gave it to your God when it belonged to me and all who lived there worshipped me. But now you have taken my greatest hope from me and now more than ever I cannot bear your schemes. Oh, how I suffer because of that accursed man! Cursed be the day on which you were born! I am so weakened that a river of tears flows from me, for my hope is taken away." The devil said all this outside, crying and lamenting, and everyone heard him. When she returned, he said to the newly-baptized girl, "My lady Pelagia, why are you doing this to me? Why have you become my Judas? For was not he also crowned with glory and honor and became an apostate by betraying his lord? This is what you have done to me!" The holy Nonnus said to her, "Make the sign of the cross in the name of Christ." And she made the sign of the cross in the name of Christ and she blew at the demon and at once he disappeared.

10. Two days later, when Pelagia was asleep in her room with the holy Romana her godmother, the devil appeared to her in the night and awakened Pelagia the servant of God, saying, "I ask you, my lady Margaret, were you not once rich with gold and silver? Did I not adorn you with gold and jewels? Tell me, how have I displeased you? Tell me, so that I may make amends, for you have made me a very great cause for mockery among the Christians." Then the handmaid Pelagia made the sign of the cross and blew at the demon, saying, "My God who snatched me out of your teeth and led me into the heavenly bridal chamber will resist you for me." At once the devil disappeared.

11. On the third day after the baptism of the holy Pelagia, she called her servant who was in charge of all her goods and said to him, "Go to my rooms and make an inventory of all the gold and silver, the ornaments and the precious clothes, and bring it to me." The servant did as his mistress told him and reported it all to her. At once she sent for holy Nonnus through the holy Romana her godmother, and she placed all she

had in his hands, saying, "Lord, these are the riches with which Satan ensnared me; I place them at your disposal; do with them whatever you think is right, for my choice is the riches of Christ." At once the bishop called the senior custodian of the church and in her presence he gave all her goods into his hands saying, "I charge you, by the undivided Trinity, do not let any of this remain with the bishop or with the church, but let it all be expended on the widows and orphans and the poor, so that whatever evil clings to it may be removed by this good use and the riches of sin become treasures of righteousness. But if you sit lightly to this promise and either you or anyone else keep any of it, let anathema come upon you and them and their houses, and let them have a part with those who cry, 'Crucify, crucify.'" Pelagia then called to all her servants, boys and girls, and set them free and gave each a collar of gold from her own hand and said, "Make haste to free yourselves from this wicked world, so full of sin, so that we who have been together in this world may remain together without grief in that life which is most blessed."

12. On the eighth day when it is the custom for the baptized to take off their white robes, Pelagia rose in the night, though we did not know it, and took off her baptismal dress and put on a tunic and breeches belonging to the holy bishop Nonnus; and from that day she was never seen again in the city of Antioch. The holy lady Romana wept bitterly, but the holy bishop Nonnus said to her, "Do not weep, my daughter, but rejoice with great joy, for Pelagia has chosen the better part like Mary whom the Lord preferred to Martha in the Gospel" (Luke 10:42). Now Pelagia went to Jerusalem and built herself a cell on the Mount of Olives and there she prayed to the Lord.

13. After a little while, the bishop of Antioch called the bishops together, so that they might all go back to their own homes. Three or four years later, I, James the deacon, wanted to go to Jerusalem to worship the resurrection of Christ and I asked the bishop to let me go. When he gave me his blessing he said to me, "Brother deacon, when you reach the city of Jerusalem, ask the whereabouts of a certain brother Pelagius, a monk and a eunuch, who has lived there for some years shut up alone; go and visit him; truly I think you will be helped by him." I did not at all understand that he was talking about the handmaid of God, Pelagia.

14. So I reached Jerusalem, and when I had joined in the adoration

of the resurrection of our Lord Jesus Christ, on another day I made inquiries about the servant of God. I went and found him on the Mount of
Olives where he used to pray to the Lord in a small cell which was closed
on all sides, with one small window. I knocked on the window and at
once she appeared and she recognized me, though I did not recognize
her. How could I have known her again, with a face so emaciated by fasting? It seemed to me that her eyes had sunk inwards like a great pit. She
said to me, ""Where have you come from, brother?" And I replied, "I was
sent to you by the order of the holy bishop Nonnus." At once she closed
the little window on me, saying, "Tell him to pray for me, for he is a saint
of God." At once she began the psalms of the third hour. I prayed beside
the cell and then left, much helped by the sight of her angelic face. I returned to Jerusalem and began to visit the brothers in the monasteries
there.

15. Throughout these monasteries, great indeed was the fame of the
monk Pelagius. So I decided to make another journey to speak with her
and receive some saving teaching. When I reached the cell and knocked,
calling her name, there was no reply. I waited a second day and also a
third, calling the name of Pelagius, but I could not hear anyone. Then I
said to myself, "Either there is no one there or he who was a monk has
left." But warned by a nudge from God, I said to myself, "I had better see
if, in fact, he has died." So I broke open the little window; and I saw that
he was dead. So I closed the opening and I was filled with sorrow. I ran
all the way to Jerusalem and told whomever I met that the holy monk
Pelagius who had wrought so many wonders was now at rest. Then the
holy fathers came with monks from several monasteries and the door of
the cell was broken in. They carried out his sacred little body as if it had
been gold and silver they were carrying. When the fathers began to
anoint the body with myrrh, they realized that it was a woman. They
wanted to keep such a wonder hidden but they could not, because of the
crowds of people thronging around, who cried out with a loud voice,
"Glory to you, Lord Jesus Christ, for you have hidden away on earth such
great treasures, women as well as men." So it was known to all the people, and monks came in from all the monasteries and also nuns, from
Jericho and from the Jordan where the Lord was baptized, bearing can-

dles and lamps and singing hymns; and the holy fathers bore her body to its burial. May the life of this harlot, this account of total conversion, join us to her and bring us all to the mercy of the Lord on the day of judgment, to whom be glory and power and honor to the ages of ages. Amen.

3. Theodora, Sarah, and Syncletica

Although the *Apophthegmata patrum*, the "Sayings of the Fathers," was compiled in the version we have today in the late sixth century, many of the sayings date to the beginnings of desert asceticism in the early fourth century. This alphabetical collection presents the spiritual reflections of anchorites (solitaries) in the Egyptian desert. Most of the anchorites were male, but there were some women who lived the ascetic life in the desert, and some of the sayings of these "ammas" (mothers) are reproduced here.

Apophthegmata patrum (selections)

Theodora

2. Amma Theodora said, "Let us strive to enter by the narrow gate. Just as the trees, if they have not stood before the winter's storms cannot bear fruit, so it is with us; this present age is a storm and it is only through many trials and temptations that we can obtain an inheritance in the kingdom of heaven."

3. She also said, "It is good to live in peace, for the wise person practices perpetual prayer. It is truly a great thing for a virgin or a monk to live in peace, especially for the younger ones. However, you should realize that as soon as you intend to live in peace, at once evil comes and weighs down your soul through *accidie* [despondency], faintheartedness, and evil thoughts. It also attacks your body through sickness, debility, weakening of the knees, and all the members. It dissipates the strength of soul and body, so that one believes one is ill and no longer able to pray. But if we are vigilant, all these temptations fall away. There was, in fact, a monk who was seized by cold and fever every time he began to pray, and he suffered from headaches, too. In this condition, he said to himself, 'I am ill, and near to death; so now I will get up before I die and pray.' By reasoning in this way, he did violence to himself and prayed. When he

had finished, the fever abated also. So, by reasoning in this way, the brother resisted, and prayed and was able to conquer his thoughts."

5. The same amma said that a teacher ought to be a stranger to the desire for domination, vainglory, and pride; one should not be able to fool him by flattery, nor blind him by gifts, nor conquer him by the stomach, nor dominate him by anger; but he should be patient, gentle, and humble as far as possible; he must be tested and without partisanship, full of concern, and a lover of souls.

6. She also said that neither asceticism, nor vigils nor any kind of suffering are able to save, only true humility can do that. There was an anchorite who was able to banish the demons; and he asked them, "What makes you go away? Is it fasting?" They replied, "We do not eat or drink." "Is it vigils?" They replied, "We do not sleep." "Is it separation from the world?" "We live in the deserts." "What power sends you away then?" They said, "Nothing can overcome us, but only humility." "Do you see how humility is victorious over the demons?"

10. Another of the old men questioned Amma Theodora saying, "At the resurrection of the dead, how shall we rise?" She said, "As pledge, example, and as prototype we have him who died for us and is risen, Christ our Lord."

Sarah

1. It was related of Amma Sarah that for thirteen years she waged warfare against the demon of fornication. She never prayed that the warfare should cease but she said, "O God, give me strength."

3. It was said concerning her that for sixty years she lived beside a river and never lifted her eyes to look at it.

4. Another time, two old men, great anchorites, came to the district of Pelusia [on the easternmost branch of the Nile] to visit her. When they arrived one said to the other, "Let us humiliate this old woman." So they said to her, "Be careful not to become conceited thinking to yourself, 'Look how anchorites are coming to see me, a mere woman.'" But Amma Sarah said to them, "According to nature I am a woman, but not according to my thoughts."

6. She also said, "I put out my foot to ascend the ladder, and I place death before my eyes before going up it."

9. She also said to the brothers, "It is I who am a man, you who are women."

Syncletica

4. Amma Syncletica said, "Do not let yourself be seduced by the delights of the riches of the world, as though they contained something useful on account of vain pleasure. Worldly people esteem the culinary art, but you, through fasting and thanks to cheap food, go beyond their abundance of food. It is written: 'He who is sated loathes honey' (Prov 27:7). Do not fill yourself with bread and you will not desire wine."

8. She also said, "If illness weighs us down, let us not be sorrowful as though, because of the illness and the prostration of our bodies, we could not sing, for all these things are for our good, for the purification of our desires. Truly fasting and sleeping on the ground are set before us because of our sensuality. If illness then weakens this sensuality the reason for these practices is superfluous. For this is the great asceticism: to control oneself in illness and to sing hymns of thanksgiving to God."

19. Amma Syncletica said, "There are many who live in the mountains and behave as if they were in the town, and they are wasting their time. It is possible to be a solitary in one's mind while living in a crowd, and it is possible for one who is a solitary to live in the crowd of his own thoughts."

21. She also said, "Just as a treasure that is exposed loses its value, so a virtue which is known vanishes; just as wax melts when it is near fire, so the soul is destroyed by praise and loses all the results of its labor."

27. She also said, "There is grief that is useful, and there is grief that is destructive. The first sort consists in weeping over one's own faults and weeping over the weakness of one's neighbors, in order not to destroy one's purpose, and attach oneself to the perfect good. But there is also a grief that comes from the enemy, full of mockery, which some call *accidie* [despondency]. This spirit must be cast out, mainly by prayer and psalmody."

WOMEN AND DOMESTIC LIFE

Marriage

During the period of the Roman Empire, marriage was a private act, usually arranged by the parents of the couple, and was regarded as legal based on the expression of intent to live as husband and wife. Legal documents and dowries were not required by law until the fifth century and, although there were ceremonial rituals that marked the transfer of the bride to the groom's residence (see selection 5 below), marriage was not regulated by religious or civic officials as it is today. Early in the imperial era, there was a shift in attitude toward marriage; under the influence of such first-century Stoic philosophers as Musonius Rufus, marriage was regarded not only as a civic duty to supply new citizens but also as a reciprocal relationship based on affection and companionship; however, sexuality in marriage was generally understood not in terms of pleasure but in terms of procreation. From New Testament texts onward, Christian attitudes toward marriage were ambivalent, and Christians eventually diverged from wider societal practices by condemning divorce and remarriage. The ascetic tendencies of early Christianity are clear in the following texts that deal with marriage; because the apostle Paul's teachings on marriage in 1 Corinthians 7 were so influential on the tone and parameters of Christian views of marriage in the patristic period, that text is included here.

1. Paul, 1 Corinthians 7 (RSV)

Written from Ephesus in 53 or 54 C.E., this letter addresses several questions that Christians in Corinth had posed to Paul, the founder of their community. One of the problems involved a group within the community that argued that their spirituality entailed sexual abstinence, even between husbands and wives. While Paul distances himself from such views, he also shows his own ambivalence, wishing on the one hand that all were unmarried as he was, but on the other hand conceding (somewhat grudgingly) that marriage had its place in Christian life ("For it is better to marry than to be aflame with passion").

1 Now concerning the matters about which you wrote. It is well for a man not to touch a woman. 2 But because of the temptation to immorality, each man should have his own wife and each woman her own husband. 3 The husband should give to his wife her conjugal rights, and likewise the wife to her husband. 4 For the wife does not rule over her own body, but the husband does; likewise the husband does not rule over his own body, but the wife does. 5 Do not refuse one another except perhaps by agreement for a season, that you may devote yourselves to prayer; but then come together again, lest Satan tempt you through lack of self-control. 6 I say this by way of concession, not of command. 7 I wish that all were as I myself am. But each has his own special gift from God, one of one kind and one of another.

8 To the unmarried and the widows I say that it is well for them to remain single as I do. 9 But if they cannot exercise self-control, they should marry. For it is better to marry than to be aflame with passion.

10 To the married I give charge, not I but the Lord, that the wife should not separate from her husband 11 (but if she does, let her remain single or else be reconciled to her husband) — and that the husband should not divorce his wife.

12 To the rest I say, not the Lord, that if any brother has a wife who is an unbeliever, and she consents to live with him, he should not divorce her. 13 If any woman has a husband who is an unbeliever, and he consents to live with her, she should not divorce him. 14 For the unbelieving husband is consecrated through his wife, and the unbelieving wife is consecrated through her husband. Otherwise, your children would be unclean, but as it is they are holy. 15 But if the unbelieving partner desires to separate, let it be so; in such a case the brother or sister is not bound. For God has called us to peace. 16 Wife, how do you know whether you will save your husband? Husband, how do you know whether you will save your wife?

17 Only, let every one lead the life which the Lord has assigned to him, and in which God has called him. This is my rule in all the churches. [Note: Verses 18–24 address an unrelated topic; Paul's comments on marriage resume in v. 25]

25 Now concerning the unmarried, I have no command of the Lord, but I give my opinion as one who by the Lord's mercy is trustworthy. 26 I think that in view of the impending distress it is well for a person to remain as he is. 27 Are you bound to a wife? Do not seek to be free. Are you free from a wife? Do not seek marriage. 28 But if you marry, you do not sin, and if a girl marries she does not sin. Yet those who marry will have worldly troubles, and I would spare you that. 29 I mean, brethren, the appointed time has grown very short; from now on, let those who have wives live as though they had none, 30 and those who mourn as though they were not mourning, and those who rejoice as though they were not rejoicing, and those who buy as though they had no goods, 31 and those who deal with the world as though they had no dealings with it. For the form of this world is passing away.

32 I want you to be free from anxieties. The unmarried man is anxious about the affairs of the Lord, how to please the Lord; 33 but the married man is anxious about worldly affairs, how to please his wife, 34 and his interests are divided. And the unmarried woman or girl is anxious about the affairs of the Lord, how to be holy in body and spirit; but the married woman is anxious about worldly affairs, how to please her husband. 35 I say this for your own benefit, not to lay any restraint upon you, but to promote good order and to secure your undivided devotion to the Lord.

36 If any one thinks that he is not behaving properly toward his betrothed, if his passions are strong, and it has to be, let him do as he wishes: let them marry—it is no sin. 37 But whoever is firmly established in his heart, being under no necessity but having his desire under control, and has determined this in his heart, to keep her as his betrothed, he will do well. 38 So that he who marries his betrothed does well; and he who refrains from marriage will do better.

39 A wife is bound to her husband as long as he lives. If the husband dies, she is free to be married to whom she wishes, only in the Lord. 40 But in my judgment she is happier if she remains as she is. And I think that I have the Spirit of God.

2. Hermas, *The Shepherd, Mandate* 4

Composed by a Roman Christian and dated to the early second century C.E., *The Shepherd* is a work composed of visions, parables, and mandates, most of which are delivered by a revelatory figure called the Angel of Repentance. Much of the material is concerned with ethical behavior; Mandate 4 addresses concerns about adultery and remarriage.

29.1 "I command you," he [the angel of repentance] said, "to guard your chastity. Do not allow the desire for another woman to enter your heart, nor any thought of fornication, or any similar vice. For to do this is to commit a great sin. If you always remember your own wife, you will never sin. But if this desire enters your heart, you will sin, and if any similar wicked desire should enter, you will commit sin. For this desire is a great sin for the servant of God. If anyone commits this wicked deed, he brings about his own death. See to it, then, that you avoid this desire. For where holiness dwells, in the heart of the righteous man, there lawlessness should not enter."

I said to him, "Lord, permit me to ask you a few questions."

"Speak," he said.

"Lord," I said, "if a man has a wife who believes in the Lord and he catches her in adultery, does the man sin if he continues to live with her?"

"As long as the man is unaware," he said, "he does not sin. But if he discovers her sin and the woman does not repent, but rather persists in her adultery, the man shares the guilt of her sin and participates in her adultery, if he continues to live with her."

"What, then," I said, "will the man do, Lord, if the woman persists in this passion?"

"He must dismiss her," he said, "and the man must live by himself. But if, after dismissing her, he should marry another woman, he himself commits adultery" [see Mark 10:11].

"And if, Lord," I said, "the woman repents after she has been dismissed and wishes to return to her husband, shall he not take her back?"

"Yes," he said, "if the man does not take her back, he sins and brings great sin upon himself, for it is necessary to welcome back the sinner who has repented. But this must not occur more than once, because the servants of God are allowed only one repentance. Therefore, for the sake of repentance the man must not marry. This course of action applies to the woman as well as to the man.

"Adultery occurs," he said, "not only when a man defiles his flesh, but also when he acts as the pagans do. So then, if a man persists in such practices and does not repent, you shall separate from him and not live with him, or else you participate in his sin. That is why you were instructed to live alone, whether you are male or female, so that repentance might be possible in these cases." . . .

32.4 Again I asked him: "Lord, since you bore with me once, please explain something else."

"Speak," he said.

"If a wife," I said, "or a husband should die, and the surviving spouse should marry, does the one who marries sin?"

"He does not sin," he said, "but if he remains single, he gains for himself more extraordinary honor and great glory with the Lord. But if he marries, he does not sin. Therefore, preserve your chastity and holiness and you will live for God."

3. Clement of Alexandria, *The Pedagogue* (selections)

In the course of the second century, many Christians read the story of Adam and Eve in Genesis 1–4 as a story about the "fall" of human beings from a spiritual existence into our present mortal condition; in this context, human sexuality was understood as a sign of sin and separation from that original paradisal state. Groups like the Gnostics, some of whom saw the creator-God as an evil figure, and the Encratites (whose name comes from the Greek word *enkrateia*, "self-control" or "chastity") taught that marriage—and thus sexuality and procreation—must be rejected so that human beings might regain the spiritual existence that was once theirs. Clement of Alexandria (ca.160–ca. 215 C.E.), a teacher and theologian who attempted to integrate Christianity with Greek culture, opposed these teachings, not only by adopting Stoic views of marriage (e.g., that marriage is a civic duty) but also by taking Scripture at its word (e.g., Gen 1:28, God's command to humans to "increase and multiply").

Book 2

10.83 Our next task is to discuss the proper time for sexual intercourse, which is solely for married persons. The purpose of intercourse is to produce children and the ultimate aim is to produce good children. In a similar manner the farmer sows seed with the aim of producing food, intending ultimately to harvest the fruit. But far superior is the farmer who sows in living soil. The one farms with the aim of producing temporary sustenance, the other does so to provide for the continuance of the entire universe. The one plants solely for himself; the other does so for God, since God himself said, "Multiply" [Gen 1:28], and we must obey. In this way the human being becomes the image of God, by cooperating in the creation of another human being. . . .

90 We must think of young men as our sons and regard other men's wives as our daughters. We must exercise restraint when it comes to the pleasures of the stomach and maintain complete mastery over the region below the stomach. If, as the Stoics say, the wise man is forbidden even to lift his finger in an irrational manner, how much more must those who pursue wisdom exercise control over the sexual organs. For it seems to me that the genitals are called the "private parts" because they must be treated with greater privacy or modesty than other members of the body.

Nature treats legitimate marriages as it does eating and drinking: it allows whatever is appropriate, useful, and dignified, and it urges us to desire to produce children. But those who indulge in excess violate the laws of nature and harm themselves in illegitimate unions. Above all, it is never right to have intercourse with young boys as if they were girls. That is why the philosophers, following Moses' lead, said: "Do not sow seed on rocks and stones because it will never take root and achieve the fruitfulness that is its nature" [Plato, *Laws* 8.838E].

91 . . . When the noble Plato recommended that "you shall abstain from every female field that is not your own" [*Laws* 8.839A], he derived this from his reading of the biblical injunction: "You must not lie with your neighbor's wife and defile yourself with her" [Lev 18:20]. "There should be no sowing of sterile, bastard seed with concubines" [*Laws* 8.841D]. Do not sow "where you do not wish seed to grow" [*Laws* 8.839A]. "Do not touch anyone except your own wedded wife" [*Laws* 8.841D].

Only with a wife are you permitted to enjoy physical pleasure for the purpose of producing descendants, for this is all that the Logos allows. We who have a share in the divine work of creation must not scatter seed randomly, nor should we act disrespectfully or sow what cannot grow.

92 That is why Moses himself even prohibited men from having intercourse with their own wives during their menstrual periods [see Lev 18:19]. For it is completely contrary to reason to defile with the impurities of the body the most fertile part of the seed, which is destined to become a human being. We must not allow it to be washed away in the filthy, impure flow of matter, for it is a seed capable of proper birth that is thus torn away from the furrows of the womb.

Furthermore, Moses left no example of any ancient Hebrew who had intercourse with a pregnant wife. For mere pleasure, even when pursued in marriage, is illicit, improper, and irrational. On the contrary, Moses ordered men to abstain from their wives until they were delivered. In fact, the uterus, which is situated below the bladder and above that part of the intestine called the rectum, extends its neck between the two into the bladder. The opening through which the seed penetrates is closed when the uterus is full. But when the uterus is emptied of the fetus, it is free again; after bearing its fruit, it can then receive the sperm. We are not ashamed to mention the organs of generation for the benefit of our hearers since God was not ashamed to create them.

93 When the uterus has conceived a thirst for childbearing, it receives the sperm and thereby escapes any blame for the act of intercourse. But after the seed has been sown, it closes its opening to completely eliminate licentiousness. Previously the body's desires were taken up with loving embraces, but now they are redirected and occupied with the development of the child within; in this way they cooperate with the Creator. It is not right to disturb nature when it is at work by engaging in acts of excessively wanton conduct. . . .

94 In general, then, this is the question to be investigated: whether we should marry or completely abstain from marriage. In my work *On Continence* I have already treated the subject. Now if we have to ask whether we may marry at all, how can we allow ourselves to make use of intercourse on every occasion, as if it were a necessity like food? It is

clear that the nerves are stretched like threads and break under the tension of intercourse. Moreover, sexual relations spread a mist over the senses and drain the body of energy. This is obvious in the case of irrational animals and in persons undergoing physical training. Among athletes it is those who abstain from sex who defeat their opponents in the contests; as far as animals are concerned, they are easily captured when they are caught in and all but dragged away from the act of rutting, for all their strength and energy is completely drained.

The sophist of Abdera called sexual intercourse a "minor epilepsy" and considered it an incurable disease. Is it not accompanied by weakness following the great loss of seed? "For a human being is born of a human being and torn away from him" [Democritus, fragment 32]. See how much harm is done: a whole person is torn out with the ejaculation that occurs during intercourse. "This is now bone of my bone and flesh of my flesh" [Gen 2:23], Scripture says. By spilling his seed a man loses as much substance as one sees in a body, for what has been expelled is the beginning of a birth. Moreover, the shaking of the body's material substance disturbs and upsets the harmony of the whole body.

95 . . . Nevertheless, marriage should be accepted and given its proper place. Our Lord wanted humanity to "multiply" [Gen 1:28], but he did not say that people should engage in licentious behavior, nor did he intend for them to give themselves over to pleasure as if they were born for rutting. Rather, let the Pedagogue put us to shame with the words of Ezekiel: "Put away your fornications" [see Ezek 43:9]. Even irrational animals have a proper time for sowing seed.

But to have intercourse without intending children is to violate nature, which we must take as our teacher. We should observe the wise precepts that her pedagogy has established concerning the proper time, by which I mean old age and childhood; the young are not permitted to marry, the old are no longer permitted to do so. Otherwise, one may marry at any time. So marriage is the desire for procreation, but it is not the random, illicit, or irrational scattering of seed.

96 Our entire life will be spent observing the laws of nature, if we control our desires from the start and if we do not kill off with devious instruments the human creature that has been conceived according to di-

vine providence. For women who, in order to conceal their incontinence, make use of death-dealing drugs that completely expel the mortal creature, abort not only the embryo, but also human kindness.

But those who are permitted to marry have need of the Pedagogue, so that they might not fulfill the mystic rites of nature during the day, nor have intercourse after coming home from church or from the marketplace or early in the morning like a rooster, for these are the proper times for prayer and reading and the other deeds done during the day. But the evening is the proper time to take one's rest, after dinner and after giving thanks for the benefits one has enjoyed.

97 Nature does not always provide the opportunity to consummate marital intercourse, and the union becomes the more desirable the more it is delayed. But one must not become intemperate at night under the pretext of the cover of darkness; rather, one should preserve modesty in the soul, as if it were the light of reason. We will be no different from Penelope at her loom [see Homer, *Odyssey* 2.104–5; Plato, *Phaedo* 84A], if during the day we weave the teachings of self-restraint, but at night undo them when we go to bed. For if we must practice self-control, as certainly we must, we ought to manifest it even more with our own wives by avoiding indecent embraces, and we should show at home the same trustworthy proof of chastity that we display toward our neighbors.

It is absolutely impossible for a man to be considered dignified by his wife, if he does not show any sign of dignity during the pleasures of intercourse. The good feeling that admittedly accompanies intercourse blossoms only for a short time and grows old along with the body. But sometimes it happens that it grows old even before the body, and desire is extinguished; this occurs when marital chastity has been violated by pleasure taken with prostitutes. The hearts of lovers have wings, and charms are quenched by a change of mind. Love frequently changes into hate if there are too many reasons for condemnation.

4. Clement of Alexandria, *Miscellanies* (selections)

Book 2

23.139 . . . Those who approve of marriage say, "Nature has made us well adapted for marriage, as is evident from the arrangement of our bodies into male and female." They constantly cry out: "Increase and multiply" [Gen 1:28].

Now even though this is the case, they should still consider it shameful if the human person, created by God, should show less restraint than the irrational beasts who do not mate with many partners indiscriminately, but with one of the same species, as do pigeons, ringdoves, and turtledoves, and animals such as these. Furthermore, they say, the childless man falls short of his natural perfection when he does not provide his own successor to take his place. For the perfect man is the one who has produced from himself his like, or rather, who sees that he has produced his like, when the begotten one attains the same nature as the one who begot him.

23.140 By all means, then, we must marry, both for the sake of our country and for the succession of children and for the completion of the world, in so far as it pertains to us. The poets also pity a marriage that is "half-complete" and childless, but they consider happy one that is "blossoming." Physical illnesses also reveal how necessary marriage is. The loving care of a wife and the depth of her faithfulness exceed the endurance of all other relatives and friends, just as she surpasses them in sympathy. Above all, she prefers to be always at his side and truly she is, as Scripture says, "a necessary help" [Gen 2:18].

23.141 . . . Now marriage is a help, especially to those who are advanced in years, when it provides a caring spouse and produces children by her to nourish one's old age. . . . Lawmakers do not entrust the highest offices to unmarried men. For example, a Spartan lawmaker established a penalty not only for failure to marry, but also for unlawful marriages, late marriages, and the single life. The noble Plato orders the unmarried man to pay into the public treasury the cost of a wife's maintenance and to give to the magistrates the appropriate expenses [see

Laws 6.774]. For if people do not marry and produce children, they contribute to the scarcity of human beings and destroy both the cities and the world that is composed of them.

23.142 What a great impiety it is to destroy divine generation! Indeed, it is unmanly and weak to avoid living with a wife and children. When the loss of something is an evil, its possession is a good; and this pertains to everything else. But the loss of children is the greatest of evils, they say. . . .

23.143 Marriage makes a father, just as a husband makes a mother. That is why Homer offers the greatest prayer for "a husband and a house," but adds the qualification "with good harmony" [*Odyssey* 6.181]. The marriage of some people is an agreement to indulge in pleasure, but the marriage of philosophers leads to a harmony that is in accordance with reason. In such a marriage wives are ordered to adorn themselves not in outward appearance, but in character; husbands are commanded not to use their wives like mistresses, with the aim of indulging bodily wantonness, but rather to preserve marriage as a help for their whole life and as an occasion for the highest form of self-restraint.

As I see it, far more honorable than the seeds of wheat and barley that are sown at the proper season is the human being who is sown, for whose sake all things grow and for whom sober farmers sow those seeds. Therefore, every foul and defiling practice must be purged from marriage, so that the couplings of irrational beasts may not be thrown in our face as being more in accord with nature than human intercourse. Some animals, following a commonly accepted limit, cease copulating as soon as the proper time commands them, leaving creation to providence. . . .

Book 3

6.45 To those who blaspheme both the creation and the holy Creator, the almighty and only God, through their supposedly sacred continence, and who teach that marriage and childbearing should be rejected and that one should not bring other unfortunate people into the world or provide further fodder for death, this is what I have to say: First, from the apostle John: "And now many antichrists have come; this is how we know it is the final hour. They went out from us, but they did not belong

to us. For if they had belonged to us they would have remained with us"
[1 John 2:18–19]. They can be refuted because they distort the very evidence that they present to make their case. For example, when Salome
asked the Lord, "How long will death reign?" she did not mean that life
was evil or that creation was corrupt. And when the Lord responded, "As
long as you women bear children," he was merely teaching what is the
natural course of things, for death always follows birth [The Gospel According to the Egyptians].

6.46 The purpose of the law is to lead us away from luxury and all
disorderly behavior; its ultimate end is to conduct us from unrighteous-
ness to righteousness, so that we choose to be self-controlled in marriage, childbearing, and civic life. The Lord "came not to destroy the law,
but to fulfill it" [Matt 5:17]. To "fulfill" does not mean that it was defec-
tive, but rather that the prophecies in the law have now been fulfilled by
Christ's coming. For before the law the elements of good conduct were
proclaimed by the Logos to those who lived righteously. Most people
know nothing of continence and live for the body, not for the spirit. But
the body without the spirit is "earth and ashes" [Gen 18:27]. Now the
Lord condemns adultery even in thought [see Matt 5:28]. What does this
mean? Is it not possible to live chastely even in marriage and not to try to
dissolve "what God has joined together" [Matt 19:6]? This is the teaching
of those who divide the body of marriage, who cause the name [of Christ]
to be blasphemed. Since they say that intercourse is impure, although
they themselves derive their existence from intercourse, does it not follow that they are impure? But I think that even the seed of those who
have been made holy is holy.

6.47 It is proper that not only our spirit be made holy, but also our behavior, our way of life, and our body. What did Paul mean when he said
that "the wife is sanctified by her husband and the husband by his wife"
[1 Cor 7:14]? What did the Lord mean when he said to those who asked
him whether it was lawful to put away one's wife, as Moses commanded:
"Moses wrote this because of your hardness of heart. But have you not
read that God said to the first man, 'You shall be two in one flesh'? Therefore, whoever puts away his wife, except because of adultery, makes her
an adulteress" [Matt 19:3–9]. But "after the resurrection," he says, "they

will neither marry nor be given in marriage" [Matt 22:30]. Furthermore, concerning the stomach and its food, it is written: "Food is for the stomach and the stomach for food, but God will destroy them both" [1 Cor 6:13]. [He said this] to refute those who wished to live like wild pigs and goats, to prevent them from eating and mating without restraint.

6.48 If, as they say, they already participate in the resurrection and for this reason reject marriage, they should also stop eating and drinking. For the apostle says that in the resurrection both the stomach and food will be destroyed. Why then do they hunger and thirst and endure the sufferings of the flesh and all the rest, when the person who through Christ attains the anticipated final resurrection will not have to endure such things? Even those who worship idols abstain from food and sex. "But the kingdom of God," he says, "is not a matter of eating and drinking" [Rom 14:17]. In fact, even the astrologers are careful to abstain from wine and meat and sex, all the while worshipping angels and demons. Just as humility is meekness, not the abuse of the body, so, too, is chastity [enkrateia] a virtue of the soul, which is hidden, not visible.

6.49 Some openly declare that marriage is fornication and teach that it was introduced by the devil. They boast that they are imitating the Lord himself who neither married nor possessed anything in the world, and they claim to understand the gospel better than anyone else. To them Scripture says: "God resists the proud, but gives grace to the humble" [Jas 4:6; 1 Pet 5:5]. Moreover, they do not know the reason why the Lord did not marry. First, he had his own bride, the church; second, he was no ordinary man who had need of a helpmate after the flesh [see Gen 2:18]. Nor did he need to beget children, since he lives eternally and was born the only Son of God. The Lord himself says: "What God has joined together, man must not separate" [Matt 19:6]. And again: "As it was in the days of Noah, they were marrying and giving in marriage, building and planting, and as it was in the days of Lot, so will be the coming of the Son of Man" [Matt 24:37–39]. To show that he is not speaking to the Gentiles, he adds: "When the Son of Man comes, will he find faith upon the earth?" [Luke 18:8] And again: "Woe to those who are pregnant and nursing in those days" [Matt 24:19], although this has to be interpreted allegorically. The reason he did not determine "the times that the Father has established in his own power" [Acts 1:7] was so that the world might continue from generation to generation. . . .

7.57 The human ideal of self-control [*enkrateia*], I mean the one found among the Greek philosophers, consists in struggling against lust [*epithumia*], and in not yielding to it so as to manifest its deeds. But among us self-control means not to experience lust at all. Our aim is not merely to be self-controlled while still experiencing lust in the heart, but rather to be self-controlled even over lust itself. But this kind of self-control is attained only by the grace of God. That is why he said: "Ask and it will be given to you" [Matt 7:7]. Moses received this grace, even though he was clothed in the needy body, so that for forty days he felt neither thirst nor hunger [see Exod 24:18]. . . .

7.58 In general, then, let this be our position regarding marriage, food, and other matters: to do nothing out of lust, but to wish only for those things that are necessary. For we are children not of lust, but of the will [see John 1:13]. The married man must exercise self-control in procreation, so that he does not feel lust for his wife, whom he must love, while he produces children by a holy and chaste will. For we have learned not to "have concern for the flesh to fulfill its lusts" [Rom 13:14], but to behave "decently as in the day," that is, in Christ and in the path that the Lord has illumined, "walking not in orgies and drunkenness, not in immorality and debauchery, not in dissension and jealousy" [Rom 13:13].

7.59 Furthermore, one should not look at self-control merely in regard to one form of it, that is, sexual relations, but also in regard to the other things that our souls lustfully crave when they are not content with the necessities and yearn for luxury. It is self-control to despise money, delicacy, property, to have little regard for outward appearance, to control the tongue, and to master wicked thoughts. Once certain angels lost their self-control and were seized by desire so that they fell from heaven down to earth. Valentinus [a Gnostic teacher and philosopher, second century C.E.] in a letter to Agathopus says: "Having undergone all things, Jesus was self-controlled. He was exercising his divine nature: he ate and drank in a unique manner, without evacuating his food. He had such power of self-control that the food within him did not undergo corruption, since he himself did not have to undergo corruption."

But we embrace the self-control that comes from the love of the Lord and from a desire for the good in itself, as we sanctify the temple of the Spirit. For it is good "to make oneself a eunuch for the kingdom of heaven" [Matt 19:12] in respect to all lust, and "to purify the conscience from dead works for the worship of the living God" [Heb 9:14]. . . .

12.79 But if by agreement sexual relations are suspended for a time for the purpose of prayer [see 1 Cor 7:5], this teaches self-control. But he adds the words "by agreement" to prevent anyone from dissolving the marriage, and the words "for a time," so that the married man who is compelled to practice self-control does not fall into sin; for if he abstains from intercourse with his own wife, he may conceive a desire for another woman. On these grounds the apostle also said that if a man thinks that he is not behaving properly by raising his daughter as a virgin, he does well to give her in marriage [see 1 Cor 7:36].

Whether one chooses to be celibate or to marry for the sake of procreation, one must remain unyielding to what is inferior. If a person can endure such a life, he will acquire for himself greater merit with God, since he practices self-control in a manner that is both pure and rational. But if he has gone too far in choosing the rule for the greater glory, he may fall short of his hope. Just like celibacy, marriage has its own distinctive services and ministries for the Lord; I refer to the care of one's children and wife. The special characteristic of the marital union, it seems, is that it gives the person who is committed to a perfect marriage the opportunity to show concern for everything that pertains to the household he shares with his wife. That is why the apostle says that bishops must be appointed who have learned how to supervise the whole church by supervising their own households [see 1 Tim 3:4–5]. So, then, let each one complete his ministry by the work to which he was called [see 1 Cor 7:24], so that he may be free in Christ and may receive the proper reward for his ministry [see 1 Cor 7:22].

5. John Chrysostom, *Homily 12 on* *1 Corinthians* (selections)

Born and raised in Antioch, the eloquent preacher and theologian John Chrysostom became a priest in 386 C.E. and served as bishop of Constantinople from 398–404. Although Chrysostom wrote one of the major early Christian treatises on virginity in which he claimed that "virginity is as much superior to marriage as heaven is to earth" (see above, Section II, "Major Treatises on Virginity") and although he pictured the miseries of marriage when he wrote against the *subintroductae* (see Section II, "The Subintroductae"), he did not disparage marriage in his later writings. The first selection indicates Christian adoption of marriage customs from the wider culture and John's rejection of them; modesty is for him one of the ideals on which marriage should be founded.

5. . . . . Marriage is deemed honorable by us as well as by those outside the church, and indeed it *is* honorable. But when wedding ceremonies are performed, ludicrous things occur about which you shall straightaway hear. Most people, misled and held fast by custom, do not realize the peculiarity of these practices but need others to teach them. There are dancing, cymbals, flutes, shameless words and songs, drunkenness, carousing—and then all the enormous trash of the Devil is introduced.

I know that I seem ridiculous in attacking these practices and that I shall be convicted of great folly by the majority for disrupting the ancient laws. As I said earlier, the deception worked by custom is great. Nonetheless, I shall not cease making my point. For surely at least some people, if not everyone, will accept us and choose to be ridiculed along with us rather than have us join them in that laughter deserving of tears, harsh punishment, and retribution.

For how can it not be worthy of the strongest condemnation that a virgin who has lived entirely within the enclosure of her home and has been instructed in modesty from her early years, is forced all at once to cast off her modesty totally, and right from the start of marriage is taught shamelessness, is placed among licentious, crude, unchaste, and effeminate men? What sort of evil will not be implanted in the bride from that day? Shamelessness, recklessness, insolence, love of extravagant glory—

for she will want all her days to be like these! Hence women become extravagant and lavish, hence result their myriad evils. . . .

6. "What?" someone asks. "Are you criticizing marriage? Speak up!" By no means—I am not *that* crazy! But I do criticize the baggage wickedly dragged along in the wake of marriage: the make-up, the eye-shadow, and all the other superfluities of this sort. Indeed, from that day she will receive many lovers, and these even before she receives her bridegroom-to-be. . . .

Then see what happens next. Not only during the day, but also in the evening, drunken men, alternately stupefied and inflamed by their carousing, are supplied to gape at the beauty of the girl's face. And they show her off not just in the house, but also strutting about in the marketplace. Late in the evening they accompany her with torches, thus exhibiting her to everyone. By these actions, they counsel nothing other than it henceforth behooves her to cast off all modesty. And they don't call a halt even here, but they lead her forth, uttering disgraceful words. This is a law with the masses. Thousands of worthless runaway slaves and sorry knaves henceforth fearlessly say whatever they wish, both to her and to the man about to dwell with her. Nothing is decent, everything is full of indecency. Will not the bride have a lovely lesson in discretion, seeing and hearing such things? A certain devilish rivalry prevails among the champions of these matters to surpass the others in uttering reproaches and shameful words by which they dishonor the group; those depart victors who hurl the most insults and the greatest terms of disgrace. . . .

"But this is the customary thing!" someone objects. Indeed, for this very reason it deserves to be mourned, because the Devil has enclosed the business in the guise of custom. For since marriage is a decorous matter that marshals our race and produces many benefits, that Evil One, being vexed and knowing that marriage was in effect a fortified outpost stationed against sexual immorality, here introduced anew in one way or another every kind of sexual immorality. In all events, many virgins have even been dishonored in such gatherings. And even if that is not always the case, for the time being it is enough for the Devil to have those evil words and songs, the exhibition of the bride, and the pompous escort of the groom through the marketplace. In addition, since these activities occur in the evening, many torches are brought in to prevent the unseemly events from remaining hidden, lest the darkness provide cover for these evils. For what do the great crowds portend? And what the drink? What the pipes? Is it not patently clear that these things take place so that those at home, sunk in deep sleep, cannot remain unaware of the events, but roused by the pipe, stooping to peer down over their balconies, become witnesses of the passing farce?

What can anyone say about the songs themselves, brimming with every sort of licentiousness, introducing disgusting amours and unlawful unions, the overthrow of households, myriad tragic episodes, frequently bandying about names like "my sweetie and boy-friend," "my darling and love"? And, what is yet sorrier, maidens who have taken off all their modesty as if their robes are present at these events. In honor of the bride, or more accurately as an insult to her, they even sacrifice their salvation, and in the midst of dissolute young men they behave disgracefully with their disorderly ditties, their shameful words, their satanic melody.

If you are still asking, *you* tell *me:* "Where do adulteries come from? Whence sexual immorality? Whence the ruining of marriages?"

6. John Chrysostom, *The Kind of Women Who Ought to be Taken as Wives* 4

In this selection, Chrysostom, while affirming marriage, provides an extended commentary on such Pauline sentiments as found in Ephesians 5:22–24 regarding the submission of wives to husbands; his view of women's proper duty as managers of the household agrees with conventional Graeco-Roman views.

Indeed, I have heard many people say, "So-and-so who used to be poor became very prosperous from his marriage. Since he married a rich woman, he's well off and now he fares sumptuously." What do you reply, O men? You neither feel shame nor do you blush, though you wish to make a profit from a wife? Why don't you prefer to sink into the ground, profiting in such a way? How can these be the words of a real man? A wife has just one purpose: to guard the possessions we have accumulated, to keep a close watch on the income, to take charge of the household.

Indeed, this is why God gave her to you, that in these, plus all other matters, she might be a helper to you.

Our life is customarily organized into two spheres: public affairs and private matters, both of which were determined by God. To woman is assigned the presidency of the household; to man, all the business of state, the marketplace, the administration of justice, government, the military, and all other such enterprises. A woman is not able to hurl a spear or shoot an arrow, but she can grasp the distaff, weave at the loom; she correctly disposes of all such tasks that pertain to the household. She cannot express her opinion in a legislative assembly, but she can express it at home, and often she is more shrewd about household matters than her husband. She cannot handle state business well, but she can raise children correctly, and children are our principal wealth. At a glance she can detect the bad behavior of the servants and can manage them carefully. She provides complete security for her husband and frees him from all such household concerns, concerns about money, wool-working, the preparation of food and decent clothing. She takes care of all other matters of this sort, that are neither fitting for her husband's concern nor would they be satisfactorily accomplished should he ever lay his hand to them—even if he struggled valiantly!

Indeed, this is a work of God's love and wisdom, that he who is skilled at the greater things is downright inept and useless in the performance of the less important ones, so that the woman's service is necessary. For if the man were adapted to undertake both sorts of activities, the female sex could easily be despised. Conversely, if the more important, most beneficial concerns were turned over to the woman, she would go quite mad. Therefore God did not apportion both duties to one sex, lest the other be displaced and be considered superfluous. Nor did God assign both to be equal in every way, lest from equality a kind of struggle and rivalry should again arise, for women in their contentiousness would deem themselves deserving of the front-row seats rather than the man! But taking precautions at one and the same time for peace and decency, God maintained the order of each sex by dividing the business of human life into two parts and assigned the more necessary and beneficial aspects to the man and the less important, inferior matters to the woman. God's plan was extremely desirable for us, on the one hand because of our pressing needs and on the other, so that a woman would not rebel against her husband due to the inferiority of her service. Understanding all these things, let us thus strive for just one goal, virtue of soul and nobility of behavior, so that we may enjoy peace, live in concord, and maintain ourselves in love unto the end.

7. John Chrysostom, *Homily 20 on Ephesians* (selections)

Here Chrysostom not only affirms marriage but emphasizes the role of love between husband and wife; his earlier stark contrast between virginity and marriage is greatly softened in this homily. Along the way, he gives practical advice about how to achieve marital harmony, especially regarding money.

(1) A certain wise man who was compiling a list of blessings numbered this one among them: "A wife who agrees with her husband" [Sir 25:1]. In another place he listed as a blessing that a wife should live in harmony with her husband [cf. Sir 40:23]. Indeed, from the very beginning God seems to have shown a special concern for this union. Speaking of the two as if they were one, he said: "Male and female he created them" [Gen 1:27]. And, in another place, "There is neither male nor female" [Gal 3:28]. For no relationship between two men is as close as that between a man and a woman, if they are joined together as they should be. When another blessed man wished to describe the highest form of love, as he was grieving over someone who was dear to him and, so to speak, one soul with him, he did not mention father, or mother, or child, or brother, or friend. No, he said: "Your love to me was wonderful, more wonderful than that of women" [2 Sam 1:26].

Truly, this love is more tyrannical than any tyrant. Other passions may be strong; this passion is not only strong, but also imperishable. For deeply implanted in our nature there is a certain desire (*eros*) that, without our noticing it, knits together these bodies of ours. . . . The man was allowed to marry his own sister; or rather, not his sister but his daughter; no, not his daughter, but rather something more than his daughter, his very own flesh. From the beginning [God] constructed the whole edifice, like a building made of stones, gathering them together into one. On the one hand, he did not create the woman apart from the man, lest the man regard her as something alien to himself. Nor, on the other hand, did he restrict marriage solely to the woman, lest the man, by withdrawing and turning in on himself, should be cut off from the rest.

. . . Nothing so welds our lives together as the love of man and woman. For the sake of love, many will lay aside even their weapons; for the sake of love, many will even give their lives. It was not without good reason that Paul showed so much concern about this matter when he said: "Wives, be submissive to your husbands, as to the Lord" [Eph 5:22]. Why is this? Because if they are in harmony, the children will be brought up well, the household will be properly ordered, and neighbors, friends, and relatives will enjoy the sweet fragrance. But if the opposite happens, everything will be turned upside down and thrown into confusion. . . .

(2) . . . Now hear what [Paul] demands of you. "Husbands, love your wives, as Christ has loved the church" [Eph 5:25]. You have seen the measure of obedience, now hear the measure of love. Would you like your wife to obey you, as the church obeys Christ? Then you must care for her, as Christ does for the church. Even if it is necessary to give your life for her, even if you must be cut into a thousand pieces, even if you must endure any suffering whatever, do not refuse it. . . . Even if you see her looking down on you and despising you and holding you in disdain, you will be able to lay her at your feet by showing great care and love and affection for her. For nothing has greater power than these bonds, especially between husband and wife.

You may be able to restrain a servant by fear; no, not even a servant, for he will soon be off and away. But she who is your life's partner, the mother of your children, the very reason for your happiness, she must not be restrained by fear and threats, but by love and a gentle disposition. What sort of union is it, when the wife trembles before her husband? What sort of pleasure will the husband himself enjoy, if he lives with a wife who is more a slave than a free woman? Even if you suffer in some ways because of her, do not criticize her, for Christ has done nothing of the sort. . . . [Note: After several more paragraphs on the topic of love, Chrysostom turns to practical advice, as follows.]

(6) . . . Do not believe anyone who slanders a husband to his wife. A husband should not believe any random accusations against his wife, nor should a wife be overly inquisitive about his comings and goings. In no case should a husband ever render himself worthy of suspicion. Why is it, tell me, that after spending the whole day with your friends and devoting the evening to your wife, you are still unable to ease her mind and free her of suspicion? Even if your wife accuses you, do not be angry. It is affection, not foolishness, that causes this; her complaints come from fervent affection, burning desire, and fear. She is afraid that someone might rob her marriage bed, that someone might destroy her most cherished goods, that someone might steal her very head, that someone might break into her marriage chamber. . . .

(7) . . . No one should reproach his neighbor's poverty; no one should lust for money; then everything will be at peace. A wife should not say to her husband, "You unmanly coward! You timid, sleepy dolt! I know a man from a low-class background, who has amassed a fortune by taking risks and travelling abroad. His wife wears gold and goes out on a pair of white mules. She rides everywhere, surrounded by a crowd of slaves and a swarm of eunuchs. But you stay put and live a useless life!" A wife should not say this or anything like this. For she is the body and she is not to give orders to the head, but to listen and obey.

"But how will she bear poverty?" you ask. "Where will she find consolation?" She should associate with those who are poorer than she is, she should think about the great number of highborn and noble young women who not only have received nothing from their husbands, but who have even given away all that they have. Let her reflect on the dangers that wealth produces and she will welcome a life free from such business. In a word, if she feels affection for her husband, she will say nothing of this sort. She will prefer to have him near her, without gaining a thing, than to have a thousand talents of gold along with the anxiety and worry that women inevitably experience when their husbands go on long journeys. . . . The husband should teach her that poverty is not an evil; he should teach her not only by his words, but also by his deeds. He should teach her to despise glory, and the wife will neither speak about nor desire such things.

The husband should act like a man who has been entrusted with the care of a sacred image. From the very first evening that he receives her into the bridal chamber, he should teach her self-restraint, moderation, how to live a holy life, rejecting the desire for money at the very outset, as soon as she comes through the door. He should instruct her in philosophy and advise her not to have pieces of gold dangling from her ears or down her neck or around her shoulders or strewn about the bedroom, nor should she have costly, golden clothing stored away. Let her be dressed elegantly, but the elegance should not degenerate into extravagance. Leave that sort of thing to the stage!

He should decorate the house with great propriety, so that it breathes temperance rather than perfume. Two, or even three, benefits will result from this. First, the bride will not be upset when the bridal chamber is opened and the clothes and the gold and silver vessels are returned to their proper owners. Second, the bridegroom will not have to worry about losing or protecting this pile of treasure. But the third and most important benefit is that the husband will be revealing his own attitude, that he takes pleasure in none of these things and that he will do away with all the rest. . . .

(9) You ought to pray together. Both should go to church, and at home the husband should ask the wife, and the wife should ask the husband, about what was said and read there. If you should experience poverty, call to mind the holy men, Paul and Peter, who are now more highly regarded than wealthy men or kings. Remember how they spent their lives in hunger and thirst. Teach her that there is nothing in this life to fear, except offending God. If you marry in this way and with these aims, you will not be much inferior to the monks; the married person will not be much less than the unmarried.

If you want to give dinner parties or banquets, there should be no disorderly or improper behavior. Rather, if you should find some poor, holy person who is able to bless your house, who is able to bestow all God's blessings simply by setting foot inside, invite him in. Let me add something else. None of you should be eager to marry a wealthy woman; choose instead someone much poorer. A wealthy wife actually causes more pain than pleasure by her wealth, because of the insults, because of her demands for more than she brought to the marriage, because of the arrogance and extravagance and vulgar language. . . .

Praise for Mothers and Sisters

In the course of the fourth century, patristic authors developed a model of the ideal woman as mentor and paradigm of the spiritual life, as we have already seen in the biographies of women presented in Section III above. Portraits of virtuous female family members were also composed at this time, the most famous of which is Saint Augustine's portrayal of his mother Monica in *The Confessions*. Authors in the Greek East also praised sisters and mothers; for example, see Gregory of Nyssa's biography of his virginal, ascetic sister Macrina in Section III. In the following selections we see praise given to married women relatives as well, with an emphasis on the domestic life as an arena for the development and exercise of Christian virtues.

1. Gregory of Nazianzus, *Funeral Oration for his Sister Gorgonia (Or. 8)* (selections)

Gregory of Nazianzus (ca. 330–390 C.E.) was one of the "Cappadocian Fathers" along with his friends Basil of Caesarea and Gregory of Nyssa. A talented orator, he is known for developing the genre of the Christian funeral eulogy as well as poetic auto-biography. In the following selections from his eulogy for his sister Gorgonia, probably delivered in about 370 on the first anniversary of her death, we see Gregory present-ing an idealized portrait of his sister as a paradigm of the Christian woman whose life as a married woman displayed virtues such as modesty, wisdom, piety, moderation. She is also presented in terms of domestic ideals of generosity, hospitality, and a well-run household. [Note: I have emended this translation in order to bring it into con-formity with twenty-first-century English usage.]

1. In praising my sister, I shall be honoring my own family. Yet, while she is a member of my family, I shall not on that account praise her false-ly, but because what is true is for that reason praiseworthy. [After develop-ing the theme that kinship should not be a barrier against praising one who truly mer-its such a eulogy, Gregory continues as follows.]

4. Who is there who does not know our new Abraham and the Sarah of our time? I mean Gregory and his wife Nonna [i.e., the parents of Gorgonia and Gregory himself]. For it is not right to omit the mention of names that are an exhortation to virtue. He was justified by faith [Gen 15:6; Rom 3:28], and she has dwelt together with the man of faith. He beyond hope has been the father of many nations [Gen 17:5], and she has brought them forth spiritually [see Gal 4:26]. He fled the bondage of his father's gods [Gen 12:1–4], and she is the daughter and the mother of the free. He went forth from his kindred and his father's house for the sake of the land of promise, and she was the occasion of his departure [i.e., Nonna was responsible for the conversion of her husband to Christianity]. In this one point, if I may speak a little boldly, she surpassed Sarah herself. He nobly undertook this migration, and she was his zealous partner. . . .

6. From them Gorgonia received both her being and her good repute. They were the source of the seeds of her piety, of her noble life, and of her joyful departure with better hopes. These, indeed, are fair blessings and such as do not easily accrue to many of those who take pride in their noble birth and puff themselves up because of their lineage. But if I must speak about her in a more philosophical and spiritual way, Gorgonia's native land was the heavenly Jerusalem [see Gal 4:26; Rev 3:12; 21.2, 10], the city not seen by the eye but perceived by the mind, the city in which we are citizens and toward which we are hastening. Christ is a citizen there and his fellow citizens celebrating the feast are "the assembly of the firstborn who are enrolled in the heavens" [Heb 12.22–23], who celebrate its great founder by the contemplation of his glory and participate in an everlasting chorus. Gorgonia's nobility lay in the preservation of the image, in her assimilation to the archetype [Gen 1:26], which is effected by reason and virtue and that pure desire, which forms ever more in the things of God, those who are truly initiated in the heavenly mysteries, and finally, in her knowledge of our origin, our nature, and our destiny. . . .

8. She so excelled in modesty and so surpassed all the women of her own day, not to mention those of old who were greatly famed for modesty, that in the two main conditions of life—I mean marriage and celibacy, the latter of which is loftier and more divine but also more difficult

and perilous, while the former is lower but safer—she avoided the disadvantages of both and chose and united the loftiness of the one with the security of the other. [Note: The word translated as "modesty"—*sophrosyne*—can also mean "temperance" or "self-control," especially concerning sexuality.] And she was modest without being proud, blending the virtue of marriage with celibacy, and showing that neither of these binds us completely to or separates us from God or the world. And so the one of its very nature is not to be altogether shunned [i.e., marriage] nor the other [celibacy] exclusively praised. But it is the mind that nobly presides over both marriage and virginity, and these, like raw materials, are ordered and fashioned to virtue by the craftsman, reason [Christ in his role as cosmic creative principle]. Although she was tied according to the flesh, she was not on that account separated from the spirit, nor because she had her husband as her head did she ignore her first Head [see 1 Cor 11:3]. When she had served the world and nature a little, to the extent that the law of the flesh willed it, or, rather, He who imposed this law on the flesh, she consecrated herself wholly to God.

But the most beautiful and noble of her actions was to convince her husband of her views [about living a chaste life], gaining not an unreasonable master but a good fellow servant. Not only that, she also made the fruit of her body, her children and her children's children, the fruit of her spirit, and dedicated to God, instead of her single soul, her whole family and household. [Note: Gorgonia converted her husband Alypios to Christianity and urged him to be baptized, just as her mother Nonna had done for her own husband, Gregory the Elder.] And she made marriage itself praiseworthy by her pleasing and acceptable life in wedlock and by the beautiful fruit of her union. She exhibited herself, as long as she lived, as an exemplar of every excellence to her children, and when she was called, she left her will behind as a silent exhortation to her family.

9. The divinely inspired Solomon, in his instructive wisdom, I mean in his Proverbs, praises the woman who keeps her house and loves her husband. And in contrast to the woman who wanders abroad [Prov 7:11], who is uncontrolled and dishonorable, who hunts precious souls with wanton ways and words [Prov 6:26; 7:10–13], he praises her who is engaged honorably at home, who performs her womanly duties with manly

courage, her hands constantly at the spindle as she prepares double cloaks for her husband [Prov 31:17–19, 22], who buys a field in season [Prov 31:16], and carefully provides food for her servants [Prov 31:15], and receives her friends at a bountiful table [see Prov 9:2], and who exhibits all other qualities for which he extols in song the modest and industrious woman. If I were to praise my sister on such counts, it would be like praising a statue for its shadow, or a lion for his claws, to the neglect of greater perfections. Who was ever more worthy to be seen, yet was seen less and kept herself more inaccessible to the eyes of men? Who knew better than she the bounds of gravity and gaiety, so that neither her gravity might seem uncouth nor her tenderness wanton, but the one prudent and the other gentle? . . . Who had such control over her eyes? Who so derided laughter that the very beginning of a smile seemed almost too much to her? Who so barred the portals of her ears? . . . Who so regulated her lips?

10. I am sure that you wish me to mention also the following special characteristic of hers. . . . She was never adorned with gold fashioned by art into surpassing beauty, or with blond hair fully or partly exposed, or with spiral curls, or with the ingenious arrangements of those who disgracefully turn the noble head into a show piece. Hers were no costly, flowing, diaphanous robes, hers no brilliant and beautiful gems, flashing color and causing the figure to glow with light. Hers were no devices and magic tricks of the painter, or that cheap beauty of the earthly creator who, by his rival craftsmanship, hides with deceitful pigments the image of God and disgraces it with adornment and exhibits to wanton eyes the divine form as an image of a prostitute. . . . The only red that pleased her was the blush of modesty, and the only pallor, that which comes from abstinence. [Note: After more praise for Gorgonia's piety, hospitality, and ascetic virtues, Gregory narrates the following specific incidents from his sister's life.]

15. . . . You know the story of her mules getting out of control and running away with her carriage, and its dreadful overturn, how she was dragged along horribly and suffered serious injuries, and the scandal it became to unbelievers because the just were allowed to suffer in this way, and the swift correction of their unbelief. Although crushed and mangled internally and externally in bone and limb, she would have no

physician except Him who had permitted the accident, both because she shrank from the eyes and hands of men, guarding her modesty even in suffering, and also because she sought her vindication from Him who had allowed her to suffer in this way. Nor from anyone else but Him did she obtain her recovery. Thus people were less struck by her misfortune than they were amazed by her unexpected recovery, and they believed that the tragedy had happened for the very reason that she might be glorified by her sufferings. . . . [Note: After more praise for his sister's miraculous healing, Gregory now reveals a secret that Gorgonia had entrusted to him alone.]

17. Gravely stricken, she was physically ill with a strange and unusual sickness. All at once her whole body became feverish, her temperature rising and her blood racing, followed by a sluggishness inducing coma, incredible paleness, and a paralysis of mind and limbs. These attacks occurred not intermittently but often. The terrible disease did not seem human. No treatment proved successful—neither the skill of physicians who carefully examined the case both singly and in consultation, nor her parents' tears, which had often proved effective, nor public prayers and supplications, which, as though for their individual preservation, all the people offered on her behalf. For they regarded her safety as their own, and her sickness and affliction as a common disaster.

18. What, then, was done by this great soul, worthy of the greatest favors, and what medicine was found for her sickness? Here lies the great secret. Despairing of all other help, she fled for refuge to the Physician of all and, waiting until the dead of night, when the disease was somewhat abated, she prostrated herself with faith at the altar and called with a loud voice, and by all of his names, the one who is honored there, and recalling all of his miraculous works, for she was familiar with those of old as well as the new, she finally committed an act of pious and noble impudence. She imitated the woman whose hemorrhage was dried up by the hem of Christ's garment [Matt 9:20–22].

And what did she do? Placing her head, with a similar cry, on the altar, and pouring abundant tears on it, as the woman of old had once watered the feet of Christ [Luke 7:37–38], she vowed that she would not let go until she had recovered her health. Then she anointed her whole body with her own medicine, even a portion of the consecrated precious body and blood which she treasured in her hand and with which she mingled her tears. Oh the wonder! At once she felt herself cured and went away relieved in body and soul and mind, having received what she hoped for as a reward for her hopes. By her strength of soul she gained that of body. . . . [Note: After several more paragraphs of praise, Gregory concludes with his sister's deathbed scene, as follows.]

22. . . . She was just passing away and was breathing her last, and around her was a group of relatives and friends, showing the customary solicitude for the dying. Her aged mother, whose soul was in agony with envy at the departure, was bent over her, while the love of all present was mingled with anguish. . . . There was profound silence and her death took on the semblance of a sacred ceremony. To all appearances she neither breathed nor stirred nor uttered any sound. Her silence seemed to indicate her dissolution, as though the organs of speech had ceased to function because of the withdrawal of the soul that moved them. But her pastor, who was carefully observing everything about her, because of the manifest wonder of the circumstances, perceived that her lips were moving slightly. He put his ear close to them, for his character and sympathy gave him confidence. . . . She was faintly murmuring a psalm, the closing words of a psalm, and truly they are a testimony of her confidence in her parting. Blessed indeed is he who can close his life with the words: "I will both lie down and sleep in peace" [Ps 4.10]. These were the words, fairest of women, that came to your lips, and they were appropriate to you. . . . And you have attained to glorious peace after your sufferings, and have received, beyond the rest common to all, that sleep due to the beloved of God, fitting indeed for one who lived and died amid the words of piety.

2. Gregory of Nazianzus on his Mother, Nonna

In his poems and funeral orations, Gregory wrote often of his admiration for his mother, Nonna. We have seen in the selection above his comparison of her with the biblical Sarah. In the following brief selections, she is presented in terms of Proverbs 31:10 ("A good wife who can find? She is far more precious than jewels") as well as the antitype of the biblical Eve and as a prophetic dreamer who at one point dreamed that her son restored her to health.

On His Own Life, 2.1.11.70–80

In these lines from one of his autobiographical poems, Gregory describes how the fulfillment of his mother's anxious wish to provide the family with a son was predicted in a dream.

God granted the favor, and in her great desire, failing not in loving prayer, she actually anticipated it. There came to her a gracious foretaste, a vision containing the shadow of her request. My likeness and my name appeared clearly to her, the work of a dream by night. Then I was born to them, the gift of God the giver if worthy of the prayer; if not, it was because of my own shortcomings.

On His Own Affairs, 2.1.1.425–32

In this, another of his autobiographical poems, Gregory describes his mother's dedication of himself to God, and includes a note on another of Nonna's dreams.

When I was delivered from my mother's womb, she offered me to you [God]. Ever since the day she had yearned to nurse a manchild on her knee, she imitated the cry of the holy Anna, "O King Christ, that I might have a boy for you to keep within your fold. May a son be the flourishing fruit of my birth pangs" [see 1 Sam 1:11]. And you, O God, granted her prayer. There followed the holy dream which gave her the name. In due time you gave a son. She dedicated me as a new Samuel (if I were worthy of the name) in the temple.

Funeral Oration For His Brother Caesarius
(Or. 7) (selection)

Gregory delivered this eulogy for his brother at his funeral on 11 October 368 C.E. He includes the following passage on his mother in order to show the origin of the piety of Caesarius.

4. Our mother was from the beginning and by ancestry consecrated to God, and her piety was a necessary legacy not only for herself but also for her children. She was truly holy dough from the holy first-fruits [see Rom 11:16]. She increased and magnified it to such an extent that some have believed and proclaimed—for I will say it out loud, though the thesis is bold—that the perfection of her husband was the work of none other

than herself. And, wonderful to say, as the reward of piety a greater and more perfect piety was given. [The reference here is to Nonna's role in inducing her husband, Gregory the Elder, to be baptized; he eventually became a bishop.]

Funeral Oration For His Father (Or. 18) (selections)

Gregory delivered this oration at his father's funeral in 374 C.E. In it he includes a description of his mother's virtues (in contrast to the biblical Eve) and also relates an anecdote concerning another of her dreams.

8. She [Eve] who was given to Adam as a helper (for it was good that the man not be alone) became an enemy rather than a helper and an opponent rather than a companion. She deceived her husband by pleasure and alienated him from the tree of life by means of the tree of knowledge [see Gen 2:18–3:24]. But she [Nonna] who was given by God to my father became not only a companion (for this would be less amazing) but also a leader, guiding him herself by deed and word toward that which is best. Even though she judged it best, according to the law of marriage, that her husband prevail in other matters [see 1 Cor 11:3], she was not ashamed to show herself to be his teacher of piety. It is fitting to admire her for this, but it is even more appropriate to admire him for yielding willingly to her.

. . . Some women excel in running the household and others excel in piety—for it is difficult to succeed in both—but she [Nonna] was superior to all in both. . . . On the one hand, she augmented her household by her attentiveness and careful planning according to the standards and laws prescribed by Solomon for the manly woman, so that she did not appear to be pious. On the other, she was devoted to God and divine things as though household cares were far from her thoughts. Neither, however, was damaged by her attention to the other; rather, she strengthened each through the other.

30. [Note: In section 29, Gregory relates the story of his father's miraculous recovery from illness. Now he turns to a similar story about his mother.] A short time later the same miracle happened to my mother, and it deserves not to be omitted. For I will honor her, since no one is more deserving of such esteem, and in so doing please my father by connecting the two of them in my narrative.

Noble, enduring, and healthy her whole life, she was attacked by an illness. . . . The worst of her many afflictions was an inability to eat; for many days, she was in danger of dying and no remedy for the illness could be found. How then did God nourish her? Not by raining manna, as of old for Israel [Exod 16:14], nor by striking the rock so that it gushed forth water for the thirsty people [Exod 17:6], nor by feeding her with the help of ravens as he did for Elijah [1 Kgs 17:6], nor did he satisfy her hunger by sending a prophet through the air, as he did for Daniel of former times when he was hungry in the pit [Bel 33–36]. In what way, then?

It seemed to her that I, her dearest (for she preferred me over the others even in dreams), suddenly stood by her in the night with a basket of shining white bread and, after praying over it and signing it with the cross as is my beloved practice, fed and encouraged her, and that she recovered bodily strength. This vision of the night was a thing of reality, for from that moment on she became herself again and had better hope. This was made known by a distinct and visible sign. For as soon as I went in to her early the next morning, I saw clearly that she was more cheerful than before. Then when I asked her as usual how the night had been and whether she needed anything, she said, "You, my child, fed me readily and lovingly, and now you ask how I am? I am very well and at ease." At once her attendants signaled to me with a nod of the head not to contradict her but to accept her answer without hesitation lest she become despondent if the truth were revealed.

3. John Chrysostom, *On the Priesthood* (selection)

Bishop of Constantinople from 398–404 C.E., Chrysostom was as a young man invited by a friend to share a residence with him. In this selection, Chrysostom explains his mother Anthusa's opposition to this move and, in a long quotation that he attributes to her, brings out some of her virtues.

1.5 But my mother's constant pleas prevented me from granting Basil this favor, or rather, prevented me from receiving it from his hands. For when my mother became aware of this scheme, she took me by the hand, led me into the part of the house reserved exclusively for her, and sat next to me on the bed on which she had borne me. She unleashed streams of tears and added words more pathetic than the tears, making a bitter lament to me in this manner: "My child," she said, "I was not permitted to enjoy your father's virtue for long, since that was the plan that seemed good to God. Your father's death followed on the birth pangs with which I bore you, designating you to be an untimely orphan and me an untimely widow, to learn the dreadful events of widowhood that only those women who have experienced them can rightly understand. For no word can match the storm and billow that the maiden is up against who has recently left her father's home and is inexperienced at business matters, but who is suddenly hurled into unrestrained grief and must necessarily bear cares beyond her years and sex.

"She must, I think, pay attention to the servants' sluggishness and carefully note their evil deeds, fend off the schemes of relatives, bear nobly the abuses of those who exact the public taxes and the harshness of the tax payments themselves. Should the dead man depart leaving behind a child and should it be a daughter, the mother will also be afforded a great concern, but nonetheless she escapes the outlay of funds, she escapes the fears. A son, in contrast, will fill her with myriad fears each day and with many anxieties. I made allowance for the expenses I had to bear for necessary goods if I wished to bring up my son as befits a free man. Yet all the same, none of these difficulties convinced me to enter into the union of a second marriage, nor to bring another bridegroom into your father's house. I remained in the midst of the stress and the confusion and did not flee the iron furnace of widowhood, aided chiefly by grace from above. Yet it brought me great comfort amid those horrors to gaze constantly at your face and to cherish for myself a living image of the departed, an image that was almost exactly like him.

"Thus while you were still a child and had not yet learned to talk, when you were at an age when children are an enormous delight to their parents, you furnished me with much comfort. I bore my widowhood nobly and you cannot say to censure me that I lessened your patrimony, something I know that many with the misfortune of being orphans have experienced. Indeed, I kept your patrimony completely intact and defrayed all expenses necessary for your honored reputation; omitting nothing, I paid for them out of my own money, money that came from my own home. Don't imagine that I say these things as a reproach! As a return for all these things, however, I ask one favor from you, that you do not invest me with widowhood a second time nor again kindle the grief already laid to rest: wait for my death. I shall perhaps depart after a short time."

FEMALE IMAGERY
AND THEOLOGY

Eve-Mary Theme

The role of Eve in causing human beings to be cast out of paradise into a world of mortality and suffering (Gen 3:1–24) provided early Christian theologians with both an image of human sinfulness as well as a justification for viewing women, the "daughters" of the first woman, Eve, as secondary to and submissive to men, and for denying them institutional authority (see Section I, "Teachers," 4: "Women, the Church, and Teaching," especially the selection from John Chrysostom). Beginning in the early second century, Mary was presented as the antitype to Eve. Using as a model the Pauline image of Christ as a "second Adam" who redeemed what the "first Adam" had lost (1 Cor 15:45–47), theologians viewed the virgin Mary as recuperating what the virgin Eve had destroyed.

1. Eve

The biblical portrait of Eve as one who was deceived and then became a deceiver herself was a powerful image in early Christianity. Already in the New Testament, for example, Paul wrote to the Corinthian community, "For I betrothed you to Christ to present you as a pure bride to her one husband. But I am afraid that as the serpent deceived Eve by his cunning, your thoughts will be led astray from a sincere and pure devotion to Christ" (2 Cor 11:2–3), thus using Eve as a figure for theological disobedience.

1 Timothy 2:11–15 (RSV)

Allegedly written by Paul, this pastoral letter expresses a view of Eve that became standard theological fare in later centuries.

11 Let a woman learn in silence with all submissiveness. 12 I permit no woman to teach or to have authority over men; she is to keep silent.

13 For Adam was formed first, then Eve; 14 and Adam was not deceived, but the woman was deceived and became a transgressor. 15 Yet woman will be saved through bearing children, if she continues in faith and love and holiness, with modesty.

Clement of Alexandria, *The Pedagogue* 2.123.3

A teacher in Alexandria who may have headed an independent school that presented Christianity as the true philosophy, Clement (ca. 160–215 C.E.) wrote extensively on Christian manners and mores (see Section II, "Female Comportment," above). In this passage, he uses Eve to critique female pride.

As the serpent deceived Eve, so jewelry made of gold, shaped enticingly like a serpent, leads other women to insolent behaviors, wearing eels and serpents in order to be fashionable.

John Chrysostom, *On Virginity* (selection)

Priest in Antioch and later bishop of Constantinople (398–404 C.E.), Chrysostom here presents a view of both Adam and Eve as originally virgins in paradise. (For the full text from which this selection is excerpted, see Section II, "Major Treatises on Virginity," 3, above.)

14.3 When the whole world had been completed and all had been readied for our repose and use, God fashioned man for whom he made the world. After being fashioned, man remained in paradise and there was no reason for marriage. Man did need a helper, and she came into being; not even then did marriage seem necessary. It did not yet appear anywhere but they remained as they were without it. They lived in paradise as in heaven and they enjoyed God's company. Desire for sexual intercourse, conception, labor, childbirth, and every form of corruption had been banished from their souls. As a clear river shooting forth from a pure source, so were they in that place adorned by virginity.

14.5 . . . Nothing either thwarted or hindered that happy life, which was far better than this. But when they did not obey God and became earth and dust, they destroyed along with that blessed way of life the beauty of virginity, which together with God abandoned them and withdrew. As long as they were uncorrupted by the devil and stood in awe of their master, virginity abided with them. It adorned them more than the diadem and golden raiment do kings. However, when they shed the princely raiment of virginity and laid aside their heavenly attire, they accepted the decay of death, ruin, pain, and a toilsome life. In their wake came marriage: marriage, a garment befitting mortals and slaves.

2. Eve and Mary

Prior to the decision of the Council of Ephesus in 431 C.E. to approve the title *Theotokos* ("God-bearer") for Mary, early Christian theological speculation about the significance of Mary focused not only on her motherhood as a way to emphasize the reality of the incarnation but also on her cosmological role in the history of salvation. In this regard, she was presented as the antitype to the biblical Eve, as seen in the selections below.

Justin Martyr, *Dialogue With Trypho* (selection)

Apologist, teacher, and philosopher, Justin was martyred in Rome in about 165 C.E. This text, written around 135 C.E. and staged as a dialogue with a Jew named Trypho, argues for an understanding of Christianity as the fulfillment of the promises and prophecies of the Old Testament. Toward the end of the text, Justin says the following about Mary and Eve. [Note: This translation has been slightly emended in order to bring it into conformity with twenty-first-century English usage.]

100.4–6 Christ became man by the virgin, in order that the disobedience that proceeded from the serpent [Gen 3:1–7] might be destroyed in the same manner in which it had its origin. For Eve, who was a virgin and undefiled, having conceived the word of the serpent, brought forth disobedience and death. But the virgin Mary received faith and joy when the angel Gabriel announced to her the good news that the spirit of the Lord would come upon her and the power of the Highest would overshadow her. . . . And by her has [Christ] been born, to whom we have shown so many Scriptures refer, and by whom God destroys both the serpent and those angels and human beings who are like him but gives deliverance from death to those who repent of their wickedness and believe in him.

Irenaeus, *Against Heresies* (selection)

Irenaeus (ca. 115–ca. 202 C.E.) was bishop of Lyons in Gaul (modern-day France). His major work, *Adversus haereses* ("Against Heresies") is a refutation of a variety of Gnostic teachings and also includes an exposition of orthodoxy as Irenaeus defined it. This selection contains Irenaeus's idea of Mary's role in the renewal of all creation effected by the incarnation and resurrection of Christ.

3.22.4 Moreover, it follows that Mary the Virgin is found to be obedient. She says, "Behold your handmaid, Lord; let it be done with me according to your word" [Luke 1:38]. Eve was disobedient, to be sure, since she did not obey when she was still a virgin. Indeed, she had a husband, Adam, but was still a virgin ("for they were both naked" in Paradise "and were not ashamed" [Gen 2:25], since they had been created only a short time before and did not understand about the production of children, for it was proper for them first to reach maturity and thus henceforth to multiply); Eve, having become disobedient, was made the cause of death both for herself and for all the human race. Thus also Mary had a husband selected for her and nonetheless was a virgin, yet by her obedience she was made the cause of salvation both for herself and for all the human race. For this reason the law calls a woman engaged to a man his wife, while conceding that she is still a virgin. This indicates a link that goes from Mary back to Eve. . . . Moreover, the knot of Eve's disobedience was loosened through the obedience of Mary. For what the virgin Eve bound through unbelief, this the Virgin Mary loosed through faith.

Epiphanius of Salamis, *Panarion* 78.17–19

Bishop of Salamis in Cyprus, Epiphanius (ca. 315–403 C.E.) was one of the major heresiologists of the early church. In this passage, he adds to the teaching of Justin and Irenaeus on the Eve-Mary theme by suggesting that Mary, not the physical Eve, was the true "mother of the living."

"Hail, full of grace, the Lord is with you" (Luke 1:28). This is she who was prefigured by Eve and who symbolically received the title of mother of the living (see Gen 3:20). For Eve was called mother of the living after she had heard the words, "You are dust and to dust you shall return" (Gen 3:19), in other words, after the fall. It seems odd that she should receive such a grand title after having sinned. Looking at the matter from the outside, one notices that Eve is the one from whom the entire human race took its origin on this earth. Mary, on the contrary, truly introduced life itself into the world by giving birth to the Living One, so that Mary has become the Mother of the living.

Indeed, the words: "Who gave woman wisdom and skill in embroidery?" (Job 38:36), refer to two women: one is the first Eve, who skillfully wove the visible garments of Adam, whom she herself had reduced to nakedness. To this toil, then, she had been destined. Just as nakedness was discovered because of her, so to her was given the task of reclothing the sensible body against visible nakedness.

To Mary, instead, God entrusted the task of giving birth, for our sakes, to him who is the lamb and the sheep; from his glory, as from a veil, by the power of his immortality, a garment is skillfully woven for us.

But we must consider another marvelous aspect of the comparison between Eve and Mary. Eve became for men the cause of death, because through her death entered the world. Mary, however, was the cause of life, because life has come to us through her. For this reason, the Son of God came into the world, and, "where sin abounded, grace superabounded" (Rom 5:20). Whence death had its origin, thence came forth life, so that life would succeed death. If death came from woman, then death was shut out by him who, by means of the woman, became our life.

And as in paradise Eve, still a virgin, fell into the sin of disobedience, once more through the Virgin came the obedience of grace, when the joyful announcement was given that eternal life in the flesh was descending from heaven. For God said to the serpent: "I will put enmity between you and the woman, between your seed and hers" (Gen 3:15). Woman's seed is found nowhere; and so it is in a figurative sense that this enmity is applied to Eve in relation to her and the serpent and to that which was represented by the serpent, namely, the devil and envy.

But all this cannot be perfectly fulfilled in her. Instead, it will be realized truly in the holy, elect, and unique seed, which comes from Mary alone and not from relations with man. This seed came to destroy the power of the dragon, that is, the tortuous and fleeting serpent, who boasted of holding possession of the whole world.

For this reason, the Only-begotten was born of a woman for the ruin of the serpent, that is to say, the ruin of false doctrine, of corruption, of deceit, error, and lawlessness. He is the one who truly opened the womb of his Mother (see Exod 13:12). For all the other firstborn sons who preceded him were not able—to speak with decency—to realize a condition of that sort. Only the Only-begotten opened the virginal womb. That happened to him alone and to nobody else.

Theodotus of Ancyra, *On the Mother of God and on Nativity* (selection)

Theodotus (d. ca. 446 C.E.) was bishop of Ancyra (in modern-day Turkey) and was one of the preeminent theologians at the Council of Ephesus in 431 C.E. A major topic at the council concerned the title "Theotokos" (God-bearer) for Mary, a title that one theologian, Nestorius, had rejected because he feared that the doctrine of Mary's divine maternity compromised the human nature of Christ. Theodotus opposed Nestorius and wrote several Marian homilies (on Nestorius and the Council of Ephesus: see "Virgin and Mother of God," below). When compared with earlier texts on the Eve-Mary theme as above, this selection demonstrates how the theme was developed in later centuries; here Mary is not simply the antitype to Eve but actually redeems her.

Divine Providence has given her [the Virgin Mary] to us, a creature worthy of the Lord, bearer of blessings. She does not incite us to disobedience but leads us to submit to God. She does not offer a deadly fruit but offers the life-giving bread. She is not timid in her reasoning but is strong in her affections. Not light in her mind, but solid in her soul. She converses with the archangel in a magnificent dialogue and shames the author of evil. Seeing the angel of the Annunciation, she was struck by wonder because he did not look like a son of Adam; nevertheless, she remained prudently attentive to what he told her, to assure herself that what was visiting her in the Temple was not the kind of deceitful benevolence that had once visited paradise. In other words, to make sure that it was not the audacity of the violator introducing himself into the house of God, as he had done in Eden. She wanted to make sure that the glad tidings were not a trick.

What did the divine messenger do then? Perceiving the Virgin's interior dispositions and perspicacity in her outward appearance and admiring her just prudence, he began to weave her a kind of floral crown with two peaks: one of joy and one of blessing; then he addressed her in a thrilling speech of praise, lifting up his hand and crying out: "Hail, O full of grace, the Lord is with you, you are blessed" (Luke 1:28), O most beautiful and most noble among women. The Lord is with you, O all-holy one, glorious and good. The Lord is with you, O worthy of praise, O incomparable, O more than glorious, all splendor, worthy of God, worthy of all blessedness.

I admire your humility, most eminent woman. "Do not fear, Mary" (Luke 1:30), spouse of God, divinely nourished treasure. To you I announce neither a conception in wickedness nor a birth in sin; instead, I bring the joy that puts an end to Eve's sorrow. To you I proclaim neither a trying pregnancy nor a painful delivery [see Gen 3:16]; rather, I foretell a birth of consolation and gladness. Do not judge divine things in a human way. For I am not telling you about a tearful labor or about giving birth in sadness; no, I am proclaiming the dawn of the light of the world.

Through you, Eve's odious condition is ended; through you, abjection has been destroyed; through you, error is dissolved; through you, sorrow is abolished; through you, condemnation has been erased. Through you, Eve has been redeemed.

He who is born of the holy (Virgin) is holy, holy and Lord of all the saints, holy and Giver of holiness. Wondrous is he who generated the Woman of wonder; Ineffable is he who precedes the Woman beyond words; Son of the Most High is he who springs from this highest creature, he who appears, not by man's willing it, but by the power of the Holy Spirit; he who is born is not a mere man, but God, the incarnate Word.

Marian Literature

Beginning in the early second century, Mary became the focus of intense theological interest, particularly regarding her status as virgin as well as her implication in the paradox of the union of the divine with the human. Early Christians were curious about her both as a historical figure as well as a crucial figure in doctrinal discussions of christology. The following selections illustrate the wide variety of discussions that the figure of Mary evoked.

1. Marian Biography

Early Christian authors did not hesitate to "fill in the gaps" of Gospel accounts of various figures, as we saw in the selection from Theodotus of Ancyra (above), who elaborated on the conversation between Mary and the angel Gabriel in the Gospel of Luke's account of the Annunciation (Luke 1:26–38). In the second and third centuries a large body of literature, now called apocryphal, was written to provide more detailed stories about the lives and acts of figures in the New Testament. Like Paul, Andrew, Peter, and others, Mary too was provided with a "biography," the most complete of which is the following.

Protevangelium of James (selections)

The unknown author of this apocryphal narrative validated the work by taking the name of James; of the two New Testament figures bearing this name, one was a witness of the Transfiguration, and the other was the leader of the Christian community in Jerusalem. Also known as *The Book of James*, this text extends the history of Mary "backwards" to her birth and childhood and also provides an elaborated account of the Annunciation. It was immensely popular in late antiquity, and many of its stories, especially those dealing with the Annunciation, were pictured in medieval and Byzantine art. [Note: Passages in angle brackets represent textual variants; passages in parentheses specify the referents of the text.]

[In the beginning of the text, Anna, who will give birth to Mary, laments that she is barren. The text continues as follows.]

4.1 And behold, an angel of the Lord came to her [cf. Luke 1:13] and said: "Anna, Anna, the Lord has heard your prayer. You shall conceive and bear [cf. Luke 1:13; Gen 16:11], and your offspring shall be spoken of in the whole world." And Anna said: "As the Lord my God lives, if I bear a child, whether male or female, I will bring it as a gift to the Lord my God [cf. 1 Sam 1:11], and it shall serve him all the days of its life [cf. 1 Sam 2:11]."

2. And behold, there came two messengers, who said to her: "Behold, your husband Joachim is coming with his flocks; for an angel of the Lord

came down to him and said to him, 'Joachim, Joachim, the Lord God has heard your prayer. Go down; behold, your wife Anna has conceived.'" 3. And Joachim went down and called his herdsmen and said: "Bring me ten lambs without blemish and without spot; they shall belong to the Lord my God. And bring me twelve <tender> calves for the priests and the elders, and a hundred kids for the whole people." 4. And behold, Joachim came with his flocks, and Anna stood at the gate and saw Joachim coming and ran immediately and hung on his neck, saying, "Now I know that the Lord God has greatly blessed me; for behold the widow is no longer a widow, and I, who was childless, have conceived." . . . 5.2 And her months were fulfilled, as (the angel) had said. In the ninth month Anna gave birth. She said to the midwife: "What have I brought forth?" And she said: "A female." And Anna said: "My soul is magnified this day" [see Luke 1:46]. And she lay down. When the days were fulfilled, Anna purified herself from her childbed and nursed the child, and called her Mary.

6.1 Day by day the child waxed strong; when she was six months old her mother stood her on the ground to try if she could stand. And she walked <twice> seven steps and came to her bosom. Anna took her up, saying, "As the Lord my God lives, you shall walk no more upon this ground until I take you into the temple of the Lord." And she made a sanctuary in her bedchamber, and did not permit anything common or unclean to pass through it. And she summoned the undefiled daughters of the Hebrews, and they cared for her amusement.

2. On the child's first birthday, Joachim made a great feast and invited the chief priests and the priests and scribes and the elders and the whole people of Israel. And Joachim brought the child to the priests, and they blessed her, saying, "O God of our fathers, bless this child and give her a name renowned for ever among all generations" [see Luke 1:48]. And all the people said: "So be it, Amen." [Note: Anna sings a song of praise, and the text now resumes as follows.]

7.1 The months passed, and the child grew. When she was two years old, Joachim said to Anna: "Let us bring her up to the temple of the Lord [see 1 Sam 1:21], that we may fulfil the promise we made, lest the Lord send (some evil) upon us and our gift become unacceptable." And Anna replied: "Let us wait until the third year [see 1 Sam 1:22], so that the child may then long no more for her father and mother." And Joachim said: "Very well." 2. When the child was three years old, Joachim said: "Let us call the undefiled daughters of the Hebrews, and let each one take a lamp, and let these be burning, in order that the child may not turn back and her heart be enticed away from the temple of the Lord." And he did so until they went up to the temple of the Lord. The priest took her and kissed her and blessed her, saying, "The Lord has magnified your name among all generations; because of you the Lord at the end of the days will manifest his redemption to the children of Israel." 3. And he placed her on the third step of the altar, and the Lord God put grace upon the child, and she danced for joy with her feet, and the whole house of Israel loved her [see 1 Sam 18:16].

8.1 Her parents went down wondering, praising and glorifying the almighty God because the child did not turn back <to them>. And Mary was in the temple nurtured like a dove and received food from the hand of an angel. 2. When she was twelve years old, there took place a council of priests, saying, "Behold, Mary has become twelve years old in the temple of the Lord. What then shall we do with her, that she may not pollute the temple of the Lord?" [See Lev 15:19–31; the reference is to the beginning of menstruation.] They said to the high priest: "You stand at the altar of the Lord; enter (the sanctuary) and pray concerning her, and what the Lord shall reveal to you we will do." 3. And the high priest took the vestment with the twelve bells and went into the Holy of Holies and prayed concerning her. And behold, an angel of the Lord (suddenly) stood before him and said to him: "Zacharias, Zacharias, go out and assemble the widowers of the people, <who shall each bring a rod [Num 17:2]>, and to whomever the Lord shall give a (miraculous) sign, his wife she shall be." The heralds went forth and spread out through all the country around Judaea; the trumpet of the Lord sounded, and all ran to it. [Joseph is chosen to be Mary's husband; the text continues as follows with an account of the Annunciation.]

11.1 [Mary] took the pitcher and went forth to draw water, and behold, a voice said: "Hail, you who are highly favored, <the Lord is with you, blessed are you> among women" [Luke 1:28, 42]. And she looked around on the right and on the left to see whence this voice came. And trembling she went to her house and put down the pitcher and took the purple and sat down on her seat and drew out [the thread for the temple veil she was weaving]. 2. And behold, an angel of the Lord (suddenly) stood before her and said: "Do not fear, Mary; for you have found grace before the Lord of all things and shall conceive of his word" [Luke 1:30]. When she heard this she doubted in herself and said: "Shall I conceive of the Lord, the living God, <and bear> as every woman bears?" 3. And the angel of the Lord said: "Not so, Mary; for a power of the Lord shall overshadow you; wherefore also that holy thing which is born of you shall be called the Son of the Highest [Luke 1:35, 32]. And you shall call his name Jesus; for he shall save his people from their sins" [Matt 1:21; Luke 1:31]. And Mary said: "Behold, (I am) the handmaid of the Lord before him; be it to me according to your word" [Luke 1:38]. . . . 12.3 Mary was sixteen years old when all these mysterious things happened.

13.1 Now when she was in her sixth month, behold, Joseph came from his building and entered his house and found her with child. He smote his face, threw himself down on sackcloth, and wept bitterly, saying, "With what countenance shall I look towards the Lord my God? What prayer shall I offer for her? For I received her as a virgin out of the temple of the Lord my God and have not protected her. Who has deceived me? Who has done this evil in my house and defiled her <the virgin>? Has the story (of Adam) been repeated in me? For as Adam (was absent) in the hour of his prayer and the serpent came and found Eve alone and deceived her and defiled her [Gen 3:13], so also has it happened to me." 2. And Joseph arose from the sackcloth and called Mary and said to her: "You who are cared for by God, why have you done this and forgotten the Lord your God? Why have you humiliated your soul, you who were brought up in the Holy of Holies and received food from the hand of an angel?" 3. But she wept bitterly, saying, "I am pure, and know not a man" [Luke 1:34]. And Joseph said to her: "Whence then is this in your womb?" And she said: "As the Lord my God lives, I do not know whence it has come to me."

14.1 . . . [Joseph says], "What then shall I do with her? I will put her away secretly" [Matt 1:19]. And the night came upon him. 2. And behold,

an angel of the Lord appeared to him in a dream, saying, "Do not fear because of this child. For that which is in her is of the Holy Spirit. She shall
bear a son, and you shall call his name Jesus; for he shall save his people
from their sins" [Matt 1:20]. And Joseph arose from sleep and glorified the
God of Israel who had bestowed his grace upon him, and he watched
over her [Matt 1:24]. [In the next sections, the Jewish high priest discovers that Mary
is pregnant and charges Mary and Joseph with transgression; both are tested and
found to be pure. Next, Mary and Joseph set out for Bethlehem, following the account in Luke 2:1, and the text resumes as follows.]

18.1 And [Joseph] found a cave there and brought her into it, and left
her in the care of his sons and went out to seek for a Hebrew midwife in
the region of Bethlehem. 2. <Now I, Joseph, was walking, and (yet) I did
not walk, and I looked up at the vault of heaven, and saw it standing still
and the birds of the heaven motionless. And I looked at the earth, and
saw a dish placed there and workmen lying around it, with their hands in
the dish. But those who chewed did not chew, and those who lifted up
anything lifted up nothing, and those who put something to their mouth
put nothing (to their mouth), but all had their faces turned upwards. And
behold, sheep were being driven and (yet) they did not come forward,
but stood still; and the shepherd raised his hand to strike them with his
staff, but his hand remained up. And I looked at the flow of the river, and
saw the mouths of the kids over it and they did not drink. And then all at
once everything went on its course (again)>.

19.1 <And behold, a woman came down from the hill-country and
said to me: "Man, where are you going?" And I said: "I seek a Hebrew
midwife." She answered me: "Are you from Israel?" And I said to her:
"Yes." She said: "And who is she who brings forth in the cave?" I said:
"My betrothed." And she said: "Is she not your wife?" I said to her: "She is
Mary, who was brought up in the temple of the Lord, and I received her
by lot as my wife. And (yet) she is not my wife, but she has conceived of
the Holy Spirit." And the midwife said to him: "Is this true?" And Joseph
said to her: "Come and see."> And the midwife went with him. 2. And he
went to the place of the cave, and behold, a dark <bright> cloud overshadowed the cave [see Matt 17:5]. The midwife said: "My soul is magnified today, for my eyes have seen wonderful things; for salvation is born
to Israel" [see Luke 2:30, 32]. And immediately the cloud disappeared from

the cave, and a great light appeared, so that our eyes could not bear it. A short time afterwards that light withdrew until the child appeared, and it went and took the breast of its mother Mary. And the midwife cried, "How great is this day to me, that I have seen this new sight." 3. And the midwife came out of the cave and Salome met her. And she said to her: "Salome, Salome, I have a new sight to tell you; a virgin has brought forth, a thing which her nature does not allow." Salome said: "As the Lord my God lives, unless I put (forward) my finger [cf. John 20:25] and test her condition, I will not believe that a virgin has brought forth."

20.1 And Salome went in and made her ready to test her condition. And she cried out, saying, "<Woe for my wickedness and my unbelief; for> I have tempted the living God; and behold, my hand falls away from me, consumed by fire!" 2. And she prayed to the Lord. 3. And behold, an angel of the Lord stood before Salome and said to her: "The Lord God has heard your prayer. Come near, touch the child, and you will be healed." 4. And she did so. . . . And Salome was healed as she had requested, and she went out of the cave. And behold, an angel of the Lord <a voice> cried: "Salome, Salome, tell <not> what marvel you have seen, before the child comes to Jerusalem."

[21.1 From this point on, the story follows the narrative of Matt 2 (the Wise Men and King Herod) and ends with the story of the death of Zechariah, whose son, John the Baptist, was sought by Herod according to this text.]

2. Virgin and Mother of God

The birth stories in the Gospels of Matthew and Luke provide the basic view of Mary as virginal mother. Matt 1:22–23 draws on the prophet Isaiah to establish the virgin birth ("All this took place to fulfill what had been spoken by the Lord through the prophet: 'Look, the virgin shall conceive and bear a son, and they shall name him Emmanuel,' which means, 'God is with us'"). The story of the Annunciation in Luke 1:26–38 likewise emphasizes Mary's virginal status by repeatedly describing her with the Greek term *parthenos,* meaning a chaste young woman or virgin. During the first three centuries patristic authors often drew on Old Testament passages to explain the virgin birth (e.g., Gen 49:9: "From a sprout, my son, you went up"; Isa 11:1: "For a shoot shall sprout from the stump of Jesse, and a branch shall flower from his roots").

During the christological controversies of the fourth and fifth centuries, Mary's role as "mother of God" (*Theotokos*) was the object of intense reflection because the doctrine of the virgin birth was crucial to reflection on Jesus' double nature as both human and divine. The title *Theotokos* was formally adopted at the Council of Ephesus in 431 C.E. and reaffirmed at the Council of Chalcedon in 451 C.E.

John Chrysostom, *Homilies on Matthew* 4.3

This text from Chrysostom, bishop of Constantinople from 398–404 C.E., is representative of patristic expressions of the mystery of the virgin birth as well as its anthropological and christological significance.

Neither the angel Gabriel nor the evangelist Matthew can say anything except that the birth of Christ was the work of the Holy Spirit, but neither of the two explains how the Spirit did this, since such a mystery is totally beyond words. Do not believe that you have understood the mystery, just because you hear the words, "of the Holy Spirit." For even after we have learned this, there remain many things we do not know about. For example: How could the Infinite be contained in a womb? How could the Virgin give birth and continue to be a virgin? Tell me, how did the Spirit fashion that temple? How did he take from his Mother, not all of her body, but only a part that he augmented and formed?

The evangelist clearly states that Christ came forth from the Virgin's body in these words: "That which is conceived in you" (Matt 1:20), and Paul does the same: "born of a woman" (Gal 4:4), in order to stop the mouths of those who say that Christ passed through his Mother's womb as if through a channel. Had it been so, what need would there have been for the Virgin's womb? And what would he have had in common with us, because his flesh would have been different from ours, since it would not have been derived from the same human substance as ours? In what way would he have been descended from the root of Jesse? How could he be called shoot and flower of this root? How could he have been called Son of man? On what pretext could Mary have been called his Mother? How would he have come forth from David's line? How did he take the form of a slave (Phil 2:7)? How could one hold that "the Word became flesh" (John 1:14)? And how could Paul have told the Romans that "from them (the Jews) came Christ according to the flesh, he who is God over all" (Rom 9:5)?

Based on all these proofs and on many others besides, we establish that Jesus came forth from us and from our human substance and that he was born of the Virgin's womb, but how this happened we do not see. So do not pry into the mystery, but humbly accept what God has revealed, and do not be curious about what God keeps hidden.

Proclus of Constantinople, *Oration to the Theotokos* (selection)

Presbyter and then bishop of Constantinople from 434–446 C.E., Proclus was noted for his Marian sermons. He was active in the christological controversy associated with the theologian Nestorius (bishop of Constantinople from 428–431 C.E.), who opposed the title *Theotokos* ("God-bearer") because he did not think that a human being could give birth to the godhead and so preferred the title *Christotokos* ("Christ-bearer"). As this sermon, delivered on Dec. 26, 428 C.E., at the Virginity Festival in Constantinople, makes clear, Proclus did accept *Theotokos* as an appropriate title for Mary.

For this reason we now call the Holy Virgin Mary "Theotokos,"
She is the unstained treasure of virginity, the expression of paradise of
    the second Adam,
She is the workshop of the union of natures, the festival of the covenant
    of salvation.
She is the bridal chamber in which the Logos wedded all flesh,
She is the living bramble bush of nature that the fire of divine birth
    pangs did not consume.
She is truly the delicate cloud, the producer of His body, above the
    Cherubim,
The purest fleece of the heavenly rain from which the shepherd clothed
    the sheep.
Mary, the servant and mother, the Virgin and heaven, the only bridge
    from God to humanity,
She is the awe-inspiring loom of the divine economy on which the gar-
    ment of unity was woven inexpressibly,
The weaver of which is the Holy Spirit, the overshadowing power from
    above, the woolworker.

3. Marian Cult

Epiphanius of Salamis, Cyprus, a fourth-century bishop and author of a heresio-logical work entitled *Panarion,* gives the only full account in antiquity of a group of women called Kollyridians, notable for ritual worship of Mary. They took their name from the sacrificial bread, *kollyris,* that they offered to Mary. If such a group really existed, it is likely that they had adapted widespread Mediterranean practices of offering bread to mother-goddesses, thus elevating Mary to the status of divinity.

Epiphanius, *Panarion* 78.23; 79 (selections)

78.23 For it is related that some women in Arabia, who come from the region of Thrace, put forward this silly idea: they prepare a kind of cake in the name of the ever-Virgin, assemble together, and in the name of the holy virgin they attempt to undertake a deed that is irreverent and blasphemous beyond measure—in her name they function as priests for women.

79.1 For some women prepare a certain kind of little cake with four indentations, cover it with a fine linen veil on a solemn day of the year, and on certain days they set forth bread and offer it in the name of Mary. They all partake of the bread. . . .

79.4 [After exposing the effrontery of these women who claim to function as priests, Epiphanius continues with the following objection.] Now certainly the body of Mary was holy, but she was not God. Indeed she was a virgin and is revered as such, but she is not given to us to be worshipped; rather she worships him who was born of her flesh, he who came from heaven from the paternal bosom. . . . 79.5 The whole narrative of this heresy is utter nonsense, an old wives' tale. What part of Scripture speaks of it? Which of the prophets allowed a human being to be worshiped, to say nothing of a woman?

79.8 These women revive the old mixed cup of Fortuna [Roman goddess of fate, luck, or fortune] and prepare their table for the devil, not for God, as it is written, "The food of ungodliness was eaten" [see Isa 65:11], as the divine word says, and, "The women threshed flour and the children collected firewood to make cakes for the heavenly army" [Jer 7:18]. Such women were silenced by Jeremiah so that they might not disturb the world—lest they say, "Let us honor the queen of heaven" [see Jer 44:18].

4. The Other Mary

The biblical Mary Magdalene was a woman from whom Jesus had cast out seven devils (Luke 8:2; Mark 16:9), and in addition she was said to have been present at the crucifixion and was a witness of the resurrection (John 19:25; 20:1–19). In the patristic period, she became a composite figure made up of several women mentioned in the New Testament (e.g., Luke 7:39; Matt 26:6–13; Mark 14:3–8). She became a popular symbol of the loving disciple and forgiven sinner. All three of the following texts demonstrate the challenges that the idea of a specifically *female* disciple and witness posed for early Christian writers.

Gospel of Thomas 114

Simon Peter said to them [the disciples], "Let Mary leave us, for women are not worthy of life." Jesus said, "I myself shall lead her in order to make her male, so that she too may become a living spirit resembling you males. For every woman who will make herself male will enter the kingdom of heaven."

Gospel of Philip 63.32–64.10

[Note: Square brackets and ellipsis marks indicate lacunae or uncertain reconstructions of words in the text.]

And the companion of the [. . .] Mary Magdalene. [. . . loved] her more than [all] the disciples [and used to] kiss her [often] on her [. . .]. The rest of [the disciples . . .]. They said to him, "Why do you love her more than all of us?" The savior answered and said to them, "Why do I not love you like her? When a blind man and one who sees are both together in darkness, they are no different from one another. When the light comes, then he who sees will see the light, and he who is blind will remain in darkness."

Gospel of Mary (selection)

At this point in the gospel, the disciples have received their missionary commission from the resurrected Jesus and are weeping in despair at the thought of the mission's dangers. This is when Mary enters the text.

Then Mary stood up, greeted them all, and said to her brethren, "Do

not weep and do not grieve nor be irresolute, for his grace will be entirely with you and will protect you. But rather let us praise his greatness, for
he has prepared us and made us into men." When Mary said this, she
turned their hearts to the Good, and they began to discuss the words of
the [Savior].

Peter said to Mary, "Sister, we know that the Savior loved you more
than the rest of women. Tell us the words of the Savior which you remember—which you know (but) we do not, nor have we heard them."
Mary answered and said, "What is hidden from you I will proclaim to
you." And she began to speak to them these words: "I," she said, "I saw
the Lord in a vision and I said to him, 'Lord, I saw you today in a vision.'
He answered and said to me, 'Blessed are you, that you did not waver at
the sight of me. For where the mind is, there is the treasure.' I said to
him, 'Lord, now does he who sees the vision see it [through] the soul [or]
through the spirit?' The Savior answered and said, 'He does not see
through the soul nor through the spirit, but the mind which [is] between
the two—that is what sees the vision. . . .'"

[At this point there are several pages missing in the text; when it resumes, Mary narrates an elaborate vision of the soul's journey through personified cosmic powers like
ignorance, desire, and wrathful wisdom, all of which it overcomes until it achieves
rest.]

When Mary had said this, she fell silent, since it was to this point that the
Savior had spoken with her. But Andrew answered and said to the
brethren, "Say what you (wish to) say about what she has said. I at least
do not believe that the Savior said this. For certainly these teachings are
strange ideas." Peter answered and spoke concerning these same things.
He questioned them about the Savior: "Did he really speak with a woman
without our knowledge (and) not openly? Are we to turn about and all
listen to her? Did he prefer her to us?"

Then Mary wept and said to Peter, "My brother Peter, what do you
think? Do you think that I thought this up myself in my heart, or that I am
lying about the Savior?" Levi answered and said to Peter, "Peter, you
have always been hot-tempered. Now I see you contending against the
woman like the adversaries. But if the Savior made her worthy, who are

you indeed to reject her? Surely the Savior knows her very well. That is why he loved her more than us. Rather let us be ashamed and put on the perfect man and acquire him for ourselves as he commanded us, and preach the gospel, not laying down any other rule or other law beyond what the Savior said."

Female Images and Metaphors

Despite the fact that early Christianity marginalized actual women by denying them priestly duties and often denigrated them—physically, by associating them with excessive sexuality and passion, and theologically, by tainting them with the legacy of Eve and thus with sin—writers often used female images to envision theological, anthropological, and institutional aspects of Christianity. God, for example, was imagined as a lactating mother, the church was personified as a woman, and the human soul and virtues were imagined to be female. Some authors, when interpreting the Song of Songs, understood the Song's lovers in Christian terms, casting Christ as the bridegroom and the soul as the bride. Not all uses of female imagery were positive, however; especially in Christian texts from Nag Hammadi, the soul-as-female as well as female dimensions of the divine world were sometimes portrayed as errant and ignorant. Thus the ambivalence that early Christian literature displayed toward women is reflected in its utilization of female imagery as well.

1. God as Mother

When the God of biblical tradition is presented by means of a familial metaphor, the paternal image of "father" is typical. In the following passages, however, early Christian writers have drawn on the image of a nourishing mother to depict the relation among God, Christ, and human beings. (See also Section I, "Prophets," above, for the Montanist Priscilla's vision of Christ as a woman.)

Irenaeus, *Against Heresies* 4.38.1

In this constructive portion of his heresiological work, Irenaeus, bishop of Lyons in the late second century C.E., imagines both God and Christ as mothers.

At this point, however, if someone objects, "What then? Was God not able to make the human being perfect from the beginning?" let that person know that for God, who is always the same and is uncreated, all things are possible. But his created beings, since their origin was later, are necessarily inferior to the one who created them. . . . Indeed, since they are later, they are infants; and because they are infants, they are neither accustomed to nor tutored in perfect knowledge. Although a mother is capable of giving adult food to her infant, the infant is not yet strong enough to receive such food; so also God himself could have given perfection to human beings from the beginning, but human beings were incapable of receiving it because they were still only infants. For this reason our Lord, in these last times when he had recapitulated all things in himself, came to us not in the way in which he was capable of coming but in the way in which we were capable of seeing him. He could in fact have come to us in his indescribable glory, but we were not yet capable of enduring the greatness of his glory. Because we were like infants, he who was the perfect bread of the Father gave himself to us as milk. This was his coming in the form of a human being, so that by being nourished as it were from the breast of his flesh and becoming accustomed through this diet of milk to eating and drinking the Word of God, we might be able to contain in ourselves him who is the bread of immortality, who is the Spirit of the Father.

Odes of Solomon 19

Variously dated between the late first and the third century C.E., the *Odes of Solomon* is considered by many to be the earliest Christian hymnbook. There is some debate over whether the language of composition was Syriac or Greek. The *Ode* given here is a poetic rendering of the metaphors of milk and breasts seen in the passage above. Note that the Holy Spirit is considered feminine; this may reflect the text's Semitic origin, since "spirit" in Hebrew and Aramaic is in the feminine gender.

1. A cup of milk was offered to me,
And I drank it in the sweetness of the Lord's kindness.
2. The Son is the cup,
And the Father is he who was milked;

And the Holy Spirit is She who milked Him;

3. Because his breasts were full,

And it was undesirable that His milk should be ineffectually released.

4. The Holy Spirit opened her bosom,

And mixed the milk of the two breasts of the Father.

5. Then She gave the mixture to the generation without their knowing,

And those who have received (it) are in the perfection of the right hand.

6. The womb of the Virgin took (it),

And she received conception and gave birth.

7. So the Virgin became a mother with great mercies.

8. And she labored and bore the Son but without pain,

Because it did not occur without purpose.

9. And she did not require a midwife,

Because He caused her to give life.

10. She brought forth like a strong man with desire,

And she bore according to the manifestation,

And acquired with great power.

11. And she loved with redemption,

And guarded with kindness,

And declared with grandeur.

Hallelujah

Clement of Alexandria, *The Pedagogue* (selections)

A teacher in Alexandria in the second century C.E., Clement wrote a long section, full of physiological detail, on milk in this treatise. Brief samples of his theological conclusions, plus part of the hymn that closes this work, follow.

1.6.43 Our nourishment, that is, the Lord Jesus, the Word of God, is Spirit become flesh, flesh from heaven made holy. This is our nourishment, the milk flowing from the Father by which alone we little ones are fed. I mean that He, the "well-beloved" [Matt 3:17], the Word, our provider, has saved mankind by shedding His blood for us. Therefore, we fly trustfully to the "care-banishing breast" [Homer, *Iliad* 22.83] of God the Father; the breast that is the Word, who is the only one who can truly bestow on us the milk of love.

1.6.45 We are nourished with milk, the Lord's own nourishment, as

soon as we leave our mother's womb; and as soon as we are born anew
we are favored with the good tidings of hope of rest, that heavenly
Jerusalem in which, as it is written, "milk and honey rain down" [see Exod
3:8]. In this material figure, we are given a pledge of the food of holiness,
for, though solid food must be put away sooner or later, as the Apostle
says [1 Cor 3:2], the nourishment that we derive from milk leads us directly to heaven, since it educates us to be citizens of heaven and companions of the angels. If the Word is an overflowing fountain of life [see Rev
21:6], and is also called a river of oil [see Deut 32:13], then certainly Paul
can use a similar figure of speech and call Him "milk," adding: "I gave
you to drink" [1 Cor 3:2]. We do drink the Word, nourishment of truth.

Hymn to the Educator (selection)
O Jesus, our Christ!
Milk of the bride,
Given of heaven,
Pressed from sweet breasts—
Gifts of Thy wisdom—
These Thy little ones
Draw for their nourishment;
With infancy's lips
Filling their souls
With spiritual savor
From breasts of the Word.

2. The "Woman Clothed with the Sun"

This mysterious figure from the book of Revelation provoked a good deal of
imaginative speculation by patristic authors. She was variously understood as
Jerusalem, the church, the Virgin Mary, and as a model for human virgins. One example of allegorical interpretation, by Hippolytus of Rome, is given here; for another, see
above in Section II, "Major Treatises on Virginity," 1: Methodius, *The Symposium* 8.4–
8.13.

Revelation 12:1–6 (RSV)

1 And a great portent appeared in heaven, a woman clothed with the sun, with the moon under her feet, and on her head a crown of twelve stars; 2 she was with child and she cried out in her pangs of birth, in anguish for delivery. 3 And another portent appeared in heaven; behold, a great red dragon, with seven heads and ten horns, and seven diadems upon his heads. 4 His tail swept down a third of the stars of heaven, and cast them to the earth. And the dragon stood before the woman who was about to bear a child, that he might devour her child when she brought it forth; 5 she brought forth a male child, one who is to rule all the nations with a rod of iron, but her child was caught up to God and to his throne, 6 and the woman fled into the wilderness, where she has a place prepared by God, in which to be nourished for one thousand two hundred and sixty days.

Hippolytus, *Treatise on Christ and Antichrist* 61

Presbyter in the church in Rome in the early third century C.E., Hippolytus is best known today for his *Refutation of All Heresies,* but he also wrote theological and exegetical works. In this treatise, he pulls together passages from both testaments of the Bible in order to picture the cosmic future, as in the selection that follows.

By the "woman then clothed with the sun," he meant most manifestly the Church, endowed with the Father's word, whose brightness is above the sun. And by "the moon under her feet" he referred to her being adorned, like the moon, with heavenly glory. And the words, "upon her head a crown of twelve stars," refer to the twelve apostles by whom the Church was founded. And those, "She, being with child, cries, travailing in birth, and pained to be delivered," mean that the Church will not cease to bear from her heart the Word that is persecuted by the unbelieving in the world. "And she brought forth," he says, "a man-child, who is to rule all the nations"; by which is meant that the Church, always bringing forth Christ, the perfect man-child of God, who is declared to be God and man, becomes the instructor of all the nations. And the words, "her child was caught up unto God and to his throne," signify that he who is always born of her is a heavenly king, and not an earthly one. . . . "And the dragon," he says, "saw and persecuted the woman who brought forth the man-child. And to the woman were given two wings of the great eagle, that she might fly into the wilderness, where she is nourished for a time and times, and half a time, from the face of the serpent" [Rev 12.14]. That refers to the one-thousand two-hundred and threescore days during which the tyrant is to reign and persecute the Church, which flees from city to city, and seeks concealment in the wilderness among the mountains, possessed of no other defense than the two wings of the great eagle, that is to say, the faith of Jesus Christ, who, in stretching forth His holy hands on the holy tree, unfolded two wings, the right and the left, and called to Himself all who believed in Him, and covered them as a hen her chickens.

3. The Church Personified as a Woman

Although St. Paul had called the church "the body of Christ" [1 Cor 12:27], from the second century onward it became conventional to speak about the church as a "female" entity as well. The marital metaphor that viewed the church as the spouse of Christ was the dominant one, although there were others, as the following selections demonstrate.

2 Clement 14.2

This text may be the oldest complete Christian sermon, possibly written in the second century C.E. Its author is anonymous.

I do not think that you are ignorant that the living Church is "the body of Christ" [Eph 1.23]. For the Scripture says: "God made man male and female" [Gen 1:27]; the male is Christ and the female is the Church. The sacred books, moreover, and the Apostles say that the Church is not of the present time, but existed from the beginning. For she was spiritual, as also our Jesus, and He was revealed in the last days to save us.

Hermas, *The Shepherd, Visions* 1.2.2; 2.1.1–3; 2.4.1

Composed in Rome, probably in the early second century C.E., the *Shepherd* is concerned with ethics, particularly regarding repentance and forgiveness. A series of the author's dreams and visions, in which an old woman appears to him, is followed by a set of mandates and parables.

1.2.2 I saw before me a great white chair of snow-white wool. Then there came a lady advanced in years, in an exceedingly brilliant garment, with a book in her hand. She was sitting alone and saluted me.

2.1.1–3 While making my way to Cumae at the same time as last year . . . once more the spirit seized me and bore me off to the same spot as in the past. . . . I . . . began praying to the Lord. . . . On rising from prayer, I beheld before me the elderly lady I had seen last year. She was walking and reading a little book. Then she said to me: "Can you report this to God's elect?" "Lady," I said, "I cannot remember so many things. Give me the book and I shall copy it." "Take it," she said, "and return it to me."

2.4.1 Brethren, a revelation was made to me in my sleep by an exceedingly beautiful young man, who said: "Who, do you think, is the elderly lady from whom you took the book?" "The Sibyl," I said. "No," he said, "you are mistaken." "Who is she, then?" I said. "The Church," he said. "Why is she elderly?" I asked. "Because she was created before all things," he said, "For this reason she is elderly and for Her sake the world was erected."

Clement of Alexandria, *The Pedagogue* 1.6.42

Here Clement continues his metaphor of the lactating mother giving nourishment (see his section under "God as Mother," above). This time, however, the mother is the church.

O mystic wonder! The Father of all is one, the Word who belongs to all is one, the Holy Spirit is one and the same for all. And one alone, too, is the virgin Mother. I like to call her the Church. She alone, although a mother, had no milk because she alone never became a wife. She is at once virgin and mother; as virgin, undefiled; as mother, full of love. Calling her children about her, she nourishes them with milk that is holy: the Infant Word. That is why she has no milk [defective text here], because this Son of hers, beautiful and all hers, the Body of Christ, is milk.

Origen of Alexandria, *Commentary on John*, frag. 45

One of the most creative and prolific of patristic theologians, Origen (ca. 185–ca. 251 C.E.) is best known today for his allegorical interpretations of the Bible, demonstrated in this passage and the next.

Just as Adam and his wife became the parents of all people, so Christ and the Church generate as their offspring all good actions, thoughts, and words.

Origen of Alexandria, *Commentary on the Song of Songs* 1.1 (selection)

"Let Him kiss me with the kisses of His mouth" [Song 1.2]. It behooves us to remember the fact to which we drew attention in our introduction—namely, that this little book which has the semblance of a marriage-song is written in dramatic form. And we defined a drama as something in which certain characters are introduced who speak. . . . And the spiritual interpretation too is equally in line with that which we pointed out in our prologue; the appellations of Bride and Bridegroom denote either the Church in her relation to Christ, or the soul in her union with the Word of God.

Reading it as a simple story, then, we see a bride appearing on the stage, having received for her betrothal and by way of dowry most fitting gifts from a most noble bridegroom; but, because the bridegroom delays his coming for so long, she, grieved with longing for his love, is pining at home and doing all she can to bring herself at last to see her spouse, and to enjoy his kisses. We understand further that the bride, seeing that she can neither be quit of her love, nor yet achieve what she desires, betakes herself to prayer and makes supplication to God, whom she knows to be her Bridegroom's Father. . . . Let us consider her . . . aflame with longing for her Spouse, vexed by the inward wound of love, pouring out her prayer to God, and saying concerning her Spouse: "Let Him kiss me with the kisses of His mouth."

This is the content of the actual story, presented in dramatic form. But let us see if the inner meaning also can be fittingly supplied along these lines. Let it be the Church who longs for union with Christ; but the Church, you must observe, is the whole assembly of the saints. So it must be the Church as a corporate personality who speaks and says: "I am sated with the gifts which I received as betrothal presents or as dowry before my marriage. For of old, while I was being prepared for my wedding with the King's Son and the Firstborn of all creation [see Rev 19:6–9; Col 1:15], His holy angels put themselves at my service and ministered to me,

bringing me the Law as a betrothal gift; for the Law, it is said, was ordained by angels in the hand of a mediator [Gal 3:19]. The prophets also
ministered to me. For they it was who uttered all the things that were to
tell me and to show me about the Son of God, to whom they were desiring to betroth me, when all these so-called betrothal gifts and dowry
presents should have been taken away. Moreover, in order to enkindle
me with love and longing for Him, they with prophetic voice proclaimed
to me about His coming; filled with the Holy Spirit, they foretold His
countless acts of power and His mighty works. His beauty also they described, His charm and gentleness, that I might be inflamed beyond all
bearing with the love of Him by all these things.

But, since the age is almost ended and His own presence is not
granted me, and I see only His ministers ascending and descending upon
me, because of this I pour out my petition to you, the Father of my
Spouse, beseeching you to have compassion at last upon my love, and to
send Him, that He may now no longer speak to me only by His servants
the angels and the prophets, but may come Himself, directly, and kiss me
with the kisses of His mouth—that is to say, may pour the words of His
mouth into mine, that I may hear Him speak Himself, and see Him teaching. The kisses are Christ's, which He bestowed on His Church when at
His coming, being present in the flesh, He in His own person spoke to her
the words of faith and love and peace, according to the promise of Isaiah
who, when sent beforehand to the Bride, had said: "Not a messenger, nor
an angel, but the Lord Himself shall save us" [see Isa 33:22].

4. The Soul as Female

The human soul, like the church, was typically personified as female, perhaps in
part for linguistic reasons (the Latin *anima* and the Greek *psyche* are both feminine-
gendered nouns). As the principle of life and freedom of choice in human beings, the
personified soul was portrayed both negatively (the sinful soul) and positively (the
soul longing for union with its creator). These two passages from Origen, Alexandrian
theologian of the third century C.E., are classic patristic dramatizations of both aspects of the soul's activities.

Origen of Alexandria, *Homilies on Genesis* 1.15

But let us see allegorically how man, made in the image of God, is male and female [Gen 1:27]. Our inner man consists of spirit and soul. The spirit is said to be male; the soul can be called female. If these have concord and agreement among themselves, they increase and multiply [Gen 1:28] by the very accord among themselves and they produce sons, good inclinations and understandings or useful thoughts, by which they fill the earth and have dominion over it. This means they turn the inclination of the flesh, which has been subjected to themselves, to better purposes and have dominion over it, while the flesh, of course, becomes insolent in nothing against the will of the spirit. But now if the soul, which has been united with the spirit and, so to speak, joined in wedlock, turn aside at some time to bodily pleasures and turn back its inclination to the delight of the flesh and at one time indeed appear to obey the salutary warnings of the spirit, but at another time yield to carnal vices, such a soul, as if defiled by adultery of the body, is said properly neither to increase nor multiply, since indeed Scripture designates the sons of adulterers as imperfect [see Wis 3:16]. Such a soul, to be sure, which prostrates itself totally to the inclination of the flesh and bodily desires, having forsaken conjunction with the spirit, as if turned away from God will shamelessly hear, "You have the face of a harlot; you have made yourself shameless to all" [Jer 3:3]. She will be punished, therefore, like a harlot, and her sons will be ordered to be prepared for slaughter.

Origen of Alexandria, *Commentary on the Song of Songs* 1.1 (selection)

This passage is the continuation of the selection from Origen's *Commentary on the Song of Songs* in subsection 3, "The Church Personified as a Woman," above, where Origen is interpreting Song of Songs 1.2, "O that you would kiss me with the kisses of your mouth." Having first allegorized the Bride and Bridegroom as the Church and Christ, he now allegorizes them as the Soul and the Word of God.

As the [next] point in our exposition, let us bring in the soul whose only desire is to be united to the Word of God and to be in fellowship with Him, and to enter into the mysteries of His wisdom and knowledge as into the chambers of her heavenly Bridegroom; which soul has already received His gifts—that is to say, her dowry. For, just as the Church's dowry was the volumes of the Law and the Prophets, so let us regard natural law and reason and free will as the soul's betrothal gifts. And let the teaching, which comes down to her from her masters and teachers, following on these gifts of her natural endowment, be to her for her earliest instruction. But, since she does not find in these the full and perfect satisfaction of her desire and love, let her pray that her pure and virginal mind may be enlightened by the illumination and the visitation of the Word of God Himself. For, when her mind is filled with divine perception and understanding without the agency of human or angelic ministration, then she may believe she has received the kisses of the Word of God Himself.

For this reason, then, and for the sake of these kisses, let the soul say in her prayer to God: "Let Him kiss me with the kisses of His mouth." For as long as she was incapable of receiving the solid and unadulterated doctrine of the Word of God Himself, of necessity she received "kisses," that is, interpretations, from the mouth of teachers. But, when she has begun to discern for herself what was obscure, to unravel what was tangled, to unfold what was involved, to interpret parables and riddles and the sayings of the wise along the lines of her own expert thinking, then let her believe that she has now received the kisses of the Spouse Himself, that is, the Word of God.

Moreover, the plural, "kisses," is used in order that we may understand that the lighting up of every obscure meaning is a kiss of the Word of God bestowed on the perfected soul. . . .

And let us understand that by the "mouth" of the Bridegroom is meant the power by which He enlightens the mind and, as by some word of love addressed to her . . . makes plain whatever is unknown and dark to her. And this is the truer, closer, holier kiss, which is said to be granted by the Bridegroom-Word of God to the Bride—that is to say, to the pure and perfect soul; it is of this happening that the kiss, which we give one to another in church at the holy mysteries, is a figure.

Exegesis on the Soul (selection)

Even more dramatic than Origen's is this text's presentation of the soul-as-woman. Part of the Nag Hammadi Library, the *Exegesis on the Soul* narrates the myth of the soul's fall and redemption, drawing on an eclectic array of biblical and Homeric texts to enhance the story, which resembles one version of the Valentinian myth of the cosmic principle Sophia (wisdom personified). For the sake of brevity, biblical passages have been noted but not quoted as they are in the text. Words in brackets and parentheses represent editorial reconstructions of textual lacunae.

Wise men of old gave the soul a feminine name. Indeed she is female in her nature as well. She even has her womb.

As long as she was alone with the father, she was virgin and in form androgynous. But when she fell down into a body and came to this life, then she fell into the hands of many robbers. And the wanton creatures passed her from one to another. . . . Some made use of her [by force], while others did so by seducing her with a gift. In short, they defiled her, and she [. . . her] virginity.

And in her body she prostituted herself, and gave herself to one and all, considering each one she was about to embrace to be her husband. When she had given herself to wanton, unfaithful adulterers, so that they might make use of her, then she sighed deeply and repented. But even when she turns her face from those adulterers, she runs to others and they compel her to live with them and render service to them upon their bed, as if they were her masters. Out of shame she no longer dares to leave them, whereas they deceive her for a long time, pretending to be faithful, true husbands, as if they greatly respected her. And after all this they abandon her and go.

She then becomes a poor desolate widow, without help; not even a measure of food was left her from the time of her affliction. . . . And her offspring by the adulterers are dumb, blind, and sickly. . . .

But when the father who is above visits her and looks down upon her and sees her sighing—with her sufferings and disgrace—and repenting of the prostitution in which she engaged, and when she begins to call upon [his name] so that he might help her, . . . saying, "Save me, my father, for behold I will render an account [to thee, for I abandoned] my

house and fled from my maiden's quarters. Restore me to thyself again."
When he sees her in such a state, then he will count her worthy of his
mercy upon her, for many are the afflictions that have come upon her because she abandoned her house. [There follow several quotations about prostitution from Jer 3:1–4, Hos 2:2–7, Ezek 16:23–26.] What does "the sons of
Egypt, men great of flesh" [Ezek 16:26] mean if not the domain of the flesh
and the perceptible realm and the affairs of the earth, by which the soul
has become defiled here, receiving bread from them, as well as wine, oil,
clothing and the other external nonsense surrounding the body—the
things she thinks she needs. . . .

Guard yourselves against the prostitution of the body but especially
that of the soul [here the text quotes 1 Cor 5:9–10; Eph 6:12]. As long as the
soul keeps running about everywhere copulating with whomever she
meets and defiling herself, she exists suffering her just deserts. But when
she perceives the straits she is in and weeps before the father and repents, then the father will have mercy on her and he will make her
womb turn from the external domain and will turn it again inward, so
that the soul will regain her proper character. For it is not so with a
woman. For the womb of the body is inside the body like the other inter-
nal organs, but the womb of the soul is around the outside like the male
genitalia, which are external.

So when the womb of the soul, by the will of the father, turns itself
inward, it is baptized and is immediately cleansed of the external pollution which was pressed upon it. . . . And so the cleansing of the soul is to
regain the [newness] of her former nature and to turn herself back again.
That is her baptism.

Then she will begin to rage at herself like a woman in labor, who
writhes and rages in the hour of delivery. But since she is female, by herself she is powerless to beget a child. From heaven the father sent her
her man, who is her brother, the firstborn. Then the bridegroom came
down to the bride. . . . She cleansed herself in the bridal chamber; she
filled it with perfume; she sat in it waiting for the true bridegroom. No
longer does she run about the marketplace, copulating with whomever
she desires, but she continued to wait for him—(saying) "When will he
come?"—and to fear him, for she did not know what he looked like: she

no longer remembers since the time she fell from her father's house. . . .
And she dreamed of him like a woman in love with a man. . . .

For since that marriage is not like the carnal marriage, those who
are to have intercourse with one another will be satisfied with that intercourse. And as if it were a burden, they leave behind them the annoyance
of physical desire and they [turn their faces from] each other. . . . But
[once] they unite [with one another], they become a single life.

5. The Virtues as Female

Lists of virtues and vices were common in Graeco-Roman ethical literature, especially in Stoicism. In early Christianity, just as the soul was often portrayed as a
woman, so also human virtues (and vices) were often personified as female.

Hermas, *The Shepherd, Parables* 9.13.1–3; 9.15.1–3

The final portion of this text is a series of visions shown to the author by a spiritual guide named the "angel of repentance." Hermas see a tower being built on a plain,
where there are also several virgins.

9.13.1–3 "Now about the tower," I said, "what is it?" "This tower," he
said, "is the Church." "And the virgins?" I said, "who are they?" "They,"
he said, "are holy spirits. It will be found that no man will enter the Kingdom of God in any other way, unless they clothe him with their raiment.
For, if he only receives the Name, without receiving raiment from them,
it is of no avail to him. The virgins are the powers of the Son of God. If
you bear the Name, without His power, you are bearing the Name to no
purpose. Now, the stones you saw rejected [from the tower]," he said, "are
those who bore the Name, but did not put on the virgins' raiment." "What
kind of garment is this raiment of theirs?" I said. "The names themselves," he said, "are the garment. Anybody who bears the Name of the
Son of God is also bound to bear their names. Even the Son of God Himself bears the names of these virgins."

9.15.1–3 "Sir, let me know," I said, "the names of the virgins and of
the women dressed in black raiment." "I shall tell you," he said, "the
names of the virgins standing at the corners, the stronger ones. The first
one is Faith, the second is Continence, the third is Fortitude, and the

fourth is Long-suffering. The others standing between them, in the middle, are called: Simplicity, Innocence, Purity, Cheerfulness, Truth, Understanding, Concord, and Love. The person who bears these names and that of the Son of God can enter into the Kingdom of God. Let me also tell you," he said, "the names of the women with the dark raiment: The first is Unbelief, the second is Incontinence, the third Disobedience, and the fourth Deceit. Their companions are called: Grief, Wickedness, Licentiousness, Irascibility, Lying, Foolishness, Slander, and Hatred. The servant of God who bears these names can, indeed, see the Kingdom of God, but cannot enter it."

Gregory of Nazianzus, *On the Misfortunes of his Soul* 2.1.45.229–66

One of the Cappadocian Fathers, Gregory of Nazianzus (ca. 329–390 C.E.), the Bishop of Constantinople in 379–381 C.E., was called simply "The Theologian" as early as the mid-fifth century. He wrote several autobiographical poems; a dream recorded in one of them is given in narrative form here.

Two women appeared to me, brilliant in clothing shining with light, virgins, and they came close to me. Both were beautiful but neglectful of the usual adornments of women—no jewelry, no cosmetics, no silk, nothing of those things invented by men for the appearance of women in order to excite passion. Veils shrouded their heads in shadows; their eyes were lowered to the ground, their cheeks colored with the rosy tint of modesty. They were like dewy rosebuds, their lips silent. It was a great joy to contemplate them, since I was sure that they were more than human. Because I had charmed them, they gave me kisses as though I were a beloved son. I asked who they were, and they replied, Chastity and Temperance, who lead human beings close to Christ the King, rejoicing in the celestial beauty reserved for virgins. "Come, child," they said, "unite your spirit to ours and bring your flaming torch to join ours so that we can take you across the sky and place you in the splendor of the eternal Trinity." With these words they raised themselves into the sky, and I watched as they flew.

APPENDICES AND
INDICES

Timeline of Early Christian Women

1ST CENTURY
Mary, mother of Jesus
Mary Magdalene
"Woman Clothed with the Sun" (f)

2ND CENTURY
Agathonicê (?)
Blandina (d. 177)
Marcosian prophets
Maximilla (ca. 150–60)
Priscilla (ca. 150–60)
Thecla (f)
Quintilla (ca. 150–60)

3RD CENTURY
Arete (f)
Marcella (f)
Polyxena (f)
Potamiena
Thallusa (f)
Xanthippe (f)

4TH CENTURY
Anthusa
Gorgonia (d. ca. 371)
Macrina (ca. 327–ca. 379)
Melania the Elder (ca. 342–ca. 410)
Melania the Younger (ca. 383–439)
Nonna (d. 384)
Olympias (ca. 365–ca. 410)

5TH CENTURY
Nun who feigned madness
Pelagia (f)
Sarah
Syncletica
Theodora

Note: Most dates are approximate (designated by "ca." for *circa*); dates of death are designated by "d." Women who were probably fictional are designated by "(f)."

Timeline of Early Christian Authors and Texts

1ST CENTURY
1 Timothy (?)
Odes of Solomon (1st–3rd c.)
Paul, 1 Corinthians (ca. 52)
Revelation (ca. 95)

2ND CENTURY
Acts of Paul and Thecla
Clement of Alexandria (ca. 160–ca. 215), *Miscellanies; The Pedagogue*
Hermas, *The Shepherd*
Ignatius (d. ca. 117), *To the Smyrneans*
Irenaeus (ca. 115–ca. 202), *Against Heresies*
Justin Martyr (d. ca. 165), *Dialogue with Trypho*
Gospel of Thomas (?)
Martyrdom of Saints Carpus, Papylus, and Agathonicê (?)
Polycarp (d. ca. 156), *To the Philippians*
Protevangelium of James (?)
2 Clement (?)

3RD CENTURY
Acts of Andrew (?)
Acts of Xanthippe and Polyxena

Note: Many dates are approximate and are designated by "ca." (*circa*) or by a question mark when uncertain; "d." designates date of death. The abbreviation "c." signifies "century."

Didascalia apostolorum

Exegesis on the Soul (?)

Gospel of Philip (?)

Gospel of Mary

Hippolytus of Rome (ca. 170–ca. 236), *The Apostolic Tradition; Refutation of All Heresies; Treatise on Christ and the Antichrist*

Hypostasis of the Archons (?)

Methodius (d. 311), *The Symposium*

Origen of Alexandria (ca. 185–ca. 251), *Against Celsus; Commentary on 1 Corinthians; Commentary on John; Commentary on the Song of Songs; Homilies on Genesis*

4TH CENTURY

Apostolic Constitutions

Athanasius (ca. 298–373), *Second Letter to Virgins* (late 360s?)

Canons of the Council of Gangra (ca. 340–360)

Debate of a Montanist and an Orthodox Christian

Epiphanius (ca. 315–403), *Panarion*

Eusebius of Caesarea (ca. 260–ca. 339), *Ecclesiastical History*

Gregory of Nazianzus (ca. 329–390), *Funeral Oration for his Brother Caesarius (Oration 7)* (368); *Funeral Oration for his Sister Gorgonia (Oration 8)* (ca. 370); *Funeral Oration for his Father (Oration 18)* (374); *On his Own Affairs; On his Own Life; On the Misfortunes of his Soul*

Gregory of Nyssa (ca. 331/40–ca. 395), *Life of Saint Macrina* (ca. 380); *On the Soul and the Resurrection* (380s?); *On Virginity* (early 370s)

John Chrysostom (ca. 347–407), *Discourse 4 on Genesis; Homilies on Matthew; Homily 12 on 1 Corinthians; Homily 20 on Ephesians; The Kind of Women Who Ought to be Taken as Wives; On the Priesthood; On Virginity; Treatises on the Subintroductae*

5TH CENTURY

Apophthegmata patrum (possibly early 6th c.)

Gerontius, *Life of Melania the Younger* (ca. 440)

James the Deacon, *Life of Saint Pelagia the Harlot* (?)

Life of Olympias, Deaconess

Palladius (ca. 365–425), *Lausiac History*

Proclus of Constantinople (d. 446), *Oration to the Theotokos* (428)

Theodotus of Ancyra (d. ca. 446), *On the Mother of God and on Nativity*

APPENDIX THREE

Suggestions for Further Reading

General Books and Articles

Castelli, Elizabeth A. "Heteroglossia, Hermeneutics, and History: A Review Essay of Recent Feminist Studies of Early Christianity." *Journal of Feminist Studies in Religion* 10 (1994): 73–98.

Clark, Elizabeth A. "Early Christian Women: Sources and Interpretation." In *That Gentle Strength: Historical Perspectives on Women in Christianity,* edited by Lynda L. Coon, Katherine J. Haldane, and Elisabeth W. Sommer, 19–35. Charlottesville: University Press of Virginia, 1990.

————. "Ideology, History, and the Construction of 'Woman' in Late Ancient Christianity." *Journal of Early Christian Studies* 2 (1994):155–84.

Clark, Gillian. *Women in Late Antiquity: Pagan and Christian Lifestyles.* Oxford: Clarendon Press, 1993.

Cloke, Gillian. *This Female Man of God: Women and Spiritual Power in the Patristic Age.* London and New York: Routledge, 1995.

Kraemer, Ross Shepard. *Her Share of the Blessings: Women's Religions Among Pagans, Jews, and Christians in the Greco-Roman World.* New York and Oxford: Oxford University Press, 1992.

MacDonald, Margaret. *Early Christian Women and Pagan Opinion: The Power of the Hysterical Woman.* New York: Cambridge University Press, 1996.

Pantel, Pauline Schmitt, ed. *A History of Women in the West.* Vol. 1, *From Ancient Goddesses to Christian Saints.* Cambridge: The Belknap Press of Harvard University Press, 1992.

Schüssler Fiorenza, Elisabeth. *In Memory of Her: A Feminist Theological Reconstruction of Christian Origins.* New York: Crossroad, 1983.

Torjesen, Karen Jo. "Reconstruction of Women's Early Christian History." In *Searching the Scriptures.* Vol. 1, *A Feminist Introduction,* edited by Elisabeth Schüssler Fiorenza, 290–310. New York: Crossroad, 1993.

Section I: Women's Roles in the Church

Boyarin, Daniel. *Dying for God: Martyrdom and the Making of Christianity and Judaism.* Stanford: Stanford University Press, 1999.

Burrus, Virginia. "The Heretical Woman as Symbol in Alexander, Athanasius, Epiphanius, and Jerome." *Harvard Theological Review* 84 (1991): 229–48.

Davies, J. G. "Deacons, Deaconesses and the Minor Orders in the Patristic Period." *Journal of Ecclesiastical History* 14 (1963): 1–15.

Eisen, Ute E. *Women Officeholders in Early Christianity: Epigraphical and Literary Studies.* Wilmington: Michael Glazier, 2000.

Frend, W. H. C. *Martyrdom and Persecution in the Early Church.* Oxford: Blackwell, 1965.

King, Karen L. "Prophetic Power and Women's Authority: The Case of the *Gospel of Mary* (Magdalene)." In *Women Preachers and Prophets through Two Millennia of Christianity,* edited by Beverly Mayne Kienzle and Pamela Walker, 21–41. Berkeley: University of California Press, 1998.

Methuen, Charlotte. "Widows, Bishops, and the Struggle for Authority in the *Didascalia apostolorum.*" *Journal of Ecclesiastical History* 46 (1995): 197–213.

Osiek, Carolyn. "The Widow as Altar: The Rise and Fall of a Symbol." *Second Century* 3 (1983): 159–69.

Shaw, Brent. "Body/Power/Identity: Passions of the Martyrs." *Journal of Early Christian Studies* 4 (1996): 269–312.

Thurston, Bonnie Bowman. *The Widows: A Woman's Ministry in the Early Church.* Philadelphia: Fortress Press, 1989.

Torjesen, Karen Jo. *When Women Were Priests: Women's Leadership in the Early Church and the Scandal of their Subordination in the Rise of Christianity.* San Francisco: HarperSanFrancisco, 1993.

Trevett, Christine. *Montanism: Gender, Authority and the New Prophecy.* New York: Cambridge University Press, 1996.

Wire, Antoinette Clark. *The Corinthian Women Prophets: A Reconstruction through Paul's Rhetoric.* Minneapolis: Fortress Press, 1990.

Section II: Women and Virginity

Brakke, David. *Athanasius and Asceticism.* Baltimore and London: The Johns Hopkins University Press, 1995.

Brown, Peter. *The Body and Society: Men, Women, and Sexual Renunciation in Early Christianity.* New York: Columbia University Press, 1988.

Burrus, Virginia. "Word and Flesh: The Bodies and Sexuality of Ascetic Women in Christian Antiquity." *Journal of Feminist Studies in Religion* 10 (1994): 27–51.

Castelli, Elizabeth A. "Virginity and its Meaning for Women's Sexuality in Early Christianity." *Journal of Feminist Studies in Religion* 2 (1986): 61–88.

Clark, Elizabeth A. "Devil's Gateway and Bride of Christ: Women in the Early Christian World." In *Women and a New Academy: Gender and Cultural Contexts,* edited by Jean O'Barr, 81–102. Madison: University of Wisconsin Press, 1989.

————. *Jerome, Chrysostom, and Friends: Essays and Translations.* Studies in Women and Religion 2. New York: The Edwin Mellen Press, 1979.

Cooper, Kate. *The Virgin and the Bride: Idealized Womanhood in Late Antiquity.* Cambridge: Cambridge University Press, 1996.

Elm, Susanna. *'Virgins of God': The Making of Asceticism in Late Antiquity.* Oxford: The Clarendon Press, 1994.

Harrison, Verna. "Gender, Generation, and Virginity in Cappadocian Theology." *Journal of Theological Studies,* n.s. 47 (1996): 38–68.

Miller, Patricia Cox. "The Blazing Body: Ascetic Desire in Jerome's Letter to Eustochium." *Journal of Early Christian Studies* 1 (1993): 21–45.

Rouselle, Aline. *Porneia: On Desire and the Body in Antiquity.* Trans. Felicia Pheasant. Oxford: Blackwell, 1988.

Section III: Portraits of Ascetic Women

Brakke, David. "The Lady Appears: Materializations of 'Woman' in Early Monastic Literature." *Journal of Medieval and Early Modern Studies* 33 (2003): 387–402.

Burrus, Virginia. *Chastity as Autonomy: Women in the Stories of the Apocryphal Acts.* Studies in Women and Religion 23. Lewiston: The Edwin Mellen Press, 1987.

————. "Macrina's Tattoo." *Journal of Medieval and Early Modern Studies* 33 (2003): 403–18.

————. *The Sex Lives of Saints: An Erotica of Ancient Hagiography.* Philadelphia: University of Pennsylvania Press, 2004.

Cameron, Averil. *Christianity and the Rhetoric of Empire: The Development of Christian Discourse.* Berkeley: University of California Press, 1991.

————. "Desert Mothers: Women Ascetics in Early Christian Egypt." In *Women as Teachers and Disciples in Traditional and New Religions,* edited by E. Puttick et al., 11–24. Lewiston: The Edwin Mellen Press, 1993.

Castelli, Elizabeth A. "Mortifying the Body, Curing the Soul: Beyond Ascetic Dualisms in *The Life of St. Syncletica.*" *differences* 4 (1992): 134–53.

Clark, Elizabeth A. *Ascetic Piety and Women's Faith: Essays on Late Ancient Christianity.* New York: The Edwin Mellen Press, 1986.

————. *The Life of Melania the Younger: Introduction, Translation, and Commentary.* New York: The Edwin Mellen Press, 1984.

Coon, Lynda L. *Sacred Fictions: Holy Women and Hagiography in Late Antiquity.* Philadelphia: University of Pennsylvania Press, 1997.

Davies, Stevan L. *The Revolt of the Widows: The Social World of the Apocryphal Acts*. Carbondale: Southern Illinois University Press, 1980.

Davis, Stephen J. "Crossed Texts, Crossed Sex: Intertextuality and Gender in Early Christian Legends of Holy Women Disguised as Men." *Journal of Early Christian Studies* 10 (2002): 1–36.

————. *The Cult of St Thecla: A Tradition of Women's Piety in Late Antiquity*. Oxford: Oxford University Press, 2001.

Frank, Georgia. "Macrina's Scar: Homeric Allusion and Heroic Identity in Gregory of Nyssa's *Life of Macrina*." *Journal of Early Christian Studies* 8 (2000): 511–30.

MacDonald, Dennis Ronald. *The Legend and the Apostle: The Battle for Paul in Story and Canon*. Philadelphia: Westminster Press, 1983.

Miller, Patricia Cox. "Is There a Harlot in This Text? Hagiography and the Grotesque." *Journal of Medieval and Early Modern Studies* 33 (2003): 419–36.

Momigliano, Arnaldo. "The Life of St. Macrina by Gregory of Nyssa." In *On Pagans, Jews, and Christians*, by Arnaldo Momigliano, 333–47. Middletown: Wesleyan University Press, 1987.

Shaw, Teresa. *The Burden of the Flesh: Fasting and Sexuality in Early Christianity*. Minneapolis: Fortress Press, 1998.

Ward, Sister Benedicta. *Harlots of the Desert: A Study of Repentance in Early Monastic Sources*. Kalamazoo: Cistercian Publications, 1987.

Section IV: Women and Domestic Life

Balch, David L., and Carolyn Osiek. *Early Christian Families in Context: An Interdisciplinary Dialogue*. Grand Rapids: Eerdmans, 2003.

Clark, Elizabeth A. "Anti-familial Tendencies in Ancient Christianity." *Journal of the History of Sexuality* 5 (1995): 356–80.

Foucault, Michel. *The History of Sexuality*. Vol. 3, *The Care of the Self*, translated by Robert Hurley. New York: Random House, 1986.

Grubbs, Judith Evans. "'Pagan' and 'Christian' Marriage: The State of the Question." *Journal of Early Christian Studies* 2 (1994): 361–412.

Hunter, David G., ed. and trans. *Marriage in the Early Church*. Minneapolis: Fortress Press, 1992.

Jacobs, Andrew, and Rebecca Krawiec. "Father Knows Best? Christian Families in the Age of Asceticism." *Journal of Early Christian Studies* 11 (2003): 257–64.

Moxnes, Halvor. *Constructing Early Christian Families: Family as Social Reality and Metaphor*. New York and London: Routledge, 1997.

Osiek, Carolyn. "The Family in Early Christianity: 'Family Values' Revisited." *Catholic Biblical Quarterly* 58 (1996): 1–24.

Reynolds, P. L. *Marriage in the Western Church: The Christianization of Marriage During the Patristic and Early Medieval Periods*. Leiden: E. J. Brill, 1994.

Section V: Female Imagery and Theology

Atwood, Richard. *Mary Magdalene in the New Testament Gospels and Early Tradition.* New York: Lang, 1993.

Benko, Stephen. *Virgin Goddess: Studies in the Pagan and Christian Roots of Mariology.* Leiden: E. J. Brill, 1993.

Cameron, Averil. "Virginity as Metaphor: Women and the Rhetoric of Early Christianity." In *History as Text: The Writing of Ancient History,* edited by Averil Cameron, 171–205. London: Duckworth, 1989.

Castelli, Elizabeth A. "'I Will Make Mary Male': Pieties of the Body and Gender Transformation of Christian Women in Late Antiquity." in *Bodyguards: The Cultural Contexts of Gender Ambiguity,* edited by Julia Epstein and Kristina Straub, 29–49. New York: Routledge, 1992.

Clark, Elizabeth A. "The Lady Vanishes: Dilemmas of a Feminist Historian after the 'Linguistic Turn.'" *Church History* 67 (1998): 1–31.

Corrington, Gail Paterson. "The Milk of Salvation: Redemption by the Mother in Late Antiquity and Early Christianity." *Harvard Theological Review* 82 (1989): 393–420.

Gambero, Luigi. *Mary and the Fathers of the Church: The Blessed Virgin Mary in Patristic Thought.* San Francisco: Ignatius Press, 1999.

King, Karen L. *The Gospel of Mary Magdala: Jesus and the First Woman Apostle.* Missoula: Polebridge Press, 2003.

_____. *Images of the Feminine in Gnosticism.* Harrisburg: Trinity Press International, 2000.

Limberis, Vasiliki. *Divine Heiress: The Virgin Mary and the Creation of Christian Constantinople.* London and New York: Routledge, 1994.

Meeks, Wayne. "The Image of the Androgyne: Some Uses of a Symbol in Earliest Christianity." *History of Religions* 13 (1974): 165–208.

Miller, Patricia Cox. "'Pleasure of the Text, Text of Pleasure': Eros and Language in Origen's *Commentary on the Song of Songs.*" *Journal of the American Academy of Religion* 54 (1986): 241–53.

Pagels, Elaine. *Adam, Eve, and the Serpent.* New York: Random House, 1988.

_____. "What Became of God the Mother? Conflicting Images of God in Early Christianity." *Signs* 2 (1976/77): 293–303.

Shoemaker, Stephen. *Ancient Traditions of the Virgin Mary's Dormition and Assumption.* Oxford: Oxford University Press, 2002.

General Index

Index of Biblical Passages

Hebrew Bible/Old Testament

Apocrypha

New Testament

Women in Early Christianity: Translations from Greek Texts was designed and composed in Walbaum by Kachergis Book Design of Pittsboro, North Carolina. It was printed on 60-pound Natures Natural and bound by Thomson-Shore, Inc, of Dexter, Michigan.